TOURISM POLICY
AND
INTERNATIONAL TOURISM

IN OECD COUNTRIES

1991 - 1992

SPECIAL FEATURE:
TOURISM STRATEGIES AND RURAL DEVELOPMENT

ORGANISATION FOR ECONOMIC CO-OPERATION AND DEVELOPMENT

ORGANISATION FOR ECONOMIC CO-OPERATION AND DEVELOPMENT

Pursuant to Article 1 of the Convention signed in Paris on 14th December 1960, and which came into force on 30th September 1961, the Organisation for Economic Co-operation and Development (OECD) shall promote policies designed:

— to achieve the highest sustainable economic growth and employment and a rising standard of living in Member countries, while maintaining financial stability, and thus to contribute to the development of the world economy;

— to contribute to sound economic expansion in Member as well as non-member countries in the process of economic development; and

— to contribute to the expansion of world trade on a multilateral, non-discriminatory basis in accordance with international obligations.

The original Member countries of the OECD are Austria, Belgium, Canada, Denmark, France, Germany, Greece, Iceland, Ireland, Italy, Luxembourg, the Netherlands, Norway, Portugal, Spain, Sweden, Switzerland, Turkey, the United Kingdom and the United States. The following countries became Members subsequently through accession at the dates indicated hereafter: Japan (28th April 1964), Finland (28th January 1969), Australia (7th June 1971) and New Zealand (29th May 1973). The Commission of the European Communities takes part in the work of the OECD (Article 13 of the OECD Convention).

Publié en français sous le titre :
POLITIQUE DU TOURISME ET TOURISME INTERNATIONAL
DANS LES PAYS DE L'OCDE 1991-1992

FOREWORD

The Tourism Committee has, for more than thirty years, published information on government policies in the field of tourism. This has been accompanied by statistics on recent trends in the development of international tourism in the OECD area.

Chapter I of this annual report presents a synthesis of the Tourism Committee's work on the potential effects of tourism strategies on rural development. It points out - *inter alia* - some of the comparative advantages regarding rural development that tourism can offer and it provides an input for the wider deliberations of the OECD horizontal programme which is being undertaken under the aegis of the Council Working Party on Rural Development.

Chapters II and III, and the Statistical Annex, study the evolution of international supply and demand in OECD Member countries and outline the trends observed in 1991-1992.

The report was adopted by the Tourism Committee which recommended its derestriction by the OECD Council. The Council decided on 28 February 1994 to make it publicly available.

Table of contents

INTRODUCTION 7

Chapter I

TOURISM STRATEGIES AND RURAL DEVELOPMENT

I.   Rural tourism defined -- the relationship between tourism and agriculture 13
     1.   The case for rural tourism 14
     2.   But what is rural tourism? 14
     3.   What is rurality? 15
     4.   Rural population densities and settlement size 15
     5.   Selected national criteria for "rural" settlements 16
     6.   Land use 16
     7.   "Traditional" social structures 16
     8.   The characteristics of "rural" and "urban" societies 17
     9.   The *continuum* concept 17
     10. Rural tourism: A concept for development and conservation 18
     11. The importance of the *continuum* - concept for rural tourism 20
     12. What types of holidays are rural? 20
     13. The relationship between tourism and agriculture 21

II. Rural tourism: its growth, its market -- promises and problems 23
     1.   Why has rural tourism grown? 23
     2.   The size of the market 25
     3.   What can rural tourism contribute to rural development? 25
     4.   Rural tourism: the problems 28

III. Managing rural tourism and rural development 31
     1.   Can tourism strategies solve the rural regeneration question? 31
     2.   But can - and should - rural tourism be managed? 32
     3.   The evolution of rural tourism management 32
     4.   Issues to be addressed if sustainable rural tourism is to be promoted
          succesfully 33
     5.   Pre-requisites before discussion can begin 33
     6.   Key issues to be solved in practice 35

IV. Future research and development programmes 37
    1.   Market information 37
    2.   How best to relate to markets? 38
    3.   Benefit assessment and enhancement 38
    4.   Management, control and operational issues 39
    5.   Sustainability indicators 40
    6.   Training 40
    7.   Community involvement and community/industry co-operation 41
    8.   Agency intervention in rural tourism development 41
    9.   International co-operation 41
    10.   Best or bad practice assessment 42

Appendix A   Education and training for rural tourism 43
Appendix B   A categorised bibliography 47

Chapter II

INTERNATIONAL TOURIST FLOWS IN MEMBER COUNTRIES

I.   International tourism in the OECD area 77
II.   International tourism in individual Member countries in 1992 82
III. Main generating countries 88

Chapter III

THE ECONOMIC IMPORTANCE OF INTERNATIONAL TOURISM IN MEMBER COUNTRIES

I.   International tourism receipts and expenditure 100
II.   The economic importance of the "travel" account in the
    balance of payments 102

STATISTICAL ANNEX 107

Trends in international tourism
in the OECD area

Main developments

Despite persistent international recession and the escalating Yugoslav conflict, the main data available for 1992 show a resumption of growth in OECD-area international tourism (see synthesis Table p. 807) :

-- Arrivals at frontiers: up 4 per cent (compared with a 1 per cent decrease the previous year);

-- Nights spent in various forms of accommodation: up 3 per cent (compared with a 0.3 per cent increase);

-- Receipts in real terms: up 5 per cent (compared with 1 per cent);

-- Receipts in current dollars: up 11 per cent (compared with 3 per cent).

In the OECD area, the situation in Europe improved with regard to both arrivals at frontiers (from North America and Asia in particular) and the number of nights spent in all forms of accommodation. The Mediterranean area benefited most (in Turkey, arrivals were up 28 per cent, versus 2 per cent in 1991, and use of accommodation rose by 73 per cent; in Greece, arrivals were up 16 per cent, compared with a 9 per cent drop in 1991, and nights spent advanced 21 per cent). On the other hand, Italy recorded a downturn by losing 1.2 million visitors, including 70 per cent from its three main markets -- Germany, France and the United Kingdom; similarly, it lost three million nights spent in various forms of accommodation (down 4 per cent).

North America saw an increase in arrivals, although the rise was smaller than in 1991 (up 3 per cent, compared with 6 per cent), the incentive effect of a weaker dollar having been partially offset by economic conditions in the region's leading markets. Canada was especially affected in 1992 by the world economy, which caused nights spent in all forms of accommodation to drop by 4 per cent and arrivals at frontiers by 1 per cent. Most importantly, the fewer nights spent by American, British and Asian tourists had a greater impact than the decline in arrivals at frontiers; only the Australian market returned to growth.

In Australasia-Japan, arrivals were up by a substantial 10 per cent, compared with 5 per cent, driven especially by Asian prosperity. Japan, however, stood still (with arrivals unchanged in 1992 after a 12 per cent rise in 1991), its competitiveness weakened by a strong yen. In Australia, nights spent in all forms of accommodation diminished for the second year in a row (down 5 per cent on 1991), whereas nights spent in hotels advanced by 8 per cent and arrivals at frontiers by 10 per cent.

Trend of international tourism in the OECD area
Per cent change over previous year

	Arrivals at frontiers[1]		Nights spent in means of accommodation[2]		Receipts in national currency		Receipts in real terms[3]	
	% 91/90	% 92/91	% 91/90	% 92/91	% 91/90	% 92/91	% 91/90	% 92/91
Austria			5.1	0.1	6.9	0.0	3.4	−3.9
Belgium[4]			−5.6	5.8	0.4	5.0	−2.7	2.5
Denmark			11.7	11.1	8.1	2.8	5.3	0.7
Finland			−10.8	1.9	7.9	18.2	3.6	14.9
France	3.5	8.3	2.3	8.2	9.6	10.1	6.3	7.5
Germany[6]			7.4	−3.6	1.6	−0.7	−1.8	−4.4
Greece	−9.4	16.1	−15.9	20.9	−1.4	52.3	−17.1	31.5
Iceland	1.2	−0.6	3.5	−0.3	−0.9	−7.9	−7.2	−11.4
Ireland	−2.3	4.2	−1.2	1.5	7.3	1.1	4.0	−2.0
Italy[7]	−14.9	−2.4	2.4	−3.6	−3.4	15.7	−9.3	9.9
Luxembourg[4]			5.9	−8.8	0.4	5.0	−2.7	2.5
Netherlands			4.5	5.2	21.5	14.2	17.0	10.2
Norway			8.0	12.0	11.3	14.1	7.6	11.5
Portugal	7.9	2.6	13.5	−8.6	7.3	−8.1	−3.6	−15.6
Spain	2.8	3.4	3.8	3.4	6.0	6.6	0.1	0.7
Sweden			−14.8	3.8	−3.6	7.2	−11.9	4.9
Switzerland	−4.5	1.6	0.4	−0.1	6.8	7.3	0.9	3.1
Turkey	2.4	28.2	−26.9	73.1	26.8	125.6	−23.6	32.7
United Kingdom	−6.1	5.8	−5.0	−2.1	−4.5	3.2	−9.8	−0.5
EUROPE[5]	−3.1	4.3	0.4	3.9			−1.5	3.6
Canada	−2.0	−1.1	0.7	−4.0	3.0	2.3	−2.5	0.8
United States	8.5	3.9			12.5	11.3	7.9	8.0
NORTH AMERICA	5.6	2.6					6.9	7.4
Australia	7.0	9.6	−1.1	−5.0	8.2	9.8	4.8	11.3
New Zealand	−1.3	9.6	−6.6	6.3	2.5	4.6	−0.1	3.5
Japan	11.9	0.0			−10.9	−1.7	−13.7	−3.3
AUSTRALASIA-JAPAN[5]	4.5	9.6	−2.4	−2.4			−4.6	3.8
OECD[5]	−1.2	4.0	0.3	3.0			0.6	4.7

1. Arrivals of tourists except in Australia, Ireland, Italy, Spain and Turkey where arrivals concern visitors.
2. Nights spent in all means of accommodation except in Finland, Iceland and Spain where nights spent concern hotels and similar establishments.
3. After correcting for the effects of inflation. For the regional and OECD totals, the receipts of the individual countries are weighted in proportion to their share in the total expressed in dollars.
4. Receipts apply to both Belgium and Luxembourg.
5. Overall trends for countries with data available from 1990 to 1992.
6. The data relate to the territory of the Federal Republic of Germany prior to 3rd October 1990. Since 1991, data for all means of accommodation include camping sites.
7. Break of series (for payments only) in 1990 due to the liberalisation of capital movements.

The eight main generators of tourism to the OECD area (in decreasing order, Italy, United States, Japan, Germany, the Netherlands, the United Kingdom, Canada and France) also continued to yield contrasting results.

Italy still constitutes one of Europe's most dynamic and most promising markets: in 1992, nights spent by people arriving from that country advanced by 13 per cent in the OECD area, whereas expenditure in dollars rose by 42 per cent. The most popular destinations were Turkey (up 75 per cent), France (up 20 per cent), Belgium (up 15 per cent) and Spain (up 14 per cent). In addition, arrivals of Italian tourists grew by 21 per cent in North America and by 3 per cent in Australasia-Japan.

Nights spent by United States tourists were up 4 per cent in the OECD area as a whole, and their spending rose 13 per cent. Americans headed mainly for Europe (nights spent up 12 per cent) and above all increased their travel to Turkey, Austria, Norway and Belgium, cutting back somewhat on trips to Canada (down 6 per cent).

After declining in 1991, Japanese demand bounced back with 2 per cent growth in nights spent and a 14 per cent rise in visits. In Europe, although arrivals from Japan rose even more sharply (up 22 per cent), such was not the case for the number of nights spent (up 2 per cent), since the average duration of stay in Europe shrank considerably.

Next in line with demand that also advanced -- albeit less so than in 1991 -- came Germany, the Netherlands, Canada and the United Kingdom. In Germany, nights spent were up 2 per cent (versus 11 per cent in 1991), whereas expenditure in dollars rose 19 per cent.

Arrivals of Dutch tourists remained at the same level in Europe but increased by 6 per cent in North America and by 12 per cent in Australasia-Japan. In the United Kingdom, demand stayed strong for the United States (arrivals up 13 per cent) and Japan (arrivals up 17 per cent).

Fewer Canadians visited the United States in 1992 (down 3 per cent), whereas their travel to other countries increased (by 10 per cent).

Lastly, tourism from France, decreased with nights spent in Europe up 2 per cent; this figure conceals a significant drop in demand for Portugal (down 20 per cent), Iceland (down 19 per cent) and Austria and Spain (down 10 per cent), whereas travel to Turkey was on the rise (up 129 per cent).

The tourism balance sheet of the OECD countries was still in the red in 1992, as the deficit swelled to nearly $12 billion, from $5 billion in 1991. Much of this was due to increased expenditure by European countries (up 16 percent) and by Australasia-Japan (up 10 per cent), the latter led by greater spending on the part of the Japanese, as a result of their government's programme to encourage outbound travel.

Besides the cyclical trends the Tourism Committee observes and analyses each year, in particular through the annual report, it also examines the industry's structural changes and interactions with other sectoral policies.

Consequently, since 1987 the Tourism Committee has been exploring the contribution of tourism policy to the development of rural areas. Since 1990 this activity has been carried out within the broader context of the OECD's Rural Development Programme, which was set up in line with the mandate given to the Organisation by the Council at its 1990 Ministerial meeting.

For many years, rural areas have experienced serious problems associated both with declining population and quality of available services. This trend has been accentuated by the dramatic changes in the agricultural economy accompanied by job losses and income erosion.

In contrast to this, however, rural tourism economic activity has expanded considerably, becoming a thriving, fast-growing sector which has also proven an increasingly significant factor for economic growth in the countries and regions where it has developed.

Under the circumstances, it is important to gauge whether tourism's growth potential can be harnessed to pull rural regions out of decline -- in particular by exploiting city-dwellers' new-found interest in the countryside and its way of life, and in preserving the landscape and its architectural heritage.

The OECD Tourism Committee has devoted several of its meetings to this issue. In particular, it has sought to determine, in the light of national experience, whether there is anything distinctive about rural tourism, whether rural tourism can develop in all rural areas and will be likely to create jobs and attract capital. In addition, the Committee has also sought to determine whether there are any negative consequences for the countryside and if such consequences call for action on the part of central government and/or local authorities.

From these discussions, a synthesis was drawn for the OECD Secretariat by Mr. Bernard Lane, Director of the Rural Tourism Unit of the University of Bristol, United Kingdom, which is contained in Chapter I. This marks a first stage in the Committee's work on the subject and provides an input for the wider deliberations of the horizontal programme undertaken by the Council Group on Rural Development.

Trends of international tourism
in Europe
(Indices 1984 = 100)

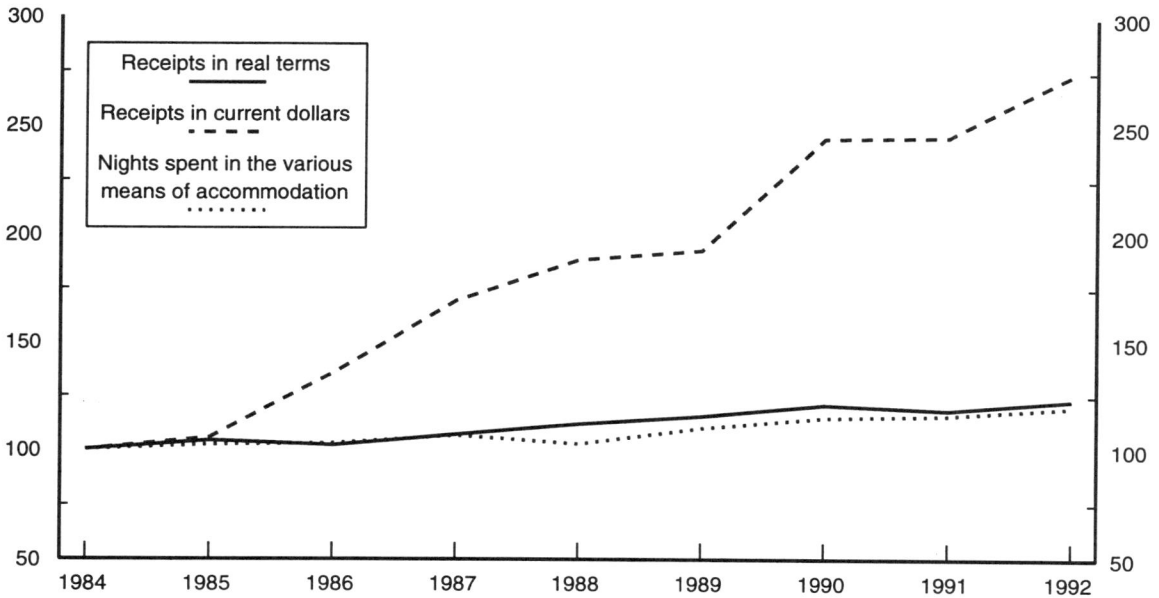

Source: OECD

Trends of international tourism
in North America
(Indices 1984 = 100)

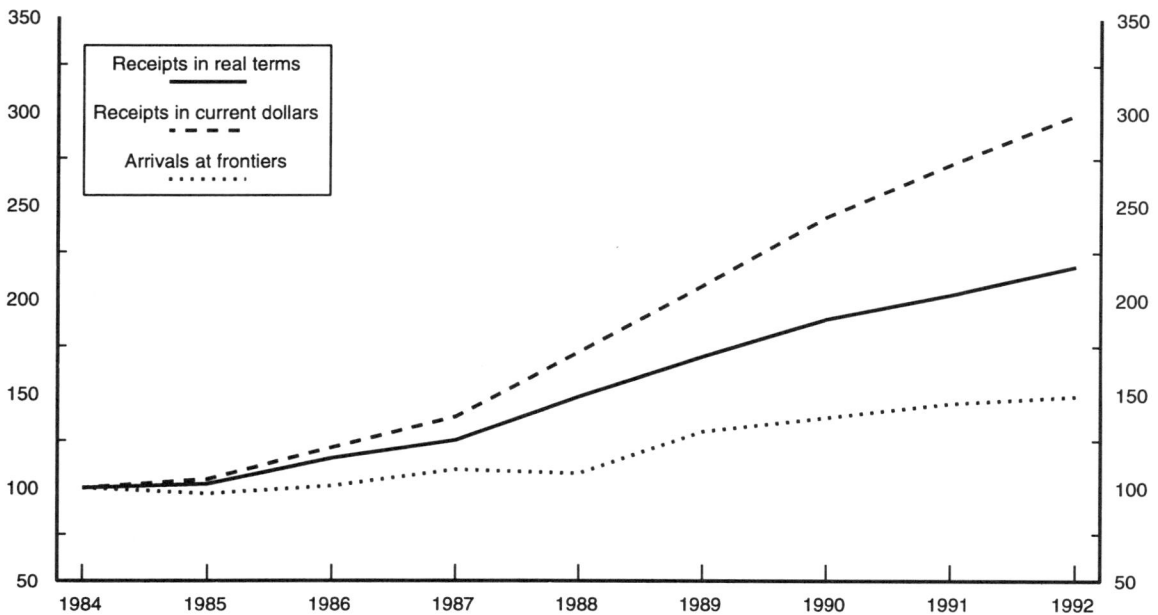

Source: OECD

Trends of international tourism
in Australasia-Japan
(Indices 1984 = 100)

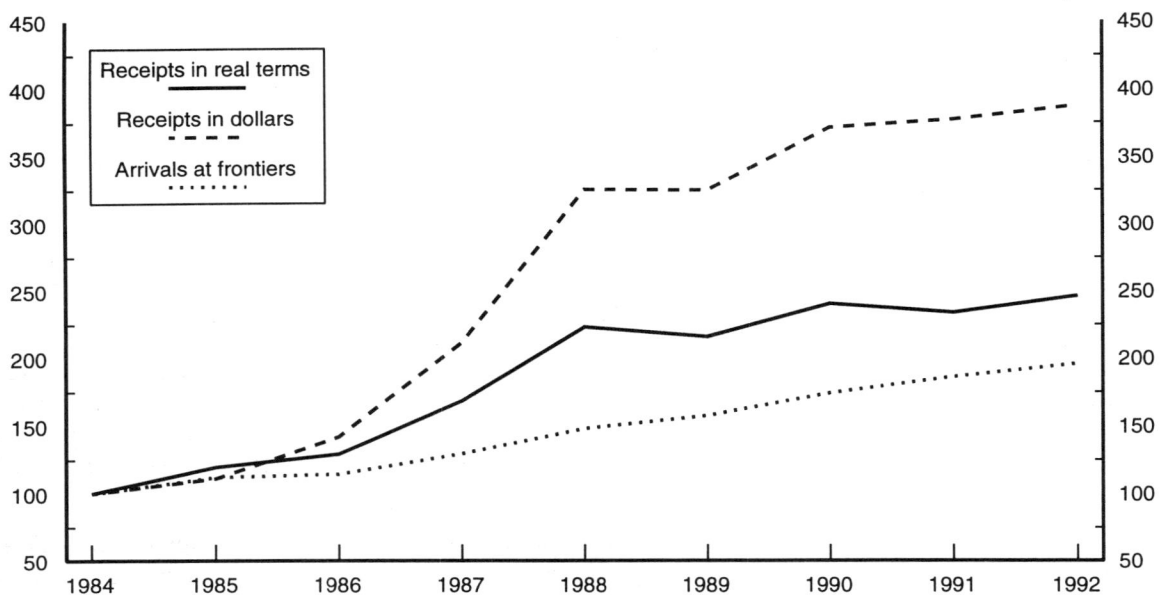

Receipts in real terms
——————

Receipts in dollars
- - - - - -

Arrivals at frontiers
· · · · · · ·

Source: OECD

Chapter I

Tourism strategies and rural development

I. Rural tourism defined -- the relationship between tourism and agriculture

Across the rural regions of the developed world the issues of population decline, economic change and community regeneration are universal. For over a century, the powerful trends of industrialisation and urbanisation have steadily altered the economic and political position of rural society. In the last 40 years those trends have intensified. Farm incomes have fallen in real terms. Technological changes have joined with falling incomes to reduce agricultural employment. In response, rural service provision has diminished: shops, schools, churches, professional services and transport facilities have all declined in numbers and in underlying vitality. Typically, rural populations have aged and become fewer in total. Many small towns and villages now struggle to retain their viability. Throughout the world, local, regional and central government agencies have intervened to address these issues, with various degrees of success.

In recent years, the rural world has seen new challenges. Nature and landscape conservation is increasingly regarded as important. Historic buildings and "traditional" rural societies are receiving more attention. In some more accessible rural regions, there has been an influx of population, of people unhappy about big city living conditions - a trend known as counter-urbanisation. But for most parts of the countryside, rural decline issues remain important.

Tourism on the contrary, presents a picture of thriving growth. From humble origins in the nineteenth century, tourism has expanded rapidly since the early 1950's. International tourist arrivals have increased from 25 millions in 1950 to an estimated 476 millions in 1992. About 60 per cent of this travel is for leisure purposes. Domestic (non-international) tourism, however, dwarfs even these massive figures. The World Tourism Organization estimates domestic travel numbers to be ten times the international total. Domestic tourism is also growing rapidly. The WTO estimates that, by 2000, tourism could be the world's largest single industry.

There are many factors behind the growth statistics. In the developed world, there has been a rapid growth in disposable income. In Britain whose economic growth in recent years has not been very strong disposable income rose by 63 per cent in real terms between 1968 and 1988. Shorter working hours and increasing numbers of paid holidays have helped. Higher levels of education have prompted a greater desire to travel, and explore. Transport networks - rail, road, air and sea - have been greatly improved. Rarely, however, have government agencies directly influenced the pace of tourism development, which has largely been driven by market forces and private enterprise. In this way, tourism differs markedly from agriculture and other rural activities.

Tourism has, until recently, been concentrated into specialist beach, lake and mountain resort areas, and into major cultural centres. It has proved to be a powerful engine for economic growth - transferring capital, income and employment from industrial, urban and developed areas to non-industrial regions. Intra OECD tourism flows dominate the world pattern. The top five tourist generating countries -Germany, United States, United Kingdom, Japan and France - account for over 51 per cent of world travel expenditure. Income flows are remarkably similar: the top five destination countries, accounting for 41 per cent of receipts, are the United States, Spain, Italy, France and the United Kingdom (1987 figures). Within that picture there have been real changes in the post war period. Foremost amongst the new destinations is Spain. Foreign visitors to Spain increased from 6 millions in 1960 to 47 millions in 1986. Foreign earnings more than doubled - (to 15 billion US dollars) - between 1983 and 1987 alone. Tourism now employs over 1.5 million Spanish people directly. Yet the vast majority of Spain's visitors are concentrated into the five coastal regions of Spain, out of the total of 16 Spanish regions.

While the Spanish example illustrates how tourism can assist national economic growth, the experience of many other countries, including Britain, Ireland, France and the United States illustrates how regional economic growth can also be linked to tourism development.

Can the power of tourism's growth potential be harnessed to pull rural regions out of decline? Already tourism to rural regions is increasing. Can - and will - that increase continue? Will rural tourism provide sufficient employment, income and capital flows to materially assist rural development? Can all rural areas be helped? Could there be drawbacks to tourism development in the countryside? Should governments and communities intervene to assist or guide tourism development? Is there evidence that this can be done successfully? What further research is needed into issues in rural tourism to help understand and foster its growth and potential? And what marks out rural tourism from other forms of tourism activity?

1. The case for rural tourism

Rural tourism is not totally new. Interest in countryside recreation grew in the nineteenth century as a reaction to the stress and squalor of the expanding industrial cities. Writers such as Wordsworth and Schiller captured the romanticism of the rural scene. The new railway companies capitalised on this emergent interest by transporting tourists to the countryside. The Alps and the American and Canadian Rockies were early rural tourism venues assisted by rail-led marketing and capital investment.

The new rural tourism of the 1970's, 80's and 90's is, however, different in several ways. Far larger numbers of visitors are involved. Over 70 per cent of all Americans now participate in rural recreation: figures for many other OECD countries reveal similar, if slightly lower, levels of participation. The penetration of those visitors is far greater. The spread of car ownership and internationally available car hire allows visitors to reach regions far beyond rail-nets and rail-heads. Most important of all, tourism has developed away from spectacularly scenic areas into countryside of all types. It has also broken free of large and specialised resorts into small towns and villages to become truly rural.

Growth in rural tourism is difficult to quantify, because few countries collect statistics in a way which separates purely rural from other forms of tourism. Most national tourism administrations agree, however, that it is a growth sector. Experience in individual rural regions provides further testimony. In the American states of Wyoming, Montana and Idaho ranch and farm hospitality enterprises have increased from five in 1985 to 90 in 1992. Australia's "Outback Queensland" area reports steady annual increases in visitor flows of up to 20 per cent p.a. Many new tourism projects in rural Austria have achieved a steady development in patronage throughout the 1980's.

2. But what is rural tourism?

At first glance, this is a simple question. Rural tourism is tourism which takes place in the countryside. But, on deeper consideration, a simple definition of rural tourism is inadequate for many purposes. Equally, it is difficult to produce a more complex definition which applies to all rural areas in all countries. Problems include:

-- Urban - or - resort-based tourism is not confined to urban areas, but spills out into rural areas.

-- Rural areas themselves are difficult to define, and the criteria used by different nations vary enormously.

-- Not all tourism which takes place in rural areas is strictly "rural" - it can be "urban" in form, and merely be located in a rural area.

-- Tourism has historically been an urban concept; the great majority of tourists live in urban areas. Tourism can be an urbanising influence on rural areas, encouraging cultural and economic change, and new construction.

-- Different forms of rural tourism have developed in different regions. Farm-based holidays are important in many parts of rural Germany and Austria. Farm-based holidays are much rarer in the rural United States and Canada.

-- Rural areas themselves are in a complex process of change. The impact of global markets, communications and telecommunication have changed market conditions and orientations for traditional products. The rise of environmentalism has led to increasing control by "outsiders" over land use and resource development. Although some rural areas still experience depopulation, others are experiencing an inflow of people to retire or to develop new "non-traditional" businesses. The once clear distinction between urban and rural is now blurred by suburbanisation, long distance commuting and second home development

-- Rural tourism is a complex multi-faceted activity: it is not just farm-based tourism. It includes farm-based holidays but also comprises special interest nature holidays and ecotourism, walking, climbing and riding holidays, adventure, sport and health tourism, hunting and angling, educational travel, arts and heritage tourism, and, in some areas, ethnic tourism. There is also a large general interest market for less specialised forms of rural tourism. This area is highlighted by studies of the important German tourism market, where a major requirement of the main holiday is the ability to provide peace, quiet and relaxation in rural surroundings.

Because rural tourism is multi-faceted, because rural areas themselves are multi-faceted and rarely either static entities or self-contained, and free from urban influence, a working and reasonably universal definition of the subject is difficult to find. However, in almost every case rurality is the central and unique selling point in the rural tourism package. The search for a definition must, therefore, begin with an understanding of the concept of rurality itself.

3. *What is rurality?*

The need for a definition of rural tourism is relatively new. The need for a definition for rurality in general is an old issue faced by geographers, sociologists, economists and planners for many years. In this wider debate on rurality three major discussion points dominate: (1) population density and size of settlements, (2) land use, and its dominance by agriculture and forestry, (3) "traditional" social structures and issues of community identity and heritage. It is worth briefly discussing each of these in turn.

4. *Rural population densities and settlement size*

Typically rural areas have low population densities: this is a result of small settlements, widely spaced apart. The natural and/or the farmed/forested environment dominates the built environment. Average rural population densities vary enormously between and within the OECD countries: an exact analysis would be valueless because of the varying sizes of the administrative units used for statistical purposes. This point is also illustrated when examining the size of settlements classified as rural by a selection of member states, given below:

5. Selected national criteria for "rural" settlements

Australia	population clusters of fewer than 1 000 people, excluding certain areas, e.g. holiday resorts.
Austria	Towns of fewer than 5 000 people
Canada	Places of fewer than 1 000 people, with a population density of fewer than 400 per square kilometre.
Denmark (and Norway)	Agglomerations of fewer than 200 inhabitants
England and Wales	No definition - but the Rural Development Commission excludes towns with more than 10 000 inhabitants.
France	Towns containing an agglomeration of fewer than 2,000 people living in contiguous houses, or with not more than 200 metres between the houses.
Portugal (and Switzerland)	Towns of fewer than 10 000 people.

Source: UN Demographic Year-books and Robinson (1991)

The OECD Rural Development Programme uses a pragmatically based series of indicators: while at local level a population density of 150 persons per square kilometre is the preferred criterion, "at the regional level geographic units are grouped by the share of their population which is rural, into the following three types: predominantly rural (>50 per cent), significantly rural (15-50 per cent) and predominantly urbanized regions (<15 per cent)".

From this array of varying definitions, two clear points stand out. Rural settlements may vary in size, but they are small, and always with a population of fewer than 10 000 inhabitants. They are almost always in areas of relatively low population density.

6. Land use

Many commentators define rural areas as those with less than 10-20 per cent of their land areas covered by the built environment. There are three important implications here. These areas will be dominated by agrarian and forest-based economic activities. They will be, to a large extent, repositories of the natural world and wild-life. For the visitor, they will give an impression of space, and a traditional non-urban, non-industrial economy. Their economies will be strongly influenced by the market for farm and forest products. Although the labour force required for farming and forestry has declined rapidly in recent years, rural areas still show a strong bias towards jobs in the farm/forest sector. Additionally, they usually exhibit low female activity rates outside the home because of the shortage of job opportunities for women in many rural areas.

7. "Traditional" social structures

The rapid urbanisation of the nineteenth and twentieth centuries produced new social structures different from the "traditional" societies of the countryside. The retention of older ways of life and thinking is important in retaining rural "character". It is this residual character which, combined with the scenic values and recreational opportunities of the countryside, attracts tourists from urban areas.

It is difficult to define the exact characteristics of rural society. There are great variations between countries and continents, and even within countries. In his article, "Communities and their Relationships to Agrarian Values" (in Rural Policy Problems, Brown, W.P. and Hadwinger, P.F. eds., pp. 19-32, Lexington, 1982), Flinn noted three very different types of traditional life styles within the rural United States:

- Small town society, closely knit, strongly believing in democracy, but often not in close contact with nature.

- Agrarian society, based on family farming, farm life and the calendar of the seasons.

- Ruralists, living outside towns, but not farming: independents who value open space, nature, and "a natural order".

The rural sociologists have struggled hard to identify the varying characteristics of rural societies. Frankenberg's urban/rural contrasts, dating from 1966, remains a valuable check list.

8. The characteristics of "rural" and "urban" societies

Rural	Urban
Community	Association
Social fields involving few but multiple role relationships	Social fields involving many overlapping role relationships
Different social roles played by same person	Different social roles played by different people
Simple economies	Diverse economies
Little division of labour	Great specialisation in labour force
Ascribed status	Achieved status
Education according to status	Status derived from education
Role embracement	Role commitment
Close-knit networks	Loose-knit networks
Locals	Cosmopolitans
Economic class is one of several divisions	Economic class is the major division
Conjunction	Segregation
Integration with work environment	Separation of work environment

Source: Frankenberg, 1966

9. The continuum concept

Faced with the complexities of the rural world discussed above, and with an array of other indices deliberately not discussed here, commentators on the rural scene have evolved the concept of the rural-urban continuum as a way of coping with the complexity of the situation, and the problem of comparing areas which are perceived to be rural, but possess many different characteristics. Rural communities can be assessed on a sliding scale with sparsely populated remote wilderness as one end of a polar typology. The other end of the scale can be represented by the so-called "world city", the ultimate expression of urbanisation. Between these extremes lie a variety of situations, largely rural or largely urban, with a mid-point represented by the outermost edge of suburbia, a cross-over point between poles, exhibiting characteristics of both rural and urban typology (see Robinson 1990).

An additional part of the "rurality" equation can be introduced here. The OECD's Rural Development Programme has developed a useful typology for assessing the economic geography of rural areas. This divides the rural world into peripheral or remote regions, "intermediate" regions, which make up the majority of the rural land mass, and economically integrated rural regions, often close to large urban complexes. The peripheral regions are characterised by sparse populations, small scale often traditional enterprises, high servicing costs and economic poverty. The economically integrated regions tend to have large farm units, a diversified economy, good services and relative affluence. The intermediate areas lie midway between these extremes. This typology can also fit the continuum concept: the three types of region are not sharply defined but blend into each other. The typology has important implications for both rural development and rural tourism which will be explained later.

The continuum concept copes not only with a variety of landscapes, life styles and demographic inheritance - but also with change. Settlements can move along the continuum, exhibiting change through time. Typically - but not always - the change tends to move districts and settlements towards the urban pole. In the OECD's economic typology, change is also common - and can also occur in either direction.

A further valuable point to note is that the continuum concept allows observers to realise that indices of rurality may change at different rates relative to each other. Thus, rural settlements may remain locationally rural while becoming functionally urban. Settlement size and population density may remain "rural", but economies may become non-agricultural, and society may display increasing numbers of urban characteristics. Different parts of rural society may display more or less urban characteristics. The American geographer Brian Berry notes the increasing development in the USA of "urban civilisation without cities" as educated, independently employed or retired urbanites seek "rustic backgrounds for sophisticated lives lived in a country setting". Commentators have, however, also noted that these newcomers to the countryside are amongst the most vocal in seeking to preserve certain rural characteristics, notably, landscapes dominated by farming, forestry or parkland, and small-scale settlements.

Throughout the debate on definitions of rurality amongst academics, planners and politicians, rurality is almost always seen as an important condition, possessing very valuable characteristics worthy of preservation. Thus, while the global condition has become steadily more urban, most commentators have stressed the importance of retaining key differences between urbanisation and the rural realm. Forty years ago, in 1951, the British government set up a special commission to review the future of that most remote and most rural part of Britain, the crofting communities of the Highlands and Islands of Scotland. (Crofting is a subsistence farming/fishing economy carried out on small holdings, usually of less than 5 hectares, far away from urban settlements.) After noting that crofting flew in the face of all modern agrarian practices, and required, even in 1951, massive levels of state subsidy, the Commission concluded that, "in the national interest, the maintenance of these communities is desirable, because they embody a free and independent way of life which, in a civilisation predominantly urban and industrial in character, is worth preserving for its own intrinsic value" (Taylor Commission, 1951). In 1990, Peter Keller, in a report for the Tourism Committee of the OECD, on "Tourism Policy and Rural Development", wrote " The countryside as a creative counterbalance to the hypercivilised urban centre is no illusion.... hill farmers must be kept on the land... highly developed economies should be able to afford the luxury of safeguarding typically rural areas". In this, Peter Keller, as an expert on the tourism industry, recognises the special value of the countryside.

The practical expression of the pro-rural sentiments quoted above has been two-fold. Government policies financially support both primary rural products and rural service provision in every OECD Member country. These financial policies are frequently backed by strong conservation policies, aimed at the retention of existing landscape areas, whole settlements, buildings and the natural world. Urban conservation policies also exist, but usually cover only fragments of cities and isolated special situations.

10. Rural tourism: a concept for development and conservation

It has been argued above that rurality as a concept is connected with low population densities and open space, and with small scale settlements, generally of fewer than 10 000 inhabitants. Land use is dominated by farming, forestry and natural areas. Societies tend towards traditionalism: the influence of the past is often strong. Government policies lean towards conservation rather than radical or rapid change.

It follows, therefore, that rural tourism should be:

-- Located in rural areas;

-- Functionally rural, built upon the rural world's special features: small scale enterprise, open space, contact with nature and the natural world, heritage, "traditional" societies and "traditional" practices;

-- Rural in scale - both in terms of buildings and settlements - and, therefore, usually small scale;

-- Traditional in character, growing slowly and organically, and connected with local families. It will often be very largely controlled locally and developed for the long term good of the area;

-- Sustainable - in the sense that its development should help sustain the special rural character of an area, and in the sense that its development should be sustainable in its use of resources. Rural tourism should be seen as a potential tool for conservation and sustainability, rather than as an urbanizing and development tool;

-- Of many different kinds, representing the complex pattern of rural environment, economy, and history.

A list of contrasting features between urban/resort tourism and rural tourism could include the following:

Urban/Resort Tourism	Rural Tourism
Little open space	Much open space
Settlements over 10 000	Settlements under 10 000
Densely populated	Sparsely populated
Built environment	Natural environment
Many indoor activities	Many outdoor activities
Infrastructure - intensive	Infrastructure - weak
Strong entertainment/retail base	Strong individual activity base
Large establishments	Small establishments
Nationally/Internationally owned firms	Locally owned businesses
Much full time involvement in tourism	Much part-time involvement in tourism
No farm/forestry involvement	Some farm/forestry involvement
Tourism interests self supporting	Tourism supports other interests
Workers may live far from workplace	Workers often live close to workplace
Rarely influenced by seasonal factors	Often influenced by seasonal factors
Many guests	Few guests
Guest relationships anonymous	Guest relationships personal
Professional management	Amateur management
Cosmopolitan in atmosphere	Local in atmosphere

Many modern buildings	Many older buildings
Development/growth ethic	Conservation/limits to growth ethic
General in appeal	Specialist appeal
Broad marketing operation	Niche marketing

11. The importance of the continuum - concept for rural tourism

Commentators seeking to define rurality have made extensive use of the concept of the rural/urban continuum to deal with many different types of area, exhibiting different characteristics, and areas undergoing active change. A similar continuum concept can be useful for those seeking to define rural tourism. Few areas will display all of the characteristics of rural tourism listed previously. Many will display some "urban" characteristics. Some will be in the process of change and development towards becoming large, urban resorts. The use of the continuum concept allows planners to recognise this trend, and to take steps either to regulate it, or to make infrastructural provision for it. It can be strongly argued that management strategies in rural tourism should aim to conserve rurality as an important resource. But, in some cases it may be valuable to allow or even encourage some change to take place.

12. What types of holidays are rural?

This is a frequently asked and extremely difficult question. Rural tourism cannot be defined solely by holiday type: intensity of use, location, style of management, integration with the community and other factors play an important part in the definition. But a broad-brush approach can be useful. Again, the continuum concept is a useful one. Many types of holiday can be developed in both urban and rural locations. Holiday-makers may be involved in both urban and rural activities on the same day. A tentative classification of holiday types is given below: it should be used with care. The listing follows the continuum concept, moving from specifically rural to specifically urban with a broad intermediate category.

Holidays which are usually specifically rural

Walking
Climbing
"Adventure" holidays/wilderness holidays
Canoeing
Rafting
Cross-country skiing
Snow-shoe tours
Low intensity downhill skiing
Nature study in outdoor settings, including bird-watching, photography etc.
Hunting
Cycling/Cycle touring
Horse riding
Landscape appreciation
Rural heritage Studies
Small town/village touring
Relaxation holidays requiring a rural milieu
Small scale conventions/conferences
Rural festivals
River and canal angling
Sports requiring natural settings, e.g. orienteering

Holidays which may be rural or urban/resort based

Swimming
Low/medium intensity beach holidays
Medium intensity downhill skiing
Sports requiring man-made infrastructure of a semi-natural type, e.g. golf
Cuisine-based holidays
General heritage holidays
Conservation holidays
Educational holidays
Cultural festivals
Craft holidays
Camping
Sightseeing/Touring
Small/medium sized conferences/conventions
Sailing/cruising
Sea angling

Holidays which are usually specifically urban/resort based

City sightseeing
Shopping
High intensity beach holidays
High intensity downhill skiing
Urban heritage/culture holidays
Zoological gardens
Health resorts
Industrial tourism
Major conferences/conventions
Entertainment holidays/gambling
Resort holidays
Sports requiring man-made infrastructure, e.g. international arena based events

13. *The relationship between tourism and agriculture*

Traditionally agriculture and forestry were central to rural life. They were the major employers of labour, the main sources of income within the rural economy, and indirectly had a powerful influence on traditions, power structures and life styles. Together, the decisions of farmers and foresters determined rural land use and landscapes.

In the late twentieth century, the central role of farming and forestry has been diminished. Both activities have shed much of their labour force. Only five OECD countries now employ more than 15 per cent of their labour force in farming, forestry and fishing: in eight OECD countries, that figure is less than 5 per cent. The economic power of farming and forestry has declined, not least because those activities are extremely dependent on state subsidies for their profitability. Traditions are waning before the combined attack of television, power farming techniques and tree processors. Even the role of agri - and arboriculturalists as "landscape gardeners" has diminished: power has begun to move to planners and conservationists.

In this evolving situation, two myths have grown up about the role of rural tourism. One is that rural tourism is farm-based tourism. The second is that diversification into tourism will universally "save" the farming community. These statements are untrue because the relationships between agriculture, forestry and tourism are extremely complex ones.

Farm-based rural tourism has been successful through many (but not all) parts of German-speaking Europe because of a powerful combination of small farm size, interesting scenery, closeness to markets, traditional town/country links caused by late migration from the countryside to city regions, the owner-occupation of farmsteads and the tradition of effective and interventionary local government and co-operative movements. Furthermore, the role of farm-based tourism has been exaggerated because it has received great attention from both agriculture ministries and academics. The Bibiliography of Rural Tourism for the OECD reveals that farm tourism is the largest single special category of rural tourism in terms of published works (see Appendix B). In areas where some or all of the factors mentioned above are lacking, farm- based tourism has been slow to develop. Reasons include:

-- Long distances to the urban holiday market;

-- Medium and large sized farms which did not need to diversify, or were amalgated to create larger units;

-- Rented farms which either failed to receive the owner's permission to diversify, or were amalgamated to create larger units;

-- Very poor and very small farms which had no surplus accommodation;

-- Coops and local councils and tourist boards which did not help with marketing and infrastructure provision;

-- Scenery/heritage/activity attractions which were poor;

-- A short, single season.

Thus, for example, over large parts of Eastern England, Sweden, Canada and the United States, farm tourism is poorly developed. But that does not mean that rural tourism is poorly developed. Many of the kinds of rural holidays discussed earlier are not dependent on farm situations. Accommodation can be provided by hotels and motels, small town and village bed and breakfasts, purpose built lodges, camping and caravan sites.

Diversification into rural tourism is frequently held up as a potential panacea for agriculture's ills. There is no doubt that in some areas, and for some businesses, tourism can be valuable. But there are serious problems in its universal application:

-- Over 75 per cent of the land of the OECD countries is rural: there are insufficient visitors to maintain all farmers in all areas.

-- Farm-based tourism does not reduce productivity on many farms. In some cases, additional tourism earnings are invested to increase agricultural productivity. Therefore, farm surpluses in OECD countries could continue to grow, leading to falling prices and quota restrictions, and a further round of farm problems.

-- Some areas are unsuitable for intensive tourism development because of remoteness, lack of scenic or heritage attractions, and other factors.

-- Successful farm tourism development seems to require effective co-operative marketing and development efforts. Many areas have no tradition of co-operation between farmers, or between farmers and governmental agencies.

The key relationship in rural tourism is between tourism development and comprehensive rural development, embracing rural services, new enterprise attraction, conservation, a wider role for women and inward investment. Agriculture has an important role to play in rural tourism, but it is but one facet amongst many: it may be of greater or lesser importance depending on local, regional and national circumstances.

II.   Rural tourism: its growth, its market - promises and problems

1.   Why has rural tourism grown?

Rural tourism is not an accidental or temporary growth phenomenon. Although the travel trade is in some senses a "fashion" industry, subject to short term trends, the forces behind the growth of rural tourism are more long term in nature. These forces are partly connected to long term changes in the travel market, partly to improvements in transport and communications and partly to the efforts of public agencies charged with assisting rural change. In total, 14 key factors can be isolated which have been responsible for rural tourism growth in the past and which will continue that growth into the future.

-- **Increasing levels of education** The post-war period has seen universal increase in free or assisted education available to the populations of the developed world. This has included longer periods of school-based education, more higher education, the spread of adult and continuing education and the growth of non-formalised education, via radio, television and other media. Research shows that increasing levels of education correlate with increased interest in outdoor recreation, eco-tourism, and special interest holidays.

-- **A growing interest in heritage** Over the last 20 years there has been a boom in the level of interest in heritage both man-made and natural. This reflects many factors: a fear of the future, a fear of rootlessness, better education, time to explore, and, not least, better heritage presentation. Freeman Tilden's pioneering book "Interpreting Our Heritage", first published in 1957 in the United States helped revolutionise and inspire the heritage industry. Rural areas are especially well suited to heritage interpretation, possessing many historic landscapes, artefacts, and linkages, and fine settings for heritage sites. With the exception of the urban zoo (an institution now in decline), rural areas have a monopoly of the natural heritage market.

-- **Increases in leisure time,** coupled with higher levels of disposable income, are important factors in developing tourism generally. One specific aspect of this equation is important for rural tourism. This is the growth of the short break, and the second or third holiday market. The European Community's 1985 Survey of Europeans on Holiday indicated that, of those taking holidays, over one-third now take two or more holiday trips involving overnight stays away from home each year. This is important because while a "traditional" resort-based holiday may still account for main holidays, rural special interest holidays can be tried for the second, often shorter, holiday without too much risk.

-- **Transport and communications** have improved so rapidly and universally in the post-war period that remoteness - in time and cost -is now no longer a major problem for rural areas. As a result, rural tourism development projects can now be carried out in places as remote as Canada's Labrador Straits (accessible only from the offshore island of Newfoundland), or the Falkland Islands in the South Atlantic. This ease of movement owes itself in part to technological changes - jet aircraft, high speed trains, motorways, and roll-on roll-off ferries, automatic telephone systems and fax machines. It has been influenced by better and more widespread money handling facilities, chief of which has been the internationally acceptable credit card. There have also been key attitudinal changes on behalf of both the travel trade and their clients. Distance and remoteness have become selling points, rather than barriers.

-- **Health consciousness** has grown and is growing steadily and in the concept of healthy living, active recreation plays an important part. Exercise and sport play central roles in healthy living strategies. Rural areas are well placed to provide outdoor recreation of all kinds from walking to cycling, orienteering, skiing and climbing. The countryside is assumed to be healthy, with overtones of fresh air and bucolic well-being. In contrast, resort holidays based on the sun/sea/sand formula have been found to offer serious health risks.   Medical researchers in Australasia, America and Scandinavia have pinpointed sunbathing as being responsible for higher levels of skin disease, ranging from premature wrinkling to deadly skin cancers. While this problem is still only fully appreciated in the southern hemisphere, it seems very likely that knowledge of the risks posed by sun-belt holidays will grow.

-- **Better outdoor clothing** has helped rural holidays in both a practical and a fashion sense. High performance fabrics enable wearers to stay warm and dry in adverse weather, allowing tourists to enjoy wet weather and out-of-season conditions. Contemporary outdoor clothing is now extremely fashionable, and available in a wide range of colours and styles. Outdoor recreation equipment has also been much improved and many items, such as the mountain bike, the wind surfer and the 4-wheel drive utility vehicle, have achieved cult fashion status.

-- **A growing interest in speciality food** is widely evident, be it wild rice from North America, non-pasturized cheeses from France, cholesterol-free, non-farmed salmon and deer from Scandinavia, or organic produce from the Alps. Considerable space in the press is devoted to speciality foods and food preparation. Rural holidays have been able to capitalise on this trend because the countryside is the source of quality non-processed foods.

-- **Green issues** have risen high on most political agendas over the last ten years. This interest has been seized upon by the marketeers of many consumer products, including holiday tour operators. Rural holidays, although not necessarily environmentally friendly, can capitalise on the wholesomeness which the countryside is felt to exude.

-- **Authenticity** is a quality which is increasingly prized. In a world of video and television entertainment, factory produced goods, and suburban anonymity, the authenticity of the countryside, and the personal touch provided by small scale communities and accommodation units is extremely valuable. An English Tourist Board survey of motives for taking rural holidays, conducted in 1987, placed this point second only to scenery as a reason for staying in the countryside.

-- **Peace and tranquility** rank high amongst the requirements of many tourists. This is hardly surprising given the high levels of mental stress experienced by many workers. A 1986 survey of the German holiday market found that "to switch off, relax" was the number one aim of those taking holidays: this aim was given by 66 per cent of respondents. 47 per cent wished to experience nature, and 32 per cent sought cleaner air and an unpolluted environment.

-- **Ageing but active populations** are becoming the norm across the OECD countries. Early retirement is now commonplace, as are active 70-year-olds. In 1971 83 per cent of British males aged 60-64 were still working in full time jobs. By 1995 it is expected that only 55 per cent of men in that age group will remain in full time work. Effective occupational pensions allow this active but ageing population to travel widely: many choose rural holidays for health reasons and to discover new non-urban experiences.

-- **REAL travel (rewarding, enriching, adventuresome and a learning experience)** has been noted by many commentators as being a growth area. The many facets of rural tourism are specially placed to fulfil the needs of this growth market.

-- **Individualism** is also a growth market, rejecting the mass activities of the past. The growth of individualism has been noted and acted upon by the car manufacturers, by clothing manufacturers, and by many other purveyors of consumer goods. Rural tourism, because of the fragmented and small scale nature of the enterprises involved, is especially capable of exploiting this market trend, although high quality selling and hospitality skills are needed.

-- **The rural agencies,** numerous in most countries, have been quick to express an interest in rural tourism and to offer aid and advice. These agencies include those connected with agriculture, with nature conservation, with community welfare, with the arts and crafts, with National Parks, with economic development, transport - the list is almost endless. Although the agencies rarely co-ordinate their activities, and are rarely organisations with any experience of tourism, they have assisted many collective projects and individual enterprises.

2. *The size of the market*

Given the many factors above, it is interesting to note that there is very little quantitative knowledge of the precise size of the rural tourism market. Estimates have been made of the size of the "Special Interest" tourism market, which is a closely related area. The World Tourism Organization estimated the special interest market to be about 3 per cent of the total domestic and international market in 1985. In 1989, a survey of U.S. travel agents revealed that special interest holidays comprised 15 per cent of all bookings. Other U.S. surveys show that eco-tourists (a related niche rural tourism market) are relatively wealthy, and spend more per holiday than conventional visitors. Repeat bookings accounted for one-third of the clients surveyed. German statistics claim that 20 per cent of main holidays are now in the special interest category.

What is clear from market surveys is that the rural holiday market is very much an affluent and well educated one, requiring quality and tending to spend above average amounts. British and American surveys confirm these points, but perhaps the most comprehensive and telling evidence comes from France. "Le Marché du Tourisme Vert", published by the French Ministry of Tourism in 1991, takes an in-depth look at the market for rural holidays in France, including both domestic and foreign markets. British visitors were noted to be largely from the leading social groups. German tourists to rural France represent "un certain snobisme". The Italian market is described as from the upper social strata, couples aged 35-40 with children aged 5-12, usually from a large city and environmentally very aware.

Therefore, if levels of income and educational attainment continue to rise across the OECD countries, the market for rural tourism should also grow. At the time of writing, recessionary trends may limit short term growth; in the long term, most authorities predict a return to slowly rising standards.

Aside from the bird-watching and hunting/fishing markets, which have a wider appeal across the whole socio-economic spectrum in many countries, rural tourism is generally supported by an up-market clientele.

3. *What can rural tourism contribute to rural development?*

The American state of Wyoming (with a population of 512 000) estimates that wildlife tourism is worth over $ 1 billion dollars annually within its borders. Britain's Countryside Commission estimated that visitors to the countryside spent £3 000 million in 1986: of this figure £1 100 million came from those spending at least one night in the countryside, and the remainder came from day trips. These are gross figures; the net figures after deduction of goods bought in to service tourism, when tax has been paid, etc., would be much lower, but, equally, they make no allowance for the multiplier effect of tourism spending.

Clearly, rural tourism, while still only a minority tourism market, is already making a valuable contribution to rural economies. Its contribution can be expressed not only in financial terms, but also in terms of jobs, contributions towards funding conservation, encouragement to the adoption of new working practices, and the injection of a new vitality into sometimes weakened economies. In total, tourism promises 17 potential benefits to rural development. These are covered in detail below.

-- **Job retention** is extremely important in rural areas where employment decline is often endemic. Tourism cash flows can assist job retention in services such as retailing, transport, hospitality and medical care. It can also provide additional income for farmers, and, in some cases, for foresters and fisherman. Job retention is not as politically glamorous as job creation, but, by helping the viability of small communities, it is critical to the survival of marginal areas. Studies of rural Austria, Sweden and Ireland have documented the role of tourism in job retention.

-- **Job creation** is a further possibility if rural tourism is successful. Job creation typically occurs in the hotel and catering trades, but can also take place in transport, retailing, and in information/heritage interpretation. Studies in Britain suggest that job creation varies by enterprise type. Farmhouse accommodation and bed-and-breakfast can create up to 23 jobs per £100 000 of tourism revenue. Job creation effects are less marked in hotels and caravan/campsites, yielding approximately six jobs per £100 000 of revenue. Similar figures of between five and six jobs per £100 000 revenue have been estimated for rural attractions of all types (see Hart, Hardy and Shaw,1990, and others).

-- **Job diversity** is encouraged by rural tourism development. Most rural areas have little job variety outside farming and basic services. Better job diversity enriches rural society, and helps retain population levels.

-- **Pluriactivity** can be a further useful by-product of tourism in the countryside. Pluriactivity is the term used when an individual or family carries out more than one type of job to maintain their income. A part-time farmer could also offer accommodation, assist the local administration in service tasks and act as a ski-instructor. Sea fishermen may take tourist parties on angling trips, on whale watching expeditions off the coast of Canada and the United States, or on bird-watching excursions off the coast of Ireland or Scotland. Pluriactivity guards against recession in any one sector. It is especially important in the rural context because of the cultural importance of the family as a unit in many traditional societies.

-- **Service retention** is vital in rural areas: rural tourism can assist in three ways. Visitor information services can be provided by existing outlets, such as shops, thus increasing income flows if payment is made for acting as information outlets. Services can also benefit by the additional customers which visitors provide. The high levels of public transport in rural Austria and Switzerland are in part due to the support they receive from holiday-makers. This additional custom is not, however, automatic: to make the most of the potential, services often need to offer new products, to be available at different times and to understand the new markets. Finally, tourism's importance to national economies can strengthen the political case for subsides to help retain services.

-- **Farm support** is a major issue on all political agendas. Many studies have shown that farm incomes can be bolstered by rural tourism, through accommodation enterprises of all kinds, by developing open farms and other attractions, by increased sales of farm produce, and by increasing female activity rates through additional off-farm employment. There are widespread variations in the levels of farmer participation in rural tourism throughout the OECD countries, varying by region, farm size, age of farmer and other factors. While surveys show that economic benefits are of first importance in prompting farmers to enter tourism enterprises, the surveys also stress that many farmers achieve a social bonus. Visitors bring variety and company to what can be a lonely and limited life style.

-- **Forestry** is an important activity in many upland and climatically marginal regions. Forest regions have suffered serious socio-economic problems in recent years, partly because of the mechanisation of tree felling and processing, and partly because of falling prices following reduced timber demand. Rural tourism can assist forestry by diversifying income sources for forest communities if the special qualities of the forest environment for recreational use are realised and developed.

-- **Landscape conservation** has become an increasingly important form of heritage protection. Although this dates back to the designation of America's Yellowstone National Park in 1872, the national park movement is still progressing and most countries now have a wide range of lesser designations covering many types of landscape. Landscape is of crucial importance to rural tourism but, equally, visitor use is vital to the landscape conservation industry. Visitor use brings political benefits, can bring economic gains, and can provide jobs in maintaining and repairing traditional landscapes worn by recreational activities.

-- **Smaller settlements** in the countryside have always been at greater risk of losing viability because they are unable to support the many services which now require larger threshold populations to support them. Rural tourism can assist these smaller settlements to survive, because smaller places have a special attraction for visitors. Careful management of this process is, however, required.

-- **Rural arts and crafts** have a special place in the cultural heritage of regions and nations. Many commentators have noted that tourism can assist arts and crafts, both by recognising their importance, and by purchasing craft products. Income flows from these activities are well documented. Support between the arts and tourism can be a two-way process. Many communities now use arts and crafts festivals as a marketing mechanism to encourage visitors to come to their areas.

-- **Cultural provision** has always been restricted in rural areas. The lack of major facilities such as theatre, opera, music and galleries has been one of the many factors encouraging rural depopulation. The festivals and other events described in the previous paragraph have enabled rural areas to broaden their cultural provision, buying in artists and ensembles and supporting those purchases by ticket sales to visitors. The English Lake District's "Theatre in the Forest" project at Grizedale is a classic example which can be repeated in most countries.

-- **Nature conservation**, like landscape conservation, is a stated goal of most modern governments. It is, however, an expensive process. Rural tourism can valorise nature conservation in a monetary sense. Many estimates have been made of the value of nature to tourism. On the grand scale, it is estimated that each elephant is worth \$14 375 to the Kenyan economy. On a lesser scale, the British Royal Society for the Protection of Birds has demonstrated that even small bird reserves can help sustain village shops by visitor purchases and by the expenditure of reserve management and maintenance staff. Visitors are prepared to pay to see nature: most reserves and many national parks successfully charge for entrance. How far charging can be extended is a much discussed point in conservation circles.

-- **The historic built environment** can benefit from rural tourism in two ways. Many historic properties now charge for admission in order to maintain their fabrics and surrounding gardens and parklands. Secondly, there are important buildings from the past which have become redundant. Churches have lost their congregations, castles have lost their wars, farm buildings have become too small for modern equipment, railway stations have lost their trains, and canal warehouses no longer have barge traffic. The tourist industry can usually use these redundant buildings profitably and imaginatively: they can become attractions in their own right. The small town of St. Jacobs in Ontario, Canada, has converted grain stores into a craft centre; in Lanarkshire, Scotland, a folly constructed in the shape of a pineapple has become sought after as a cottage for holiday lets; in the Swiss valley of Safiental, a timber farm-house is maintained in its original pre-twentieth century condition by using it as a Youth Hotel.

-- **Environmental improvements** such as village paving and traffic regulation schemes, sewage and litter disposal can be assisted by tourism revenues and political pressures from tourism authorities. These help develop pride of place, important in retaining existing population and businesses, and in attracting new enterprises and families.

-- **Small fishing communities** are suffering badly from dwindling fish stocks, quota restrictions and international bans on some activities. A number of these communities can successfully diversify into sports fishing, bird and seal watching, and coastal sightseeing. Some environmental groups claim that potential revenue from whale and dolphin watching could exceed revenue from catching whales for meat.

-- **The role of women** within the rural community was, in the past, a restricted one. Farming, forestry and mining were very much male occupations. Alternative jobs for women were few. Women were rarely involved in local politics. The widespread emancipation of women, coupled with the possibilities which rural tourism offers, have together done much in many areas to release the under-utilised talents and energies of the female half of the population. Studies show that tourism enterprises have increased the power of women within both the family and the community. Experience in Spain, Greece, France, Britain and Ireland has demonstrated how the flexible and open-minded approach of women towards new ideas and co-operative working has helped develop and lead successful rural tourism projects. The development of the role of women could do much for the economic and social well-being of many rural areas.

-- **New ideas and initiatives** will be essential if rural communities are to prosper into the twenty-first century. Efforts to support agriculture, forestry and service provision by state subsidies have done much to develop a culture of dependency within the countryside. The new challenges and the fiercely competitive nature of the tourism market could do much to encourage enterprise and new methods. There is also evidence that rural tourism can act as a catalyst to bring new businesses of many kinds into rural communities. Research in the English county of Cornwall shows that good holiday experiences by business people were instrumental in encouraging them to re-locate their businesses to the county. Since 1971, the area has been able to reverse a century of depopulation, and it is now experiencing a population renewal.

4. *Rural tourism: the problems*

While many benefits can flow from rural tourism development, there can be problems. All economic structural re-alignments can disrupt sensitive environments. And, as the records of numerous rural aid agencies will testify, rural communities can be extremely resistant to new ideas. The problems in developing and managing rural tourism are listed below: they lead on to Section IV which asks: can rural tourism pay? will it make a sufficiently large contribution to alleviate rural problems? and can it be managed?

-- **The environmental threat.** Rural tourism operates within sensitive natural environments. Some of the most attractive tourism destinations have the most sensitive environments. These include sea and lake shorelines, wetlands, high mountain areas, and polar areas. Many studies have highlighted the threats which tourism has already brought to the environment. Intensive skiing has destroyed vegetation and encouraged land-slips; climbing erodes rock faces, and, with modern equipment, destroys their natural condition; walking and riding wears out paths in heavily used areas; noise and litter drive out and injure wild creatures; existing farming practices are upset by fire, dogs and competition for labour. The peace, quiet and authentic nature of the countryside can be seriously compromised. All these issues can be tackled to some extent by the skilled management of the countryside; management of the order required is as yet rarely available (see later in this review).

-- **The socio-cultural threat**. Just as the influx of large numbers of visitors can disrupt the natural world, so also can visitors impinge upon the small scale, static, and well ordered socio-cultural world of the rural community. Earnings patterns change, success/failure relationships are altered, power structures are challenged. More fundamentally, sociologists have long recognised that the impact of "advanced" cultures on "traditional" cultures almost always brings change to the traditional culture and not in the other direction. This process has been examined in detail in the Mediterranean and in the Alpine lands. But the process is most marked where special ethnic or linguistic groups are involved. The Irish-speaking Gaeltacht areas of Ireland have long experience of the problem: a recent positive step towards an answer has been the appointment of a project officer to try to develop tourism which is friendly towards the Irish language. In North America, the relationship of the Indian tribes and Inuit peoples to tourism development is a difficult issue still in the process of re-assessment.

-- **The housing question**. Some successful rural tourism areas - in the Canadian Rockies, in South-West England, in parts of the Alps - have found that success in the visitor market has brought accommodation problems for local people. Small communities rarely have very much surplus housing. If they are to retain their character they must not expand too much or too rapidly. Visitor demand has three types of effect. Housing can be taken over for visitor accommodation, usually in the self-catering sector. Housing purchased as second-homes by city people is often rarely used, and brings little economic benefit to the local community. Housing can be purchased as retirement homes by holidaymakers who fall in love with their holiday areas. On retirement, the one-time holidaymakers gradually create a tendency towards a gerontocracy. All these impacts raise prices and create tension within rural societies.

-- **The incoming entrepreneur**. For reasons which will be discussed later, many local farmers and businesses do not decide to enter the tourism market when opportunities present themselves. Surveys show that, in extreme cases, up to 80 per cent of tourism-related businesses in small towns and villages are owned, managed or controlled by incoming or non-local entrepreneurs. In some respects incomers can provide a valuable transfusion of contacts, capital and skill. But they can also present problems. They may be insensitive to local tradition, cultures, working practices and architectural styles. They may use non-local suppliers for goods and services. They may repatriate their profits and capital gains out of the area. They have little loyalty to their new base of operations and often leave when trading conditions deteriorate. Less tangibly, but equally important, they set up tensions between locals and incomers, and do little to change the dependency culture common to many rural places.

-- **Traffic congestion** - usually road traffic, but in some cases sea and air traffic - can be a major problem if an area is successful in attracting tourists. Narrow roads can easily be choked by traffic both inside and outside settlements, parking becomes an issue, non-tourism business can suffer and, in extreme cases, emergency services cannot make urgent calls. The attractiveness of the area as a destination can decline, taking it down-market. There can be side effects on landscape and nature conservation. Traffic management techniques and better use of public transport can help, but the funds and skills necessary are not usually available.

-- **The issues of planning, local control, public participation and partnership** bring together many of the points covered so far in this section. In an ideal world, local people and businesses would control tourism development in such a way that the problems discussed earlier would be minimised and benefits maximised. Planning controls would ensure a carefully worked out balance of development between tourism-related and other land uses. Different types of tourism activity would be zoned into the regions best suited for those types of development. Employers and employees would undertake regular training courses to learn the skills of marketing, hospitality, interpretation and tourism planning. The community would feel that it had "ownership" of its industry in a broad sense. As a result the visitor would feel a genuine sense of welcome from the host population. But real world is rarely ideal.

The financial power of the incoming entrepreneur, and the power of skilled outsiders including tour operators and tourist board officials, means that local control is seldom achieved. When locals do have power, they often do not have the foresight, experience or skills necessary. In some areas local politicians resent and resist development. In others, the promise of new jobs and income can be too great a temptation, leading to the acceptance of damaging schemes. In most cases tourism management is not practised because of cost and political implications.

There have, however, been many experiments in introducing local participation into rural tourism development projects. Most are so recent that evaluation is not yet complete. Canada has pioneered the most widespread attempts at community participation in rural tourism planning. Alberta has been especially active in this field, initiating its Community Tourism Action Plan, involving 426 out of 429 eligible communities, in 1987. Local committees have been encouraged and assisted to draw up tourism development plans through extensive consultation. Similar actions have been carried out in British Columbia and Saskatchewan. Heritage Canada has been involved in exemplary local participation work in Labrador. While it is difficult to assess the results of this work at this stage, it is already becoming clear that there are widespread variations in the quality of the plans produced. Regional co-ordination has been found to be necessary and is now being developed. Much has been learned about how to assist the work of local committees as a result of these experiences.

Other important efforts at establishing local control have taken place in Britain, Ireland and Switzerland. In Switzerland, the community of Waltensburg successfully built and operates a 70-bed hotel, to high environmental standards, with profits flowing to assist other local development schemes. This project is a model of good practice, even though it is unlikely that the concept could be transplanted fully to other rural communities. In Britain and Ireland, project leaders have assisted communities and districts to grapple with control and planning issues. Sometimes these project leaders have been educationalists; in other cases they have been rural development agency workers. Areas covered include the Ballyhoura Mountains in Ireland, the Berwick, Shropshire, West Dorset and West Somerset regions of England, and the Taff and Cleddau Rural Initiative in Wales. Further valuable experience as well as commercial success has come from these projects.

In some areas comprehensive community businesses have been formed to ensure local control and profit retention. The Connemara West Company, based in Letterfrack, Galway, Ireland is an oft quoted example. Community business, however, seems to be successful only in special circumstances.

-- **Can all rural areas successfully develop rural tourism?** Over 75 per cent of the land area of the OECD is rural. It seems unlikely that all of this vast area can participate in tourism development. Some types of area have important natural advantages for rural tourism. Experience suggests that six factors are involved in determining the suitability of areas for investment purposes. But experience also suggests that these factors are not exclusive, and that because the tourist industry is highly dynamic, and subject to changes in fashion, the factors may not remain constant in the future. Furthermore, an area's possession of any one - or even all - of these factors does not guarantee success. The factors are:

.   Scenic value - including mountains, seashores, lakes, islands, rivers and special interest scenery such as wetlands or mixed decidous forest.

.   Special wildlife assets.

.   Cultural assets including historic buildings/ towns/villages/ sites and/or ethnic heritage of all types.

.   Special facilities for sports including hunting, fishing, skiing, hiking etc.

.   Ease of access by large populations.

.   Effective promotional, commercial and management skills.

The OECD Rural Development Programme's typology for rural areas differentiates between remote areas, intermediate areas and economically integrated areas. The typology forms a useful additional set of criteria to consider when assessing conditions for the growth of tourism activities. The economically integrated areas are usually close to large cities, offering considerable leisure market potential. Closeness to cities may, however, result in a higher level of day-visit recreational use, which is less valuable in financial terms than overnight stays. Remote areas are, by definition, more likely to attract guests who stay overnight, leading to greater net revenue potential per visitor. If teamed with mountain or lake scenery, remoteness - if not too daunting - can be a considerable attraction. But remoteness without fine scenery generally means that there will be little likelihood of rural tourism development.

The OECD Rural Development Programme typology can also be a valuable indicator when considering the likelihood of local people taking up new initiatives such as tourism. Peripheral areas may try new enterprises because of a high "desperation factor", brought about by poverty and decline. Economically integrated areas may, paradoxically, also be keen to try new enterprises - not because of desperation, but because of spare capital and the large potential markets nearby. It is in the intermediate areas that it can be most difficult to change attitudes and develop new tourism businesses.

-- **Farmers** are critical in maintaining both the basic rural economy and the scenery on which rural tourism depends. Yet farmers have responded unevenly and often only slowly to the opportunities available through tourism. Some farmers are strongly anti-tourist, resenting visitors on their territory, especially where footpaths or riding trails cross their land. Many would prefer better prices for farm produce rather than incentives to move into the visitor industry. When farmers do diversify into tourism, they often do so together with other farmers, rather than with local communities, and thus potential co-operative benefits are lost.

At the root of many of the problems encountered in involving farmers in tourism is a basic question of knowledge and training. A hotelier would be incapable of working in the farming industry without a lengthy period of training, yet farmers (or their wives) are expected to diversify into providing visitor services of all kinds with little or no training.

-- **Training deficiences** are not confined to agriculturalists. Many business people and employees working in rural tourism have little or no training in the many skills required for this complex and competitive industry. Lack of training is one of the reasons why some studies have noted a high incidence of business failures in the rural tourism field. Training needs are covered in Appendix A.

-- **Failure to group and to set up co-operative ventures** is a common but not universal problem. Because rural tourism enterprises are small, co-operation with other businesses can bring major savings in marketing and training and in the purchase of supplies. Co-operative groupings can also negotiate with government bodies to fund infrastructural improvements, and can work with the major players in the international tourism market, the tour operators. Interest and success in co-operative ventures owes much to the history and experience of the regions concerned. Where there is a tradition of co-operation, usually in farming, tourism co-operatives seem to work.

III. Managing rural tourism and rural development

1. Can tourism strategies solve the rural regeneration question?

Given the long list of problems outlined above, can tourism strategies make an effective contribution to rural development?. The answer according to most authorities, is a carefully qualified yes. It will be shown below that in order to minimise the problems and maximise the benefits, sustainable tourism management strategies should be employed. It will be further argued that more research and development is necessary to help ensure the success of the strategy approach. However, even given a successful management strategy, tourism alone would not be able to solve all rural regeneration issues. It would be disastrous if it could. Tourism can contribute to regeneration, but an area would suffer in the long term if tourism came to be a dominant activity. The aim of any tourism strategy should be to assist the balanced development of an area, not to convert it into a resort complex dependent solely on the travel trade.

2. But can - and should - rural tourism be managed?

Many texts have been written on tourism management: one of the latest, by Edward Inskeep, promises "an integrated and sustainable development approach". Little, however, has been written specifically on effective rural tourism management - although there have been books on recreation management, and on countryside management.

The case against the managed approach is three-fold. The expansion of modern tourism has not been the product of planning but of a largely free market. Tourism is a consumer industry: central planning in this area has had an uneven record. Third, there is the claim that the tourism industry is different - it is unmanageable. In the words of Professor Butler of the University of Western Ontario, Canada - "tourism development is like pregnancy - one cannot become just a little bit pregnant".

The case for managing rural tourism rests on four points.

First, the tourist industry is now well established and mature. Clients are more discerning and many seek a carefully managed, quality environment on holiday, rather than just a holiday. The industry is beginning to realise that it has long term environmental responsibilities, and management techniques can help it to meet those responsibilities.

Second, rural tourism is different from resort tourism because it operates in a very sensitive human and fragile physical environment. Management is, therefore, essential if the very qualities on which the rural holiday relies are not to be lost through inappropriate or over-development.

Third, because of the many new and inexperienced small enterprises involved in the rural tourism sector, some unifying strategy is essential for business planning purposes. The initial development of this new sector frequently requires public sector finance; some form of strategic plan is normally necessary to gain access to that finance.

Finally, tourism management is beginning to evolve into something more flexible and enterprise-orientated than simple land use and infrastructure planning. This process may still have a long way to go, but most commentators and many experienced members of the industry see management as a necessary future tool. On balance, therefore, it seems that there is a powerful case for the creation of rural tourism management strategies.

3. The evolution of rural tourism management

Current thinking in rural tourism development and management has three distinct sources.

-- **Recreation management** ideas have evolved in North America over the last 50 years, largely through national park administrations. Key areas of discussion centre around visitor and vehicle control, zoning policies, wildlife and vegetation management, trail design and maintenance, carrying capacity assessment and interpretation policies. Most of these ideas are useful to rural tourism management but the recreational management approach is essentially non-commercial and does not, therefore, answer many of the question which rural tourism management poses. Recreational management techniques were usually evolved in non-farmed areas, free of settlements of any size, and in areas where land ownership was in the hands of the managing authorities. The authorities usually had considerable powers of planning control, and long term funding to carry out their ideas.

-- **The concept of sustainable tourism** was developed in the alpine regions of Europe by German, Swiss, Austrian, French and Italian academics, conservationists and tourism professionals. It is known by a number of other names green tourism, responsible tourism, post-industrial tourism, meta-tourism and alternative tourism are but a few. It was developed as an answer to the pressing problems of mass tourism in the Alps and the Mediterranean. It can best be described as a system of long term tourism planning which is friendly towards the long term well-being of communities and habitats, the visitor, and the tourist industry. It envisages these three players in the tourism equation being in a triangular relationship. In unplanned mass tourism, the industry dominates decision making, to the detriment of all parties because of the operation of the "resort cycle" theory, which envisages that a resort will have a finite life because of eventual overcrowding and deterioration. The Sustainability Concept gives power and knowledge in equal amounts to each party, resulting in careful, slow optimisation of each other's aims. (see Krippendorf, Zimmer and Glauber 1988, and Bramwell and Lane 1993).

Sustainable tourism is a powerfully attractive concept to the rural tourism manager. It provides a useful philosophy and check-list for proposed actions. Because of its all-embracing scope, because of its utopian aims, and because it is still new, it remains largely untested over time. A number of British, Austrian and other areas are now implementing sustainable rural tourism strategies.

-- **Rural tourism project management** is also in its infancy, but over the last ten years there have been many rural tourism development projects throughout the world. These have been variable in aims and quality. They have been handled by a variety of professionals including community social workers, economic development officers, marketeers, educationalists, historians and interpretation experts, land use planners, and farm advisors. Most projects have been of short duration - up to three years - and many have been unable to develop tangible long lasting benefits in that time.

Rural tourism management in the future should try to combine the experience and knowledge of all the sources discussed above. But much more work is required before long term effectiveness and success can be achieved. The issues to be addressed, and the type of research and development work necessary are described below.

4.   Issues to be addressed if sustainable rural tourism is to be promoted successfully

Over the last 20 years, many businesses and communities have participated in the growth of tourism in rural areas. As the bibliography on rural tourism in Appendix B shows, there has been great interest in this trend from many parts of the world. But several important problems remain to be addressed before the development of rural tourism is fully understood and before the benefits of that development are available to all regions in all countries. Perhaps the most important issue is how a sustainable form of rural tourism can be developed - a form of tourism which would retain the intrinsic values of the countryside, while sustaining its economic life, and helping ensure the long-term profitability of the travel industry interests involved in the transfer of visitors both inter-regionally and internationally.

5.   Pre-requisites before discussion can begin

To agree a definition of the term "rural tourism"

This may seem a somewhat arid way to begin the discussion: it is, however, vital. It sets the content and the boundaries of the discussion. Section I covers this question in detail. It defines rural tourism as being located in rural areas, and as being functionally rural - that is, firmly based on the rural world's special features of open space, contact with nature, rural heritage and society. Its scale should be in keeping with the landscape and settlements in which it operates: those settlements are normally of fewer than 10 000 people. While including farm tourism within its remit, its overall focus should also encompass the whole range of suitable businesses and settlement types in the countryside.

Its aim should be to help ensure the long-term sustainability of the life of the region: it should be a force for the conservation of rurality rather than a force for urbanisation.

The definition above is given in terms of rural tourism's location and impact. A recent Australian Department of Tourism discussion paper (Tourism discussion paper No.1 - Rural Tourism, Canberra 1993) further defines rural tourism in terms of product:

- the natural environment, the landscape and wildlife;

- the farming process;

- the country towns, the rural people, their cultures, communities and activities;

- the indigenous communities, their way of life, their identity and relationship with the land and nature.

Finally, it should be noted that because of the rich variety of physical backgrounds in the rural world and the complex palimpsest of history which overlays its physical frame, there will always be a need to adjust any definition to accommodate local, regional and national variations.

To agree the need for special care in the development and management of tourism in rural areas

While there is clearly a need for care in all forms of tourism development, there is an especially pressing case to be made for care in the countryside. Because of the fragile nature of the industry's raw material - rurality itself - all activities should be subject to special scrutiny to ensure that they pass the test of sustainability. In practice this will mean the recognition that:

- not all areas are suitable for development

- not all communities wish to be developed or are suitable for development

- not all forms of tourism activity are acceptable in every location

- there may have to be limits to growth in any one area.

- special visitor management techniques may have to be employed to prevent and/or repair environmental damage caused by visitor pressure.

To agree the aims of rural tourism development

Aims may include a wide range:

- job retention, creation and diversification;

- the conservation of traditional buildings and habitats;

- community support;

- transport system support;

- agriculture / forestry support;

- the development of a better quality of life for rural peoples;

- the development of new roles for disadvantaged/under-employed groups;

- quality-of-life enhancement for visitors from urban areas, last in this list but a crucial aim in many respects.

Rural tourism strategists need to determine their aims before commencing development; those aims should be reviewed periodically.

To recognise that there will be a need for special partnership arrangements to help rural areas develop tourism

These partnerships may be between businesses, between businesses and the community, and between businesses, communities and public sector institutions. They will be necessary because of the fragility of the rural world itself, and the fragility of many of its small enterprises. They will be necessary because of the need to restructure the rural economy. And the partnership concept will also be necessary because of the peculiar nature of tourism itself in a rural area. Tourism is a special form of economic activity in any area because of its powerful impact on the public domain. While car manufacturing or office work can be hidden away in industrial estates or science parks, tourism's basic acts of sightseeing, shopping and touring are totally public. In rural areas there is an additional intrusion: tourism frequently intrudes onto the private domain, as visitors seek access to private land, to private lakesides and sea shore. Partnerships between interests are, therefore, vital to deal with the conflicts of interest which can easily arise.

6. Key issues to be solved in practice

Successful development and management will require both public and private sector participation. Traditionally, public sector involvement in rural areas has been very considerable, both because of the need to conserve and control national food supplies and because of the long term structural weaknesses within the rural economy. Because of this inherited position, and because there seems little likelihood of most rural economies strengthening in the near future, the public sector's role will continue to be a powerful one. But tourism in non-rural areas is essentially a private sector initiative, and experience shows that it functions best in private hands. Therefore, while there will always be a strong regulatory and co-ordinating role for the public sector within rural tourism, steps should be taken wherever possible to stimulate private sector involvement. Public sector involvement is likely to be greatest in the early stages of an area's development, with private sector responsibilities then gradually taking on a more important role.

The need to understand and relate to the market

Without markets, any discussion on rural tourism must remain academic. The size, type, elasticity and demands of the market influence all the issues listed later. Lack of market knowledge, and lack of knowledge about how to relate to markets, are common problems for many rural tourism initiatives. The two parts to this issue are:

- The need to understand the size, location, characteristics, perception and requirements of markets;

- The need to understand how to relate to, influence and win markets via marketing campaigns, liaison with travel agents, travel companies and tour operators.

It is most likely that basic market research is best initiated and funded by the public sector in order to ensure that this fundamental information is available to all businesses. Marketing campaigns and promotions may be begun by the public sector, but the role of that sector should gradually change to one of co-ordinator rather than funder as development proceeds.

The development of an environmentally sustainable enterprise milieu

This complex phrase embraces a number of issues:

- The provision of effective planning and conservation legislation, and bodies to implement that legislation - a public sector responsibility.

- The development of regional and local sustainable rural tourism strategy plans to assess an area's strengths, weaknesses, opportunities and threats, to guide both public and private sector investment, and to assess environmental and community requirements. This is usually a public sector responsibility, but requires close consultation with the private sector and with environmental and community interests.

-   The provision of business advice and training - typically a public sector responsibility, but not necessarily delivered directly by the public sector. The importance of training in the development of rural tourism should not be underestimated: a separate Appendix covers this issue.

-   The development of an ongoing monitoring and evaluation process to review the success of tourism as an industry, and to provide a response mechanism for environmental and community interests. This is usually a private/public sector partnership, with a secretariat provided by the public sector. This secretariat may also be responsible for initiating research and development programmes.

The development, improvement and monitoring of accommodation

Lack of accommodation or of suitable accommodation is one of the key development problems in many rural tourism areas. Accommodation is essentially a private sector responsibility, but it may require advice / grant aid in the early stages. Quality control may be a public sector responsibility, but some of the quality control systems can be devolved to industry associations as development proceeds.

The development and improvement of visitor attractions

Although the rural world is itself the key attraction, there are many cases where special emphasis can be given to aspects of rurality by the careful development of visitor attractions. These developments are normally private sector responsibilities. The role of the public sector is that of guidance, encouragement/discouragement, regulation and, in special cases, grant aid may be necessary: in peripheral areas community-based developments may be both necessary and useful.

The need to provide and manage infrastructure

Infrastructure includes:

-   Transportation facilities and services - either a public or private sector responsibility, although rural public transport is often assisted by public subsidy even if provided by private operators.

-   Information facilities - usually, but not always or necessarily, a public sector provision. In some rural areas the private sector can be very effective at providing information on a franchised basis from a public authority.

-   Interpretation of landscape, heritage, nature. These facilities are typically a public sector responsibility, especially if carried out for a wider region. Private provision is also possible, either as a form of private visitor attraction, or as part of the work of special interest groups (such as the National Trust in the United Kingdom, or the National Trust for Historic Preservation in the United States).

-   Access for walkers / riders / cyclists. Access issues (to paths, to mountains, lake or sea shores) are usually regulated by the public sector although access often occurs across private land. Rural tourism development thrives on a good partnership here: Austria, Switzerland and Germany are classic models of good practice. In contrast, the situations in Ireland and Scotland are classic examples of unresolved access issues slowing the development of tourism because of weaknesses in the regulatory system.

-   Environmental protection and repair is normally a public sector responsibility. Payment for protection, and especially for repair, is however, a difficult issue: the principle of "the polluter pays" is increasingly threatened or invoked by the public sector in an effort to reduce the charge on the public purse. These problems, if unresolved, can produce serious disagreements between the community, the tourist trade and visitors.

Research into the development and management of rural tourism.

Research and development is important in all industries: it is particularly important in a new field like rural tourism. Research can find ways of lessening the impact of tourism on the environment and new ways of attracting and retaining visitors, and can help keep areas in the front rank of the internationally competitive business of tourism. Normally, research will be led by the public sector, but private sector participation is extremely important if the work is to be relevant and acted upon. A fuller explanation of the areas into which research is required can be found in the next section.

The requirement for leadership

Many small businesses and numerous public sector organisations are involved in rural tourism. The successful promotion of development and management planning requires more than usually informed, skilled and dedicated leadership. This is an intangible factor, but one of great importance. It can help persuade business interests to be kinder to the environment; it can steer difficult government institutions to more pragmatic interpretations of their roles; it can influence the doubting farmer; it can bring new ideas to communities of no hope.

Leadership can be provided by enlightened individuals from the private sector, by politicians, by public sector agencies, by local/regional administrations and administrators, by tourist boards, and by powerful land owners; what is important is that there be leadership, that it be carefully fostered not feared, and that it be fostered in depth, so that when one individual or agency fails, the whole momentum of development is not lost. A number of North American educational institutions provide short courses in leadership for rural politicians and administrators.

IV. Future research and development programmes

All successful industries devote resources to research and development. Rural tourism is still a relatively new area of business, and, therefore, much basic research is needed. That basic research is especially critical because of the highly competitive nature of the free enterprise tourism market. The countryside may have intrinsic advantages because of the growth of special interest, independent holiday-making, but existing resorts and mass tourism enterprises are already researching how best to improve their marketing and their products to regain market share.

In almost all business sectors research and development involves a partnership between the public and private sectors. The need for partnership is very important if rural tourism and its development are to succeed. Rural areas and enterprises have a history of public sector intervention. Rural tourism is growing in a fragmented and *ad hoc* way: public sector partnerships can co-ordinate activities. Since many of rural tourism's activities take place in the public domain, careful research into environmental and visitor management is necessary to maintain established community goals such as landscape, nature and heritage protection during the re-structuring of the rural economy away from primary production towards a greater reliance on the service sector.

This section outlines ten areas where future research and development should be concentrated.

1. *Market information*

Market information studies for rural tourism are few, and this is a major problem in determining the size, characteristics and requirements of the market. Without this information, it is difficult to plan infrastructure investment, to provide effective business training, to encourage suitable numbers and types of new entrants into rural tourism provision and, of course, to develop marketing campaigns.

Market information studies need to cover market groups already taking rural holidays, and those who do not. For both groups, basic positioning information should include age/family size/occupational characteristics/area of origin/holiday patterns during current year and previous years/ perceived requirements of holidays/likely accommodation type/likely method of travel/method of choosing holidays/knowledge and perception of specified "control" areas.

For those not taking rural holidays, additional questions should cover reasons why alternatives were taken, perception of specific types of rural holiday, perception of specific rural areas, and likely future trends in holiday choice.

For those taking rural holidays, additional questions should review propensity to take holidays in various types of rural area, repeat visit likelihood, major strengths and weaknesses of previous rural holidays, the importance of various types of infrastructure, and likely future trends in holiday choice.

The development of a standard way of obtaining and analysing this market information would assist rural groups with limited skills and resources, and also enable inter-regional and international comparisons to be made.

A particularly valuable part of this programme would be the production of information on price sensitivity (do people look for rural holidays as economical holidays?); on the importance of scenery (are specific types of landscape more or less worthwhile in investment terms?); on the importance of infrastructive such as heritage and interpretative centres (are they valuable, or simply wet weather facilities?), and on desired accommodation requirements (are private facilities vital, is personal contact really important, can historic buildings command a premium, do visitors care about the style of new buildings?)

2. How best to relate to markets?

Directly linked with the market information question comes the issue of how best to relate to markets. Major resorts and tour operators use sophisticated, expensive and sometimes wasteful methods to reach their customers. Rural tourism areas often - but not always - have weak and amateur links to their markets. There would be value in the publication of an evaluated good-practice guide looking at a range of successful areas and the techniques they have employed to relate to their markets. Special emphasis should be given to evaluating:

-- Brochure/leaflet design and distribution;
-- co-operative marketing ventures;
-- product versus area promotion;
-- repeat visit potential;
-- direct mail;
-- mailing list swaps/purchases;
-- niche marketing;
-- tour operator relationships;
-- the use of telecommunications;
-- evaluation techniques.

3. Benefit assessment and enhancement

Rural tourism investment is undertaken largely to improve the economic, environmental and social well being of rural areas. Relatively little is known about the levels of return on different types of investment: almost nothing is known about the long term impact of less tangible forms of investment such as training, strategy planning etc. Typical problems faced by investment planners in rural areas are gaps in knowledge on returns from:

-- Display boards;
-- tourism information centres;
-- visitor and heritage centres;
-- craft workshops and galleries;
-- on-road cycle route provision;

-- off-road cycle route provision;
-- public transport enhancement;
-- scenic road construction;
-- training in business skills;
-- training in hospitality skills;
-- strategy planning exercises.

Closely allied to the above enquiry is another. How could rural areas retain more revenue from their existing tourist industry. Can farmers be trained and organised to make more of the visitor market through sales to local hotels and restaurants, and direct sales to visitors? Can marketing retain visitors in an area for longer periods? Can co-operative purchasing groups re-invest money locally? There are close linkages between this field and point 4 below.

The OECD's Rural Development Programme has an ongoing project to devise internationally acceptable indicators to measure the work of rural development programmes. Any research on the benefits flowing from rural tourism development should, where possible, be linked with the project on rural indicators to ensure international compatibility and comparability.

4. *Management, control and operational issues*

Section III of this report discussed the need for skilled management if rural tourism was to flourish in an environmentally and community friendly way. Research is necessary to evaluate the management, control and operational questions involved in creating sustainable rural tourism. Evaluation should be made in terms of job retention, creation and diversification, visitor satisfaction, capital and manpower requirements, environmental protection and community participation and partnership.

Special consideration should be given to two fields:

i) For long term strategic planning, an increasing number of rural regions and localities are developing tourism strategy plans. These plans assess tourism assets, weaknesses and environmental carrying capacities. After a review of market opportunities, the long term plan looks at how best to develop and manage specific areas, communities and ecosystems. The plans discuss infrastructure requirements, traffic management schemes, new enterprise development, training for tourism businesses and marketing techniques. Five-to ten-year time scales are usually adopted.

There are many different ways of drawing up and implementing long term strategy plans. Some, for example are based on intensive community consultation techniques; others adopt a much more "top-down" approach. Research and evaluation is needed to assess the effectiveness of strategy planning in general, and of specific types of planning in detail. Effectiveness should be measured in terms of the cost of strategy development and administration, commercial success, effectiveness in environmental and community conservation, and in terms of job retention, creation and diversification.

ii) At the tactical level, the implementation of strategy plans requires detailed knowledge of issues such as visitor management schemes, heritage interpretation, ways of encouraging new entrants to tourism, the validity of co-operative marketing schemes, rural public transport schemes, historic building conservation and ways of successfully integrating nature conservation and tourism. These are just a selection of issues which face tourism administrations and businesses on a regular basis.

Work on the bibliography of rural tourism (Appendix B) revealed a remarkable lack of easily available material on the "mechanics" of rural tourism development. Visitor management information is especially rare. What written work is available is scattered in many books, from numerous countries and in several languages. There is a case, therefore, for the publication of a "reader" on this subject, bringing scattered sources together, with research being commissioned to fill gaps in existing knowledge and published material.

5. *Sustainability indicators*

The quality of the natural and human environment is an important asset for tourism to the countryside. Much is written about the need to sustain the qualities involved: most of that writing is in generalised terms.

In 1992 the World Tourism Organization (WTO) set up an International Working Group on Indicators of Sustainable Tourism. The working group reported to the WTO's Environment Committee in early 1993. It recommended the development of a series of measures and indicators of sustainability, including warning indicators, pressure/stress indicators, measures of management impact, and destination attractivity indices. Indicators were felt to be necessary at national level, and also for critical areas/"hot spots". It also recommended pilot testing of these indicators at a number of sites during 1993/4.

Collaborative research with the WTO on sustainability indicators for rural tourism would be extremely valuable. It would help back up the economic assessments already mentioned as research areas. It would give firm guidelines for decisions on management and control policies. It would help provide protection against over-development and loss of a unique selling point: rurality.

6. *Training*

Training is accepted as important in all spheres of economic activity. Training in rural tourism is generally poorly developed: this is a major stumbling block to development. Rural tourism requires relatively little new capital: the physical landscape, natural and built heritage, farming pattern, and, in many cases, redundant buildings, are all there. But, successful rural tourism requires totally new skills: in marketing, in hospitality, in catering, in heritage interpretation and guidance, in visitor management, in festival and event promotion, in building conversion, and in rural tourism strategy planning itself.

A number of organisations have begun to develop training programmes. These include:

-- The United Nations Food and Agricultural Organisation through its Rome Office

-- COFRAT (Comité de formation des ruraux aux activities du tourisme) in France's Loire-Atlantique Region

-- In Austria, the OEAR, the Österreichische Arbeitsgemeinschaft für Eigenständige Regionalentwicklung (the Austrian Association for Regional Development through Self-Help)

-- The University of Bristol's Rural Tourism Unit in the United Kingdom

-- The University of Minnesota's Tourism Center in the United States: this organisation has developed manuals and videos, and hosted a national interactive tele-conference. It was the base for America's National Rural Tourism Development Project from 1988 to 1991.

-- The University of Calgary in Canada, in its Management Faculty, through Continuing Education, and through the specialist Center for Livable Communities.

Training has tended to concentrate on small businesses and employees. It has usually been short term, with little linkage between courses, and no long term training plan. Existing business courses have usually been adapted: little specifically tailor-made material has been produced on rural tourism.

Training for rural tourism professionals, planners and administrators is less well developed. The market is smaller, but paradoxically, the need is probably greater. Planners and professionals are the industry's leaders, acting as brokers between businesses, between businesses and politicians, and frequently, between businesses and markets. Once again, training materials are usually adapted from other subject materials, and short courses with little linkage are the norm. Formal qualifications in Rural Tourism Development/Management are unknown. Closely allied to this area of training is the concept of training trainers for the farm/small businesses/employee sector.

A more detailed discussion of training and education possibilities is given in Appendix A, Education and Training for Rural Tourism. This suggests possible curriculum frameworks, and the idea of international compatibility and comparability between programmes. One of the keys to this development would be the setting up of an international Rural Tourism Training Network, bringing institutions and agencies together to learn of each others' skills, successes and failures, and common problems. The network would avoid duplication of research effort, and bring the hybrid vigour which can often stem from such collaborative ventures. The network need not be fully global, but could also function concurrently on a continental scale with groups in Europe, North America, Australasia and Asia.

7. *Community involvement and community/industry co-operation*

Community involvement and community/industry co-operation are special features of rural tourism in some places. They can bring local capital investment into play, can lessen conflicts between visitor interests and local interests, and can contribute towards the authenticity of rural holidays which many visitors seek. Yet community involvement is unsuccessful in some places, while very valuable in others. Research is needed to ascertain whether there are any basic ground rules for this type of work, whether involvement is only successful in the short term, and what exactly can and cannot be delivered in co-operation with rural communities. This area of research should also consider the role of local tourism associations, and the requirements of leadership touched upon in Section III. Its findings should be disseminated via the various publications and training materials envisaged elsewhere in this Section.

8. *Agency intervention in rural tourism development*

Many public sector agencies are involved in rural tourism development, management and marketing. Few of the agencies involved were designed specifically to work on rural tourism, or, in many cases, on tourism of any kind. Examples of their diverse origins include agricultural advisory services, national park authorities, regional and local planning agencies, state forestry authorities, rural development agencies, local government planning services, leisure services and general administrative services, and, of course, all embracing tourist boards ranging from national through regional to local level. Some public sector involvement in tourism and development in rural areas will probably always be needed. Whether, however, public sector agencies should carry out the full range of roles, or should be limited to a regulatory function, is not clear. Certainly, in some areas, co-operatives, semi-state agencies and private consultancies carry out roles reserved elsewhere for the state sector. This area of research would, therefore, examine, compare and evaluate the ways in which rural tourism is being developed and arranged by different forms of agency. The recently formed (1993) Rural Tourism Development Foundation in the United States should be included in this work.

9. *International co-operation*

International co-operation can yield valuable insights into problems and act as a powerful educational device. Many international agencies are already involved in rural tourism, including OECD, FAO, the Council of Europe, ECOVAST, EUROTER, the European Community, some travel trade groups and informal organisations such as the Anglo-American Countryside Stewardship consortium.

This area of research would look at what international links already exist and how they operate. It would examine the success (or otherwise) of different types of co-operation and exchange, and consider ways of co-ordinating schemes, and expanding (or contracting) them where advantageous. The investigation would not be limited to "executive" or "public agency" schemes, but would also bring together operators and small businesses of all kinds. Much could probably be learned from the extensive programme of exchanges between farmers common in most OECD countries

10. Best or bad practice assessment

There are many examples of rural tourism initiatives across the OECD countries. Few are known about beyond their national or even regional boundaries. Written evaluations of the initiatives are usually published in obscure places. Comparisons of one initiative with another are rarely possible because different criteria are used in each case. Perhaps most important of all, only succesful schemes are normally covered. Yet, much can be learnt from failures and, in an experimental field, failures are a necessary risk if new ideas are to be tested.

There are grounds, therefore, for the publication on a standardized basis of project assessments to help inspire, educate and assist practitioners within this field. This work could be used to form a companion volume to that discussed under heading 4 which put the case for a "reader" on the mechanics of rural tourism management. The volume under discussion here would cover the broader field of regional development, integrated project management and area based schemes. Both volumes would provide excellent material to assist the development of the training programmes covered under heading 6.

Appendix A

Education and training for rural tourism

One of the major issues in the development of rural tourism is the need for education and training. It is frequently overlooked because many people, having experienced holidays as consumers, and having been involved in other types of business, assume that little further knowledge or skill is required to enter the tourism industry. But tourism is a complex and highly professional enterprise: success rarely comes without considerable expertise. Rural tourism requires additional and specialised skills.

It is readily admitted that the restructuring of the rural economy will entail new capital inputs. To use that new capital effectively, trained administrators, managers, operators and employees are necessary. The need for agricultural education has been recognised for over a century. An hotelier would be unlikely to survive as a farmer without several years of training. But farmers and other rural people are commonly expected to enter the world of tourism with either no training, or training which lasts only a few days. In-service training or continuing professional development is also poorly developed.

Training and education programmes in rural tourism should bring a number of benefits. They should help develop more care and commitment amongst all those involved. They should help businesses become more effective and profitable, by encouraging better marketing, organisation and co-operative working and helping gain repeat visits from guests. They should help professional planners and administrators understand the need to plan rural tourism in a sustainable and profitable way. Finally, there is the critical but hard-to-define point that well-thought-out training programmes help widen horizons, raise standards and create professional and positive attitudes.

This paper sets out the client groups who need training in rural tourism, evaluates their requirements and suggests possible outline curricula, discusses the constraints on the development of rural tourism education programmes and puts forward a framework for research and development.

Client groups

i) Individual entrepreneurs in accommodation, attractions or other tourism related businesses,

ii) Employees in the rural tourism field,

iii) Professionals including planners, tourism administrators, land agents and estate managers,

iv) Community and co-operative groups,

v) Trainers in all the above fields.

Clearly the requirements of the five groups noted above will be very different in some respects. There are likely to be considerable differences amongst clients in the standards of previous educational attainment. A common core curriculum for all groups is unlikely to be feasible. But there will be many areas where similar forms of education and teaching materials can be employed.

Needs, and outline curricula

i) Individual entrepreneurs

Basic knowledge of the tourism industry's structure, facts and trends - basic knowledge of the trends in rural economy and society - principles of sustainable tourism and the operation of the planning system - skills in lodging and attraction management - basic business skills - marketing skills - assertiveness training, negotiating and hospitality skills - linguistic skills as required - a knowledge of the history, traditions and geography of the local area.

ii) Employees

Requirements here will vary considerably according to the type and grade of job under discussion. The aim should be to help people to perform their jobs more effectively, to gain greater job satisfaction, and to progress towards promotion or self employment.

Curricula suggestions would include: basic knowledge of the tourism industry's workings - assertiveness training, negotiating and hospitality skills - linguistic skills as required - knowledge of the history, traditions and geography of the local area - plus other items according to job specification.

iii) Professionals

In-depth knowledge of the tourism industry's structure, facts and trends - in-depth knowledge of trends in the rural economy and in society - adequate grounding in ecology - detailed knowledge of the implementation of the concept of sustainable tourism and the operation of the planning system - knowledge of funding systems in both the private and public sectors - skills in drawing up tourism strategy plans - marketing and management skills for areas, accommodation units, and attractions - assertiveness training and negotiating skills - visitor management techniques - community group creation and mechanics - legal and operational requirements of co-operative and partnership schemes -linguistic skills as required.

iv) Community groups

Skills similar to those required by the curriculum for entrepreneurs outlined above, but with the addition of group working skills, survey techniques and knowledge of the history and legal requirements of co-operative ventures.

v) Trainers

All the requirements of the fields to be taught plus teaching and testing skills.

Constraints on the implementation of a rural tourism training programme

i) Funding problems for long term investments such as training are always a constraint.

ii) The need for training is not recognised by the industry itself or by governments.

iii) There are few incentives for individuals to undertake education or training.

iv) There is a lack of easily available teaching materials and nationally, (or internationally) recognised curricula.

v) Some rural areas require distance learning or residential provision because of their isolation and sparse population densities.

vi) There is a lack of co-operation between institutions which could help provide training. Sometimes this occurs at national level because of jealousy, competition between agencies, or the fact that rural tourism training is cross-sectoral. It occurs at the international level because of ignorance, disinterest, language barriers and the perceived cost of travel.

Ways forward to overcome the constraints

There are several institutions in various countries which have begun to develop training programmes in rural tourism. These include the University of Minnesota (United States), the University of Calgary (Canada), in France, University College, Dublin (Ireland), CERT (the state tourism training agency) in Ireland, COFRAT (a development of the state agricultural training agency)in France, the University of Bristol (England), and a number of British agricultural colleges. There are probably many others within and without the countries mentioned. Several tourist boards are examining ways of incentivising training programmes, either by offering benefits in kind for businesses undertaking training, or by subsidising training costs. It should be possible to further encourage these moves by:

-- Drawing up an inventory of training programmes offered within the OECD countries;

-- Encouraging all interested parties to discuss, on a national basis, the need for training, how that training should be structured, what curricula should be developed, and what qualifications could be offered. The results of those national discussions should be reported back to OECD;

-- Setting up an international rural tourism training network, to encourage cross-border collaboration, pooling of material and the harmonization of programmes. This network could be developed at both continental and global levels. Early work on an Anglo-North American network, and on a European network has already begun;

-- Holding a workshop amongst practitioners from the OECD countries to act, in the first instance, as a "think-tank" on all the proposals listed above and, secondly, as a "ginger-group" to encourage and lead towards progress in the field.

-- Creating distance learning materials, and programmes, for the client groups already noted.

A categorised bibliography

I.   General Studies - Works on Tourism and Rural Tourism

ABEGG, Bruno (1991), "Spezialisierung oder Diversifikation im Tourismus" (Specialisation or Diversification in Tourism), *Wirtschaftsgeographie and Raumplanung*, Vol. 13. Geographisches Institut der Universititäet, Züerich, Switzerland.

AIREY, D. (1983), "European government approaches to tourism," *Tourism Management*, vol.4, pp. 234-44.

AMOS, C.J., and POTTS T.D., (1993), *Home Town Discovery: A Development Process for Tourism,* Clemson University, South Carolina.

ANGIOLINI, S. (1989), *Agriturismo in Toscana: protagonisti, tendenze, problemi (Agricultural tourism in Tuscany)*, Italy.

ARAMBERRI J. (1983), Tourism and Sociocultural Change - Contextual Approach, Spanish Institute of Tourism.

ARCHER, B. (1973), *The Impact of Domestic Tourism*, Bangor Occasional Papers in Economics No. 2, University of Wales Press, Bangor.

ARCHER, B.H. (1982), "The value of multipliers and their policy implications", *Tourism Management,* Vol.3, (pp. 236-41).

ARCHER, B.H. (1977), *Tourism Multipliers: The State of the Art,* Bangor Occasional Papers in Economics No.11, University of Wales Press, Bangor.

ARNOLD, R., DAVIES, S. and PEARCE, D. (1989), *Some Economic Implications of Tourism Expansion:* Inquiry into Travel and Tourism Discussion Paper No. 2, Australian Government Publishing Service, Canberra.

ARZENI, S. (1989), *International tourism: Past trends and prospects,* IIEC Discussion Paper.

ASSOCIATION POUR LA PROMOTION DU TOURISME RURAL (1992), *Standardisation des produits de tourisme rural*, Groupe LEADER, Luxembourg, May.

AYUNTAMIENTO DE CIUDAD RODRIGO (ed) (1992), *Encuentro Hispano-Luso de Turismo en Espacio Rural* (Spanish-Portuguese Conference on Rural Tourism), Salamanca.

BOCKSTAEL, N.E., STRAND, I.E. and HANEMANN, W.M., (1987), "Time and Recreational Demand Model," *American Journal of Agricultural Economics*, Vol. 69 (2), pp. 293-302.

BOTE GOMEZ, V. *(1988) Turismo en Espacio Rural. Rehabilitacion del patrimonio sociocultural y de la economia local* (Rural Tourism: Restoring the sociocultural heritage and the local economy), Madrid.

BOUQUET, M. and WINTER, M. *(1987), Who From Their Labours Rest? Conflict and Practice in Rural Tourism* London.

BOYER, M. (1972), *Le Tourisme* Editions du Seuil, Paris.

BRAMWELL, B. (ed) (1990), *Shades of Green: Working Towards Green Tourism in the Countryside,* London.

BROWNE, R-J., and NOLAN, M.L., (1989), "Western Indian Reservation Tourism Development", *Annals of Tourism Research,* Vol. 16 (3), pp. 360-376.

BRITISH TOURIST AUTHORITY (1976), *Tourism patterns of overseas motorists in Great Britain, summer, 1975*, British Tourist Authority, London.

BRITISH TOURIST AUTHORITY /ENGLISH TOURIST BOARD (1988), *Regional Estimates of Jobs in Tourism*, BTA/ETB London.

BURKART, A.J.and MEDLIK, S. (1974), *Tourism: past, present and future*, Heinemann, London.

BUTLER, R.W. (1980), "The concept of a tourist area cycle of evolution: Implications for the management of resources, *Canadian Geographer*, Vol 24. pp. 5-12.

BUTLER, R. W. (1989), "Alternative Tourism: Pious Hope or Trojan Horse?", *World Leisure and Recreation.*

CECOD. (1983), *Le tourisme en France: Edition 1982 Réactualisée,* Centre d'étude du commerce et de la distribution, Paris.

CERT (1988), *The Scope of the Tourism Industry in Ireland,* CERT and CHL Consultants, Dublin.

CLARK, R.N., HENDEE, J.C., and CAMPBELL, F. (1971), Values, behaviour and conflict in modern camping culture. *Journal of Leisure Research*, 143-159, Vol. 3.

CLAWSON, M. (1959), *Methods of measuring demand for, and value of outdoor, recreation,* Washington, D.C..

CLAWSON, M. (1985), "Outdoor recreation: 25 years of history, 25 years of projection", *Leisure Sciences*, 73-99, Vol 7.

CLAWSON, M. and KNETSCH, J.L. (1971), *The Economics of Outdoor Recreation*, Baltimore.

COMMISSION OF THE EUROPEAN COMMUNITIES (1986), *Action in the Field of Tourism.* Bulletin of the European Communities, Supplement 4/86, European Commission, Brussels.

COMMISSION OF THE EUROPEAN COMMUNITIES (1987), *Rural Tourism in the 12 Member States of the European Economic Community,* European Commission, Brussels.

COMMONWEALTH DEPARTMENT OF TOURISM (1993), *Rural Tourism,* Tourism Discussion Paper No.1, Canberra.

COUNCIL OF EUROPE, (1989), *Freizeit und Erholung auf dem Lande* (Leisure and Recreation in the Countryside), proceedings of a conference held in St. Peter Ording, Bonn/Strasbourg.

COPPOCK, J.T. and DUFFIELD, B.S. (1975), *Recreation in the Countryside: a Spatial Analysis,* Macmillan, London.

COPPOCK, J.T.(ed.) (1977), *Second Homes: curse or blessing?* Pergamon, London.

DALE, P. (ed) (1987), *Adventure tourism seminar: current issues and future management,* Vol. 2 South Island seminar, Hillary Commission for Recreation and Sport, Wellington.

DE KADT, E. (1979), *Tourism: passport to development? Perspectives on the social and cultural effects of tourism in developing countries,* Oxford University Press, Oxford.

DERNOI, L.A. (1983), *Situation actuelle du tourisme rural en Europe,* United Nations.

DEVALL, B. and HARRY, J. (1981), Who hates whom in the Great Outdoors: The impact of recreational specialization and technologies of play, *Leisure Sciences,* Vol 4.

DICKMAN, S. (1989), *Tourism: An Introductory Text,* Edward Arnold, Caulfield East.

DIRECCION GENERAL DE POLITICA TURISTICA (1992), "Seminario sobre Turismo Rural" (Seminar on Rural Tourism), *Estudios Turisticos,* No. 110.

DREZEWIECKE, M. (1992), *Rural Recreational Space,* Warsaw. (In Polish)

DREZEWIECKI, M. (1986), *Conditions for recreation in vacation villages,* Warsaw. (In Polish)

DUFFIELD, B.S. (1977), *Tourism: a tool for regional development,* University of Edinburgh: Tourism and Recreation Research Unit.

DUNLAP, R.E. and HEFFERNAN, R.B. (1981), Outdoor recreation and environmental concern: An empirical examination. *Rural Sociology,* Vol. 40, pp. 18-30.

EDINGTON, J.M., ECOLOGY, RECREATION & TOURISM, Cambridge University Press, Cambridge.

EDWARDS, A. *Leisure spending in the European Community - forecasts to 1990,* London, Economist Intelligence Unit.

ENGLISH TOURIST BOARD (1986), *Jobs in tourism and leisure: An occupation review,* London.

ENGLISH TOURIST BOARD (1987), *A Study of Rural Tourism,* Rural Development Commission P.A., Cambridge Economic Consultants Ltd.

ENGLISH TOURIST BOARD (1988), *Visitors in the Countryside: Rural Tourism - A Development Strategy,* London.

ENGLISH TOURIST BOARD (1991), *Tourism and the Environment: Maintaining the Balance.* Plus four associated reports of the Countryside Working Group, the Heritage Sites Working Group, the Historic Towns Working Group and Visitor Management Case Studies, London.

EUROPEAN COMMUNITY (1991), *Opinion of the Economic and Social Committee and the Community Action Plan to assist Tourism.* EC - Economic and Social Committee (CES 1513/91 PO/I/SLW/PMas), Brussels, pp. 11-12.

EUROTER (1991), *Tourism in Rural Europe. Village que j'aime: 51 Demonstration Projects for Village Tourism,* Nogent sur Marne.

EUROTER (1992), *Le tourism rural dans l'espace communitaire,* Nogent sur Marne.

FAGENCE, M. (1991), *Rural tourism and the small country town,* University of Queensland, Australia.

FALUDI, E. (1991) "Tasks in rural tourism" *Construction Business Review,* Hungary. (In Hungarian)

FAULKNER, B. and Fagence M. (eds) (1988), *Frontiers in Australian Tourism: The Search for New Perspectives in Policy Development and Research,* Bureau of Tourism Research, Canberra, pp. 103-13.

FEDERAL DEPARTMENT OF FORESTRY, (1980), "A case study of the growth of ski tourism and environmental stress in Switzerland", in *Case studies on the Impact of Tourism on the Environment,* pp. 261-318, OECD, Paris.

FEIFER, M. (1985), *Tourism in History From Imperial Rome to the Present,* Stein & Day, New York.

FILIPE, J. L. "Turism no espaco rural", *Technicas e Equipamentos Munici pais,* Lisbon.

FINNISH TOURIST BOARD (1991), *Defining and Classifying Services,* MALO Project, Helsinki. (In Finnish).

FINNISH TOURIST BOARD (1991), The *financing and profitablity of a country holiday enterprise,* MALO Project, Helsinki. (In Finnish)

FITTON, M. (1979), "Countryside Recreation - the problems of opportunity", *Local Government Studies,* Vol 5, No 4, London.

FRAZER, I.M. *Leisure - Tourism: Threat and Promise,* World Council of Churches.

FREZZA, P. (1989), *Vacances à la Campagne en Suisse - Chances et limites,* Diplomarbeit, Hochschule St Gallen.

FROMMER, A. (1989), *The new world of travel* Prentice Hall, New York.

GAIL, A. and HARTMANN, R. (eds) (1992), *Mountain Resort Development,* Proceedings of the 1991 Vail Conference, British Columbia.

GETZ, D. (1991), *Festivals, Special Events and Tourism,* Van Nostrand Rheinhold, New York.

GOODMAN, N. and JONES, L. (eds) (1991), *A training guide for rural tourism development,* University of Minnesota.

GROLLEAU, H. and RAMUS, A. (1986), *Espace rural, espace touristique; le tourisme à la campagne et les conditions de son developpement en France,* La documentation francaise, Paris.

GROLLEAU, H. (1987), *Rural Tourism in the 12 Member States of the EEC,* EEC tourism unit DG XXIII.

GUNN, C.A. (1979), *Tourism Planning,* Crane Rusak, New York.

H.M.S.O. (1985), *Pleasure, Leisure and Jobs,* London.

HALL, C. M. (1991), INTRODUCTION TO TOURISM IN AUSTRALIA: IMPACTS, PLANNING AND DEVELOPMENT, Longman Cheshire.

HALL, C.M. (1989), "Special Interest Travel: A prime force in the expansion of tourism?" pp. 81-90 in WELCH, R. (ed), GEOGRAPHY IN ACTION, University of Otago, Dunedin;

HARDY, S., HART, T., and SHAW Tim. (eds) (1990), *The Role of Tourism in the Urban and Regional Economy,* Regional Studies Association, London.

HARGREAVES, J. (1986), *Sport, power and culture,* Polity Press, Cambridge.

HAUKELAND J.V. (1984), *Sociocultural Impacts of Tourism in Scandanivia,* Studies in Three Host Communities in Tourism Management.

HAWKINS, D.E., SHAFER, E.L. and ROVELSTAD, J.M. (1980), *Tourism Planning and Development Issues,* Washington, D.C.

HAWKINS, D.E., SHAFER, E.L. and Rovelstad, J.M. (1980), *Tourism Marketing and Management Issues,* Washington, D.C.

HOLLOWAY, J.C. (1983), *The business of tourism,* Macdonald and Evans, London.

IUOTO (1973), *Health tourism,* United Nations, Geneva.

JAFARI J. (1982), *Understanding the Structure of Tourism - An Avant Propos to Studying its Costs and Benefits",* AIEST.

JANSEN-VERBEKE, MYRIAM (1990), *The Potentials of Rural Tourism and Agritourism in EEC.* University of Nijmegen, The Netherlands.

JANSEN-VERBEKE, Myriam (1991), *Proposal for an International Pilot Study. European Regions in Creative Contrast: Preconditions for Developing and Marketing Rural and Cultural Tourism.* Department of Regional Planning, Nijmegen Catholic University, The Netherlands.

KARIEL, H.G. (1992), "Noise in Rural Recreational Environments", *Canadian Acoustics*, Vol 19, pp. 97-104.

KARIEL, H.G. and DRAPER, D.L. (1992), "Outdoor Recreation in Mountains", *GeoJournal*, Vol 27, 97-104.

KEANE, M.J and QUINN, J. (1990), *Rural Development and Rural Tourism.* Social Sciences Research Centre, University College Galway, Ireland.

KOTH, B., KREAG, G., AND SEM., J. (1991), *Rural Tourism Development Training Guide,* University of Minnesota.

KRIPPENDORF, J., ZIMMER, P., AND GLAUBER, H. (1988), *Füer einen andern Tourismus,* Fischer Taschenbuch Verlag, Frankfurt.

KRIPPENDORF, J. (1987), *The holiday makers: understanding the impact of leisure and travel,* Heinemann, Oxford.

LANE, B. (1990), "Small Scale Rural Tourism Initiatives: The Role of a British University" (in German), in *Freizeit und Erholung auf dem Lande,* Council of Europe, Bonn/Strasbourg.

LANE, B. (1989), "The Future for Rural Tourism" in *Insights*, 1989, English Tourist Board, London.

LANE, B. (1988), "What is Rural Tourism ?" in *Changing Land Use and Recreation*, Proceedings of the 1988 CRAAG conference, Bristol.

LANE, B. (1991), "Will Rural Tourism Succeed ?" in HART, T., HARDY, S., AND SHAW, T. *The Role of Tourism in the Urban and Regional Economy*, Regional Studies Association, London.

LAWSON, F. and BAUD-BOVY, M. (1977), *Tourism and Recreation Development: A Hand-book of Physical Planning,* The Architectural Press, London.

LE FLOC'H, J-P.(1972), *Recherche sur le tourisme rural (l'exemple breton)* Doctoral thesis in law, Faculté des sciences juridiques, Université de Rennes.

LEGIENIG, H. (1986), "Tourism in rural areas", *Institute of Tourism Infomation Bulletin*, Warsaw. (In Polish).

LEITE, A. (1990), *Que turismo rural?*, Porto.

LEITE, A. (1992) "O Agroturismo no Ordenamento do Espaco e Desenvolvimento Rural" in *Congresso Municipalisom e Desenvolvimento do Noroeste Peninsular Marco de Canavezes.*

LINDGREN, G. and Maers, J. (1989), *Wild region and living landscape - a good soil for small scale tourism*, Braecke. (In Swedish)

LOGOTHETIS, M. (1989), *Rural Tourism*, Athens. (In Greek)

LONG, P., and NUCKOLLS, J., (1992), "Rural Tourism Development: Balancing Costs and Benefits", *Tourism Recreation Research*, Vol. 18 (3).

LONG, P.T. and PERDUE, R.R (1990), "The Economic Impacts of Rural Festivals and Special Events: Assessing the Spatial Distribution of Expenditures", *Journal of Travel Research*, 28 (4).

LOPEZ PASTOR, A. T. (1992), *El turismo rural como factor de desarrollo local: cooperacion institucional en torno a el* (Rural Tourism as an agent of local development: the role of institutional co-operation), Madrid.

LUNDBERG, D.E. (1972), *The Tourist Business*, Cahners Books, Boston.

MANGUN, W.R., and LOOMIS, J. (1987), "An Economic Analysis of Funding Alternatives for Outdoor Recreation in the U.S.A.", *Policy Studies Review*, Vol. 7 (2) pp. 412-431.

MARQUES, H.T. (1988), Turismo e autarquias, *Cadernos municipais*, Lisbon.

MARSH. J.(1990), *Tourism Principles, Practices, Philosophies,* 6th Edn, John Wiley & Sons, New York.

MASIUKIEWICZ, P.R (1986),"Rural tourism in the years 1981-84" *Institute of Tourism Information Bulletin*, Warsaw. (In Polish).

MATHIESON, A. and Wall, G. (1982), *Tourism: Economic, Physical and Social Impacts, Longman,* London and New York.

MINISTERE DU TOURISME (1993), *Un plan pour le tourisme rural,* Paris.

MOYNAHAN, B. (1985), *The Tourist Trap,* Pan Books, London.

MURPHY, P.E. (ed.) (1983), "Tourism in Canada: selected issues and options", *Western Geographical Series* Vol. 21, University of Victoria, Victoria.

NEUFELDT, L. (1984) *Current problems of development of tourist villages*, University of Gdansk. (In Polish)

NOE, F.P., SNOW, R., and HAMPE, G. (1987), "Visitor Use of the Outdoors : Missing Links between Policy and Recreation", *Policy Studies Review,* Vol.7 (2) pp. 377-384.

NORONHA, R. (1979), *The social and cultural dimensions of Tourism: A review of the literature in English*, Washington, D.C., 1979.

O'GRADY, R. (1990), *The challenge of tourism*, Ecumenical Coalition on Third World Tourism, Bangkok.

O'RIORDAN, T. and TURNER, R.K. (eds) (1983), *An Annotated Reader in Environmental Planning and Management,* Pergamon Press, Oxford.

OECD (1980), *The impact of Tourism on the Environment*, Paris.

OECD (1992), *Tourism Policy and International Tourism in OECD Member Countries*, Paris.

OUTDOOR RECREATION RESOURCES REVIEW COMMISSION (1962), *Projection to the years 1976 and 2000: Economic growth, population, labor force and leisure and transportation,* ORRRC Study Report No. 13, Government Printing Office, Washington D.C.

PAPAKONSTANTINIDIS, L.A. (1992), *Rural Tourism and balanced Development (Two Models),* Athens. (In Greek)

PAPAKONSTANTINIDIS, L.A.(1992), *Rural Tourism: A Station Towards Local Development,* Athens. (In Greek)

PATMORE, J.A. (1983), *Recreation and Resources*, London.

PEARCE, D. (1989), *Tourism development*, 2nd ed., Longman Scientific and Technical, Harlow.

PEARCE, D. (1987), *Tourism today: a geographical analysis* Longman, London.

PEARCE, P.L. (1988), *The Ulysses factor: evaluating visitors in tourist settings,* Springer-Verlag, New York.

PRIEWASSER, R. (1983), *Stand und entwicklung der Freizeitangebote*, Linz.

PRINCIPADO DE ASTURIAS (1992), *Seminario Internacional de Turismo de Verd* (International Seminar on Green Tourism), Oviedo.

PRINCIPADO DE ASTURIAS (1986), *Turismo en Espacio Rural* (Tourism in Rural Areas), Oviedo.

READ, S.E., HAWKINS, E.L., SHAFER and Rovelstad J.M. (eds) (1980), "A prime force in the expansion of tourism in the next decade: special interest travel", in *Tourism Marketing and Management Issues,* George Washington University, Washington D.C., pp. 193-202.

RELPH, E. (1976), *Place and Placelessness,* Pion, London.

REV. PAPERS DE TURISME (1989), *Numero Especial sobre Turismo Rural* (Special Issue on Rural Tourism), Valencia.

ROBINSON, H. (1976), *A Geography of Tourism*, Mac Donald and Evans, London.

ROSS G., (1991), "The impact of Tourism on regional Australian communities", *Regional Journal of Social Issues,* 25 pp. 15-21.

RURAL FORUM REPORT (1984), *Tourism in the Rural Economy,* Rural Forum, Edinburgh.

SANDOR, Dr. J. (1989) "Report of the Conference of the Hungarian Rural Host's Union" in *Trade Review* Hungary. (In Hungarian).

SANDOR, Dr. J. (1989), "Rural tourism as a special form of tourism" in *The Development of Settlements*, Hungary. (In Hungarian).

SCHNELL, P. (1977), "Die Bedeutung des Fremdenverkehrs im Rahmem der Wirtschaftlichen Forderung strukturschwacher Gebiete" in *Tourism - factor for national and regional development,* Sofia, University of Sofia, Kliment Ohridski, Chair of Geography of Tourism/Union of the Scientific Workers in Bulgaria/ Bulgarian Geographical Society, pp. 92-110.

SCHREIBER, Irmgard (1992), *Urlaub auf dem Lande - Voraussetzungen und Chancen (Holidays in the Countryside - Requirements and Chances).* Paper presented at the DLG Conference about "Farm/Rural Tourism" in Frankfurt, October.

SEATER (1976), *Hébergement et restauration en milieu rural,* Ministère de l'Industrie, Paris.

SEM, J. (ed) (1989), *Using tourism and travel as a community and rural revitalization strategy* (Proceedings of the National Extension Workshop), University of Minnesota.

SIVERTSEN, K. A. (1988), *Turisme i landbruket,* Zurich.

SMITH, V.L. (ed) (1989), *Hosts and guests: the anthropology of tourism* 2nd ed University of Pennsylvania, Philadelphia. SPECIALITY TRAVEL INDEX: Directory of Special Interest Travel, Alpine Hanson Publishers, San Anselmo, California.

STEINECKE, Prof. *et al* (1992), *Strategisches Tourismuskonzept für das Grossherzogtum Luxemburg*, Europaisches Tourismus Institut.

STURESSON, C.G. (1988), *Rural tourism*, Stockholm. (In Swedish).

THIBAL, S. (1991), *Pour une signalétique européenne harmonisée dans le domaine du tourisme rural et analyse des circuits d'information, de distribution et de vente*, EUROTER, Paris.

TISDELL, C. (1984), *Tourism, the environment, international trade and public economics* Asian-Australian Joint Research Project, Australian National University, Canberra.

UNITED STATES CONGRESS (1989), *Report of the Federal Task Force on Rural Tourism to the Tourism Policy Council,* Washington D.C., 25 September.

UNIVERSIDAD DE CANTABRIA (1991), *Seminario sobre Turismo Rural* (Seminar on Rural Tourism) unpublished.

UYSAL, M. and CROMPTON, J.L. (1985), "An overview of approaches used to forecast tourism demand", *Journal of Travel Research* Vol 23 (4), pp. 7-15.

WALES TOURIST BOARD (1988), *Tourism in Wales: Developing the Potential,* Cardiff.

WALL, G. (ed) (1989), *Outdoor Recreation in Canada,* Toronto.

WATSON, A. and WATSON, R.D. (1983), *Tourism, land use and rural communities in mountain areas: the Swiss approach and its relevance for Scotland,* Aberdeen: Grampian Regional Council.

WEAVER, G. (1993), *Tourism Development: A Guideline for Rural Communities,* University of Missouri.

WEILER, B. and HALL, C.M. (1992), *Special Interest Tourism* Belhaven / Halsted Press, London.

WILLIAMS, A., SHAW, G., GREENWOOD, J. and HENNESSY, S. (1986), *Tourism and economic development: a review of experiences in Western Europe,* University of Exeter, Department of Geography, Cornish Tourism Project, Discussion Paper no. 2 Exeter.

WORLD TOURISM ORGANISATION (1983), *Prospects for Restructuring Tourist Flows, Destinations and Markets,* WTO, Madrid.

YAMAZAKI, M., OYAMA, Y., and OHSHIMA, J. (1983), *Green Tourism* , Tokyo. (In Japanese)

YOUNG, G. (1973), *Tourism: Blessing or Blight?* Penguin, Harmondsworth.

II. Rural development issues

ARMSTRONG, J., McCLELAND, D., and O'BRIEN, T.A. (1989), *A Policy for Rural Problem Areas in Northern Ireland,* Belfast, University of Ulster.

BARKER, S. and LANE, B. (1990), *Local Authorities and Rural Tourism,* University of Bristol.

BETEILLE, R. (1981), *La France du vide,* Litec., Paris.

BITTA, D., ALBERT, J., LOUDON, D.L., BOOTH G.G., and WEEKS R.R. (1977), "Estimating the Economic Impact of a Short Term Tourist Event", *Journal of Travel Research,* Vol 16.(2), pp. 10-15.

BOGGS, B. BRADFORD, C. and DUNCAN, W. (1987), *Commercial Credit and Rural Economic Development,* a paper presented to the Rural Economic Policy Program Symposium sponsored by the Aspen Institute, Morgantown, West Virginia (November).

BRADLEY, T. and LOWE, P. (eds) (1984), *Locality and Rurality,* Geo Books, Norwich.

BRADSHAW, T.K. and BLAKELY, E.J. *Rural Economic Development in the 1980's: Preparing for the future,* U.S. Department of Agriculture, Economic Research Service, Washington, D.C.

BROWN, D.L. and DEAVERS, K.L. (1989), *Economic Dimensions of Rural America.*

BURDGE, R.J. (1982), "Needs assessment surveys for decision makers", In Dillman D.A. and Hobbs, D.J. (eds.), *Rural society in the U.S.: Issues for the 1980's,* Westview Press, Boulder, Colorado.

CANADIAN COUNCIL ON RURAL DEVELOPMENT (1975), *Tourism and Outdoor Recreation in Rural Development,* Ottawa.

CARTER ADMINISTRATION (1980), *Small Community and Rural Development Policy,* U.S. Government Printing Office, Washington, D.C.

CASTAGNARI, G. (1975), "La campagna come investimento", *Nord e Sud,* Vol.22, pp. 151-60.

CERNEA, M.M. (ed) (1985), *Putting People First. Sociological Variables in Rural Development,* Oxford University Press and the World Bank.

CIML (Centre for Improving Mountain Living) (1989), *Strategies for the Economic Future of Western North Carolina,* Cullowhee, NC.

CLOUT, H. (1984), *A Rural Policy for the EEC?,* Methuen, London.

COHEN, Anthony P. (ed) (1979), *Belonging: Identity and Social Organisation in British Rural Cultures.* Manchester U.P.

COMMISSION OF THE EUROPEAN COMMUNITIES (1988), European Commission, Brussels. "The Future of Rural Society" *Bulletin of the EC* Supplement 4/88.

COMMISSION OF THE EUROPEAN COMMUNITIES (1990), *Objective 5(b) - Rural Development: Adoption of the Community Support Framework.* Communication of the Agriculture and Rural Development Commissioner, European Commission, Brussels.

COMPTROLLER OF THE CURRENCY (1984), *Community banks and rural markets: Case studies in economic development.* U.S. Department of the Treasury, Washington, D.C.

COUNCIL OF STATE POLICY AND PLANNING AGENCIES (1989), *101 Ideas for Stimulating Rural Entrepreneurship and New Business Development* (January), Washington.

COUNTRYSIDE COMMISSION (1984), *A Better Future for the Uplands,* CCP 162 Cheltenham.

COUNTRYSIDE COMMISSION (1987), *New opportunities for the countryside,* Cheltenham.

CRAMER, G.L.O., and JENSEN, C.W. (1982), *Agricultural economics and agribusiness.* (2nd ed.), Wiley, New York.

DIXON, J.A., CARPENTER, R.A., FALLON, L.A., SHERMAN, P.B. and MANOPIMOKE, S. (1988), *Economic Analysis of the Environmental Impacts of Development Projects,* Earthscan Publications, London.

DYKEMAN, F.W. (1990), *Entrepreneurial and sustainable rural communities,* Mount Allison University, Canada.

ECKSTROM B.L. and LEISTRITZ, F.L. (1988), *Rural community decline and revitalization: an annotated bibliography,* New York.

EEC The Future of Rural Society (1988), Commission of the European Communities *Bulletin of the European Communities,* Supplement 4/88, CEC, Brussels.

ELKINGTON, J., and BURKE, T. (1987), *The Green Capitalists,* London.

ESTABROOKES, M. and LAMARCH, R. (eds) (1987), *Telecommunications: A Strategic Perspective on Regional Economic and Business Development,* Canadian Institute for Research on Regional Development, New Bruswick.

FLORA, J.L., CHRISS, J.J., GALE E., GREEN G.P., SCHMIDT, F.E., and FLORA, C., (1991), *From the Grassroots: Profile of 103 Rural Self Development Projects,* Staff Report No. AGES 9123, U.S.Dept of Agriculture, Economic Research Service, Washington, D.C.,

FREDERICK, M. (1992), *Tourism as rural economic development tool: an exploration of the literature* USDA, Washington, D.C.

FRITZ, R.G. (1982), "Tourism, Vacation Home Development and Residential Tax Burden: A Case Study of the Local Finances of 240 Vermont Towns" *American Journal of Economics and Sociology,* Vol. 41 (4), pp. 375-385.

GADANT, J. (1987), *Aménagement et développement rural,* Paris.

GILLESPIE, A.E. (ed) (1983), *Technological Change and Regional Development,* Pion, London.

GILLESPIE, A.E. and HEPWORTH, M.E. (1986), *Telecommunications and Regional Development in the Information Society,* Newcastle Studies on the Information Economy, Working paper No. 1.

GILLESPIE, A.E. GODDARD, J.B. HEPWORTH, M.E. and WILLIAMS, H. "Information and communications technology and regional development: an information economy perspective", *STI Review*, OECD, Paris, (April).

GILLESPIE, A.E., GODDARD, J.B., ROBINSON, J.F. SMITH, I.J. and THWAITES, A.R. (1984), *The Effects of New Information Technology on the Less Favoured Regions of the Community,* Studies Collection, Regional Policy series No. 23, CEC, Brussels.

GODDARD, J.B. and GILLESPIE, A.E. (1986), "Advanced telecommunications and regional economic development", *The Geographical Journal*, No. 3 pp. 383-397.

GREGORY, G.N.F. (ed) (1987), *Isolated communities: a major report on the needs of inland Australia.* Proceedings of the Needs of the West Conference, University of New England, Australia.

HAID, H. (1989), *Vom neuen Leben. Alternativen Wirtschafts und Lebensformen in der Alpen*, Innsbruck.

HOLDSWORTH, D. (ed) (1985), *Reviving Mainstreet*, Toronto.

JAMIESON, W. (1990), *Maintaining and Enhancing the Sense of Place for Small Communities and Regions.* University of Calgary 1990.

JOHNSON, P. and THOMAS, B. (1990), "Measuring the Local Employment Impact of a Tourist Attraction: An Empirical Study", *Regional Studies*, Vol 24. (5), pp. 395 - 403.

JOHNSTONE, D., NICHOLSON, C., STONE, M.K. and TAYLOR R. (1990), *Countrywork,* Acre, Cirencester.

KIESELBACH, S., SCOTT, R., and LONG, P.T. (1990), "Tourism and the Rural Revitalization Movement", *Parks and Recreation,* Vol. 25 (3), pp. 62-66.

LAPPING M.B., DANIELS T.L and KELLER, J.W. (1989), *Rural Planning and Development in the United States*, New York.

LAWRENCE, G. (1987), *Capitalism and the Countryside*, Pluto Press, Sydney.

LEDIS (1989), *Rural development in Wales*, UK.

LEE, R. and OGDON, P. (eds) (1976), *Economy and Society in the EEC: Spatial Perspectives,* Saxon House, Farnborough.

LEVI-STRAUSS, L. and MENDRAS, H. "Rural community studies in France' in DURAND-DROUHIN, J-L. SZWENGRUB, L-M, and MIHAILESCU, I. (eds) *Rural Community Studies in Europe,* Pergamon Press, Oxford.

LIONEL, J.B. (ed) (1988), *The Rural South in Crisis: Challenges for the Future,* Westview Press, Boulder, Colorado.

LOUKS, K. (1988), *Training Entrepreneurs for Small Business Creation: Lessons from Experience.* International Labour Office, Geneva.

LOWE, P. et al (1986), *Countryside Conflicts,* Gower/Temple Smith, London.

MACEWEN, M. and Sinclair, G. (1983) *New Life for the Hills,* Council for National Parks, London.

MARTINOS, H. (1989), *The Management of Local Economic Development Strategies*. Report prepared as part of the Local Employment Development Action (LEDA) programme of the Commission of the European Communities, DG.V. London: Local and Regional Development Planning.

MESL, Mateja (1992), *How Rural/Agri Tourism Can Assist Economies in Transition*,   Paper presented at the FAO workshop on Rural/Agri Tourism Development in Europe, Rinn bei Innsbruck, Austria, 2-4 December 1992, Studio for Rural Development, Ravne na Koroskem, Slovenia.

MESSERLI, H.R., (1990), *Enterprise Zones and Rural Tourism Development: Policy Issues and Options* U.S. Dept. of Commerce, Washington, D.C.

MORMONT, M. (1987), "Tourism and Rural Change: the Symbolic Impact", in BOUQUET, M., and WINTER, M. (eds), *Who From Their Labours Rest? Conflict and Practice in Rural Tourism*, London.

NATIONAL MAINSTREET CENTRE (1989), *Revitalizing Downtown*, Washington D.C.

O'CINNEIDE, M.S. and Cuddy, M. (1992),   *Perspectives on Rural Development in Advanced Economies*, Centre for Development Studies, University College Galway.

O'CINNEIDE, M.S. and Grimes, S. (1992), *The Planning and Development of Marginal Areas*, Centre for Development Studies, University College Galway.

O'CINNEIDE, M.S. and KEANE, M.J. (1988), *Local Socioeconomic Impacts Associated with the Galway Gaeltaecht*. Research Report No. 3, Social Sciences Research Centre: University College Galway.

O'CONNOR, J. and LYONS M. (1983), *Enterprise - The Irish Approach*, The Industrial Development Authority, Dublin

OEAR (Austrian Association for Self-Reliant Regional Development) (1988), *Advice for Self-Help Projects in Disadvantaged Regions*, Vienna (in German).

OECD (1986), *Rural Public Management*, Paris.

OECD (1988), *New Trends in Rural Policy Making*, Paris.

OECD (1990), *Partnerships for Rural Development*, Paris.

OECD (1992), *Local Intitiatives for Job Creation. Businesses and Jobs in the Rural World*, Paris.

OECD (1993), *What Future for our Countryside: A Rural Development Policy*, Paris.

PAPAKONSTANTINIDIS, L.A. (1992), *EEC LEADER/RURAL TOURISM: A station towards local development*, Athens (in Greek).

POPOVITCH, M. and BUSS, T.F. (1987), *Rural Enterprise Development: An Iowa Case Study*, Council of State Policy and Planning Agencies, Washington, D.C.

REYNOLDS, B. and HEALEY, S.J. (eds) (1991), *Rural Development Policy: What Future for Rural Ireland?* Conference of Major Religious Superiors (Ireland).

ROBINSON, G. (1990), *Conflict and change in the countryside*, London.

ROMEISS-STACKE, F. (1986), *Freizeitnachfrage - Naturbedürfnis - Siedlungsstruktur*, Munich.

ROTHWELL, R. and ZEGFIEL, W. (1982), *Innovation and the Small and Medium Sized Firm; Their Role in Employment and in Economic Change*, Frances Pinter, London.

RURAL DEVELOPMENT COMMISSION (1984), *Guidelines for Joint Rural Development Programmes*, London.

RURAL ECONOMIC POLICY PROGRAM (1986), *Commercial Bank Credit and Economic Development: Issues and Analysis*. Draft report of proceedings of symposium held in Shakertown, Kentucky, sponsored by the Aspen Institute and the Ford Foundation, 20-22 October.

SARGENT, F.O. (1976), *Rural environmental planning*. South Burlington.

SARGENT, F.O., LUSK, P., RIVERA, J.A. and VARELA, M. (1991), *Rural Environmental Planning for Sustainable Communities,* Washington, D.C.

SCHUTZ, K. and CHEMAINUS, B.C. (1984), "The Little Town That Did!", *Small Town*, Vol 15, No 2, pp. 2-13, Washington D.C.

SCOTT, I., DENMAN, J., and LANE, B. (1989), *Doing by Learning: a Handbook for Organisers and Tutors of Village Based Community Development Courses*, ACRE, Cirencester.

SEM, J. (ed) (1989), *Using tourism and travel as a community and rural revitalization strategy* (Proceedings of the National Extension Workshop), University of Minnesota.

SEROKA, J. (ed.) (1986), *Rural public administration: Problems and prospects, Greenwood Press* Westport, Connecticut.

SHOARD, M. (1980), *The Theft of the Countryside*, Maurice Temple Smith, London.

SHOVER, J. (1976), *First majority - last minority: The transformation of rural America*. DeKalb: Northern Illinois University Press.

SIEHL, G.H. (1990), *Amenity Resources and Rural Economic Growth: Report on a National Policy Symposium,* Congressional Research Service, The Library of Congress, Washington, D.C.

SMITH, M. (1989), *Behind the Glitter: The Impact of Tourism on Rural Women in the South East,* S-E Women's Employment Coalition Lexington, Kentucky.

SQUIRE, L., and VAN DER TAK, H.G. (1975), *Economic Analysis of Projects*. Baltimore, Maryland, Johns Hopkins University Press.

STOKES, S.N., and WATSON, E. (1989), *Saving America's Countryside: Guide to Rural Conservation, Baltimore*

SZABO, G. (1993), "Rural tourism as one of the chances of the development of small enterprises in the countryside", in *JUSS*, periodical Hungary. (In Hungarian)

U.S. CONGRESS HOUSE COMMITTEE ON SMALL BUSINESS (1990), *Tourism as a tool for rural development* Hearing before the Subcommittee on Procurement, Tourism, and Rural Development of the Committee on Small Business, House of Representatives, One Hundred First Congress, second session, Independence, Missouri, June.

U.S. DEPARTMENT OF AGRICULTURE (USDA) (1983), *Better country: A strategy for rural development in the 1980's*. U.S. Government Printing Office, Washington D.C.

U.S. DEPARTMENT OF AGRICULTURE (USDA) (1984), *Rural community and the American farm,* U.S. Government Printing Office, Washington D.C.

U.S. DEPARTMENT OF AGRICULTURE (USDA), *The rural resources guide,* Washington D.C. U.S. Government Printing Office, 1987.

USDA (1989), *A Hard Look at USDA's Rural Development Programs: Report of the Rural Revitalization Task Force to the Secretary of Agriculture*, Washington, DC.

VARLEY, T., BOYLAN, T.A. and CUDDY, M.P. (1990), *Rural Crisis: Perspectives on Irish Rural Development*.

WORLD COMMISSION ON ENVIRONMENT AND DEVELOPMENT (1987), *Our Common Future,* Oxford University Press, New York.

III. Community involvement in rural tourism development and management

ALBERTA TOURISM (1988), *Community Tourism Action Plan Manual,* Edmonton.

ALBERTA TOURISM (1991), *Market Planning Skills Program: Community Participants Guide,* Edmonton.

ALLEN, L.R., LONG, P.T., PERDUE, R.R., and KIESELBACH, S.R, (1988), "The impact of tourism development on residents' perceptions of community life", *Journal of Travel Research,* Vol. 27 (1), pp. 16-21.

AROCENA, J. (1986), *Le développement par l'initiative locale. Le cas francais,* L'Harmattan, Paris.

ARONSSON, L. (1992), *Principles for Planning Tourism with Local Support* in O'CINNEIDE., M.S., and GRIMES, S. *Planning and Development of Marginal Areas*, University College Galway.

BAMBERGER, M. (1986), *The Role of Community Participation in Development Planning and Project Management* World Bank, Washington D.C.

BLANK, U. (1989), *The community tourism industry imperative: the necessity, the opportunities, its potential,* Pennsylvania.

COMMISSION OF THE EUROPEAN COMMUNITIES (1986), *Community action in the field of tourism,* Documents, com. (86) 32 final, Brussels.

EUROPEAN PARLIAMENT, *Tourism in the Community,* Official Journal of the European Communities, No. C49/157. European Commission Brussels.

HAWKER, C. and MACKINNON, N. *et al (1989), Factors in the Design of Community Based Rural Development Initiatives in Europe*, The Arkleton Trust (Research) Ltd (UK).

HAYWOOD, M.K. (1988), "Responsible and Responsive Tourism Planning in the Community", *Tourism Management* Vol. 9 (2), pp. 105-118.

HENNING, S.A. (1990), *Measuring Leadership Perceptions of Recreation and Tourism Development in Rural Coastal Zones* Mississippi State University, Southern Rural Development Centre.

HONADLE, G. and VANSANT, J. (1985) "Enhancing Local Action" in Implementation of Sustainablility: Lessons from Integrated Rural Development, Kumarian Press Connecticut.

KEOGH, B. (1990), "Public participation in community tourism planning", *Annals of Tourism Research.*

LANKFORD, S. (1992), "A method for involving residents in the tourism and recreation development process" *Conference paper, International Symposium on Tourism and Leisure Management,* Taiwan.

LEWIS, Andrew *et al.* (1992), *Feasibility of Agricultural and Community Based Tours,* Centre for Integrated Agricultural Systems, University of Wisconsin, Madison.

MOULIN, C.L. (1980), "Plan for Ecological and Cultural Tourism Involving Participation of Local Population and Associations" in HAWKINS, D.D., SHAFER, E.L., and ROVELSTAD, J.M., eds., *Tourism Planning and Development Issues* Washington, D.C.

MURPHY, P.E. (1985), *Tourism - A Community Approach,* Methuen.

MURPHY, P.E. (1988), "Community Driven Tourism Planning", *Tourism Management,* Vol 9. (2), pp. 96-104.

PIZAM, A. (1978), "Tourism's Impacts: The Social Cost to the Destination Community as Perceived by its Residents", *Journal of Travel Research*, Vol. 16 (4), pp. 8-12.

ROEHL, W.S., DITTON, R.B., and FESENMAIER, D.R. (1989), "Community Tourism Ties", *Annals of Tourism Research*, Vol. 16 (4) pp. 504 - 513.

SASKATCHEWAN ECONOMIC DEVELOPMENT AND TOURISM (1988), *Community Tourism Planning Guide*, Regina.

SEM, J. (ed) (1989), *Using Tourism and Travel as a Community and Rural Revitalization Strategy* University of Minnesota.

SMITH, V.L., HETHERINGTON, A., and BRUMBAUGH, M.D.D.(1986), "California's Highway 89: Regional Tourism Model" *Annals of Tourism Research* Vol 13, (3), pp. 415-433.

TAUB, R.P. (1988), *Community Capitalism,* Harvard Business School Press, Boston, Massachusetts

WILLIAMS, S. "Self Help Tourism" (1989), in REEVES, D. (ed), in Rural communities: Determining their future, *Proceedings of the fourth annual conference of the society for the provision of Education in Rural Australia*, Launceston, Tasmania.

IV. Eco-Tourism and the relationship between natural environments and tourism

BERGSTROM, J.C., STOLL, J.R., and RANDALL, A. (1990), "The Impact of Information on Environmental Commodity Valuation Decisions", *American Journal of Agricultural Economics,* Vol. 72. (3) pp. 614-620.

BOO, E. (1990), *Ecotourism: The Potentials and Pitfalls,* Volumes 1 and 2, World Wildlife Fund, Baltimore, Maryland.

CLAWSON, M. (1975), *Forests for whom and for what?* : John Hopkins University Press, Baltimore.

COSTA, A., and FONTES, L. T. (1990), *Conciliar a natureza e o desenvolvimento*, Porto.

COTTINGHAM, D. and LANGSHAW, R. (1981), *Grizzly, bear and man in Canada's mountain parks,* Summerthought, Banff.

DECKER, D.J and GOFF, G.R. (1987), *Valuing wildlife: economic and social perspectives*, Westview Press Boulder, Colorado.

FILION, F.L., JAQUEMOT, A., and REID, R. (1985), *The importance of wildlife to Canadians*, Ottawa.

HANLEY, N., and CRAIG, H. (1991), "The Economic Value of Wilderness Areas" in DIETZ, F. VAN DER PLOEG, F., VAN DER STRAATEN, J. (eds), *Environmental Policy and the Economy*, Amsterdam.

HEALY, R.G. (1988), "Economic consideration in nature-orientated tourism: the case of tropical forest tourism," *Forestry Private Enterprise Initiative Working Paper no 39*, Southeastern Center for Forest Economics, Research Triangle Park, North Carolina.

JACOBSON, S.K. and ROBLES, R. (1992), "Ecotourism, sustainable development and conservation education: development of a tour guide training program in Tortuguero, Costa Rica", *Environmental management,* Vol 16,pp. 701 -713, New York.

JANSEN-VERBEKE, M. Ecotourism (1991), Prevention is Better than Cure, *World Leisure Recreation Association congress paper.*

JAYAL, N. D. (1986), *Conservation, tourism & mountaineering in the Himalayas*, India.

KAZA, S. (1982), "Recreational whalewatching in California: a profile", *Whalewatcher*, vol. 16 no. 1, pp. 6-8.

KRUTILLA, J. V. and FISHER, A. R. (1975), *The Economics of Natural Environment*, Baltimore.

LINDBERG, K. (1991), *Economic policies for maximising nature tourism's contribution to sustainable development*, Washington, D.C.

MAIER, J. (1986), *Naturnaher Tourismus im Alpenraum - Möglichkeiten und Grenzen (Nature-oriented Tourism in the Alpine Region - Possibilities and Limitations)*, Arbeitsmaterialien zur Raumordnung und Raumplanung, Heft 37. Institut Für Wirtschaftsgeographie and Regionalplanung, University of Bayreuth, Germany.

MARSH, J. (1986), "Wilderness tourism", in *Tourism and the Environment: Conflict or Harmony*, Canadian Society of Environmental Biologists - Alberta Chapter, Edmonton, pp. 47-59.

MASTERTON, A. M. (1991), "Ecotourism: an economic issue", *Tour and Travel News,* Issue 228.

MURPHY, P.E. (1986), "Tourism as an agent for landscape conservation: an assessment", *The science of the total environment*, Vol 55 p. 387-395, Amsterdam.

NATURE CONSERVATION COUNCIL OF NEW SOUTH WALES (1988), *Policy on Tourism*, Sydney.

PANNEL, KERR, FORSTER and Co. (1971), *Great Barrier Reef Visitor Plan,* Melbourne.

TUCKER, M. (1989), *Whales and whale watching in Australia,* Australian National Parks and Wildlife Service, Canberra.

VALENTINE, P.S. (1984), "Wildlife and tourism: some ideas on potential and conflict" in O'Rourke, B. (ed) *Contemporary issues in Australian tourism,* Dept of Geography, University of Sydney, Sydney.

VICKERMAN, S. (1982), "Stimulating tourism and economic growth by featuring new wildlife recreation opportunities", 414-423 in *Transactions 53rd North American wildlife and natural resources conference.*

WHELAN, T. (ed) (1991), *Nature Tourism: Managing for the Environment*, Island Press, Washington, D.C.

WHITLOCK, W., VAN ROMER, K. and BECKER, R. H. (1991), *Nature Based Tourism: an annotated bibliography*, South Carolina.

WILLIS, K. G. and BENSON, J.F. (1988), A Comparison of User Benefits and Costs of Nature Conservation at Three Nature Reserves, *Regional Studies.*

WILSON, M.A. and Laarman, J.G. (1987), "Nature tourism and enterprise in Ecuador", *Forestry private enterprise initiative working paper no 27*, Southeastern Center for Forest Economics, Research Triangle Park, North Carolina.

V. Farm tourism

AGRITOURIST (1989), *Esperienze e prospettive dell'agriturismo,* Rome.

AISLEITNER, J. (1986), *Formen und Auswirkungen des bauerlichen Nebenerwerbs (Various Types of, and the Effects of, Part-Time Farming),* Institut für Geographie, University of Innsbruck, Austria.

ARNOLD, K. (1981), *Urlaub auf dem Bauernhof,* Vienna.

AUSTRIAN FARM HOLIDAYS ASSOCIATION (1992), *Urlaub am Bauernhof - Darstellung der Bauerlichen Vermietung in Oesterreich (Farm Holidays - Presentation of the farmer's room-letting in Austria)*, Vienna.

BODENSTEDT, A.A. *Has Agritourism a Chance Against Mass-Tourism?*

BORD FAILTE (1989) *Grant Scheme for Investments in Agri Tourism under the Revised Programme for Western Development, Bord Failte,* Dublin.

BOWEN, R., COX, L., and FOX, M. (1991),"The interface between tourism and agriculture", *Journal of Tourism Studies,* Vol.2. (2).

BRAUN, A. (1992), *Tourismus und Landwirtschaft: Modell Tirol (Tourism and Agriculture: Tyrol as a model),* Paper presented at the Conference "Tourismusforum Oberwallis" in Naters, 12 November 1992, Ecole Suisse de Tourisme, Sierre, Switzerland.

BUCHANAN, J. (1982), *Report of a Visit to the United Kingdom, Ireland, France and Sweden in 1981 to Study the Potential to be Gained by Farmers from Tourism,* Nuffield Farming Scholarships Trust, Olney, Bucks.

BUCHUNGSZENTRALE (1992), *"Ferien auf dem Bauemhof"* (Course material about Farm Holidays), Training course 27 March 1992, Schweizerischer Bauernverband, Brugg, Switzerland.

BULL, C. and WIBBERLEY, G.P. (1976), *"Farm Based Recreation in South East England Studies"* in Rural Land Use Report 12, Wye College.

CANNATA, G. (1984), *La domanda de agriturismo nelle campagne italiane,* Anagritur, Rome.

COMMITTEE OF AGRICULTURAL ORGANISATIONS IN THE EC/GENERAL COMMITTEE FOR AGRICULTURAL CO-OPERATION IN THE EC. (1983). *The Situation Of And Prospects For Agri-Tourism in The European Community, Pr(834)17, COPA/ COGECA,* Brussels.

CRUZ, J.M. (1991), *L'Agrotourisme dans la CEE: Utopie ou Realite,* EURAGRITOUR, Brussels,

DART (1984), *Farm Recreation and Tourism in England and Wales,* Countryside Commission CCP 83, Cheltenham.

DAVIES, E.T., *Tourism on Devon Farms - a Physical and Economic Appraisal,* University of Exeter Agricultural Economic Unit, Report 188.

DENMAN, R. *Recreation on Farms, Crofts and Estates* Scottish Tourist Board, 1978.

DENMAN, R. and DENMAN, J. *A study of farm tourism in the West Country,* West Country Tourist Board, Exeter, 1990.

DERNOI, L.A. *Present conditions for farm tourism in Europe,* New York, 1983.

EISELT, B. *Der Urlaub am Bauernhof im oberoesterreichischen Alpenvorland,* University of Linz, 1976.

EMBACHER, HANS. *'Farm Holidays in Austria - The Austrian Model of Promoting Rural Tourism.* Paper presented at the FAO workshop on Rural/Agri Tourism Development in Europe, Rinn bei Innsbruck, Austria, 2-4 December 1992. Austrian Farm Holidays Association, Vienna, Austria, 1992.

EXETER UNIVERSITY AGRICULTURAL ECONOMICS UNIT *The Role of Farm Tourism in the Less Favoured Areas of England and Wales,* Report No 218, 1982.

FAC/ECE WORKING PARTY ON AGRARIAN STRUCTURE & FARM RATIONALISATION *Symposium on agriculture and tourism in Finland,* Geneva, 1982.

FEEHAN, J. (ed) *Tourism on the Farm.* Environmental Institute, University College Dublin, 1992.

FOLEY, C. *Understanding Historic Monuments on the Farm.* Historic Monuments and Buildings Branch, Dept of the Environment for Narthern Ireland and Dept for Agriculture for Northern Ireland, 1988.

FRATER, J. *Farm Tourism in England and Overseas* Research Memorandum 93, Centre for Urban Studies, University of Birmingham, 1982.

FRY, P. *Farm Tourism in Western Australia: Report of a Pilot Study,* Rural and Allied Industries Council, Perth, 1984.

GANNON, A. *A Strategy for the Development of Agri Tourism*, Dublin, 1988

GANNON, A. *Agri-Tourism in Austria*, 1989.

GANNON, A. *The Global Management Approach for Farm Development and Family Living*, Dublin, 1987.

GANNON, AGNES. *A Strategy for the Development of Agri-Tourism.* F.A.O. Regional Office for Europe, Rome, Italy, 1989.

GANNON, A., B. HENNELLY, and C. FOX. *Agri-Tourism in Austria Study Tour Report.* Dublin: ACOT, 1987.

GEALE, P. (1985), *Farm Tourism*, Queensland Tourist and Travel Corporation, BRISBANE.

GELDOF, W. (1992), *Agritourism and Regional Development: A Case Study in a Bulgarian Village*. Centre for Recreation Studies, Wageningen Agricultural University, The Netherlands.

HORBER, Rudolf (1983), "Landwirtschaft und Tourismus im schweizerischen Berggebiet" (Agriculture and Tourism in the Mountainous Regions of Switzerland) in: *Berichte uber die Landwirtschaft, 61* Verlag Paul Parey, Hamburg and Berlin (1990), p.302-313.

JANSEN-VERBEKE, Myriam and KLOEZE, Jan W. te. (1990), *An International Study on the Marketing Aspects of Agritourism,* Department of Regional Planning, Nijmegen Catholic University and Department of Sociology Centre for Recreation Studies, Wageningen Agricultural University, The Netherlands.

JANSEN-VERBEKE, Myriam (1990), *The Potentials of Rural Tourism and Agritourism in EEC*, University of Nijmegen, The Netherlands.

JENKINS, D.L. (1989), *Choices and challenges: farming alternatives for Queensland*, Brisbane, Australia.

JONES, W. Dyfri and GREEN D.A.G. (1986), *Farm Tourism in Hill and Upland Areas of Wales*. Aberystwyth: Department of Agricultural Economics and Marketing, The University College of Wales.

KELLY, O'MAHONY, HESLIN (1987), *Agri-Tourism in England*, Dublin.

KINSEY, B.H. (1987), *Agri-Tourism and Rural Enterprises*. Croom Helm, Sydney, 1987.

KLOEZE, J.W. (1990), Farm Camping in the Netherlands, The First Nation-Wide Research on Relevant Aspects of Agritourism, Paper presented at the Institute of Sociology International Conference *"Bulgarian Agriculture in the Future"*, Sofia, Bulgaria, 20-24 November.

KLOEZE, Jan W.te. (1992), *Agritourism and Regional Development: A Case Study in a Bulgarian Village*. Paper presented at the Joint Conference of the British Leisure Studies Association and the Dutch Vereniging voor de Vrijetijdssector *'Internationalization and Leisure Research'* Tilburg University, The Netherlands, 10-13 December.

LBL (1992), *Ferien auf dem Bauernhof (Holidays on Farms),* Hints and Recommendations, Landwirtschaftliche Beratungszentrale (Agricultural Extension Services Center), Lindau, Switzerland.

LEIMGRUBER, W. (1985), "Farmhouse holidays and rural development", paper given to a conference on *"The Management of Rural Resources"* held at the University of Guelph, Canada, University of Fribourg, Switzerland, 1985.

LEWIS, Andrew *et al.* (1992), *Feasibility of Agricultural and Community Based Tours.* Centre for Integrated Agricultural Systems, University of Wisconsin, Madison.

LODER-SYMONDS, R.F. (1976), "How can British agriculture benefit from the expansion of tourism?" *Farmers' Club Journal.*

MAGAGNOTTI, P. (1978), "Urlaub auf dem Bauernhof", *Agriturismo,* Bologna.

MANNHART, Andreas E. *Landwirtschaft und Tourismus: Konkurrenz oder Erganzung? (Agriculture and Tourism: Competitors or Complementary Elements?).* Regionalstudie Sarganserland-Walensee, Geographisches Institut der Universität, Zürich, Switzerland.

MAUDE, A.J.S. and REST, D.J. (1985), "The social and economic effects of farm tourism in the United Kingdom", *Agricultural Administration,* Vol. 20.

MESL, Mateja (1992), *How Rural/Agri Tourism Can Assist Economies in Transition.* Paper presented at the FAO workshop on Rural/Agri Tourism Development in Europe, Rinn bei Innsbruck, Austria, 2-4 December 1992, Studio for Rural Development, Ravne na Koroskem, Slovenia.

MOOR, U. (1989), *Marketing-Konzept für "Ferien auf dem Bauernhof",* Diplomarbeit, Schweizerische Schule für touristik.

MOYER, Harriett (1987), *Agriculture and Tourism in Wisconsin.* Report On the First Agri-Tourism Conference, The Recreation Resources Center, University of Wisconsin, Madison, p.6-7.

NATIONAL FARMERS UNION (1973), *Farm Tourism in Wales,* N.F.U. Council for Wales, Welshpool.

NATIONAL FARMERS' UNION/PEAT MARWICK MCLINKTOCK (1988), *The Leisure Market,* London.

PALMINSKOSKI, Unto (1983), "Tourismus als landwirtschaftlicher Nebenerwerb in Finnland" (Tourism as a source of additional income for farmers in Finland), in: *Berichte uber die Landwirtschaft, 61.* Verlag Paul Parey, Hamburg and Berlin. p.314-316.

PALMINKOSKI, U. (1991), *The feasibility of existing farm buildings for country holidays,* Helsinki (in Finnish).

PARENTE, A. (1980), *"L'agriturismo",* in Corna-Pellegrini G. and Brusa C. (eds), *La ricerca geografica in Italia 1960-1980* Ask, Varese.

PETRIN, Tea (1992), *Networking System for Rural/Agri Tourism.* Paper presented at the FAO workshop on Rural/Agri Tourism Development in Europe, Rinn bei Innsbruck, Austria, 2-4 December 1992. Ljubljana, Slovenia.

PEVETZ, W. (1985), "Fremdenverkehr und Landwirtschaft im oesterreichischen Berggebiet (Tourism and Agriculture in the mountainous regions in Austria)," in: *Der Forderungsdienst, Sonderheft,* Vienna, p.35-47.

PEVETZ, W. (1992), "Erscheinungsformen, Voraussetzungen und Chancen des Agrotourismus," in *Monatsberichte über die oesterreichische Landwirtschaft/Bundesanstallt f. Agrarwirtschaft,* Vienna.

PIZAM, A. (1980), *The benefits of farm tourism to rural communities: the Massachusetts case,* Massachusetts.

POTTHOFF, Hilda. (1983), "Tourismus und Landwirtschaft (Agriculture and Tourism)," in: *Berichte uber die Landwirtschaft,* Verlag Paul Parey, Hamburg and Berlin. p.274-279.

PROBST, Dennis P. and COMBRINK, Thomas E. (1990), *The Interrelations of Agriculture and Tourism in Michigan.* Cooperative Extension Service, Michigan State University, East Lansing.

PRUCKNER, G. (1991), *Bewertung überbetrieblicher Leistungen und negativer externer Effekte der Landwirtshcaft*, Linz.

QUINN, J. (1989), *Rural Development through Agri-Tourism*, Galway.

REUR TECHNICAL SERIES 14 (1990), *Rural Development Through Agri-Tourism, A Guide to Developing an Agri-tourism Enterprise*, Food and Agricultural Organisation of the United Nations, Rome.

RIEDER, S. (1984), *Der Bauernhoftourismus - seine Verbreitung in der Schweiz und seine Anwendungsmöglichkeiten im Jura*, Universität Basel.

SCHULZ-BORCK, H. (1986), *Urlaub auf dem Bauernhof - die Analyse des Angebots*, Bonn.

SKOOG, G. (1988), *Which possibilities has tourism as a production branch in farming*, Uppsala (in Swedish)

STAIKOV, Z., KOZHOUHAROVA, V. und DRAGANOVA, M. *Rural and Agritourism in Bulgaria*, Institute of Sociology, Sofia, Bulgaria.

STOKES, R. (1991), "Psychological, environmental and economic factors relevant to farm tourism supply", *Australian Psychologist*, Vol.26 (3).

TAMBLYN, C., and POWELL, R. *Input/output study of the North Coast agricultural and fisheries industries*. University of New England, Australia.

TRANTER, R.B. (ed) (1983), *Strategies for Family-Worked Farms in the UK*, CAS Paper 15, Centre for Agricultural Strategy, Reading.

US DEPT OF AGRICULTURE (1962), *Rural Recreation. A new family-farm business*, Washington, D.C.

VINCENT, J.A. (1980), "The political economy of alpine development: tourism or agriculture in St Maurice" *Sociologia Ruralis*, vol. 20, No 3-4.

WALES TOURIST BOARD, (1977), *The Farmers Guide to Tourism*, Cardiff.

WINTER, M. (1981), "The agricultural economy of the New Forest" chapter in Social Research Consultancy, *The New Forest Common Grazing System*, Report to the Countryside Commission.

WINTER, M. (1984), "Farm-based tourism and conservation in the uplands", *Ecos: A Review of Conservation*, Vol. 5, No. 3.

WOHLMANN, Rainer and LOHMANN, Martin (1986), *Urlaub auf dem Bauernhof, Urlaub auf dem Land (Holidays on the Farm, Holidays in the Countryside*, Studienkreis für Tourismus, Starnberg, Germany.

VI. Rural heritage interpretation

ADAMS, J. *et al* (1986) *Aboriginals and recreation*. Workshop held in Canberra, 23-24 June.

ALBERTA HISTORICAL RESOURCES DIVISION (1992), *The Economic Impact of Provincial Heritage Facilities in Alberta*, Edmonton.

BORD FAILTE (1990), *Developing Heritage Attractions - A Conference to plan the Development of Culture and Heritage-Based Tourism Attractions in Ireland*, Dublin.

BORD FAILTE (1992), *Heritage and Tourism - Second Conference on the Development of Heritage Attractions in Ireland*, Dublin.

FOLEY, C. (1988), *Understanding Historic Monuments on the Farm.* Historic Monuments and Buildings Branch, Dept of the Environment for Narthern Ireland and Dept for Agriculture for Northern Ireland.

FOWLER, N. (1987), *Making the Most of Heritage,* HMSO, London.

GROLLEAU, H. (1988), *Rural Heritage and Tourism in the EEC,* EEC tourism unit DG XXIII.

HAM, S.H. (1992), *Environmental Interpretation: A Practical Guide for People with Big Ideas and Small Budgets,* Golden, Colorado.

HEWISON, R. (1987), *The Heritage Industry: Britain in a Climate of Decline,* Methuen, London.

JOHNSON, D. (ed) (1991), *Pride of Place - the arts in rural areas,* The Arts Development Association, Dartington.

LANE, B. (1991), "Sustainable tourism: A new concept for the Heritage Interpreter", *Interpretation Journal,* No. 49, London.

LONG, P.T. and PERDUE, R.R (1990), "The Economic Impacts of Rural Festivals and Special Events: Assessing the Spatial Distribution of Expenditures", *Journal of Travel Research,* 28 (4).

MAWSON, R. (1984), *Summary Report: Who Visits Historic Houses and Why ?* National Trust for Historic Preservation, Washington D.C.

MYERSCOUGH J. (1989), *The Economic Importance of the Arts in Britain,* Policy Studies Institute, London.

STEINECKE, Prof., HAART, N. *et al* (1993), *Inventaire des sites touristiques des equipements sportifs et culturels de la region/Evaluation du potential de developpement touristique,* Europaisches Tourismus Institut.

THE EUROPEAN CENTRE FOR TRADITIONAL AND REGIONAL CULTURES (1990), *Study of the Social Cultural and Linguistic Impact of Tourism in and upon Wales,* Cardiff.

TILDEN, F. (1977), *Interpreting Our Heritage,* University of North Carolina Press.

UZZELL, D. (ed) (1989), *Heritage Interpretation,* Vols 1 & 2, Belhaven Press, London.

VII.   Marketing for rural tourism

AHLGREN, H. (1991), *Developing Country Holidays into a Brand Product,* MALO Project, Finnish Tourist Board, Helsinki. (In Finnish)

ALBERTA TOURISM (1991), *Market Planning Skills Program: Community Participants Guide,* Edmonton.

COWELL, D.W. (1984), *The Marketing of Services,* Heinemann, Oxford.

CROMPTON, J.L. (1979), "Motivations for Pleasure Travel" *Annals of Tourism Research,* 6.

DYKEMAN, F.W. (1989), *Rural tourism opportunity recognition: insightful marketing and development concepts,* Mount Allison University, Canada.

EAGLES, P.J.F. (1984), *The Planning and Management of Environmentally Sensitive Areas,* London.

GILBERT, D. (1989), "Rural Tourism and Marketing", *Tourism Management* Vol.10, (1), pp. 39-50.

GOODALL, B. and Ashworth, G.(eds) (1988), *Marketing in the Tourism Industry: The Promotion of Destination Regions,* Routledge, London.

HAWKINS, D.E., SHAFER, E.L. and Rovelstad, J.M. (eds) (1980), *Tourism Marketing and Management Issues*, George Washington University, Washington, D.C.

HEISE, D.A. (1991), Promoting tourism in rural America, *Rural Information Center publication series*, Maryland, December.

JANSEN-VERBEKE, Myriam and KLOEZE, Jan W. (1990), *An International Study on the Marketing Aspects of Agritourism*, Department of Regional Planning, Nijmegen Catholic University and Department of Sociology Centre for Recreation Studies, Wageningen Agricultural University, The Netherlands.

KING, B. and HYDE, G. (eds) (1989), *Tourism Marketing in Australia*, Hospitality Press, Melbourne.

KNABL, J. (1984), *Marketing-Konzept für Urlaub am Bauernhof in Tirol*, Innsbruck.

MINISTERE DU TOURISME (1991), *Le Marche du Tourisme Vert: Clientèles Européennes* Paris.

MOOR, U. (1989), *Marketing-Konzept für "Ferien auf dem Bauernhof"*, Diplomarbeit, Schweizerische Schule für Touristik.

NATIONAL FARMERS' UNION/PEAT MARWICK MCLINKTOCK (1988), *The Leisure Market*, London.

NEUBAUER, S. (1989), *DLG-Marktnischen-Katalog. Einkommensalternativen für Landwirte*, Frankfurt.

PLANQUE, V. (1975), *La promotion du tourisme vert*, Conseil supérieur du Tourisme.

THIBAL, S. (1991), *Pour une signalétique européenne harmonisée dans le domaine du tourisme rural et analyse des circuits d'information, de distribution et de vente*, EUROTER, Paris.

VENTH, O. (1985), *Umweltsensibilität und Konsequenzen für das Tourismusmarketing*, Gesellschaftliches Wertesystem, Berlin 1985.

WALES TOURIST BOARD (1984), *Rural Tourism: A New Marketing Initiative*, Internal W.T.B. Consultative Paper, Cardiff.

WEILER, B. and HALL, C.M. (1992), *Special Interest Tourism*, Belhaven/Halsted Press, London.

VIII. National Parks and Protected Areas

AITCHISON J., HUGHES E.J. and JONES, G. (1983), The *Llyn Peninsula: an Assessment of the Heritage Coast & AONB*, Dwyfor District Council, Pwllheli.

BATESON, P., NYMAN, S. and SHEPPARD, D., (eds) (1989), *National parks and tourism*, Royal Australian Institute of Parks and Recreation and New South Wales National Parks and Wildlife Service, Sydney.

BRAHTZ, J.F.P. (ed.) (1972), *Coastal Zone Management: Multiple use with conservation*, Wiley, New York.

BROOKS, P.R. (ed.) (1980), *Proceedings of the New York State Forest Resources Planning Symposium*. New York State Department of Environmental Conservation, Albany.

CENTRE FOR LEISURE RESEARCH (1986), *Access to the Countryside for Recreation and Sport*, Report to the Countryside Commission and Sports Council.

CLAWSON, M. and Knetsch, J.K. (1966), *Economics of Outdoor Recreation*, John Hopkins, Baltimore.

COPPOCK, J.T. and Duffield, B.S. (1975), *Recreation in the Countryside: a Spatial Analysis*, Macmillan, London.

COPPOCK, J.T.(ed) (1977), *Second Homes: curse or blessing?* Pergamon, London.

COUNCIL OF EUROPE (1993), *Nature Conservation and Tourism in Protected Areas*, Environmental Encounters No. 15, Strasbourg.

COUNCIL OF NATURE CONSERVATION MINISTERS (CONCOM) WORKING GROUP FOR THE MANAGEMENT OF NATIONAL PARKS (1986), *Guidelines for Reservation and Management of Wilderness Areas in Australia, Canberra 1986.*

COUNTRYSIDE COMMISSION (1982), *National Parks: A Study of Rural Economics* (with University of Edinburgh), CCP 144, Cheltenham.

COUNTRYSIDE COMMISSION (1984), *National Countryside Recreation Survey,* CCP 201, Cheltenham.

COUNTRYSIDE COMMISSION (1987), *Recreation 2000 - Enjoying the Countryside,* a Consultation paper on Future Policies, Cheltenham.

COUNTRYSIDE COMMISSION (1990), *Tourism in National Parks: A Guide,* Cheltenham.

COUNTRYSIDE RECREATION RESEARCH ADVISORY GROUP (CRRAG) (1988), *Changing Land Use and Recreation*, CRRAG, Bristol.

CROMPTON, J.L. and Richardson, S.L. (1986), "The tourism connection: where public and private leisure services merge" *Parks and Recreation*, October.

DOUGLASS, R.W. (1975), *Forest recreation,* Pergamon Press, New York.

DOWNING, K.B. (1985) "Visitor demands and services: the western United States experience", 177-183 in Dooling, P.J. (ed) *Parks in British Columbia*, symposium on parks in British Columbia 17-19 February 1984, University of British Columbia, Vancouver.

DUFFIELD, B.S. and VAUGHAN D.R. (1981), *The Economy of Rural Communities in the National Parks of England and Wales*, Tourism and Recreation Research Unit, University of Edinburgh.

EWERT, A.H. (1989), *Outdoor adventure pursuits: foundations, models and theories,* Publishing Horizons, Inc, Columbus.

FROME, M. (1992), *Regreening the National Parks*, University of Arizona.

FRUEH, S. (1988), *Report to World Wildlife Fund on Tourism to Protected Areas,* mimeo, World Wildlife Fund - U.S., Washington, D.C.

HAMMITT, W.R., and COLE, D. (1987), *Wildland recreation ecology and management,* John Wiley and Sons, New York.

JORGENSON, G.M. (1974), *Recreation and leisure: a bibliography and review of the New Zealand literature,* New Zealand Ministry of Works and Development, Wellington.

LAWSON, F. and BAUD-BOVY, M. (1977), *Tourism and Recreation Development: A Hand-book of Physical Planning*, The Architectural Press, London.

MACEWAN, A., and MACEWAN, M. (1974), *Greenprints for the Countryside? The story of Britain's National Parks* Allen & Unwin, London.

MACEWEN, A. and MACEWEN, M. (1982), *National Parks: Conservation or Cosmetics?*, George Allen and Unwin, London.

MARSH, J. (1986), "Wilderness tourism", in *Tourism and the Environment: Conflict or Harmony,* Canadian Society of Environmental Biologists - Alberta Chapter, Edmonton, pp. 47-59.

MCNEELEY, J.A. and THORSELL, J.W. (1987), *Guidelines for the development of terrestrial and marine national parks for tourism and travel* IUCN, Gland.

MCNEELY, J.A. and MILLER, K.R. (eds) (1984), *National Parks, conservation, and development,* Smithsonian Institution Press, Washington, D.C.

MITCHELL, R.G. (1983), *Mountain Experience: The Psychology and Sociology of Adventure,* The University of Chicago Press, Chicago.

MOORE, M. (1987), Opening speech (presented by Sir Ron Scott) pp. 5-10 in Dale, P. (ed) *Adventure tourism seminar: current issues and future management,* Vol. 2, *South Island seminar,* Hiliary Commission for Recreation and Sport, Wellington.

NATIONAL PARK SERVICE OF AMERICA (1992), *National Parks for the 21st Century: the Vail Agenda,* Washington.

NATIONAL PARKS DIVISION (NPD) (1986), *Khao Yai National Park Management Plan, 1987-1991.* National Parks Division, Royal Forest Department, Bangkok.

PEARCE, D.G. (1982), *Westland National Park Economic Impact Study,* Department of Lands and Survey/Department of Geography, University of Canterbury, Christchurch.

PETERSON, J.P., SUNDSTROM, T., and STEWART, S. (1987), *A profile of Great Lakes diver activity, travel, and expenditure patterns,* Michigan Sea Grant College Program, Ann Arbor.

PIGRAM, J.J., (1983), *Outdoor recreation and resource management,* Croom Helm, London.

POSNER, B., CUTHBERTSON, C. TOWLE E. and REEDER, C. *Economic Impact Analysis for the Virgin Islands National Park,* Island Resources Foundation St. Thomas.

PRESIDENT'S COMMISSION ON AMERICANS OUTDOORS (PCAD) (1987), *Americans and the outdoors,* US Government Printing Office, Washington D.C.

PYBUS, V. (1989), *Adventure holidays* 12th ed., Vacation Work, Oxford.

SINGH, T.V. and Kaur, J. (eds) (1982), *Studies in tourism and wildlife parks conservation,* Metropolitan Book Company, New Delhi.

THOMPSON, P.T. (1971), *The Use of Mountain Recreational Resources: a comparison of recreation and tourism in the Colorado Rockies and the Swiss Alps,* University of Colorado, Boulder.

WORLD TOURISM ORGANISATION (1985), *The role of recreation management in the development of active holidays and special interest tourism and consequent enrichment of the holiday experience,* World Tourism Organisation, Madrid.

WORLD TOURISM ORGANISATION (1985), *The State's Role in Protecting and Promoting Culture as a Factor of Tourism Development and the Proper Use and Exploitation of the National Cultural Heritage of Sites and Monuments for Tourism,* World Tourism Organization, Madrid.

WRIGHT, R.G. (1992), *Wildlife research and management in the National Parks,* University of Illinois.

IX. Project reports and area studies

ADAC (1979), "Bausteine für eine umweltverträgliche Tourismusentwicklung (Material for Environmentally Adjusted Tourism Development)" in: *Mehr Wissen - Mehr Handeln,* Allegemeiner Deutscher Automobil-Club e.V., Munich.

ALI, S., BLAKELY, K., and LEWIS, D.E. (1979), Development of Tourism in the Illawarra: Economic Effects and Prospects. An independent study undertaken for and supported by the Department of Tourism, New South Wales,. Economic Research Bulletin 11, Dept of Economics, University of Wollongong.

ALTMAN, J.C. (1987), *The Economic Impact of Tourism on the Warmun (Turkey Creek) Community,* East Kimberly Working Paper No.19, Centre for Resource and Environmental Studies, Australian National University, Canberra.

AN FORAS FORBATHA (1973), Brittas Bay: a planning and conservation study, Dublin.

BORD FAILTE (1989), *Developing for Growth - A Framework Plan for Irish Tourism,* Dublin.

BOTE (1984), *Importancia de la demanda turistica en el espacio rural en Espana,* Consejo superior de investigaciounes Scientificas, Madrid.

BROWN, T.L., and CONNELLY, N.A. (1986), "Tourism and Employment in the Adirondack Park", *Annals of Tourism Research* Vol. 13 (3), pp. 481-489.

BRYDEN, J.M. et AL (1988), *Training for Rural Scotland,* The Arkleton Trust (Research) Ltd (UK).

BURTENSHAW, D.(1981), "Austria", pp. 335-46 in Clout H. (ed.), *Regional Development in Western Europe* (2nd ed), Wiley, Chichester.

BUSINESS AND ECONOMIC PLANNING *The Economic and Social Impact of Tourism on Cornwall,* Tourism Consultative Committee, (undated).

BYRNE, J.H. (1977), *Study of the Economic Effects of Tourism on the Gosford-Wyong Sub-Region,* P.A. Consulting Services, Planning and Environment Commission of New South Wales, Sydney.

BYRON SHIRE COUNCIL (1985), *Keeping Byron Unique: A Tourism Strategy,* Byron Bay, Australia.

CARTER, M.R. (1977), A method of analysing patterns of tourist activity in a large rural area: the Highlands and Islands of Scotland, *Regional Studies* 5.

CHADWICK, J.W., Houston J.B. and Mason J.E.W. (1972), *Ballina,* A Local Study in Regional Economic Development, Institute of Public Administration, Dublin.

CHIEF EXECUTIVE OF CLWYD COUNTY COUNCIL AND 6 ASSOCIATED DISTRICT AND BOROUGH COUNCILS (1987), *A Tourism Strategy for Clwyd,* January.

CHON, K-S. and Evans, M.R. (1989), "Tourism in a Rural Area - A Coal Mining County Experience", *Tourism Management* Vol. 10 (4) pp. 315-321.

CLARY (1977), D. *La façade littorale de Paris: le tourisme sur la cote normande, étude géographique,* Editions Ophrys, Paris.

CORK/KERRY TOURISM. *Fermoy, Co.Cork. A Marketing and Development Plan 1989-1991,* Report by Cork/Kerry Tourism Organisation, Cork.

DAHMS, F. (1991), "Economic revitalization in St Jacobs, Ontario: ingredients for transforming a dying village into a thriving small town", *Small Town,* Vol 21, May, Washington, D.C.

DARTMOOR NATIONAL PARK (1986), *Dartmoor Area Tourism Development Action Programme,* Mss., Bovey Tracey.

DEPT OF TOURISM AND TRANSPORT (1990), *Ireland - Operations Programme for Tourism 1989 to 1993,* Dublin.

DEPT. OF GEOGRAPHY (1987), *Tourism in Cornwall,* Project No. 1, Dept. of Geography, Exeter University.

DEVELOPMENT BOARD FOR RURAL WALES (1988), *Annual Report 1987/8.*

DUIGOU, S. (1979), *La Bretagne ayant dansé tout l'été,* Le Signor, Le Guilvinec, Finistère, 1979.

FOX, C. (1979), *Integrated Rural Development Plan for the Ballyhoura sub-region,* Programme prepared for EEC, Dublin.

GREER, J.V., and Murray M.R. (1988), A Recreation Strategy for the Mourne Area of Outstanding Natural Beauty, The Sports Council for Northern Ireland, Belfast.

HAAS, V. (1976), *The Impact of Mass Tourism on a Rural Community in the Swiss Alps,* The University of Michigan.

HASSLACHER, P. *"Sanfter Tourismus-Virgental"*, Innsbruck: Oesterreichischer Alpenverein.

HENNESSY, S., GREENWOOD, J., SHAW, G. and WILLIAMS, A. (1986), *The role of tourism in local economies; a pilot study of Looe, Cornwall*, Exeter, University of Exeter, Department of Geography, Tourism in Cornwall Project, Discussion Paper no. 1.

HODGESON, G. and DIXON, J.A. (1988), *Logging versus Fisheries and Tourism in Palawan: An Environmental and Economic Analysis,* EAPI Occasional Paper, Honolulu, Hawaii; East-West Centre.

HOUSE OF COMMONS COMMITTEE OF WELSH AFFAIRS (1987), *Tourism in Wales Vol. 1* Report together with the Proceedings of the Committee, House of Commons Paper 256 - 1 HMSO.

IRISH TOURIST INDUSTRY CONFEDERATION (1989), *Doubling Irish Tourism - A Market-Led Strategy*, Dublin.

JENKINS, J. (1988), *Issues in the development of fossicking as a recreational activity and tourist attraction in the New England Region*, unpublished honours thesis, Department of Geography and Planning, University of New England, Armidale.

JOHNSON, R. (1992), Small town bed and breakfasts: St Jacobs, Ontario, tries an alternative form of tourist accommodation. *Small Town*, June, Washington, D.C.

LABRADOR STRAITS AND BATTLE HARBOUR RESOURCE TEAM (1992), *Labrador Straits Report*, Heritage Canada, Quebec.

LANE, B. (1991), *Berwick upon Tweed: A Strategy for Sustainable Rural Tourism,* University of Bristol.

LE FLOC'H, J-P. (1972), *Recherche sur le tourisme rural* (l'exemple breton). Thése pour le doctorat en droit. Faculté des sciences juridiques, Université de Rennes.

LEDIS (1989), *Agrotourism Initiatives in Greece*, Overseas E58, UK, August.

MONTEMAGNO, G. (1990), "The Development of Tourism and Recreation in Rural Society - Possibilities and Limits in Italy" in *Freizeit und Erholung auf dem Lande*, Council of Europe, Bonn/Strasbourg.

NORTH COAST ENVIRONMENTAL COUNCIL (1987), *Tourism and the Environment, A Position Paper on Tourism Development by the North Coast Environment Council,* North Coast Environmental Council, Lismore.

O'CNAIMSHI, S. (1987), *Tourism Development in South West Donegal: Parish of Glencolumkille,* Bord Failte and Donegal/Sligo/Leitrim Tourism Organisation, Letterkenny.

PAPAKONSTANTINIDIS (1986), L.A. *Integrated Program for Rural Tourism (Akrotiri Irinis/Crete area)*, Athens (in Greek).

PAPAKONSTANTINIDIS, L.A. (1988), *Integrated Program for Rural Tourism (Kollines Arkadia/Pelopenessos area)*, Athens (in Greek).

PAPAKONSTANTINIDIS, L.A. (1989 a), *Integrated Program for Rural Tourism Donousa/Cyclades Island group*, Athens (in Greek).

PAPAKONSTANTINIDIS, L.A. (1988 b), (*Integrated Rural Tourism Program for Vartholomio*, Athens, 1989 (in Greek)

PAPAKONSTANTINIDIS, L.A. (1989 c), *Integrated Rural Tourism Program for Ypati Fthiotide area*, Athens (in Greek).

PAPAKONSTANTINIDIS, L.A. (1990), *Integrated Rural Tourism Program for Kymi Eboia Island*, Athens (in Greek).

PLETTNER, H.J. (1979), *Geographical Aspects of Tourism in the Republic of Ireland*, Research Paper No. 9, Social Sciences Research Centre, University College, Galway.

POPOVITCH, M. and BUSS, T.F. (1987), *Rural Enterprise Development: An Iowa Case Study* Council of State Policy and Planning Agencies, Washington, D.C.

PRICE WATERHOUSE (1987), *Improving the Performance of Irish Tourism*, The Stationery Office, Dublin.

PRIME MINISTER OFFICE (1990), *A White Paper on Tourism in Japan*, (in Japanese).

QUINN, J. (1989), *The Development of Ballyhoura: Past and Present.* Paper presented at IRD Conference, Kilfinane, Limerick, January.

RICHARDSON, S. (1991), *Colorado Community Tourism Action Guide*, University of Colorado.

SIMMS, D. M. (1971), *Tourism, Entrepreneurs and Change in Southwest Ireland,* Michigan: University Microfilms International.

SZABE, G. "Chances of reviving and developing rural tourism in two groups of settlements in Baranya County" in *Regional Research Center Scientific Institute of the Hungarian Academy of Science, in Transdanubia* (in Hungarian).

SZABO, G. and Caordas, L. (1973), "Alfold project VI" in *JUSS* periodica, Hungary, (in Hungarian).

TAKEUCHI, K. Some Remarks on the Geography of Tourism in Japan, *GeoJournal.*

TAYLOR, D.T., FLETCHER, R.R., and CLABAUGH, T. (1990), *Tourism in the Big Horns: A Profile of Visitors, Attractions and Economic Impacts*, University of Wyoming.

TRRU (1975), *Economic Implications of Tourism; A Case Study of Greater Tayside*, Tourism and Rural Recreation Unit, University of Edinburgh.

UPPER YARRA VALLEY AND DANDENONG RANGES AUTHORITY (1988), *Draft Tourism Strategy for the Upper Yarra Valley and Dandenong Ranges Region*, Lilydale, Australia.

VAUGHAN D.R. and WILKES K. (1985), *Tourism in South East Dorset: The Economic Implications,* Southern Tourist Board, Eastleigh.

WATERWAYS COMMISSION. *Managing an Estuary: An Overview of a Management Programme for the Peel Inlet and Harvey Estuary and their Environs,* Waterways Commission/Peel Inlet Management Authority, Perth.

WEST COUNTRY TOURIST BOARD, (1980), *A strategy for tourism in the West Country*, Exeter.

WOLMAN ASSOCIATES, (1978), *Yukon Tourism Development Strategy,* Department of Tourism and Information, Yukon, Canada.

X. Sustainability issues

AUSTRALIAN TOURISM INDUSTRY ASSOCIATION (1990), *Code of environmental practice for the Australian tourism industry,* Canberra.

BRAMWELL, B. and LANE B. (1993), "Sustainable Tourism : An Evolving Global Approach", *Journal of Sustainable Tourism*, Vol.1 (1), pp. 1-5.

CIPRA. *Sanfter Tourismus: Schlagwort oder Chance für den Alpenraum? (Soft Tourism: Buzz-word or a Chance for the Alpine Region?).* Commission Internationale pour la Protection des Regions Alpines. Vaduz, Lichtenstein. 1985.

COMMUNITY AID ABROAD (1990), *Travel wise and be welcome: A guide to responsible travel in the 90s,* Community Aid Abroad, Melbourne.

CRONIN, L. (1990), "Sustainable development and tourism", in *Environment, Tourism and Development; An Agenda for action? A Workshop to Consider Strategies for Sustainable Tourism Development,* Valletta, Malta, Centre for Environmental Management and Planning, Old Aberdeen.

CROSBY, A. "Social and Environmental Effects of the Introduction of Integrated (Soft) Rural Tourism on the Countryside". (in German) in *Freizeit und Erholung auf dem Lande,* Council of Europe, Bonn/Strasbourg, in German.

COUNCIL OF EUROPE (1992), *The Challenges Facing European Society with the Approach of the Year 2000: Strategies for Sustainable Quality Tourism,* European Regional Planning, No 53, Council of Europe Press.

DE KADT, E. (1990), *Making the Alternative Sustainable: Lessons from Development for Tourism* Institute of Development Studies.

DUTTON, I. and HALL, C.M. (1989), "Making tourism sustainable: the policy/practice conundrum", *Proceedings of the Environment Institute of Australia, Second National Conference,* Melbourne.

EBER, S. (ed) (1992), *Beyond the Green Horizon: A Discussion Paper on Principles for Sustainable Tourism.* World Wildlife Fund, London.

ENGLISH TOURIST BOARD/COUNTRYSIDE COMMISSION (1989a), *Principles for Tourism in the Countryside.*

ENGLISH TOURIST BOARD/COUNTRYSIDE COMMISSION (1989b), *Principles for Tourism in National Parks.*

ENGLISH TOURIST BOARD (1991), *The Green Light: Guide to Sustainable Tourism,* London.

GONSALVES, P.S. (1987), "Alternative tourism - the evolution of a concept and establishment of a network", *Tourism Recreation Research* 12 (2): 9-12.

HASSLACHER, P. (1984), *"Sanfter Tourismus-Virgental".* Innsbruck: Oesterreichischer Alpenverein.

HAWKES, S., and WILLIAMS, P., (1993), *The Greening of Tourism: A Casebook of Best Environmental Practice* Simon Fraser University, British Columbia.

HONADLE, G. and VANSANT, J. (1993), "Enhancing Local Action" in *Implementation of Sustainablility: Lessons from Integrated Rural Development,* Kumarian Press, Connecticut.

JEFFREYS, A. (1987), "A draft policy for a conservation council", in *Tourism and the Conservation Movement,* (ed. Corkhill J.,) North Coast Environment Council, Lismore, Australia pp. 2-11.

JENNER, P. and SMITH, C. (1992), *The Tourism Industry and the Environment* Economic Intelligence Unit (EIU) Special Report No 2453, London.

KRIPPENDORF, J., ZIMMER, P. and GLAUBER, H. (1988), *Fuer einen andern Tourismus,* Fisher Taschenbuch Verlag, Frankfurt.

LANE, B. (1990), "Developing Sustainable Rural Tourism" in *Proceedings of the Irish National Planning Conference,* Dublin.

LANE, B. (1991), "Sustainable Tourism: a new concept for the Heritage Interpreter" *Interpretation Journal,* No.49, London.

LANE, B. (1992), *The Hotel Ucliva, Switzerland: A Rural Hotel built and operated on Ecological Principles* University of Bristol.

LINDBERG, K. (1989), *Tourism as a Conservation Tool,* Mimeo, Johns Hopkins University (SAIS), Washington, D.C.

LOBRY, J. (1986), *Le tourisme vert, un tourisme de liberte*, Paris.

MEADOWS, D. H., MEADOWS, D. L., and RANDERS, J. (1992), *Beyond the Limits - Global Collapse or a Sustainable Future* Earthscan Publications.

MICHAUD, J.-L. (1993), *Le tourisme face à l'environnement,* Presses Universitaires de France, Paris.

MITCHELL, B. (Nd) (1991), *Resource Management and Development*, Toronto.

MITCHELL, P.A.M. (1988), *The Traveller's Guide to Good Manners*, Gooday Publishers, West Sussey.

OECD (1990), *The impact of Tourism on the Environment*, Paris.

O'RIORDAN, T. and TURNER, R.K. (eds) (1983), *An Annotated Reader in Environmental Planning and Management,* Pergamon Press, Oxford.

ORTUNO, M. (1987), *Por un turismo limpio* Madrid.

PEARCE, D., MARKANDYA, A. and BARIBIER, E. (1989), "Sustainable Development - The Business Approach. International Chamber of Commerce" in *Blueprint for a Green Economy*, Earthscan Publications, 1989.

RESEARCH AND PLANNING DIVISION WEST AUSTRALIAN TOURISM COMMISSION (1986), "Tourism as a sustainable use of natural resources", McDAVITT, C.(ed), in *Towards a State Conservation Strategy Invited Review Papers,* Bulletin 251, Department of Conservation and Environment, Perth, pp. 43-52.

TRIGANO, G. (1984), *Tourism and the Environment: The Club Mediterranee Experience* UNDP Industry and Environment Office Newsletter, UNDP, Paris.

WHEELLER, B. (1990), "Is responsible tourism appropriate?' in *Tourism research into the 1990s* University College, Durham.

XI. Transport issues

BMA (1982), *Cycling Towards Health and Safety*, Oxford University Press.

CHEW, J. (1987), "Transport and Tourism in the Year 2000" *Tourism Management*, June.

COUNTRYSIDE COMMISSION (1989), *Managing the Rights of Way Network: An Agenda for Action*, CCP 273, Cheltenham.

COUNTRYSIDE COMMISSION/SPORTS COUNCIL (1985), *A Step in the Right Direction: The Marketing of Circular Walks,* CCP 195, Cheltenham.

DEPARTMENT OF TRANSPORT (1990), *Transport Statistics Great Britain 1979-89*, HMSO, London.

FOE *Pro-Bike: A Cycling Policy for the 1990s.* Friends of the Earth, London (undated).

NEVEL, B. and HARNIK, P. (1990), *Railroads recycled: how local initiative and Federal support launched the Rails to Trails movement*, Washington, D.C.

RUNTE, A. (1990), *Trains of Discovery: Western Railroads and the National Parks*, Colorado.

SCHWEKE, T., SPREHN, D, HAMILTON and S., & GRAY, J. (1989), *A Look at Visitors on Wisconsin's Elroy - Sparta Bike Trail* University of Wisconsin.

XII.   Visitor management

DUNLAP, R.E. and HEFFERNAN, R.B. (1981), Outdoor recreation and environmental concern: An empirical examination. *Rural Sociology*, Vol. 40, pp. 18-30.

GETZ, D. (1983), "The capacity to absorb tourism: Concepts and Implications for Strategic Planning" *Annals of Tourism Research*, Vol 10, pp. 239-263.

GRIEF, F. (1987), *Wintersporteinrichtung und ihre auswirkungen auf die Land- und Forstwirtshaft.*

KARIEL, H.G. (1991), "Noise in Rural Recreation Environments" *Canadian Acoustics*, Vol 19, pp. 3-10.

KUSS, F.R. and GRAEFE, A.R. (1992), Effects of Recreation in Mountains, *GeoJournal*, Vol 27, pp. 97-104.

LINDSAY, J.J. (1980), " Compatibility Planning for Different Types of Outdoor Recreation and Natural Resources" in *Tourism Planning and Development Issues*, by HAWKINS, D.D. and SHAFER, E.L., and ROVELSTAD, J.M., eds. Washington, D.C.

PANNEL, KERR, FORSTER AND CO. (1971), *Great Barrier Reef Visitor Plan* Melbourne.

SHELBY, B. and HABERLEIN, T.A. (1986), *Carrying Capacities in Recreation Settings*, Oregon.

TRAVIS, A. (1982), Managing the Environmental and Cultural Impacts of Tourism and Leisure Development, *Tourism Management.*

VAN-LIERE, K.D. and NOE, F.P. (1984), "Outdoor Recreation and Environmental Attitudes: Further examination of the Dunlap-Heffernan thesis", *Rural Sociology*, Vol 46, pp. 501-513.

WEAVER, T. and DALE, D. (1978), "Trampling effects of hikers, motorcycles and horses in meadows and forests", *Journal of Applied Ecology,* vol. 15, pp. 451-7.

Chapter II

International tourist flows in Member countries

This Chapter brings together, in the form of summary tables, the most recent data available on international tourist flows to OECD Member countries. The tables give regional totals for each of the three geographical areas of the OECD -- Europe, North America and Australasia-Japan -- plus the OECD total.

Annual data by country of origin of foreign tourists or visitors, for 1991 and 1992, are set out in the Statistical Annex.

Section I outlines the general trends noted in 1992 over the whole OECD area.

Section II records changes in international tourist flows in each Member country in 1992. The data cover:

a) Arrivals at frontiers either of tourists (persons spending more than one night in the country being visited) or, where such figures are not available, all visitors (tourists plus same-day visitors). For further details of how travellers are classified, please refer to Chart A in the Statistical Annex.

b) The number of nights spent by foreign tourists in hotels and similar establishments (generally speaking, hotels, motels, inns and boarding houses).

c) The number of nights spent in all forms of accommodation without distinction.

For further details on types of accommodation covered by the data for each receiving country, please refer to Table C in the Statistical Annex.

Lastly, Section III describes international flows from the OECD's main generating countries: Canada, France, Germany, Italy, Japan, the Netherlands, the United Kingdom and the United States.

I. International tourism in the OECD area

After a somewhat gloomy year in 1991, indicating that international tourism is vulnerable to external shocks, growth in international tourism resumed in the OECD area in 1992, in spite of the continuing economic recession and escalation of the Yugoslav conflict.

According to the World Tourism Organisation (WTO), in 1992, international tourism expressed in terms of arrivals rose world-wide by 4.6 per cent to about 476 million arrivals. The fastest growth was observed in the Far East/Pacific region (+ 8.2 per cent), followed by South Asia (+ 7.6 per cent), Africa (+ 7.2 per cent) and the Middle East (+ 6.9 per cent). The growth rate in Europe was 3.5 per cent.

Growth resumed in Europe, the largest tourism market in the world, due to the buoyant long-haul markets. Tourism within the EC remained steady in spite of weak European economies and rising unemployment.

The 1992 figures in the OECD area are as follows:

-- arrivals at frontiers in Europe: + 4 per cent (against - 3 per cent in 1991);

-- nights spent in hotels and similar establishments in Europe: + 5 per cent (against - 1 per cent);

-- nights spent in all forms of accommodation in Europe: + 4 per cent (against + 0.2 per cent);

-- arrivals at frontiers in North America: + 3 per cent (against + 6 per cent);

-- arrivals at frontiers in Australasia-Japan: + 10 per cent (against + 5 per cent);

-- nights spent in all forms of accommodation in Australasia-Japan: - 2 per cent (against - 2 per cent).

Arrivals at frontiers (Table 1)

Of the 19 European Member countries, only 12 collect data or provide estimates on foreign tourist or visitor flows at frontiers. Two of these 12 countries, Austria and Germany, record all traveller arrivals at frontiers, a much broader yardstick than is used for analysing tourist flows, since it includes travellers in transit. These figures have not, therefore, been included in Table 1, but are shown for information in Table 6 of the Statistical Annex.

Fifteen countries, including ten European ones, collect figures on arrivals at frontiers. Although regional trends are satisfactory (ranging from + 3 to + 10 per cent), there are variations depending on the destinations concerned.

Europe is recovering part of its market, especially from North America and Asia, which it had lost in part in 1991 because of the impact of the Gulf War. Mediterranean countries, as the main countries of destination in the OECD area, are markedly improving. Among these, Turkey (+ 28 per cent arrivals against + 2 per cent in 1991), Greece (+ 16 per cent arrivals against - 9 per cent in 1991) and France (+ 8 per cent arrivals against + 4 per cent in 1991) stand out. In these three countries, arrivals from the United States (+ 130 per cent, + 55 per cent and + 22 per cent, respectively) and the other major markets sparked increased tourism activity. Spain, which had organised the Olympic Games and the Universal Exhibition in Seville, showed a 3 per cent increase in the number of arrivals.

Growth resumed in the United Kingdom (+ 6 per cent arrivals) due to the expansion of its main markets, especially North America.

Italy and Iceland were the only countries to show a slowdown in tourist flows (- 2.4 per cent and - 0.6 per cent, respectively). Italy lost about 1.3 million visitors, of which 70 per cent from its three main markets, France, Germany and the United Kingdom.

Arrivals in **North America** rose by 3 per cent (against + 6 per cent). The United States remains a particularly attractive destination (+ 4 per cent arrivals) as the dollar continued to drop relative to most European currencies as well as the yen. However, the dollar effect was partly cancelled by the economic sluggishness of United States' main markets. Canada (- 1 per cent arrivals) was badly affected by its economic situation and its main market, the United States, which represents eight-tenths of the total number of tourists, fell by 2 per cent. The 6 per cent increase in the Canadian dollar relative to the United States dollar was also an appreciable contributory factor.

In the **Australasia-Japan** region, arrivals rose twice as fast as in 1991 at a rate of 10 per cent against + 5 per cent. Growth in New Zealand resumed (+ 10 per cent against - 1 per cent in 1991), thanks to a healthy economic situation in Asian countries and also a sharp increase in arrivals from European markets.

Japan held back (+ 0 per cent against + 12 per cent in 1991), mainly during the second half of 1992. Because of the strength of the yen relative to other currencies, Japan was less competitive and earnings in real terms continued to fall (- 3 per cent) for the second year in a row. Lastly, international tourism in Australia performed well (+ 10 per cent) with continued growth in the main traditional markets.

Nights spent in hotels and similar establishments (Table 2)

Eighteen European countries plus Australia compile data on nights spent in hotels and similar establishments; generally speaking, these data concern nights recorded in hotels, motels, boarding houses and inns (see Table C in the Statistical Annex).

After a 1 per cent fall from 1991 to 1990, **Europe** recorded a 5 per cent increase in 1992. Although this appears to be a rather satisfactory situation, trends varied markedly among European countries.

Germany recorded a further decrease (- 3 per cent) reflecting the downturn of all its main European markets and Canada. Nights spent by tourists from the United States, however, (+ 3 per cent) and Japan (+ 5 per cent) continued to rise. Portugal also lost 6 per cent of its customers, spread across many of its markets. This is partly due to a shift towards Spain, where many international events were held in 1992.

France, Greece and Turkey confirmed the positive trends observed in terms of arrivals. Finally, Belgium rose by 17 per cent, mainly through the return of French, German, Dutch and United Kingdom customers.

Outside Europe, Australia performed well with strong growth (+ 8 per cent), especially from European countries and Japan.

Nights spent in all forms of accommodation (Table 3)

Nineteen countries (16 European countries plus Australia, Canada and New Zealand) compile data on nights spent in all forms of accommodation. This category includes hotel and non-hotel accommodation -- youth hostels, camp sites, holiday villages etc. -- (for further details see Table C in the Statistical Annex).

Most countries showed good results in 1992 (overall increase in the number of nights spent, + 3 per cent). In Northern Europe, Scandinavian countries showed an overall good performance (+ 10 per cent), including a slight resumption of growth in Sweden after two poor years. These results are partly due to the increase in nights spent by tourists from France, Germany, the United Kingdom and the United States.

In the Mediterranean area, there was a sharp increase in Turkey (+ 73 per cent) and Greece (+ 21 per cent) following marked reductions in 1991. On the other hand, Italy lost 3 million nights spent in all forms of accommodation (- 4 per cent). The same trend was shown in Portugal (- 9 per cent) where the average duration of stay was shorter.

Canada was down by 4 per cent, representing a loss of more than 3 million nights. This was mainly accounted for by reductions in the number of nights spent by United States (- 6 per cent) and United Kingdom (- 3 per cent) tourists. Similarly, Australia showed a 5 per cent decrease, in spite of the higher number of nights spent in hotels.

Table 1. Annual growth rates of number of arrivals of foreign tourists at frontiers[1]

	T/V	% 90/89	% 91/90	% 92/91	1992 Millions of arrivals
Austria					
Belgium					
Denmark					
Finland					
France[4]	T	7.4	3.5	8.3	59.6
Germany					
Greece	T	9.8	−9.4	16.1	9.3
Iceland	T	10.4	1.2	−0.6	0.1
Ireland	V	12.3	−2.3	4.2	3.1
Italy	V	9.4	−14.9	−2.4	50.1
Luxembourg					
Netherlands					
Norway					
Portugal	T	12.7	7.9	2.6	8.9
Spain	V	−3.7	2.8	3.4	55.3
Sweden					
Switzerland[2]	T	4.8	−4.5	1.6	12.8
Turkey[3]	V	20.9	2.4	28.2	7.1
United Kingdom	T		−6.1	5.8	17.0
EUROPE[1]		5.4	−3.1	4.3	
Canada	T	0.4	−2.0	−1.1	14.7
United States[5]	T	8.1	8.5	3.9	44.6
NORTH AMERICA		5.8	5.6	2.6	
Australia	V	6.5	7.0	9.6	2.6
New Zealand	T	8.3	−1.3	9.6	1.1
Japan	T		11.9	0.0	2.1
AUSTRALASIA-JAPAN[1]		7.0	4.5	9.6	
OECD[1]		5.5	−1.2	4.0	

V Visitors.
T Tourists.
Note: Canada, Italy and Portugal dispose of both series (V and T); see annex.
1. Overall trend for all countries with data available from 1989 to 1992.
2. Estimates.
3. Travellers.
4. Changes of series in 1989 and in 1991: new frontiers' survey.
5. New series from 1989.

Table 2. Annual growth rates of nights spent by foreign tourists in hotels and similar establishments[1]

	% 90/89	% 91/90	% 92/91	1992 Millions of beds-nights
Austria	0.8	3.7	0.0	64.2
Belgium	4.5	−4.4	17.0	7.7
Denmark	11.1	9.8	3.6	6.2
Finland	−2.0	−10.8	1.9	2.2
France	5.5	−2.8	12.3	59.6
Germany[3]	4.9	−6.7	−3.1	26.9
Greece	6.3	−14.7	21.4	36.3
Iceland	−30.7	3.5	−0.3	0.4
Ireland	8.5	13.8	−1.0	9.3
Italy	−3.1	−0.3	−3.7	63.4
Luxembourg	5.8	−0.4	−6.1	1.0
Netherlands	12.9	−1.3	6.3	8.5
Norway	3.1	10.7	9.2	4.3
Portugal	8.0	14.2	−6.3	17.9
Spain	−8.4	3.8	3.4	76.9
Sweden	−5.2	−11.5	−0.8	2.8
Switzerland	2.7	−3.2	−0.6	20.2
Turkey	5.7	−21.1	66.8	13.6
United Kingdom				
EUROPE[1]	0.6	−0.8	4.5	
Canada				
United States				
NORTH AMERICA				
Australia[2]	19.0	−8.3	8.3	12.5
New Zealand				
Japan				
AUSTRALASIA-JAPAN[1]				
OECD[1]	1.1	−1.0	4.6	

1. Overall trend for all countries with data available from 1989 to 1992.
2. New series from 1989.
3. The data relate to the territory of the Federal Republic of Germany prior to 3rd October 1990.

Table 3. **Annual growth rates of nights spent**
by foreign tourists in all means of accommodation[1]

	% 90/89	% 91/90	% 92/91	1992 Millions of beds-nights
Austria	−0.2	5.1	0.1	99.8
Belgium	5.9	−5.6	5.8	12.9
Denmark	8.9	11.7	11.1	11.6
Finland				
France[4]	10.5	2.3	8.2	428.4
Germany[3]	3.8	7.4	−3.6	36.1
Greece	6.3	−15.9	20.9	36.9
Iceland				
Ireland	7.4	−1.2	1.5	33.8
Italy	−2.5	2.4	−3.6	83.6
Luxembourg		5.9	−8.8	2.3
Netherlands	16.1	4.5	5.2	18.1
Norway	5.4	8.0	12.0	7.1
Portugal	6.1	13.5	−8.6	20.1
Spain				
Sweden	−13.3	−14.8	3.8	5.8
Switzerland	2.6	0.4	−0.1	37.0
Turkey	11.8	−26.9	73.1	16.8
United Kingdom	4.7	−5.0	−2.1	182.4
EUROPE[1]	5.9	0.2	4.0	
Canada	−8.7	0.7	−4.0	79.4
United States				
NORTH AMERICA[1]				
Australia[2]	16.9	−1.1	−5.0	61.4
New Zealand	9.5	−6.6	6.3	20.5
Japan				
AUSTRALASIA- **JAPAN** [1]	15.0	−2.4	−2.4	
OECD[1]	5.4	0.1	3.0	

1. Overall trend for all countries with data available from 1989 to 1992.
2. New series from 1989.
3. The data relate to the territory of the Federal Republic of Germany prior to
   3rd October 1990. Since 1991, includes camping sites.
4. Changes of series in 1989 and in 1991: new frontiers' survey.

II. International tourism in each Member country in 1992

Australia. For the second year in a row, the number of nights spent in all forms of accommodation fell, in 1992 (-5 per cent) compared with 1991. The main losses were recorded in Europe (-10 per cent) and North America (-11 per cent).

Over the same period, however, the number of nights spent in hotels rose by 8 per cent and arrivals at frontiers by 10 per cent. Using arrivals at frontiers (the most comprehensive statistical series) a more detailed analysis of the recent trend in tourism by foreign visitors in Australia shows that growth rates were sustained, especially for emerging markets from Asia.

In terms of arrivals, Japan remains the largest market for Australia with 630 000 visitors in 1992. This represents a 19 per cent increase over 1991 and accounts for 24 per cent of arrivals in 1992.

The remainder of arrivals from Asia rose by 31 per cent. This reflects both the economic buoyancy of this region, inducing more and more people to travel, but also the attractiveness of Australia as a destination. The devaluation of the Australian dollar relative to many currencies in Asian countries also improved the competitiveness of the Australian tourist product for Asian visitors. The markets which grew most strongly out of Asia are Taiwan (+83 per cent) and Korea (+42 per cent). Thailand and Singapore also expanded (+36 per cent and +33 per cent, respectively).

Arrivals from United Kingdom/Ireland and the rest of Europe grew by 9 per cent and 8 per cent, respectively, in 1992, following a decline in 1991.

The only major markets to have declined in 1992 were the United States and New Zealand (-3 per and -7 per cent, respectively). Arrivals from the United States had picked up markedly in 1991 due to the many discounts offered by airlines on the United States/Australia links. The fall in arrivals from New Zealand followed a 15 per cent increase in the previous year.

Austria. All indicators show that Austrian tourism remained stable in 1992 after a fairly good performance in 1991. The number of nights spent in all forms of accommodation, in hotels and similar establishments and arrivals at accommodation stayed the same as in the previous year.

The number of nights spent in all forms of accommodation in Austria -- the series considered to be the most representative for analytical purposes -- fell by 0.3 per cent for tourists from Europe in spite of the 1 per cent increase from the leading market, Germany (65 per cent of nights spent). The other major markets, namely the Netherlands and the United Kingdom were down by about 3 per cent. However, the largest decrease is from former Yugoslavia (-31 per cent), followed by Spain and Finland (-17 per cent). Finally, European non-Member countries performed well, with an 11 per cent increase. Following the collapse of the Communist bloc, Vienna and Austria are once again at the heart of greater Europe, lying at the crossroads of the European routes which will boost tourism in this region.

Outside Europe, after a very poor performance in 1991, North American tourists flocked back into Austria (+25 per cent) as did Japanese tourists (+10 per cent).

Belgium. In 1992, tourism in Belgium resumed growth, recovering equivalent or higher levels than those in 1991 in terms of volume. The number of nights spent in all forms of accommodation rose by 6 per cent, due to the 17 per cent increase in the number of nights spent in hotels and similar establishments.

The best increases in the number of nights spent in Belgium concerned Japan (+48 per cent), Spain (+35 per cent) and the United States (+21 per cent). Belgium's second market, Germany (+10 per cent) and third market, the United Kingdom (+20 per cent), which together account for almost one-third of the total number of nights spent, continued to strengthen their positions.

The situation of the leading market, the Netherlands, gives more cause for concern with a 12 per cent drop between 1990 and 1992. Belgium has lost about 600 000 nights spent in all forms of accommodation by Dutch tourists in two years. However, this decrease does not concern hotels, where more nights have been spent by tourists from the Netherlands -- an extra 65 000 nights. The largest percentage losses are shown by Norway (-24 per cent), Africa (-26 per cent) and Luxemburg (-21 per cent), which represent small markets for Belgium.

Canada. In 1992, generating and receiving international tourism in Canada faced the full impact of the world-wide recession. The poor economic situation of the main generating countries for Canada had the overall result of diminishing consumer confidence and hence expenditure on all goods and services, including international tourism. On the other hand, the devaluation of the Canadian dollar relative to most other currencies had a relatively positive impact on travel in Canada. The combined effect of these two factors led to a relative decrease in the number of nights spent in all forms of accommodation of 4 per cent and a 1 per cent decrease in the number of arrivals of tourists at frontiers.

The poor figures are chiefly due to the fewer nights spent by United States (58 per cent of nights spent and a drop of 6 per cent from 1991) and United Kingdom tourists, their second market (8 per cent of nights spent and a 3 per cent decline). On the other hand however, arrivals of United States tourists (80 per cent of arrivals) only fell by 2 per cent and arrivals of United Kingdom tourists even rose by 1 per cent, this difference being attributable to a shorter duration of stay.

On the whole, the nights spent by tourists from Europe remained steady (+0.5 per cent) in spite of large trend variations: Norway, Greece and the Netherlands rose by over 30 per cent whereas Finland, Sweden and Turkey fell by 13 to 15 per cent.

The decrease in the number of nights spent by Japanese tourists (-5 per cent) and by tourists from the Asia/Oceania region (-7 per cent) should also be noted, in spite of the booming Chinese market (+40 per cent). In Latin America, the Argentinian and Brazilian markets were the weakest. The Australian market picked up again (+10 per cent).

Denmark. In 1992, Denmark recorded 33 million nights spent in all forms of accommodation (hotels, camp sites, holiday homes and youth hostels) which drops to 11.6 million when holiday homes are excluded.

1992 was the fourth year in succession that tourism expanded in Denmark. The number of nights spent in all forms of accommodation (including holiday homes) rose by 13 per cent in 1992. The number of nights spent in holiday homes rose by 20 per cent whereas those spent in hotels, camp sites and youth hostels rose by 4 per cent, 13 per cent and 0.3 per cent, respectively.

In terms of nights spent in all forms of accommodation (excluding holiday homes) by country of origin, the main markets for Denmark are Germany (40 per cent of nights spent), Sweden (23 per cent) and Norway (10 per cent of nights spent and +7 per cent over 1991). The markets with the strongest growth were the Netherlands (+59 per cent) -- this increase is chiefly due to camping (+73 per cent) -- Japan (+19 per cent) and Germany (+16 per cent). The Finnish market, which is small for Denmark, fell by 18 per cent in 1992. The French market fell by 1 per cent and the Swedish market remained steady (+2 per cent).

Finland. After declining in 1991 (-11 per cent), the number of nights spent in hotels and similar establishments rose again in 1992 (+2 per cent), and the trend continued during the first ten months of 1993 with an increase of 16%. One of the main reasons was the improved competitiveness due to the devaluation and subsequent floating of the Finnish mark, together with a strengthened marketing policy.

Tourism from Germany continued to grow (+7 per cent) due to the new price levels in Finland and increased demand from German tourists for environment-friendly products. After falling for two years in a row, the Norwegian market picked up again at +8 per cent. Likewise, following the impact of the Gulf war in 1991, the number of nights spent by tourists from the United States rose by 5 per cent.

On the other hand, Finland's main market, Sweden (23 per cent of nights spent), fell by 3 per cent. The number of nights spent by United Kingdom tourists fell by 4 per cent.

France. 1992 featured several major events (Winter Olympic Games in the Alps and the opening of Eurodisney near Paris) which partly accounted for the steady and marked growth in the various indicators of international tourism. The number of arrivals of tourists grew by 8 per cent and nights spent in all forms of accommodations by 8 per cent, that in hotels by 12 per cent.

Long-haul markets (United States in particular + 23 per cent) rose overall compared with 1990 and 1991, which had admittedly been affected by the Gulf crisis.

The deterioration in the European economic situation therefore had little impact on tourist flows in 1992, and as well as the devaluations in early autumn of the pound sterling, lira and peseta.

Germany. Since 1991 the statistics concerning all forms of accommodation include camp sites. Consequently, they cannot be compared with the statistics from previous years. For analytical purposes, the data used refer to the only former Federal Republic of Germany, since the 1991 figures for the former German Democratic Republic are not available.

The downward trend in the number of nights spent in all forms of accommodation that had been observed in 1991 continued in 1992. The total number of nights spent was 36 million in 1992, down 4 per cent from 1991.

This tendency is chiefly due to the lower number of nights spent by tourists from the main European generating countries: the Netherlands (-6 per cent), Denmark (-15 per cent), Sweden (-13 per cent) and France (-6 per cent).

A positive feature is the marked increase in the number of nights spent by tourists from countries overseas, such as the United States (+4 per cent) and Japan (+5 per cent), reversing the trend recorded in 1991.

Greece. 1992 was an excellent year with over 9 million tourists. An additional 16 per cent tourists came to Greece, boosting the level beyond the 1990 record. More Germans (+ 25 per cent), Italians (+ 20 per cent) and French (+ 15 per cent) travelled to Greece and the main market, the United Kingdom, increased by 29 per cent. Growth in the number of tourists from Central and Eastern European countries was sustained (+ 12 per cent) although much less than in the previous year. Arrivals from North America rose by 49 per cent, from Japan by 89 per cent and from Asia by 40 per cent.

The 1992 figures for nights spent in hotels and similar establishments by country of origin were not yet available at the time of drafting this chapter but an overall increase of 21 per cent was anticipated.

The upswing and the good performance in 1992 are partly due to the end of the Gulf War but also because additional access routes have been developed to offset the impact of the war in former Yugoslavia. This is chiefly reflected by an increase in the number of arrivals from Italy and that of arrivals by charter flights.

Iceland. The number of arrivals of tourists fell slightly in 1992 (- 1 per cent). This was particularly apparent concerning the United States (- 4 per cent), Sweden (- 2 per cent) -- which account for 15 per cent and 11 per cent of arrivals, respectively -- but also smaller markets such as Switzerland (- 16 per cent) and France (- 21 per cent).

However, the poor results were offset by the performance of the main market, Germany (+ 10 per cent growth, and a 17 per cent share of the total number of arrivals), Denmark (+ 5 per cent) and Norway (+ 8 per cent). Outside Europe, the Australasia-Japan region performed best.

Ireland. The number of nights in all forms of accommodation rose by 2 per cent in 1992 and the number of arrivals at frontiers by 4 per cent whereas the number of nights spent in hotels fell by 1 per cent.

The increase in the number of nights spent in all forms of accommodation was mainly due to an increase in tourists from the United States and Canada (+ 10 per cent and + 12 per cent, respectively).

The other regions were less represented in Ireland. In Europe, a decrease in the number of United Kingdom tourists for the second year running (- 6 per cent and - 2 per cent in 1992) and the decrease associated with the Netherlands market (- 16 per cent) offset the good performance of the other main European markets. Germany (+ 6 per cent) and France (+ 10 per cent) showed an increase, as did Belgium (+ 41 per cent) which recovered a more reasonable level after a significant drop in 1991 (- 52 per cent).

Italy. For all forms of accommodation -- a 4 per cent decrease was recorded in the number of nights spent: the largest decreases concerned Finland (- 33 per cent), Sweden (- 16 per cent), France (- 11 per cent) and the Netherlands (- 11 per cent).

The non-European major markets, however, were well up on 1991. More specifically, the number of nights spent by tourists from the United States in all forms of accommodation grew by 25 per cent, that of Canadian tourists by 5 per cent and that of Japanese tourists by 35 per cent.

Arrivals at frontiers fell by 2 per cent, corresponding to a loss of 1.2 million tourists over the previous year. This particularly concerned Switzerland (- 1 per cent), Germany (- 5 per cent), France (- 4 per cent), Austria (- 4 per cent) and the Netherlands (- 21 per cent).

Japan. Arrivals of foreign tourists (+ 0 per cent) in Japan did not rise as fast as arrivals of visitors (+ 1 per cent). From Europe, the United Kingdom, which accounts for almost two-thirds of the market, rose by 17 per cent. Germany increased its share (+ 15 per cent). However, this trend conceals the more negative trend shown by all the other main markets, namely France (- 2 per cent), Italy (- 15 per cent) and the Netherlands (- 1 per cent).

The United States and Canadian markets picked up again (+ 3 per cent and + 7 per cent, respectively) and now account for 16 per cent of the market.

The number of visitors from the "Chinese market" (Taiwan, Hong-Kong and China) increased by 14 per cent compared to the previous year and exceeded the total of one million of visitors.

Luxemburg. In 1992 tourism stagnated, depending on the regions and market segments concerned. Luxemburg seems to have been less affected by the economic recession than its neighbours and other countries in the European Community.

While hotel bookings rose by 4 per cent, the average duration of stay fell again. Meanwhile, there were slightly fewer Belgian and Dutch tourists, which continued to account for the largest market shares, whereas the German and French markets rose slightly.

Camp sites, youth hostels and farm accommodation rose slightly with an average duration of stay ranging from 6 days (camp sites) to two weeks (farm accommodation).

Netherlands. The nights spent in hotels and in all forms of accommodation rose respectively by 6 per cent and by 5 in 1992. In all forms of accommodation, the leading market Germany accounted for just over half the nights spent, and was up by 8 per cent, and the second market, the United Kingdom, by 6 per cent. The French market also increased (+ 4 per cent).

However, the number of nights spent by tourists from the United States (+ 12 per cent), Australia (+ 15 per cent) and Japan (+ 27 per cent) showed the biggest increases, reaching or even exceeding the level recorded in 1990 in terms of volume, after 1991, when Europe had been avoided due to the Gulf war.

In 1992, the Netherlands organised the Floriade, the flower exhibition held every 10 years. This event drew 3.2 million visitors, of which 37 per cent from abroad.

New Zealand. The number of tourist arrivals rose by 1.1 million in 1992, representing an increase of 10 per cent over 1991. Nights spent in all forms of accommodation increased by 6 per cent.

The four main markets (which account for about 60 per cent of the total nights spent) increased, North America by + 1 per cent, the United States by + 4 per cent and Canada by - 7 per cent. The

Japanese, United Kingdom and Australian markets rose by 12 per cent, 1 per cent and 3 per cent, respectively.

The other markets which showed strong percentage increases were Spain (+ 45 per cent), Germany (+ 21 per cent) and the Netherlands (+ 15 per cent). On the other hand, the main decreases concerned Finland (- 35 per cent), Sweden (- 24 per cent) and Ireland (- 17 per cent).

Asia continued to be a dynamic market, increasing by 31 per cent over 1991. Strong growth was recorded in South Korea (+ 100 per cent), Taiwan (+ 69 per cent), Thailand (+ 44 per cent), Indonesia (+ 27 per cent), Malaysia (+ 15 per cent) and Singapore (+ 10 per cent).

Norway. The significance of the travel industry for the Norwegian economy strengthened in 1992. Norway recorded a 9 per cent growth in the number of nights spent in hotels and similar establishments, and increased its shares in priority markets. All the main markets except Sweden (- 3 per cent) were up: Germany (+ 19 per cent), Denmark (+ 2 per cent), the United Kingdom (+ 23 per cent), France (+ 16 per cent), the Netherlands (+ 16 per cent), the United States (+ 25 per cent) and Japan (+ 18 per cent).

The inflation rate rose by only 2.4 per cent in 1992, which was lower than for Norway's most important trading partners. Given the low inflation rate in the period 1989-1991, the competitiveness of the travel industry has improved. According to the national authorities, quality, competitiveness on price and nature-based activities intertwined in a "green" profile have had a favourable impact on Norwegian results in the international tourism market. There has also been a growing interest in off-season products.

Portugal. Following the very good performance in 1991, there was a marked decrease in the number of nights spent in all forms of accommodation in 1992: - 9 per cent for all forms of accommodation and 6 per cent for hotels and similar establishments. Arrivals at frontiers alone continued to rise: + 3 per cent tourists and + 6 per cent for same-day visitors.

In 1992 the average duration of stay of foreign tourists was 7.3 days, slightly shorter than in 1991, reinforcing the long-term trend observed since the beginning of the 1980s (it used to be about 10 days). This partly accounts for the discrepancies between the figures on arrivals at frontiers and those for nights spent in all forms of accommodation. Of the five leading markets, the United Kingdom (29 per cent of nights spent) was well ahead while the other four markets, Germany, Spain, the Netherlands and France which together accounted for 44 per cent of nights spent fell by 4 per cent, 15 per cent, 14 per cent and 20 per cent, respectively.

The same tendency was shown by non-European markets although not to the same extent. The North America market declined by 2 per cent and Australasia-Japan 5 per cent. However, the nights spent by tourists from the United States rose by 10 per cent and the Japanese market picked up slightly (+ 2 per cent).

Good results were also shown by the Central and Eastern European market (+ 10 per cent). Latin America lost 11 per cent and Africa 3 per cent.

Spain. In 1992, Spain organised two major events: the summer Olympic Games in Barcelona and the Universal Exhibition in Seville. The results shown by Spanish tourism reflect the impact of these events. Spain received 55 million visitors in 1992, or 3 per cent more than in 1991, an additional 2 million visitors. 72 per cent of these visitors were tourists. The number of nights spent in hotels also rose by 3 per cent (+2.5 million nights spent).

In terms of nights spent in hotels, the most significant data, trends for the individual countries differ from those observed for arrivals at frontiers. This is partly due to the fact that only 22 per cent of nights are spent in hotels, representing approximately 77 million nights spent out of a total, for all forms of accommodation, of 357 million. There are several possible explanations: relatively shorter durations of stay, greater development of other forms of accommodation such as apartments and condominiums in Spain, and the share of same-day visitors in certain frontier markets.

Among the main generating markets for the Spanish hotel industry, Germany (33 per cent of the market) showed a decline of 3 per cent whereas the United Kingdom, Spain's second market with 25 per cent of nights spent, increased its share by 2 per cent. France fell by 10 per cent and Belgium increased by 4 per cent. Portugal rose by 5 per cent. Long-haul markets performed well: North America grew by 16 per cent and Japan by 14 per cent. The performance of two small European markets should also be noted, Ireland (+196 per cent or over 336 000 nights spent) and Norway (+120 per cent or 360 000 nights spent).

The duration of stay averaged nine days in the country as a whole and six days for the hotel industry. The longest durations of stay concerned Scandinavian (11.1 days), German (10.8 days), United Kingdom (10.4 days) and Japanese tourists (7.7 days).

Sweden. In 1992, the number of nights spent by foreigners in all forms of accommodation increased by 4 per cent while that of nights spent in hotels were down by 1 per cent. The discrepancy was largely due to the good performance of camp sites (+ 13 per cent).

International tourists demand totalled about 6 million nights in all forms of accommodation. The nights spent by tourists from the other Scandinavian countries were down by 2 per cent due to a 21 per cent decline in the Finnish market. The number of nights spent by tourists from Denmark rose by 3 per cent and from Norway by 5 per cent. Demand from other European countries rose by about 10 per cent. Since 1991, Germany has been Sweden's leading market with about 1.5 million nights spent in all forms of accommodation (+ 15 per cent). An 11 per cent increase was recorded for North America. Lastly, the Japanese market fell by 4 per cent.

The depreciation of the Swedish crown at the end of 1992 together with the fact that the value-added tax for hotel services and camping was reduced to 12 per cent in July 1993, increased Sweden's competitiveness as a tourist country and it has experienced a 5 per cent growth for the first nine months in 1993 compared to the first nine months in 1992.

Switzerland. In 1992, the situation remained steady with a total of 37 million nights spent in all forms of accommodation (- 0.1 per cent). Nights spent in hotels fell by 1 per cent. This was chiefly due to fewer European tourists (- 1 per cent): demand from Germany (- 1 per cent) amounting to 43 per cent of the total number of nights spent in all forms of accommodation and France (- 6 per cent) fell. On the other hand, demand from Belgium (+ 6 per cent), Italy (+ 3 per cent), the United Kingdom (+ 2 per cent) and the Netherlands (0.3 per cent) increased.

The total number of nights spent by non-European tourists rose by about 4 per cent. In the year following the Gulf war, the number of nights spent by United States (+ 17 per cent) and Japanese tourists (+ 12 per cent) increased.

Turkey. Following the decline in 1991 due to the Gulf war, international tourism picked up considerably in 1992, exceeding the record levels of 1990. The number of nights spent in all forms of accommodation rose by 73 per cent (after a 27 per cent fall), in hotels by 67 per cent (after - 21 per cent) and arrivals at frontiers by 28 per cent (after + 2 per cent).

All OECD markets boomed, the most spectacular increases being shown by Japan (+ 136 per cent), France (+ 129 per cent), Belgium and Austria (around 120 per cent). This is partly due to the situation in that region being back to normal but also to the promotion efforts by tourist activities, improved back-up of hotel management in marketing activities and further diversification of tourist products (e.g. rafting, trekking, thermal cures, etc.) leading to a longer tourist season.

A decline was recorded in East Anatolia because of the Nevrutz events. These decreases concerned Central and Eastern countries in particular.

United Kingdom. Tourism in 1992 was resilient. In most key markets, the recession continued unabated for much of 1992, impacting on disposable income. The pound sterling was also strong against foreign currencies, especially dollar-related currencies, which further exacerbated a fragile market situation. Devaluation of the pound sterling came after the main holiday season and the full effects did not begin to show until the turn of the year.

In spite of these problems the number of foreign visitors rose by 6 per cent (about 18 million arrivals) and that of nights spent in all forms of accommodation fell slightly by 2 per cent. Nights spent by tourists from North America had dropped sharply in 1991 owing to the Gulf War and the recession. In spite of a 4 per cent increase, the 1990 level was not equalled. For the other OECD regions, there was a marked decrease from the Australasia-Japan region (- 10 per cent) and a sharp decrease from New Zealand (- 33 per cent). Europe was less affected (- 3 per cent) although three major markets, Germany, Ireland and Spain declined. France increased by 1 per cent and the highest percentage increases were shown by Greece (+ 41 per cent), Iceland (+ 29 per cent) and Austria (+ 22 per cent).

The poor performance was partly caused by the shorter duration of stay. The number of visits increased, especially from long-haul markets (North America and South East Asia). Expenditure did not rise as fast as visits because of the downward trend in trade, the shorter duration of stay and the large discounts offered by the tourism industry to attract customers.

United States. Although the overall growth was twice as small in 1992 (+4 per cent and 44.6 million arrivals) as in 1991 (+9 per cent), the number of European tourists continued to rise at a fairly rapid pace (+13 per cent in 1992 and +11 per cent in 1991). The three main European markets expanded in the United States, namely the United Kingdom (+13 per cent), Germany (+18 per cent) and France (+2 per cent). The OECD countries from the Australasia-Japan region increased by 9 per cent and only New Zealand decreased (-4 per cent).

The main market, Canada, which accounts for 42 per cent of arrivals, fell by 3 per cent. This is partly due to the poor economic situation in Canada and the exchange rate variations between the two countries.

The number of tourists from Latin America rose by 7 per cent, the same rate as arrivals from Mexico, which exceeded the total of 8 million in 1992. Several small markets, Argentina, Chile, Colombia and Venezuela showed growth rates of +18 to +20 per cent. In Asia-Oceania, China, Korea and Saudi Arabia were the leading markets (+19 to +22 per cent).

III.   Main generating countries

This section describes recent trends in the main countries generating international tourism to the OECD area (see Tables 4, 5, 6 and 7), namely Canada, France, Germany, Italy, Japan, Netherlands, United Kingdom and the United States. For a more detailed picture of historical trends in these main generating countries as a whole summary tables for the period 1991-1992 are available in annex.

This section does not aim to present a detailed account of the stays and travellers from the main generating countries in OECD but to outline the main patterns followed by the residents of these countries when travelling abroad. Destinations are analysed in terms of nights spent or arrivals at frontiers depending on the data available in the receiving countries. This section is chiefly concerned with flows within the OECD area.

However, in order to explain and analyse the behaviour patterns of customers from the 24 OECD countries, the Tourism Committee plans to publish a comprehensive study on national tourism (domestic tourism and outbound travel) for the period 1970-1992 at the end of 1994. The study will therefore describe the travel patterns of residents within their own countries and abroad.

The eight countries were selected on the basis of their contribution to their international tourism growth as expressed in terms of dollar expenditures, the standard unit of account for the "Travel" item in the Balance of Payments. Taken together they accounted for about 77 per cent of total expenditure in the OECD Member countries in 1992 (for further information see Table 2 in Chapter III).

For **Canadian** outbound travel, the decline of the Canadian dollar was reflected in a decrease in the number of Canadians visiting the United States (- 3 per cent). On the whole, there was a 2 per cent fall in the number of tourists and a 1 per cent fall in dollar expenditures. It should be noted however that this downturn came after 5 years of strong growth in Canadian travel to the United States and was concentrated in the automobile market. Canadian travel to countries other than the United States rose by 10 per cent in 1992, in spite of the weaker Canadian dollar, thus rebounding from depressed levels recorded in 1991 as a result of the Gulf war.

French outbound travel in the OECD area remained stable in 1992, accounting for about 4 per cent of the total nights spent in Europe. The expenditure in dollars, however, increased by 13 per cent. The number of French visitors rose sharply in Turkey (+ 129 per cent) and also in Norway and Ireland. Conversely, demand slumped for some of the popular destinations such as Portugal (- 20 per cent), Iceland (- 19 per cent), Austria and Spain (- 10 per cent). While New Zealand (+ 10 per cent) and Australia (+ 11 per cent on visits) received more French tourists, Japan also showed a decline (- 2 per cent).

In Europe, the **German** market is in the lead with 25 per cent of the total number of nights spent. In 1992, German demand rose by only 4 per cent in terms of nights spent compared with 1991, against 11 per cent in the previous year whereas expenditure on international tourism expressed in dollars rose by 19 per cent. In 1992, Germany continued to absorb the financial cost of unification, which has turned out to be larger than expected. The number of German tourists rose markedly for several Scandinavian countries (Denmark, Norway and Sweden), Turkey (+ 70 per cent) and New Zealand. Declines were also shown in Portugal (- 4 per cent) and Spain (- 3 per cent) where German tourists accounted for 35 per cent of nights spent.

Italian demand continued to strengthen in 1992 and the number of nights spent by travellers from Italy rose an additional 13 per cent in the OECD area. During the same period, expenditure in dollars rose by 42 per cent. The Italian market continues to be one of the most flourishing in Europe and retains a promising growth potential. Italians favoured Turkey (+ 75 per cent), France (+ 20 per cent), Belgium (15 per cent) and Spain (+ 14 per cent). On the other hand, fewer went to Finland, the Netherlands, Portugal, Sweden and the United Kingdom. Arrivals of Italian tourists rose by 21 per cent in North America and 3 per cent in Australasia-Japan, tempered by the decline recorded in Japan (- 15 per cent).

After a slump in **Japanese** demand in 1991, a marked upswing was recorded in 1992 with a 2 per cent growth in terms of nights spent and 14 per cent in terms of visits. While arrivals of Japanese tourists rose faster in Europe (+ 22 per cent) than in other regions, the same does not apply to nights spent (+ 2 per cent) which did not increase as much. In other words, the average duration of stay of Japanese tourists in Europe is appreciably shorter. However, the nights spent in Turkey rose by 136 per cent, Belgium 48 per cent and the Netherlands 23 per cent. Australasia-Japan (+ 12 per cent) and the United States (+ 10 per cent of arrivals) remained very popular destinations. Fewer Japanese tourists went to Canada (- 5 per cent in terms of nights spent). The expenditure in dollars rose by 12 per cent.

In 1992 the nights spent by **the dutch** tourists rose by 4 per cent in Europe. However, the number of arrivals of tourists remained unchanged whereas it rose by 6 per cent in North America and 12 per cent in Australasia-Japan. Most Netherlands tourists went to Denmark (+ 59 per cent) and Germany (+ 13 per cent) but fewer went to Belgium (- 4 per cent) where they accounted for 36 per cent of nights spent. Two other destinations also suffered losses: Portugal (- 14 per cent) and the United Kingdom (- 11 per cent). In 1992, expenditure by Dutch tourists rose roughly at the same pace as the average for OECD countries (+ 17 per cent).

	T/V	Total Variation % 92/91	From France		From Germany		From United Kingdom		From United States	
			Relative share % 91	Variation % 92/91	Relative share % 91	Variation % 92/91	Relative share % 91	Variation % 92/91	Relative share % 91	Variation % 92/91
Austria										
Belgium										
Denmark										
Finland										
France (R)	T	8.3			21.3	7.3	14.7	1.2	3.0	22.2
Germany										
Greece (N)	T	16.1	5.9	15.1	19.4	24.6	20.8	28.7	2.2	54.6
Iceland (N)	T	−0.6	7.0	−21.3	15.7	9.1	10.2	−5.2	15.7	−3.6
Ireland (R)	V	4.2	7.3	−0.9	6.5	13.9	57.7	1.7	10.4	16.9
Italy (N)	V	−2.4	17.8	−3.5	17.9	−4.6	3.3	−5.8	2.2	13.8
Luxembourg										
Netherlands										
Norway										
Portugal (N)	T	2.6	7.7	−2.9	9.1	3.3	13.4	9.8	1.7	9.1
Spain (N)	V	3.4	22.5	−2.2	14.3	1.3	11.5	6.0	1.2	26.5
Sweden										
Switzerland										
Turkey (N)	V	28.2	2.1	111.5	14.1	49.4	3.6	56.7	1.4	130.2
United Kingdom (R)	T	5.8	11.7	6.0	12.4	6.0			14.3	16.0
EUROPE		4.6	12.2	−1.2	16.8	4.3	10.3	5.3	3.2	20.6
Canada (R)	T	−1.1	2.1	1.1	1.8	6.4	3.6	1.1	80.5	−1.5
United States (R)	T	3.9	1.8	3.3	3.3	18.3	5.8	13.2		
NORTH AMERICA		2.6	1.9	2.7	2.9	16.4	5.2	11.1	20.7	−1.5
Australia (R)	V	9.6	1.0	11.9	3.3	15.7	11.1	9.9	11.5	−3.3
New Zealand (R)	T	9.6	0.5	14.7	3.6	33.3	9.1	9.8	13.8	−1.0
Japan (N)	T	0.0	1.0	−1.7	1.1	14.7	5.8	16.9	13.8	2.8
AUSTRALASIA-JAPAN		5.9	0.9	6.3	2.5	20.0	8.7	11.7	12.8	−0.3
OECD		4.2	9.7	−1.0	13.5	5.0	9.2	6.2	7.2	6.0

V Visitors.
T Tourists.
(R) Tourist count by country of residence.
(N) Tourist count by country of nationality.

In the **United Kingdom**, residents increased their dollar expenditures by 10 per cent in 1992. The number of nights spent by British tourists rose slightly by 1 per cent in Europe, now accounting for about 12 per cent of the total nights spent. In Ireland, where British tourists are the main clients -- 44 per cent of nights spent -- the number of nights spent fell by 2 per cent. Austrian and Finnish destinations also showed a downward trend (- 3 per cent and - 4 per cent, respectively). However, as in all the other generating countries, the number of visitors to Turkey picked up again (+ 108 per cent).

For North America, the number of nights spent in Canada fell by 3 per cent in spite of a 1 per cent increase in the number of visits. The trend was even more marked in Australia (- 13 per cent for nights spent and + 10 per cent for arrivals).

Finally, United Kingdom demand remained very high in the United States (+ 13 per cent of arrivals) and Japan (+ 17 per cent).

The number of nights spent by **United States** residents rose by 4 per cent throughout the OECD area. Europe was the main area of destination in 1992 (+ 12 per cent in terms of nights spent). The countries that fared best from this recovery were Turkey, Austria, Norway and Belgium. There was a marked decline in Iceland however (- 13 per cent). Lastly, in 1992 fewer United States travellers went to Canada (- 6 per cent). On the other hand, according to USTTA estimates, Mexico remained the favourite destination with an 11 per cent increase in the number of visits. In 1992, recovery from the Gulf war and the US recession of 1991 resulted in an increase in US travel payments abroad (+ 13 per cent). 1992 registered gains in payments to all world regions and/or countries except Canada (- 4 per cent).

	T/V	Total Variation % 92/91	From Japan		From Netherlands		From Canada		From Italy	
			Relative share % 91	Variation % 92/91	Relative share % 91	Variation % 92/91	Relative share % 91	Variation % 92/91	Relative share % 91	Variation % 92/91
Austria										
Belgium										
Denmark										
Finland										
France (R)	T	8.3	0.8	3.1	10.8	4.5	0.9	17.8	10.7	21.6
Germany	T	16.1	0.7	89.4	5.6	21.4	0.6	27.0	6.4	20.4
Greece (N)	T	−0.6	0.9	14.1	2.1	29.0	0.7	22.3	3.4	−13.5
Iceland (N)	V	4.2					1.0	30.0		
Ireland (R)	V	−2.4	1.1	32.6	3.0	−21.4	0.7	2.2		
Italy (N)										
Luxembourg										
Netherlands										
Norway										
Portugal (N)	T	2.6	0.3	−3.8	3.8	3.6	0.7	5.4	2.9	3.2
Spain (N)	V	3.4	0.3	19.2	4.0	−1.9	0.3	6.1	3.3	4.8
Sweden										
Switzerland										
Turkey (N)	V	28.2	0.3	97.0	1.9	91.4	0.3	49.1	1.2	146.6
United Kingdom (R)	V	6.2	2.7	16.6	6.5	−11.1	3.2	12.1	4.2	7.6
EUROPE		4.7	0.9	21.7	5.8	−0.2	0.8	11.8	4.6	17.6
Canada (R)	T	−1.1	2.6	−0.2	0.6	−2.9			0.6	8.6
United States (R)	T	3.9	7.7	10.0	0.7	8.0	44.5	−2.8	1.1	23.2
NORTH AMERICA		2.6	6.4	8.9	0.7	5.7	33.0	−2.8	1.0	20.9
Australia (R)	V	9.6	22.3	19.2	0.9	9.8	2.3	−8.4	1.0	12.8
New Zealand (R)	T	9.6	11.9	12.4	0.8	28.3	3.1	−14.6	0.4	5.2
Japan (N)	T	0.0			0.3	−1.3	1.8	17.1	0.6	−14.7
AUSTRALASIA-JAPAN		5.9	11.8	18.0	0.6	11.8	2.2	−2.1	0.8	3.4
OECD		4.2	2.3	13.5	4.6	0.1	8.0	−1.6	3.7	17.7

V Visitors.
T Tourists.
(R) Tourist count by country of residence.
(N) Tourist count by country of nationality.

Table 6. **Annual growth rates of nights spent in the various means of accommodation from main generating countries**

	H/A	Total Variation % 92/91	From France		From Germany		From the United Kingdom		From the United-States	
			Relative share % 91	Variation % 92/91	Relative share % 91	Variation % 92/91	Relative share % 91	Variation % 92/91	Relative share % 91	Variation % 92/91
Austria (R)	A	0.1	3.2	−10.2	64.5	0.7	4.2	−3.2	1.2	28.1
Belgium (R)	A	5.8	10.0	7.8	17.0	9.6	10.3	20.1	4.2	21.4
Denmark (N)	A	11.1	1.5	−1.2	37.7	16.4	3.5	4.1	3.0	4.2
Finland (R)	H	1.9	3.7	3.5	15.9	7.3	6.0	−3.7	6.5	4.9
France (R)	A	8.2			20.3	6.1	15.3	0.5	3.6	23.2
Germany (R)	A	−3.6	4.9	−5.8			8.8	−2.9	9.1	3.2
Greece (N)										
Iceland	H	−0.3	7.6	−18.7	21.4	2.1	10.7	−1.5	8.2	−13.7
Ireland (R)	A	1.5	9.1	9.7	9.7	6.3	44.2	−2.4	11.6	9.9
Italy (N)	A	−3.6	7.2	−11.0	41.5	−7.8	6.2	0.2	4.6	24.8
Luxembourg (R)	A	−8.8	5.1	−7.2	8.1	1.0	3.4	15.6	2.0	11.7
Netherlands (R)	A	5.2	4.4	3.7	48.6	8.4	11.3	6.2	4.9	11.8
Norway (N)	H	9.2	5.3	16.3	18.2	19.3	8.9	23.4	7.2	25.4
Portugal (N)	A	−8.6	6.8	−19.5	18.1	−3.5	26.3	0.7	2.3	10.1
Spain (N)	H	3.4	9.0	−9.9	34.9	−2.9	25.6	1.5	1.7	15.9
Sweden (N)	A	3.8	2.9	1.4	23.6	14.6	4.9	4.7	4.5	11.5
Switzerland (R)	A	−0.1	6.7	−5.9	43.6	−1.0	6.9	2.2	4.9	17.3
Turkey (N)	A	73.1	6.5	129.3	45.9	70.2	4.3	107.5	3.0	36.8
United Kingdom (R)	A	−2.1	7.9	1.0	10.4	−1.2			13.4	6.1
EUROPE		3.4	4.2	−1.9	26.1	2.4	11.6	0.9	5.6	13.2
Canada (R)	A	−4.0	4.6	0.8	4.4	−1.2	7.6	−3.1	59.6	−6.2
United States										
NORTH AMERICA										
Australia	A	−5.0			4.8	4.8	23.3	−13.2	10.3	−6.7
New Zealand	A									
Japan		6.3	0.5	9.5	5.9	21.4	16.3	1.0	9.9	3.7
AUSTRALASIA-JAPAN		6.3	0.5	9.5	5.9	21.4	16.3	1.0	9.9	3.7
OECD		2.9	4.1	−1.7	24.2	2.4	11.4	0.7	9.6	4.2

H Hotels and similar establishments.
A All means of accommodation.
(R) Tourist count by country of residence.
(N) Tourist count by country of nationality.

Table 7. **Annual growth rates of nights spent in the various means of accommodation from main generating countries**

	H/A	Total Variation % 92/91	From Japan		From Netherlands		From Canada		From Italy	
			Relative share % 91	Variation % 92/91	Relative share % 91	Variation % 92/91	Relative share % 91	Variation % 92/91	Relative share % 91	Variation % 92/91
Austria (R)	A	0.1	0.4	9.7	9.3	-2.6	0.2	5.9	3.3	9.1
Belgium (R)	A	5.8	1.3	47.7	36.0	-3.6	0.7	-3.9	3.1	14.9
Denmark (N)	A	11.1	0.9	18.7	6.0	59.2			2.1	6.6
Finland (R)	H	1.9	2.6	-0.2	2.4	17.1	1.1	-15.5	3.7	-6.4
France (R)	A	8.2	0.5	-0.9	14.1	6.3	1.2	14.8	8.9	20.0
Germany (R)	A	-3.6	3.1	5.0	22.3	-6.0	0.9	-2.6	5.2	-5.9
Greece (N)										
Iceland					3.0	-16.0	1.3	30.2	3.9	2.3
Ireland (R)	A	1.5	1.6	35.1	3.7	-10.7	0.7	5.4		
Italy (N)	A	-3.6								
Luxembourg (R)							1.0	-2.3	4.0	-6.9
Netherlands (R)	A	5.2	1.0	27.0					4.0	0.2
Norway (N)	H	9.2	2.2	17.5	3.8	15.9	1.3	-22.0	3.2	-8.9
Portugal (N)	A	-8.6	0.3	1.9	9.8	-14.3	0.2	16.5	6.2	13.6
Spain (N)	H	3.4	0.8	13.9	3.3	-3.1	0.3	0.5	2.4	-2.9
Sweden (N)	A	3.8	1.6	-4.4	5.7	5.1	0.6	-2.2	5.3	2.6
Switzerland (R)	A	-0.1	2.0	12.3	9.2	0.3	0.2	51.0	3.8	75.0
Turkey (N)	A	73.1	0.9	135.8						
United Kingdom (R)	A	-2.1	2.3	-4.1	3.5	-11.1	4.1	-3.1	4.9	-3.0
EUROPE		2.7	1.1	6.4	9.8	1.2	1.5	3.0	6.0	13.1
Canada (R)	A	-4.0	3.2	-5.4	1.3	0.0			1.1	2.1
United States										
NORTH AMERICA										
Australia	A	-5.0	6.6	22.8			3.5	-24.7		
New Zealand	A	6.3	6.7	12.2	1.7	14.6	3.5	-6.9	0.3	12.8
Japan										
AUSTRALASIA-JAPAN		6.3	6.7	12.2	1.7	14.6	3.5	-6.9	0.3	12.8
OECD		2.3	1.4	4.8	9.0	1.3	1.4	2.5	5.5	12.9

H Hotels and similar establishments.
A All means of accommodation.
(R) Tourist count by country of residence.
(N) Tourist count by country of nationality.

Trends of international tourism
in Europe, from:
(Overnights in accommodation, indices 1984=100)

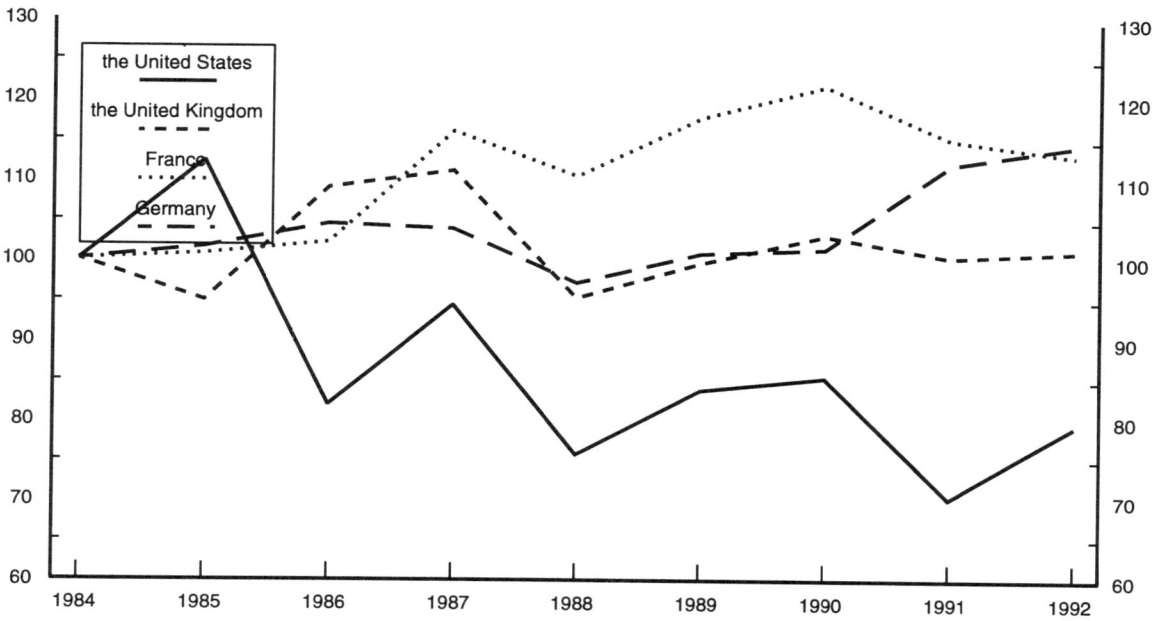

the United States

the United Kingdom

France

Germany

Source: OECD

Trends of international tourism
in Europe, from:
(Overnights in accommodation, indices 1984=100)

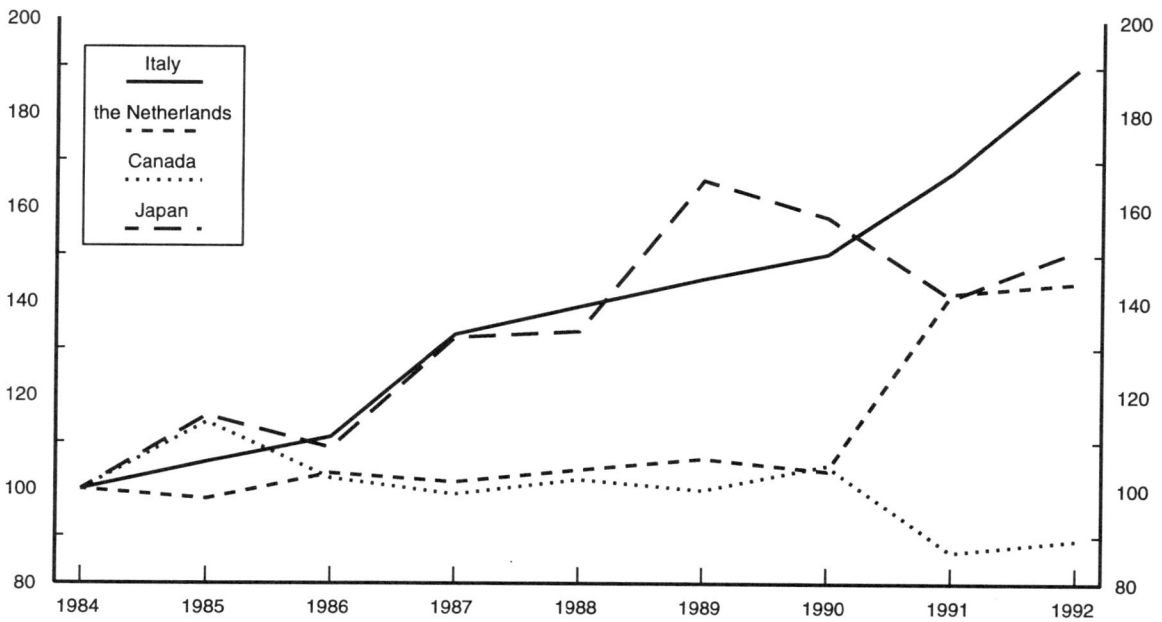

Italy

the Netherlands

Canada

Japan

Source: OECD

Trends of international tourism
in North America, from:
(Arrivals at frontiers, indices 1984 = 100)

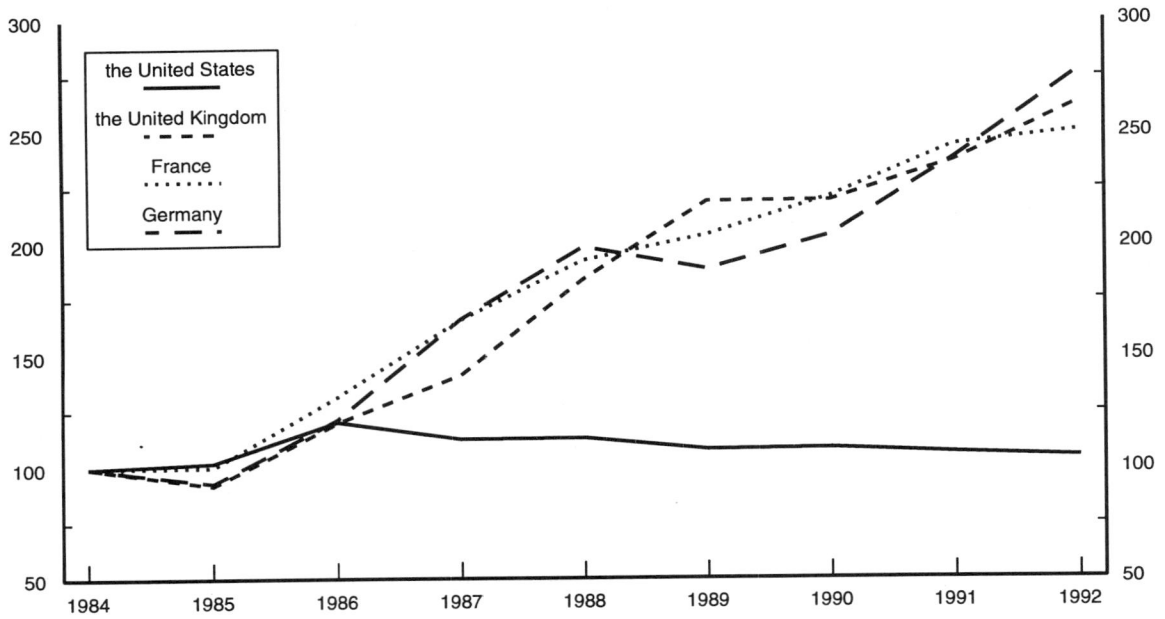

Source: OECD

Trends of international tourism
in North America, from:
(Arrivals at frontiers, indices 1984 = 100)

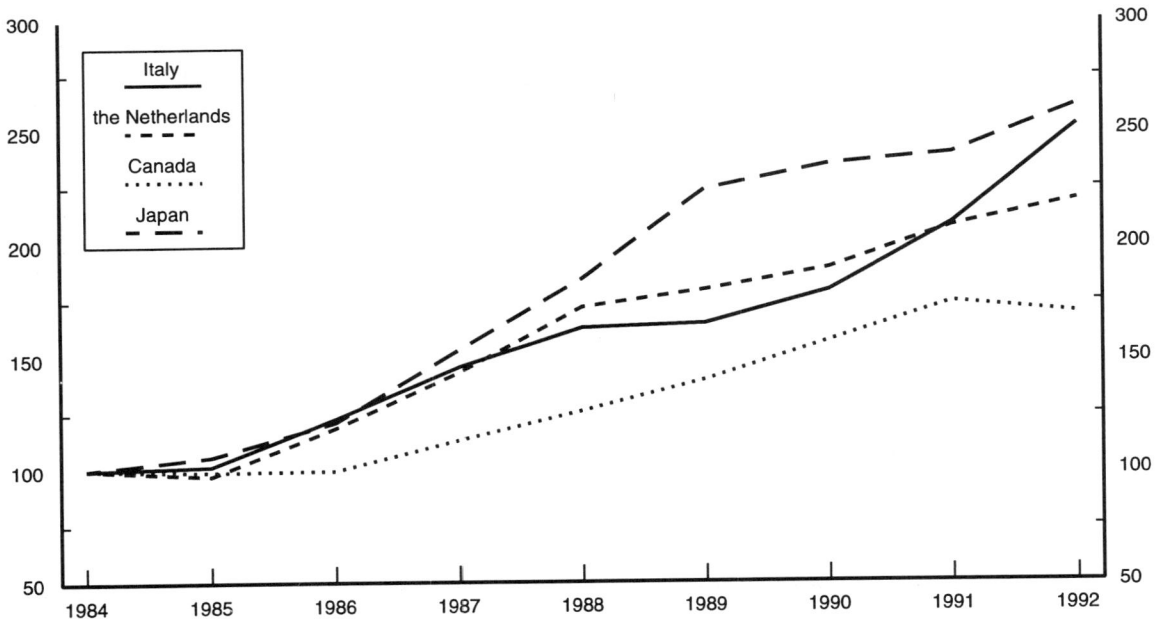

Source: OECD

Trends of international tourism
in Australasia-Japan, from:
(Arrivals at frontiers, indices 1984 = 100)

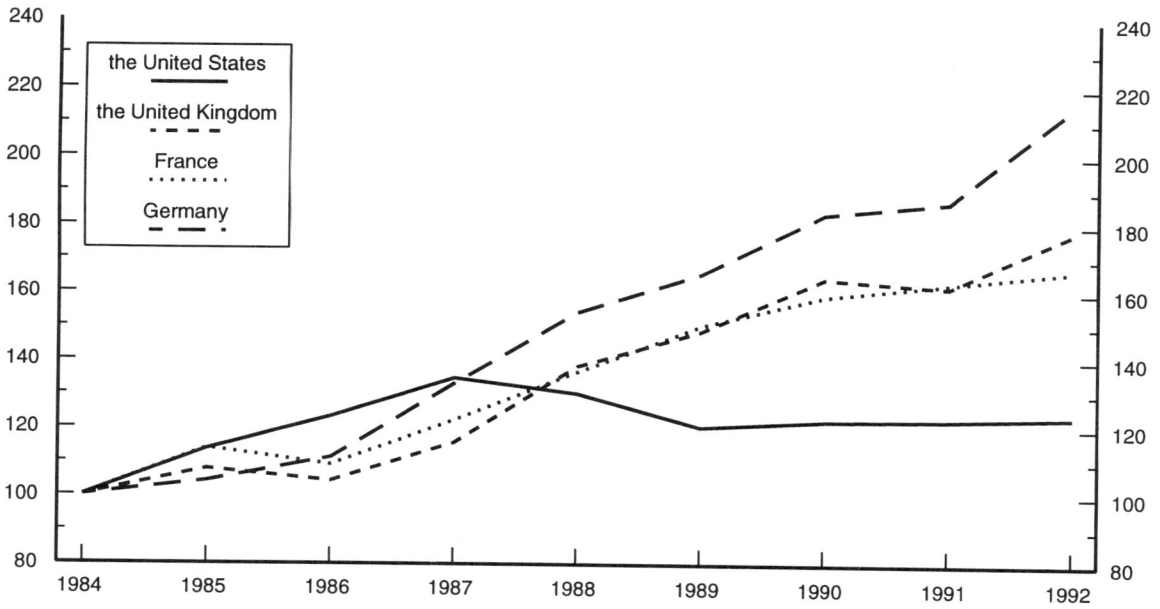

Legend:
- the United States
- the United Kingdom
- France
- Germany

Source: OECD

Trends of international tourism
in Australasia-Japan, from:
(Arrivals at frontiers, indices 1984 = 100)

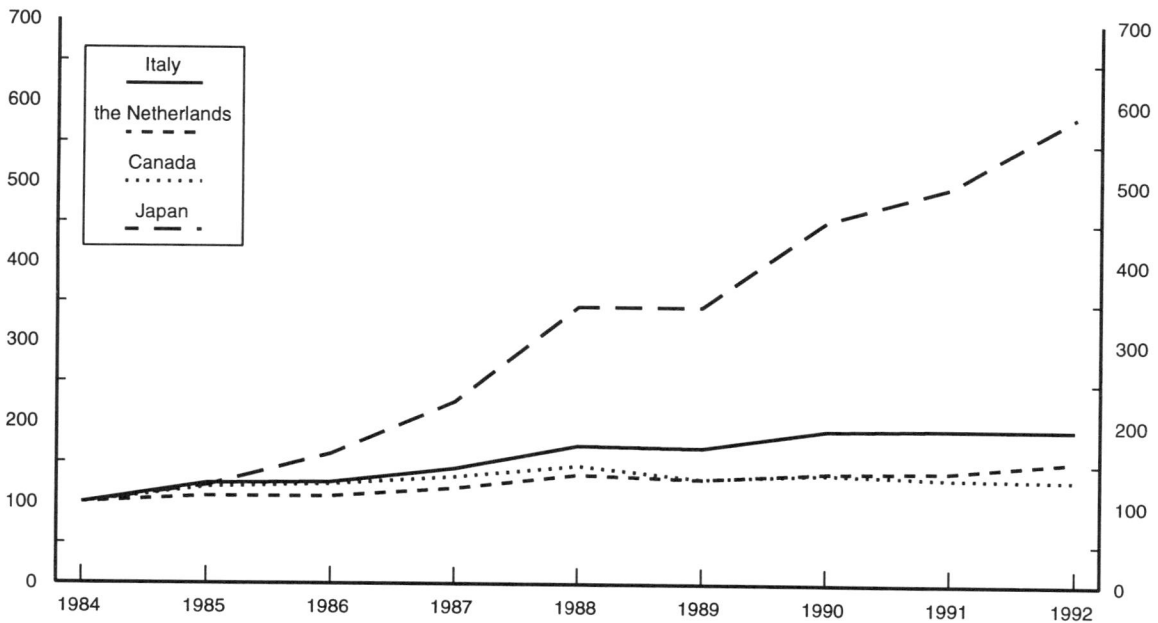

Legend:
- Italy
- the Netherlands
- Canada
- Japan

Source: OECD

Chapter III

The economic importance of international tourism
in Member countries

This Chapter brings together the most recent data available on international tourism receipts and expenditure in 1992 for the 24 OECD Member countries. The figures do not include international fare payments, except where explicitly stated (see Table 18 in the Statistical Annex).

The first part of the Chapter (Section I) considers:

a) receipts expressed in both national currencies and US dollars, first in current terms and then in real terms, i.e. adjusted for the effects of inflation and for changes in parities between the dollar and national currencies;

b) expenditure, again in both national currencies and US dollars, in current terms;

c) the tourism balance sheet for the OECD area and its three constituent regions.

The dollar was used as the common unit of account to evaluate trends for a range of countries. However, when considering the tables that give figures in "current dollars", the reader must take into account the marked fluctuations that have taken place in recent years in most OECD currencies against the dollar.

In 1992, the dollar declined in relation to most European currencies (see Table 17 of the Annex). However, it gained in value compared to the Turkish lira and the Finnish markka (by 65 per cent and 11 per cent respectively) and, to a lesser extent, against the Greek drachma (by 5 per cent) and the pound sterling (by 0.5 per cent). Outside Europe, the pattern was generally reversed, as the dollar strengthened in relation to other OECD currencies, with the notable exception of the still-rising Japanese yen (against which it lost 6 per cent).

The Secretariat would like to emphasise the analytical limitations of these figures, and thus that any conclusions from data expressed in dollars must be drawn with caution.

Section II compares the data on receipts and expenditure with a number of major macroeconomic indicators -- gross domestic product, private final consumption, and exports and imports of goods and services. They cover the period 1989-1991, as comprehensive data for these indicators for 1992 are not yet available.

The comparability of the figures provided by Member countries on receipts and expenditure for international tourism is still insufficient, and its improvement is a continuing priority for the Statistical Working Party of the OECD Tourism Committee.

The main source of divergence lies in the different survey methods used. Most countries use the "bank reporting method", which is based on the sales and purchases of foreign currency before or after travel abroad. The main drawback of this method is that it gives data on the currency concerned but not on the country visited. The "estimation method" is based on sample surveys carried out among residents at entry or departure points. Such surveys can provide extensive information but because of their cost are conducted by only a few countries. Lastly, some countries use a "mixed method" involving limited surveys to give adjustment factors to apply to bank-derived data. Progress towards data comparability is being made, however. (For further information, the notes in the Statistical Annex should be consulted.)

I.   International tourism receipts and expenditure

Dollar receipts and expenditure for the OECD area as a whole were up by 11 per cent and 14 per cent respectively (compared, respectively, with a 3 per cent rise and a 1 per cent fall in 1991) -- a trend that was amplified by the strengthening of most European currencies (except those of four countries) against the dollar.

In Europe, receipts advanced by 12 per cent and expenditure by 16 per cent. In Australasia-Japan, expenditure rose at triple the pace of receipts. In real terms, receipts in the OECD area increased by 5 per cent, up sharply from 1991's 1 per cent rise.

International tourism receipts

The revival of international tourism flows in 1992 (see Chapter II) is confirmed by the rise in receipts in national currencies (see Table 1). Receipts were up in 20 of the OECD's 24 Member countries, with the four others (Germany, Portugal, Japan and Iceland), which lost receipts in their national currencies, being among the Organisation's minor receiving countries.

The increase in receipts in current dollars was greater in 1992 than in 1991 (see Table 2). The highest growth rates were recorded in Greece (up 46 per cent), Turkey (up 37 per cent), the Netherlands (up 22 per cent) and France (up 17 per cent). In volume terms, receipts rose by $5.5 billion in the United States and by $3.6 billion in France. Conversely, receipts declined in Iceland (down 6 per cent), Canada and New Zealand (down 3 per cent) and Portugal (down 2 per cent).

For the OECD area as a whole, receipts totalled $214.4 billion in 1992, whereas world-wide, according to preliminary estimates of the World Tourism Organisation, the total came to $279 billion, up 7 per cent from $261 billion in 1991. This slightly increased the OECD countries' share of the global total, to 77 per cent.

The countries benefiting most from international tourism -- in dollar terms -- were the United States, which represented a quarter of the OECD total, followed by France (in second place with 12 per cent) and Italy (with 10 per cent). The combined receipts of the OECD's top six receiving countries (i.e. including Spain, Austria and the United Kingdom) accounted for approximately 70 per cent of the OECD total.

In real terms (see Table 3), i.e. after adjustment for the effects of inflation and fluctuations in exchange rates against the dollar, North America experienced sharper growth than the OECD area as a whole (up 7 per cent, compared with 5 per cent), and Europe and Australasia-Japan recorded increases of 4 per cent in 1992, after respective downturns of 2 and 5 per cent in 1991.

Greece, Turkey, Finland and Australia had the strongest growth rates. On the other hand, several countries regressed -- for the second year in a row: Portugal (down 16 per cent), Iceland (down 11 per cent), Germany (down 4 per cent), Japan (down 3 per cent) and the United Kingdom (down 1 per cent).

Table 1. **International tourist receipts and expenditure in national currencies**

In millions

	Currency	Receipts			Expenditure		
		1991	1992	%92/91	1991	1992	%92/91
Austria	Schilling	163 000	163 000	0.0	86 999	92 000	5.7
Belgium-Luxembourg	Franc	124 100	130 300	5.0	190 600	212 300	11.4
Denmark	Krone	22 222	22 839	2.8	21 590	22 811	5.7
Finland	Markka	4 821	5 699	18.2	10 672	10 526	−1.4
France	Franc	120 509	132 621	10.1	69 500	73 659	6.0
Germany [2]	Deutsche Mark	17 137	17 011	−0.7	51 175	57 451	12.3
Greece	Drachma	401 585	611 759	52.3	164 061	220 322	34.3
Iceland	Krona	8 036	7 404	−7.9	17 276	16 569	−4.1
Ireland	Pound	939	949	1.1	694	797	14.8
Italy [1]	Lira	22 853 073	26 441 462	15.7	14 451 448	20 368 274	40.9
Netherlands	Guilder	7 994	9 131	14.2	15 323	16 750	9.3
Norway	Krone	10 751	12 264	14.1	21 159	24 033	13.6
Portugal	Escudo	539 786	496 137	−8.1	148 324	155 723	5.0
Spain	Peseta	1 991 100	2 123 200	6.6	473 400	482 200	1.9
Sweden	Krona	16 517	17 714	7.2	36 990	38 980	5.4
Switzerland	Franc	10 115	10 855	7.3	8 180	8 610	5.3
Turkey	Lira	11 064 289	24 965 671	125.6	2 467 995	5 323 814	115.7
United Kingdom	Pound	7 449	7 687	3.2	9 966	11 090	11.3
Canada	Dollar	6 690	6 846	2.3	12 955	13 563	4.7
United States	Dollar	48 384	53 861	11.3	35 322	39 872	12.9
Australia	Dollar	5 076	5 571	9.8	5 032	5 433	8.0
New Zealand	Dollar	2 615	2 734	4.6	1 720	1 821	5.9
Japan	Yen	462 322	454 653	−1.7	3 223 097	3 396 060	5.4

Notice: for statistical coverage, see notes in table 18 in annex.
1. Break of series in 1990 due to the liberalisation of capital movements.
2. The data relate to the territory of the Federal Republic of Germany prior to 3rd October 1990. Since July 1990, data include all transactions of the former German Democratic Republic with foreign countries.

Table 2. **International tourist receipts and expenditure in current dollars**

In millions

	Receipts			Expenditure		
	1991	1992	%92/91	1991	1992	%92/91
Austria	13 962.5	14 830.6	6.2	7 452.3	8 370.7	12.3
Belgium-Luxembourg	3 632.7	4 053.4	11.6	5 579.4	6 604.2	18.4
Denmark	3 473.5	3 782.4	8.9	3 374.8	3 777.7	11.9
Finland	1 192.4	1 270.5	6.5	2 639.5	2 346.5	−11.1
France	21 363.8	25 052.8	17.3	12 320.9	13 914.6	12.9
Germany	10 331.0	10 891.0	5.4	30 850.8	36 782.2	19.2
Greece	2 205.7	3 211.9	45.6	901.1	1 156.7	28.4
Iceland	136.0	128.5	−5.5	292.3	287.6	−1.6
Ireland	1 510.7	1 615.3	6.9	1 116.5	1 356.6	21.5
Italy	18 420.3	21 461.8	16.5	11 648.3	16 532.3	41.9
Netherlands	4 275.7	5 193.8	21.5	8 195.7	9 527.5	16.3
Norway	1 658.5	1 973.5	19.0	3 264.1	3 867.3	18.5
Portugal	3 739.3	3 680.1	−1.6	1 027.5	1 155.1	12.4
Spain	19 157.6	20 734.5	8.2	4 554.9	4 709.0	3.4
Sweden	2 732.2	3 041.4	11.3	6 118.7	6 692.6	9.4
Switzerland	7 055.6	7 722.0	9.4	5 705.8	6 125.0	7.3
Turkey	2 654.0	3 639.0	37.1	592.0	776.0	31.1
United Kingdom	13 141.0	13 493.7	2.7	17 581.4	19 467.2	10.7
EUROPE	130 642.5	145 776.0	11.6	123 216.0	143 448.7	16.4
Canada	5 837.6	5 663.7	−3.0	11 303.4	11 219.7	−0.7
United States	48 384.0	53 861.0	11.3	35 322.0	39 872.0	12.9
NORTH AMERICA	54 221.6	59 524.7	9.8	46 625.4	51 091.7	9.6
Australia	3 953.3	4 089.6	3.4	3 919.0	3 988.3	1.8
New Zealand	1 512.3	1 469.9	−2.8	994.7	979.0	−1.6
Japan	3 437.4	3 589.2	4.4	23 964.2	26 809.7	11.9
AUSTRALASIA-JAPAN	8 903.0	9 148.7	2.8	28 877.9	31 777.0	10.0
OECD	193 767.1	214 449.3	10.7	198 719.3	226 317.4	13.9

International tourism expenditure

Expenditure in national currencies rose in almost all OECD Member countries, except Finland (down 1 per cent) and Iceland (down 4 per cent) (see Table 1). The steepest increases were in Turkey (up 116 per cent), Italy (up 41 per cent) and Greece (up 34 per cent).

In terms of dollar expenditure (see Table 2), the main generating countries confirmed their economic impact on international tourism, with volume growth led in order by Germany, Italy, the United States, Japan, the United Kingdom and France; the greatest percentage changes were those of Italy (up 42 per cent), Turkey (up 31 per cent) and Greece (up 28 per cent). Aggregate expenditure for all OECD countries amounted to $226.3 billion in 1992, up 14 per cent from the previous year.

Expenditure progressed most sharply in Europe (up 16 per cent), despite decreases in Finland (down 11 per cent) and Iceland (down 2 per cent). It rose by 10 per cent in North America and Australasia-Japan. Within these two regions, the Japanese and the Americans boosted their spending substantially, by some 12 to 13 per cent, whereas Canada and New Zealand posted slight declines.

The tourism balance sheet

The tourism deficit (see Table 4) of the OECD countries took another plunge in 1992 -- to $11.9 billion, just shy of its 1990 level. This was due mainly to the rapid rise in expenditure in Europe (up 16 per cent between 1991 and 1992) and in Australasia-Japan (up 10 per cent), where the deficit now exceeds $22 billion. The upswing was partly driven by a surge in spending by the Japanese, in large part because of government efforts to encourage more of Japan's people to travel abroad. In addition, with North American receipts rising three times faster than expenditure between 1990 and 1992, the region's surplus increased ninefold in just three years.

II. The economic importance of the "travel" account in the balance of payments

For some years, the Tourism Committee's Statistical Working Party has been working to apply the System of National Accounts (SNA) to pin-point the economic importance of tourism, principally in monetary terms. The SNA is the only available framework for coherent analysis of the economic contribution of tourism, because it brings together commodities, supply and use and sets them against activities and final users. It also allows links with other parts of the system, such as income and outlays.

The Manual on Tourism Economic Accounts was adopted in April 1991. Available free of charge under the reference OECD/GD(91)82, it provides a basis for the compilation of data on production, consumption, value added, gross fixed capital formation and employment in the tourist industries. The Manual will be tested over a three-year trial period which started in 1992. During that time, countries are to compare experience, conduct new surveys to provide the best possible responses to the Manual's requests for data and resolve methodological problems. At the same time, the OECD Secretariat is examining data quality in terms of comparative international analysis. Ultimately, this system will be used as a basic tool to assess the importance of tourism to Member country economies.

Inasmuch as data on the economic accounts of tourism are not yet ready for publication, the Secretariat is still using other indicators which, albeit less satisfactory, are the only ones that give an idea of the macroeconomic importance of tourism.

The final section of this chapter considers the importance of tourism in individual Member countries as measured by four indicators. The tables cover the period 1989 to 1991, since 1992 data are not yet available. Admittedly it would have been useful to include international passenger transport payments but, as only a few Member countries break down their "transport" account in this way (see Table 16 in the Statistical Annex), the data would not be comparable.

102

Share of "travel account" receipts in gross domestic product

"Travel account" receipts (see Table 5) amounted to 1.1 per cent of GDP for the OECD area as a whole. The increase in receipts as a proportion of GDP between 1989 and 1991 was especially significant in Denmark (from 2.2 to 2.7 per cent) and Ireland (from 3.1 to 3.5 per cent). Conversely, the ratio declined markedly in Portugal (from 6.0 to 5.4 per cent), Spain (from 4.3 to 3.6 per cent) and Turkey (from 3.2 to 2.5 per cent) -- three countries in which tourism plays a distinct role and had expanded considerably in recent years. It must be borne in mind, however, that because of the momentous political developments throughout the world, 1991 cannot be considered a benchmark in international tourism.

Share of "travel account" expenditure in private final consumption

From 1989 to 1991, "travel account" expenditure as a proportion of private final consumption in all Member countries combined remained stable at 1.9 per cent (see Table 6). The sharpest increases took place in Iceland (from 6.3 to 7.3 per cent) and Canada (from 3.1 to 3.8 per cent), whereas the steepest declines were in Austria (from 8.9 to 8.1 per cent) and Switzerland (from 5.7 to 5.1 per cent).

Share of "travel account" receipts in exports of goods and services

The share of international tourism receipts in OECD-area exports of goods and services is rising gradually and came to 5.0 per cent in 1991 (see Table 7). The most pronounced decreases were in Spain (from 22.5 to 19.8 per cent) and Turkey (from 13.5 to 11.5 per cent), whereas increases were recorded in Italy (from 6.4 to 7.5 per cent), the United States (from 5.7 to 6.8 per cent) and Australia (from 6.4 to 7.3 per cent).

Share of "travel account" expenditure in imports of goods and services

Between 1989 and 1991, the share of "travel account" expenditure in imports of goods and services remained level (inching from 5.1 to 5.2 per cent) (see Table 8); the only region to increase was North America, from 4.9 to 5.4 per cent. In Europe, rises in Finland, Iceland and Portugal just offset the declining proportion of tourism expenditure in Germany (from 6.8 to 6.1 per cent) and Austria (from 11.0 to 9.8 per cent). In North America, Canada's ratio increased substantially, from 5.8 to 7.5 per cent.

Table 3. **Trends in international tourist receipts in real prices[1]**

	1987 = 100					Relative share in percentage of total	
	1988	1989	1990	1991	1992	1991	1992
Austria	109.0	121.0	126.0	130.3	125.3	7.6	7.0
Belgium-Luxembourg	111.2	103.7	102.0	99.2	101.7	2.0	1.9
Denmark	102.5	101.5	120.1	126.4	127.3	1.8	1.8
Finland	107.5	106.7	103.2	106.9	122.8	0.6	0.6
France	112.1	136.8	140.3	149.2	160.4	11.7	12.0
Germany[5]	106.2	111.8	114.1	112.0	107.1	5.7	5.2
Greece	101.9	84.2	87.6	72.7	95.6	1.1	1.3
Iceland	115.1	125.1	142.9	132.6	117.5	0.1	0.1
Ireland	113.6	125.9	141.2	146.8	143.9	0.8	0.8
Italy[4]	97.4	93.2	126.3	114.6	126.0	9.2	9.6
Netherlands	103.0	116.2	115.2	134.8	148.5	2.4	2.5
Norway	106.2	98.0	98.6	106.1	118.3	0.9	0.9
Portugal	105.9	114.4	119.5	115.2	97.2	1.6	1.3
Spain	101.6	94.1	86.1	86.2	86.7	8.4	8.1
Sweden	105.3	112.7	106.7	94.0	98.6	1.3	1.3
Switzerland	102.6	108.4	106.5	107.4	110.8	3.8	3.8
Turkey	133.4	126.4	124.7	95.2	126.4	1.1	1.4
United Kingdom	95.3	98.4	101.0	91.1	90.6	6.1	5.8
EUROPE[1]	104.3	108.0	113.1	111.4	115.3	66.1	65.3
Canada	104.5	104.3	108.9	106.2	107.1	2.8	2.7
United States	121.2	141.2	159.0	171.6	185.4	26.6	27.4
NORTH AMERICA	118.8	135.9	151.8	162.2	174.1	29.3	30.1
Australia[3]	129.3	113.0	124.2	130.1	144.9	1.8	2.0
New Zealand[2]	163.6	155.3	165.4	165.3	171.0	0.8	0.8
Japan	123.2	141.4	163.3	141.0	136.3	1.9	1.8
AUSTRALASIA-JAPAN[1]	132.1	131.3	146.8	140.1	145.3	4.6	4.6
OECD[1]	108.7	115.2	123.1	123.9	129.7	100.0	100.0

1. After correcting for the effects of inflation in each country. For the regional and OECD totals, the receipts of the individual countries are weighted in proportion to their share in the total expressed in dollars.
2. Changes of series in 1986 and in 1987.
3. Change of statistical coverage in 1987.
4. Break of series in 1990 due to the liberalisation of capital movements.
5. The data relate to the territory of the Federal Republic of Germany prior to 3rd October 1990. Since July 1990, data include all transactions of the former German Democratic Republic with foreign countries.

Table 4. **Tourism balance sheet**
In billions of current dollars

	1990	1991	1992
EUROPE			
Receipts	130.2	130.6	145.8
Expenditure	123.6	123.2	143.4
Balance[1]	6.6	7.4	2.3
NORTH AMERICA			
Receipts	48.6	54.2	59.5
Expenditure	47.7	46.6	51.1
Balance[1]	0.9	7.6	8.4
AUSTRALASIA-JAPAN			
Receipts	8.8	8.9	9.1
Expenditure	30.0	28.9	31.8
Balance[1]	−21.3	−20.0	−22.6
OECD			
Receipts	187.5	193.8	214.4
Expenditure	201.3	198.7	226.3
Balance[1]	−13.8	−5.0	−11.9

1. Minus signs indicate deficits. Due to rounding of figures, balances are not always equal to difference between receipts and expenditure.

International tourist receipts
in real terms (1)
(Shares of the various regions within the OECD)

Relative shares

1984 = 100

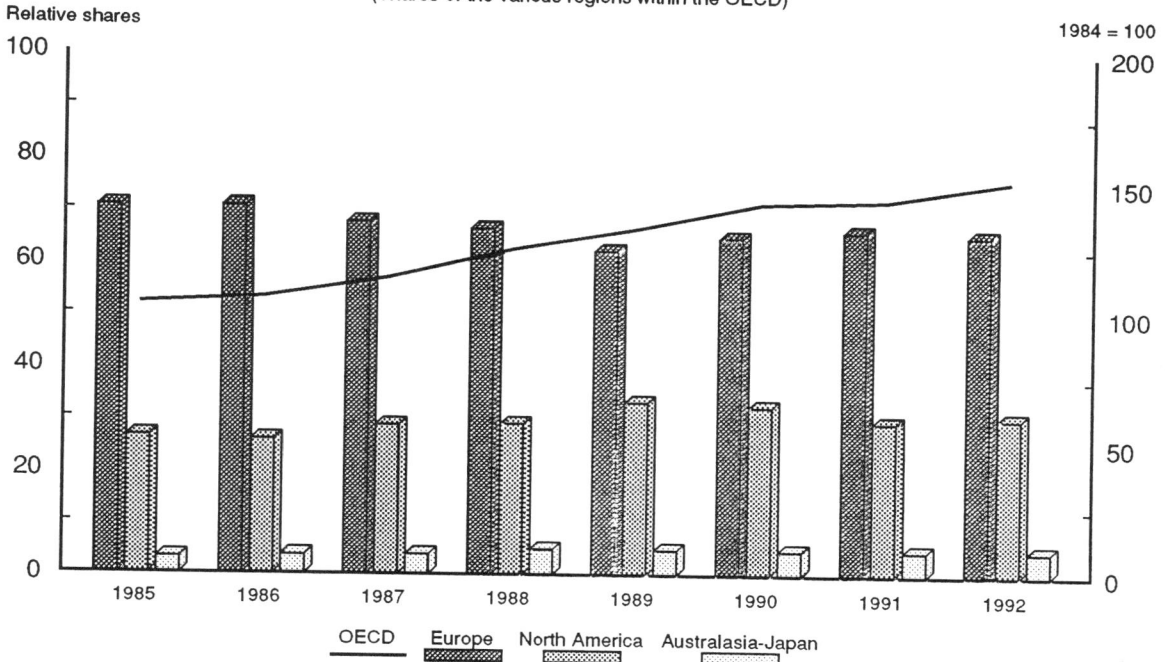

OECD   Europe   North America   Australasia-Japan

1. New series for Italy from 1990 affecting regional as well as overall OECD volumes.
Source: OECD

International tourist receipts
Importance of the OECD area in the world total
(in current dollars)

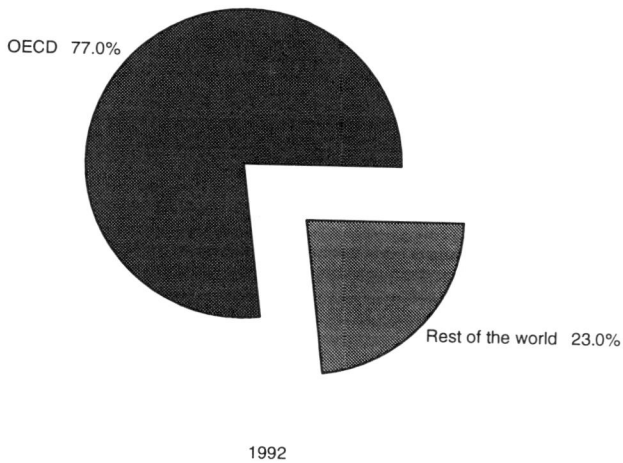

OECD 77.0%

Rest of the world 23.0%

1992

Source: OECD

International tourist receipts
Share of the various regions within the OECD
(in real terms)

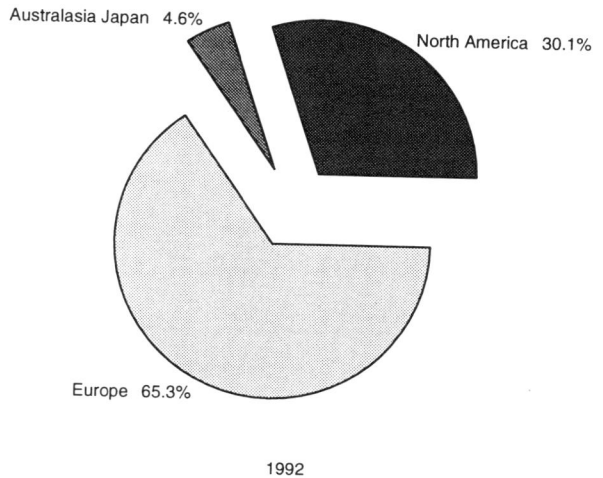

Australasia Japan 4.6%

North America 30.1%

Europe 65.3%

1992

Source: OECD

105

Table 5. Ratio of the "Travel" account receipts to the gross domestic product (%)

	1989	1990	1991
Austria	8.5	8.5	8.4
Belgium-Luxembourg	2.0	1.9	1.8
Denmark	2.2	2.6	2.7
Finland	0.9	0.9	1.0
France	1.7	1.7	1.8
Germany	0.7	0.7	0.7
Greece	3.6	3.9	3.7
Iceland	2.0	2.3	2.1
Ireland	3.1	3.3	3.5
Italy	1.4	1.8	1.6
Netherlands	1.3	1.3	1.5
Norway	1.5	1.5	1.6
Portugal	6.0	5.9	5.4
Spain	4.3	3.7	3.6
Sweden	1.3	1.3	1.1
Switzerland	3.2	3.0	3.1
Turkey	3.2	3.0	2.5
United Kingdom	1.4	1.4	1.3
EUROPE	1.8	1.9	1.8
Canada	1.1	1.2	1.2
United States	0.7	0.8	0.9
NORTH AMERICA	0.7	0.8	0.9
Australia	1.1	1.3	1.4
New Zealand	2.3	2.4	2.4
Japan	0.1	0.1	0.1
AUSTRALASIA-JAPAN	0.2	0.3	0.2
OECD	1.0	1.2	1.1

Source: OECD, Balance of Payments Division and *National Accounts of OECD Member Countries.*

Table 6. Ratio of the "Travel" account expenditure to the private final consumption (%)

	1989	1990	1991
Austria	8.9	8.8	8.1
Belgium-Luxembourg	4.5	4.6	4.5
Denmark	5.3	5.5	5.0
Finland	3.4	3.9	3.9
France	1.7	1.7	1.7
Germany	3.6	3.6	3.6
Greece	2.1	2.3	2.0
Iceland	6.3	7.6	7.3
Ireland	5.0	4.8	4.6
Italy	1.3	2.1	1.6
Netherlands	4.8	4.4	4.7
Norway	6.6	6.8	6.4
Portugal	2.0	2.3	2.4
Spain	1.3	1.4	1.4
Sweden	5.1	5.2	4.8
Switzerland	4.9	4.6	4.3
Turkey	1.2	0.8	1.0
United Kingdom	2.9	2.9	2.7
EUROPE	2.9	3.0	2.9
Canada	3.1	3.7	3.8
United States	1.0	1.0	0.9
NORTH AMERICA	1.2	1.3	1.2
Australia	2.4	2.4	2.2
New Zealand	3.6	3.5	3.7
Japan	1.4	1.5	1.3
AUSTRALASIA-JAPAN	1.5	1.6	1.4
OECD	1.9	2.0	1.9

Source: OECD, Balance of Payments Division and *National Accounts of OECD Member Countries.*

Table 7. Share of "Travel" account receipts in exports of goods and services

	1989	1990	1991
Austria	18.8	18.5	18.3
Belgium-Luxembourg	1.9	1.8	1.7
Denmark	5.3	6.0	5.8
Finland	3.4	3.4	4.1
France	5.9	5.9	6.0
Germany	2.0	2.0	2.0
Greece	17.7	19.4	17.6
Iceland	5.5	6.3	6.1
Ireland	4.3	4.9	5.0
Italy	6.4	8.0	7.5
Netherlands	2.1	2.0	2.4
Norway	3.3	3.1	3.3
Portugal	15.5	15.5	16.1
Spain	22.5	21.0	19.8
Sweden	3.7	3.6	3.4
Switzerland	6.1	6.1	6.4
Turkey	13.5	14.7	11.5
United Kingdom	3.6	3.7	3.4
EUROPE	5.1	5.3	5.2
Canada	4.2	4.3	4.4
United States	5.7	6.2	6.8
NORTH AMERICA	5.4	5.9	6.4
Australia	6.4	7.1	7.3
New Zealand	8.6	8.5	8.4
Japan	0.8	0.8	0.7
AUSTRALASIA-JAPAN	1.5	1.6	1.5
OECD	4.7	4.9	5.0

Source: OECD, Balance of Payments Division.

Table 8. Share of "Travel" account expenditure in imports of goods and services

	1989	1990	1991
Austria	11.0	10.8	9.8
Belgium-Luxembourg	2.7	2.7	2.6
Denmark	6.7	6.8	5.9
Finland	5.9	6.9	7.7
France	3.7	3.6	3.4
Germany	6.8	6.5	6.1
Greece	4.6	5.0	4.5
Iceland	10.0	11.8	11.6
Ireland	3.8	3.6	3.5
Italy	3.4	5.4	4.5
Netherlands	4.7	4.5	4.8
Norway	7.5	8.1	7.8
Portugal	2.7	3.0	3.4
Spain	3.5	3.9	3.8
Sweden	7.1	7.3	7.6
Switzerland	6.0	5.7	5.9
Turkey	2.6	1.8	2.1
United Kingdom	4.4	4.4	4.5
EUROPE	4.9	5.1	4.9
Canada	5.8	7.1	7.5
United States	4.7	5.0	4.9
NORTH AMERICA	4.9	5.4	5.4
Australia	5.7	6.0	5.8
New Zealand	7.0	6.9	7.4
Japan	6.4	6.2	5.9
AUSTRALASIA-JAPAN	6.3	6.2	5.9
OECD	5.1	5.3	5.1

Source: OECD, Balance of Payments Division.

Statistical Annex

Notes and sources 110-113

Table A: Classification of international visitors 116
Table B: Series available by country 117
Table C: Types of accommodation covered by the statistics 118

Tourist flows in the OECD area
1. Tourism from European Member countries 119
2. Tourism from Canada and the United States 119
3. Tourism from Australia, New Zealand and Japan 120
4. Tourism from all OECD countries 120
5. Tourism from non-Member countries 121
6. Tourism from all countries 121
7. Tourism from the United States -- Expenditure of United States
   residents travelling abroad 122
8. Tourism from the United States -- Number and expenditure of
   United States residents travelling overseas 122

Accommodation
9. Average length of stay of foreign tourists 123
10. Nights spent by foreign and domestic tourists in all means of
    accommodation 124
11. Nights spent by foreign and domestic tourists in hotels and similar
    establishments 124
12. Nights spent by foreign and domestic tourists in supplementary means
    of accommodation 125
13. Capacity in hotels and similar establishments 126
14. Capacity in supplementary means of accommodation 127
15. Monthly hotel occupancy rates 128

Payments
16. International fare payments 129
17. Nominal exchange rates of national currencies against the
    dollar 129
18. International tourist receipts and expenditure in dollars 130-131

Motives
19. Foreign tourism by purpose of visit 132

Transport
20. Foreign tourism by mode of transport 132

Employment
21. Staff employed in tourism 133

Prices
22. Trends in tourism prices 134

International tourist flows from main generating

Methodological notes 136

From all foreign countries
23. Arrivals of tourists/visitors at frontiers 137
24. Arrivals and nights of tourists at/in hotels 138
25. Arrivals and nights of tourists at/in all means of
    accommodation 139

From Germany
26. Arrivals of tourists/visitors at frontiers 140
27. Arrivals and nights of tourists at/in hotels 141
28. Arrivals and nights of tourists at/in all means of
    accommodation 142

From Canada
29. Arrivals of tourists/visitors at frontiers 143
30. Arrivals and nights of tourists at/in hotels 144
31. Arrivals and nights of tourists at/in all means of
    accommodation 145

From the United States
32. Arrivals of tourists/visitors at frontiers 146
33. Arrivals and nights of tourists at/in hotels 147
34. Arrivals and nights of tourists at/in all means of
    accommodation 148

From France
35. Arrivals of tourists/visitors at frontiers 149
36. Arrivals and nights of tourists at/in hotels 150
37. Arrivals and nights of tourists at/in all means of
    accommodation 151

From Italy
38. Arrivals of tourists/visitors at frontiers 152
39. Arrivals and nights of tourists at/in hotels 153
40. Arrivals and nights of tourists at/in all means of
    accommodation 154

From Japan
41. Arrivals of tourists/visitors at frontiers 155
42. Arrivals and nights of tourists at/in hotels 156
43. Arrivals and nights of tourists at/in all means of
    accommodation 157

From Netherlands
44. Arrivals of tourists/visitors at frontiers 158
45. Arrivals and nights of tourists at/in hotels 159
46. Arrivals and nights of tourists at/in all means of
    accommodation 160

From United Kingdom
47. Arrivals of tourists/visitors at frontiers 161
48. Arrivals and nights of tourists at/in hotels 162
49. Arrivals and nights of tourists at/in all means of
    accommodation 163

International tourist flows by receiving country
Australia 164
Austria 167
Belgium 171
Canada 173
Denmark 176
Finland 178
⨉ France 179
Germany 183
⨉ Greece 187
Iceland 188
Ireland 189
⨉ Italy 194
Japan 199
Netherlands 201
New Zealand 205
Norway 207
⨉ Portugal 208
⨉ Spain 214
Sweden 217
Switzerland 219
Turkey 223
United Kingdom 228
United States 230

Notes

This Annex reproduces the main international tourism statistical series available in Member countries. For 1992, data are in certain cases provisional. It illustrates recent tourism developments in the OECD (over a two or three-year period).

Some of the data contained in the text itself may not always correspond exactly to that included in the Annex: the discrepancies can be explained by a different statistical coverage (e.g. the use of GNP instead of GDP) or by the use of material of a more analytical nature (data derived from gross figures).

Finally, certain tables are prepared from data available for other OECD work (e.g. Balance of Payments and National Accounts). In some cases, these statistics, which have been standardised to follow existing international guidelines, may differ from the ones supplied by countries in response to the annual questionnaire of the Tourism Committee.

Three tables of general interest for the use of the statistical series are presented at the beginning of the Annex:

A. Classification of travellers;

B. Series available by countries;

C. Types of establishments covered by the statistics.

Main elements of the terminology used

This section indicates the main methods used for collecting statistics and deals with international tourism.

Table A gives an overview of the international classification of travellers.

International inbound tourism (i.e. tourism performed in a given country by non-residents) is usually measured by the receiving country as monthly, quarterly or annual number of arrivals and/or nights spent, using one of three methods:

-- *Border controls*: these can provide only a limited amount of information about volumes, means of transport, etc. (as used in Japan, New Zealand and Spain);

-- *Sample surveys*: these provide a large amount of quantitative and qualitative information (as used in Canada, Portugal and the United Kingdom);

-- *Registration in means of accommodation*: this method, which is used in Finland, Italy and Switzerland among others, provides more accurate information, but with a more limited scope. However, by definition, it excludes excursionists and certain types of accommodation that are not registered for tax or other reasons, such as that provided by relatives or friends.

In estimating tourism supply, it is necessary to take account of all the goods and services required by tourism i.e. the resources, infrastructure and industries producing such goods and services, whether in the tourism field itself or indirectly related to the tourist industries.

The various means of accommodation are an essential part of this supply. They can be divided into two broad categories: hotels and similar establishments, and supplementary means of accommodation.

The first category (hotels and similar establishments) normally covers four types of establishments: hotels, motels, boarding houses and inns. However, in order to reflect the actual situation in a country more accurately, similar establishments are also often included (in which case the statistical coverage is indicated in Table C or in the methodological notes for each country).

The second category (supplementary means of accommodation) can include seven types of establishemnt: youth hostels, camping sites, holiday villages, mountain hust and shelters, rented rooms, houses and flats, sanatoria and health establishments and children's holiday camps. The list can also be extended in some cases.

The data on international tourism receipts and expenditure are those found under the "travel" heading in the Balance of Payments. They are available in varying degrees of disaggregation by country/region of origin or country/region of destination.

Data concerning international tourism payments follow, in practice, the recommendations of the World Tourism Organisation.

International tourism receipts: they are defined as the receipts of a country resulting from consumption expenditures, i.e., payments for goods and services, made by visitors out of foreign currency. They should, however, exclude all forms of remuneration resulting from employment, as well as international fare receipts.

International tourism expenditure: they are defined as consumption expenditures, i.e., payments for goods and services, made by residents of a country visiting abroad. They should, however, exclude all forms of remuneration resulting from employment, as well as international fare payments.

Three different methods are currently used by the Member countries:

- In most countries, data are collected by the central bank using a method called the *bank reporting method*. When a traveller purchases or sells currency before or after a trip abroad, the bank or authorised agency records the transaction. Under this method, data are broken down according to the currency used and not according to the traveller's country of origin or destination.

- The *estimation method* is based on sample surveys that are usually carried out at the points of entry or departure for non-residents, or at the re-entry points for returning residents. Data are broken down according to tourists' country of origin or destination. These surveys provide the most reliable and most detailed statistics.

- The *mixed method*, which is used by only a few countries, was developed to remedy the shortcomings of the bank reporting method. It uses parallel sources (surveys of visitors, comparison with data provided by receiving countries, etc.), allowing the statistics obtained by the bank reporting method to be adjusted.

However, these data have their limitations. First, the volumes obtained by the bank reporting method in most countries are not an accurate measure of international tourist trade, since they represent net balances and not gross volumes; tourist transactions therefore tend to be understated. Second, it was noted that items unrelated to international tourism were included under the "travel" heading. Third, large discrepancies are found when any attempt is made to compile bilateral balances by comparing a given country's receipts, broken down by country of origin, with the expenditure reported by generating countries, broken down by country of destination.

Geographic coverage

Belgium-Luxembourg: Balance of payments statistics refer to the Belgo-Luxembourg Economic Union.

Other OECD-Europe: include OECD European countries for which no breakdown is available.

Other European countries: include non-OECD European countries for which no breakdown is available.

Origin country unspecified: includes non-OECD countries which cannot be broken down into any specific large geographic (other European countries, Latin America, Asia-Oceania, Africa).

Conventional signs:

/ Break of series.

Sources

The principal national bodies for each OECD Member country dealing with tourism statistics are as follows:

Australia

    Bureau of Tourism Research

    Australian Bureau of Statistics

Austria

    Osterreichisches Statistisches Zentralamt

    Osterreichische Nationalbank

Belgium

    Institut National de Statistiques

    Banque nationale de Belgique

    Institut Belgo-Luxembourgeois du Change

Canada

    Statistics Canada, International Travel Section

    Industry, Science and Technology Canada, Tourism

Denmark

    Danmarks Statistik

    Danmarks National Bank

Finland

    Central Statistical Office

    Bank of Finland

France

    Ministère du Tourisme, Direction des Industries touristiques

    Banque de France

Germany

    Statistisches Bundesamt

    Deutsche Bundesbank

Greece

    National Statistical Service of the National Tourist Organisation of Greece

    Bank of Greece

Iceland

    Icelandic Immigration Authorities

    Iceland Tourist Board

    Central Bank of Iceland

Ireland

    Central Statistics Office

    Irish Tourist Board (Bord Failte)

Italy

    Ministero del Turismo e dello Spetacolo

    Instituto Centrale di Statistica

    Banca d'Italia

Japan

    Ministry of Transport, Department of Tourism

    Japan National Tourist Organisation

    Bank of Japan

Luxembourg

    Service Central de la Statistique et des Etudes Economiques (STATEC)

    Institut Belgo-Luxembourgeois du Change

Netherlands

    Ministry of the Economy

    Central Bureau of Statistics

    Dutch Central Bank

New Zealand

    New Zealand Tourism Department

Norway

    Central Bureau of Statistics

    Bank of Norway

Portugal

    Direcçao-Geral de Turisme

    Instituto Nacional de Estatistica

    Banco de Portugal

Spain

Instituto Nacional de Estadisticas

Banco de Espana

Sweden

Statistics Sweden

Central Bank of Sweden

Switzerland

Office Fédéral de la Statistique, Section du Tourisme

Turkey

Ministry of Tourism

Central Bank

United Kingdom

Department of Employment, Office of Population Censuses and Surveys

British Tourist Authority

United States

Department of Commerce, United States Travel and Tourism Administration (USTTA)

Department of Commerce, Bureau of Economic Analysis

Graph A. Classification of international visitors

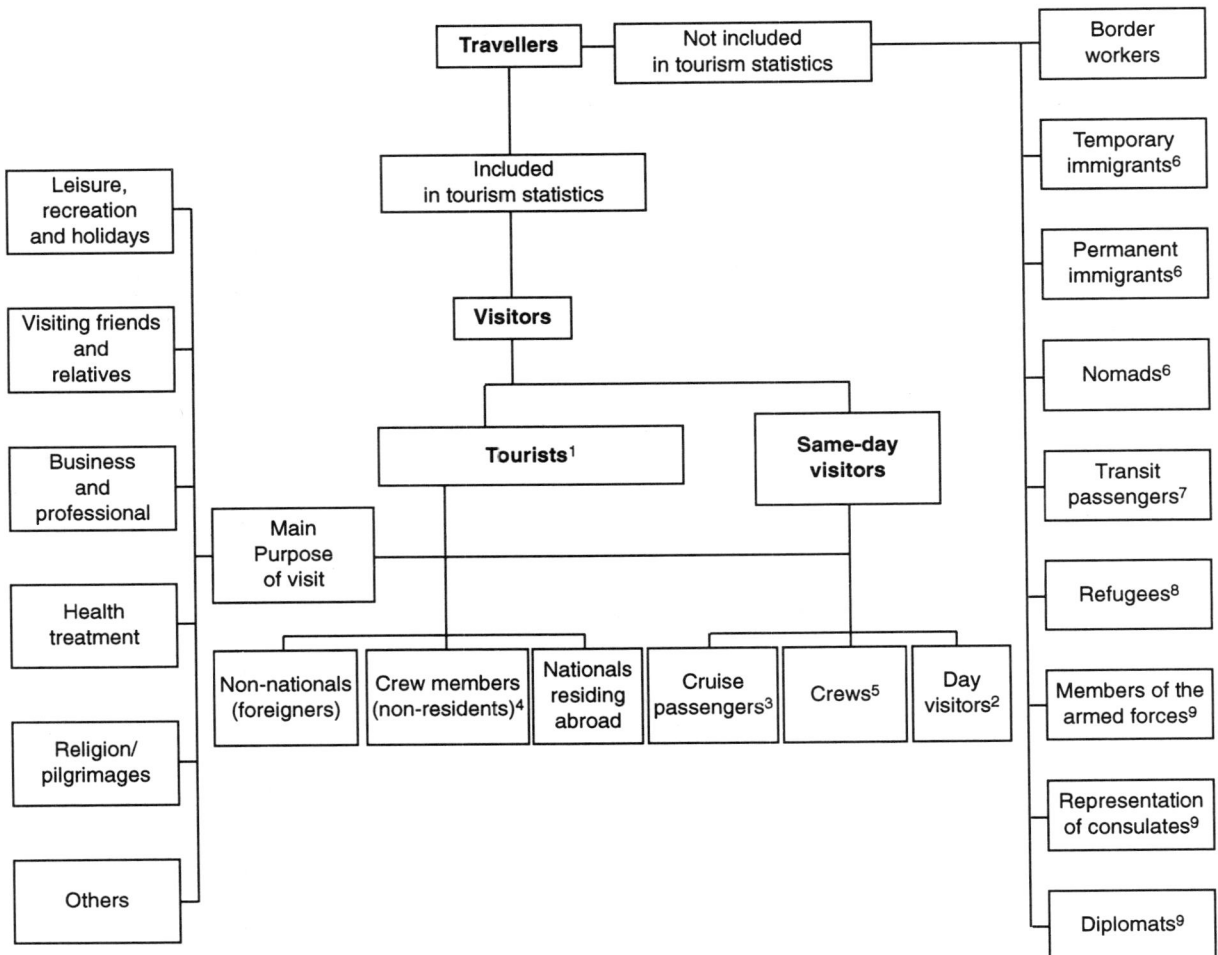

Travellers

Not included in tourism statistics
- Border workers
- Temporary immigrants[6]
- Permanent immigrants[6]
- Nomads[6]
- Transit passengers[7]
- Refugees[8]
- Members of the armed forces[9]
- Representation of consulates[9]
- Diplomats[9]

Included in tourism statistics

Visitors
- Tourists[1]
- Same-day visitors

Main Purpose of visit
- Non-nationals (foreigners)
- Crew members (non-residents)[4]
- Nationals residing abroad
- Cruise passengers[3]
- Crews[5]
- Day visitors[2]

- Leisure, recreation and holidays
- Visiting friends and relatives
- Business and professional
- Health treatment
- Religion/pilgrimages
- Others

1. Visitors who spend at least one night in the country visited, but less than one year.
2. Visitors who arrive and leave the same day for leisure, recreation and holidays; visiting friends and relatives; business and professional; health treatment; religion/pilgrimages and other tourism purposes, including transit day visitors en route to or from their destination countries.
3. Persons who arrive in a country aboard cruise ships [as defined by the international Maritime Organization (IMO), 1965] and who spend the night aboard ship even when disembarking for one or more day visits.
4. Foreign air or ship crews docked or in lay over and who use the accommodation establishments of the country visited.
5. Crews who are not residents of the country visited and who stay in the country for the day.
6. As defined by the United Nations in the Recommendations on Statistics of International.
7. Who do not leave the transit area of the airport or the port, including transfer between airports or ports.
8. As defined by the United Nations High Commissioner for Refugees, 1967.
9. When they travel from their country of origin to the duty station and vice-versa (including household servants and dependants accompanying or joining them).

Source: World Tourism Organisation (WTO).

B. Series available by country

Arrivals of foreign tourists at frontiers

Canada	Iceland	Portugal
France	New Zealand	United States
Greece	Japan	

Arrivals of foreign visitors at frontiers

Australia	Italy	Spain
Canada	Japan	Turkey (travellers)
Ireland	Portugal	United Kingdom

Arrivals of foreign tourists at hotels and similar establishments

Austria	Italy	Spain
France	Netherlands	Switzerland
Germany	Portugal	Turkey
Ireland		

Arrivals of foreign tourists at all means of accommodation

Austria	Italy	Switzerland
Germany	Netherlands	Turkey
Ireland	Portugal	

Nights spent by foreign tourists in hotels and similar establishments

Australia	Germany	Portugal
Austria	Ireland	Spain
Belgium	Italy	Sweden
Denmark	Netherlands	Switzerland
Finland	Norway	Turkey
France		

Nights spent by foreign tourists in all means of accommodation

Australia	Germany	Portugal
Austria	Ireland	Sweden
Belgium	Italy	Switzerland
Canada	Netherlands	Turkey
Denmark	New Zealand	United Kingdom
France		

C. Types of accommodation covered by the statistics

Countries	Hotels and similar establishments[11]					Supplementary means of accommodation[12]							
	Hotels[1]	Motels[2]	Boarding houses[3]	Inns[4]	Others[5]	Youth hostels[6]	Camping and caravan sites	Holiday villages	Mountain huts and shelters	Rented rooms, flats and houses[7]	Sanatoria, health establishments	Recreation homes for children[8]	Others[9]
Australia	X	X	X		X	X	X			X			X
Austria[10]	X					X	X	X	X	X	X	X	X
Belgium	X		X		X		X			X	X	X	X
Canada	X	X				X	X						X
Denmark[10]	X						X						
Finland	X		X										
France	X						X						
Germany	X	X	X	X	X	X	X	X		X	X		X
Greece	X	X	X	X	X		X						X
Ireland	X		X			X	X						
Italy	X		X		X	X	X			X			X
Netherlands	X				X	X	X						
Norway[10]	X					X	X					X	
Portugal	X	X	X	X	X		X					X	
Spain	X						X						X
Sweden	X	X	X	X		X	X	X					
Switzerland	X	X	X	X		X	X			X	X		X
Turkey	X	X	X	X	X		X	X					

Countries not listed in this table do not dispose of data by type of accommodation.

1. Includes: Germany: hotels serving breakfast only; Belgium: motels, boarding houses and inns; Finland: motels, boarding houses and inns; France: motels; Ireland: motels; Portugal: studio-hotels; Spain: "Paradores" and Casas de Huespedes"); Sweden: motels; Switzerland: boarding houses; Turkey: thermal hotels.
2. Includes: Greece: bungalows.
3. Includes: Portugal: bungalows.
4. Includes: Finland: inns; Ireland: inns; Sweden: resort hotels.
5. Includes: Portugal: private and state-owned inns.
6. Includes: Australia: hotels and motels without facilities in most rooms and not necessarily providing meals and alcoholic drinks; Belgium: non-licensed establishments; Finland: lodging houses and part of youth hostels; Greece: bungalow-hotels, studio-hotels and recreation homes for children; Netherlands: youth hostels in Amsterdam; Portugal: holiday flats and villages; Spain: fondas; Sweden: boarding houses, inns, and resort hotels; Turkey: special licensed hotels, studio-hotels and thermal hotels. Germany: mountain huts and shelters.
7. Includes: Australia: cabins and flats; Finland: holiday village cottages.
8. Includes: Portugal: youth hostels.
9. Includes: Australia: rented farms, house-boats, rented camper-vans, boats, cabin cruisers, camping outside commercial grounds; Austria: mountain huts and shelters; Belgium: youth hostels, holiday villages and social tourism establishments; Canada: homes of friends or relatives, private cottages, commercial cottages and others (universities, hostels); Germany: recreation and holiday homes, institutions providing educational services; Greece: holiday centres; Italy: recreation homes for children, mountain huts and shelters, holiday homes and religious establishments; Spain: secondary residences, private apartments, chalets and bungalows; Switzerland: dormitories in recreation homes for children, tourist camps, mountain huts and shelters, holiday villages.
10. Total available without breakdown for "hotels and similar establishments".
11. Includes: Denmark: hotels with more than 40 beds.
12. Includes: Denmark: hotels with more than 40 beds. Denmark: January and February (hotels only), March (hotels and campings January to march), October (hotels and campings October to December), November and December (hotels only).

1. Tourism from European Member countries[1]

	Arrivals at frontiers[2]			Arrivals at all means of accommodation[3]			Nights spent in all means of accommodation[4]		
	Volume 1992 (thousands)	% 92/91	% 91/90	Volume 1992 (thousands)	% 92/91	% 91/90	Volume 1992 (thousands)	% 92/91	% 91/90
Austria				16 778.5	− 1.2	6.0	93 784.6	− 0.3	8.4
Belgium							11 010.2	4.8	− 4.4
Denmark							10 730.5	11.9	14.6
Finland							1 539.4	1.4	− 1.6
France	51 816.0	6.8	8.6	51 816.0	6.8	8.6	351 758.0	6.0	12.3
Germany[5]				10 209.1	− 6.3	9.3	24 588.5	− 6.1	17.5
Greece	7 685.3	23.0	− 11.1						
Iceland	113.7	− 0.6	1.7						
Ireland	2 613.0	2.4	1.5	2 316.0	− 7.3	0.8	24 445.0	− 0.8	− 8.8
Italy	39 653.2	− 4.1	− 8.5	14 092.6	− 5.2	1.9	65 247.0	− 7.4	5.1
Luxembourg									
Netherlands				5 053.1	2.7	4.9	15 910.8	4.5	7.5
Norway							3 571.0	7.6	17.1
Portugal	8 292.4	2.6	9.6	3 820.5	− 10.1	12.1	18 520.9	− 9.0	16.4
Spain	46 589.3	− 5.5	4.4	10 154.8	2.8	4.8	70 036.3	3.4	5.6
Sweden							4 617.6	3.8	− 15.0
Switzerland				7 562.6	− 1.9	3.4	30 949.0	− 0.9	4.5
Turkey	3 007.3	63.7	− 36.4	2 663.8	75.4	− 50.0	14 301.2	85.9	− 33.0
United Kingdom	11 399.0	4.0	3.8				89 424.0	− 2.6	0.9
Canada	1 606.3	2.9	1.9				19 093.7	0.5	4.3
United States	8 064.2	12.8	10.7						
Australia	562.5	9.2	− 2.8				23 703.9	− 10.3	− 5.2
New Zealand	196.7	14.2	4.8				6 119.3	5.4	21.6
Japan	255.4	9.9	1.9						

1. Derived from tables by receiving country (see corresponding notes).
2. *Tourist* or *visitor arrivals*. When both available: *tourist arrivals*.
3. Arrivals *in all means of accommodation* or *in hotels and similar establishments*. When both available: arrivals *in all means of accommodation*.
4. Nights spent *in all means of accommodation* or *in hotels and similar establishments*. When both available: nights spent *in all means of accommodation*.
5. The data relate to the territory of the Federal Republic of Germany prior to 3rd October 1990.

2. Tourism from Canada and the United States[1]

	Arrivals at frontiers[2]			Arrivals at all means of accommodation[3]			Nights spent in all means of accommodation[4]		
	Volume 1992 (thousands)	% 92/91	% 91/90	Volume 1992 (thousands)	% 92/91	% 91/90	Volume 1992 (thousands)	% 92/91	% 91/90
Austria				710.3	30.0	− 44.8	1 734.3	25.0	− 41.9
Belgium							705.3	17.6	− 19.9
Denmark							324.2	4.2	− 26.2
Finland							172.2	1.9	− 26.3
France	2 589.0	21.2	− 16.4	2 589.0	21.2	− 16.4	22 905.0	21.1	− 17.0
Germany[5]				1 876.0	4.0	− 31.8	3 863.1	2.7	− 26.8
Greece	338.7	48.9	− 34.6						
Iceland	22.9	− 2.5	− 1.3						
Ireland	405.0	18.1	− 21.0	417.0	17.1	− 19.6	4 825.0	11.9	− 10.7
Italy	1 652.1	11.1	− 21.5	2 160.5	26.7	− 29.1	5 568.7	22.2	− 25.2
Luxembourg									
Netherlands				530.5	8.5	− 20.6	1 105.7	9.5	− 18.9
Norway							351.5	25.4	− 23.1
Portugal	222.9	8.0	− 22.8	265.5	2.9	− 29.3	774.9	− 1.6	− 26.7
Spain	971.8	23.0	− 20.5	730.0	15.8	− 26.4	1 641.9	15.9	− 26.2
Sweden							299.9	10.8	− 27.1
Switzerland				1 060.1	20.4	− 38.1	2 332.7	15.1	− 34.2
Turkey	208.8	115.4	− 59.7	174.7	73.3	− 42.2	423.7	37.7	− 20.4
United Kingdom	3 303.0	15.2	− 22.2				33 833.0	3.9	− 13.0
Canada	11 818.7	− 1.5	− 2.0				46 289.4	− 6.2	0.2
United States	18 578.5	− 2.8	10.7						
Australia	311.8	− 4.1	6.8				7 920.4	− 11.3	5.6
New Zealand	157.2	− 3.5	− 6.2				2 593.7	0.9	− 11.3
Japan	341.7	4.4	− 3.9						

1. Derived from tables by receiving country (see corresponding notes).
2. *Tourist* or *visitor arrivals*. When both available: *tourist arrivals*.
3. Arrivals *in all means of accommodation* or *in hotels and similar establishments*. When both available: arrivals *in all means of accommodation*.
4. Nights spent *in all means of accommodation* or *in hotels and similar establishments*. When both available: nights spent *in all means of accommodation*.
5. The data relate to the territory of the Federal Republic of Germany prior to 3rd October 1990.

3. Tourism from Australia, New Zealand and Japan[1]

	Arrivals at frontiers[2]			Arrivals at all means of accommodation[3]			Nights spent in all means of accommodation[4]		
	Volume 1992 (thousands)	% 92/91	% 91/90	Volume 1992 (thousands)	% 92/91	% 91/90	Volume 1992 (thousands)	% 92/91	% 91/90
Austria				299.2	8.1	− 21.0	647.2	5.0	− 15.7
Belgium							233.4	47.7	− 2.6
Denmark							110.9	18.7	− 13.5
Finland							57.2	− 0.2	− 10.1
France	435.0	3.1	− 43.7	435.0	3.1	− 43.7	1 959.0	− 0.9	− 29.4
Germany[5]				890.2	7.8	− 17.9	1 521.2	3.8	− 13.5
Greece	187.4	40.9	− 40.1						
Iceland	2.0	9.8	0.8						
Ireland	53.0	6.0	− 24.2	71.0	31.5	− 21.7	566.0	− 35.2	33.7
Italy	957.6	26.1	− 17.2	1 201.2	29.9	− 14.8	2 565.2	27.8	− 13.7
Luxembourg									
Netherlands				197.2	22.1	− 14.8	405.3	21.3	− 11.0
Norway							99.8	17.5	0.6
Portugal	45.5	− 0.9	− 15.2	55.2	2.1	− 10.3	123.8	− 4.9	− 4.1
Spain	296.1	16.7	− 19.4	340.6	− 0.3	− 31.4	702.4	13.9	− 29.7
Sweden							85.9	− 4.4	− 7.5
Switzerland				633.3	14.9	− 17.9	1 087.3	6.8	− 13.8
Turkey	74.6	61.8	− 45.9	136.3	126.6	− 37.6	245.6	119.0	− 34.5
United Kingdom	1 137.0	9.9	− 21.0				17 799.0	− 10.4	− 6.3
Canada	523.9	0.6	− 6.7				3 978.1	− 0.7	− 0.6
United States	4 279.2	8.7	1.7						
Australia	1 077.4	6.8	12.3				12 431.6	− 6.0	− 8.2
New Zealand	499.1	8.4	− 0.8				7 006.2	3.7	0.1
Japan	39.3	15.8	− 2.4						

1. Derived from tables by receiving country (see corresponding notes).
2. *Tourist* or *visitor arrivals*. When both available: *tourist arrivals*.
3. Arrivals *in all means of accommodation* or *in hotels and similar establishments*. When both available: arrivals *in all means of accommodation*.
4. Nights spent *in all means of accommodation* or *in hotels and similar establishments*. When both available: nights spent *in all means of accommodation*.
5. The data relate to the territory of the Federal Republic of Germany prior to 3rd October 1990.

4. Tourism from all OECD countries[1]

	Arrivals at frontiers[2]			Arrivals at all means of accommodation[3]			Nights spent in all means of accommodation[4]		
	Volume 1992 (thousands)	% 92/91	% 91/90	Volume 1992 (thousands)	% 92/91	% 91/90	Volume 1992 (thousands)	% 92/91	% 91/90
Austria				17 788.0	− 0.1	2.6	96 166.1	0.1	6.9
Belgium							11 948.9	6.1	− 5.3
Denmark							11 165.6	11.7	12.4
Finland							1 768.7	1.4	− 5.0
France	54 840.0	7.4	6.5	54 840.0	7.4	6.5	376 622.0	6.8	9.9
Germany[5]				12 975.3	− 4.1	− 0.7	29 972.7	− 4.6	7.8
Greece	8 211.4	24.3	− 13.1						
Iceland	138.6	− 0.7	1.1						
Ireland	3 071.0	4.2	− 2.3	2 804.0	− 3.6	− 2.8	29 836.0	0.1	− 8.2
Italy	42 262.9	− 3.1	− 9.2	17 454.4	− 0.2	− 3.2	73 380.9	− 4.7	2.1
Luxembourg									
Netherlands				5 780.8	3.7	1.4	17 421.8	5.1	4.9
Norway							4 022.4	9.2	12.2
Portugal	8 560.7	2.7	8.3	4 141.1	− 9.2	8.2	19 419.6	− 8.7	13.8
Spain	47 857.2	− 5.0	3.7	11 225.4	3.5	0.7	72 380.5	3.7	4.2
Sweden							5 003.4	4.1	− 15.7
Switzerland				9 256.0	1.3	− 4.3	34 369.0	0.3	0.4
Turkey	3 290.7	66.2	− 38.4	2 974.8	77.1	− 49.2	14 970.5	84.5	− 32.6
United Kingdom	15 839.0	6.5	− 4.4				141 056.0	− 2.2	− 3.6
Canada	13 948.9	− 1.0	− 1.8				69 361.2	− 4.2	1.2
United States	30 921.9	2.4	9.5						
Australia	1 951.7	5.5	6.8				44 055.9	− 9.3	− 4.2
New Zealand	853.0	7.2	− 0.8				15 719.2	3.9	4.9
Japan	636.5	7.2	− 1.6						

1. Derived from tables by receiving country (see corresponding notes).
2. *Tourist* or *visitor arrivals*. When both available: *tourist arrivals*.
3. Arrivals *in all means of accommodation* or *in hotels and similar establishments*. When both available: arrivals *in all means of accommodation*.
4. Nights spent *in all means of accommodation* or *in hotels and similar establishments*. When both available: nights spent *in all means of accommodation*.
5. The data relate to the territory of the Federal Republic of Germany prior to 3rd October 1990.

5. Tourism from non-Member countries[1]

	Arrivals at frontiers[2]			Arrivals at all means of accommodation[3]			Nights spent in all means of accommodation[4]		
	Volume 1992 (thousands)	% 92/91	% 91/90	Volume 1992 (thousands)	% 92/91	% 91/90	Volume 1992 (thousands)	% 92/91	% 91/90
Austria				1 309.7	2.4	− 22.5	3 587.4	− 0.8	− 26.7
Belgium							931.1	2.3	− 8.3
Denmark							422.5	− 3.6	− 1.4
Finland							474.0	3.9	− 27.8
France	4 750.0	20.1	− 24.3	4 749.0	20.0	− 24.3	51 759.0	19.7	− 34.6
Germany[5]				2 171.8	2.3	5.5	6 113.8	1.8	5.3
Greece	1 119.9	− 21.7	12.2				36 251.3	21.4	− 14.7
Iceland	4.0	3.7	4.3						
Ireland	53.0	1.9	0.0	312.0	194.3	1.9	3 941.0	13.6	186.7
Italy	7 825.8	1.5	− 37.1	2 970.6	8.2	− 1.2	10 261.7	5.5	4.6
Luxembourg									
Netherlands				302.1	12.2	− 9.8	677.2	7.0	− 5.0
Norway							252.8	8.6	− 8.4
Portugal	323.4	− 0.4	− 0.9	203.4	− 2.6	− 4.8	644.9	− 6.3	4.1
Spain	7 473.5	138.7	− 10.3	1 261.5	4.9	− 2.8	4 553.8	− 2.2	− 2.4
Sweden							811.1	2.4	− 9.4
Switzerland				1 009.5	3.9	0.2	2 626.7	− 4.9	0.9
Turkey	3 785.4	7.0	62.5	745.8	3.8	28.0	1 815.0	14.4	29.3
United Kingdom	2 340.0	3.6	− 8.2				41 357.0	− 1.8	− 9.4
Canada	791.9	− 4.4	− 4.6				10 062.3	− 3.3	− 2.6
United States	13 705.6	7.6	6.3						
Australia	646.4	24.1	8.0				17 388.1	8.2	9.9
New Zealand	202.7	20.7	− 3.5				4 789.1	15.2	− 33.3
Japan	1 466.6	− 2.9	18.4						

1. Derived from tables by receiving country (see corresponding notes).
2. *Tourist* or *visitor arrivals*. When both available: *tourist arrivals*.
3. Arrivals *in all means of accommodation* or *in hotels and similar establishments*. When both available: arrivals *in all means of accommodation*.
4. Nights spent *in all means of accommodation* or *in hotels and similar establishments*. When both available: nights spent *in all means of accommodation*.
5. The data relate to the territory of the Federal Republic of Germany prior to 3rd October 1990.

6. Tourism from all countries[1]

	Arrivals at frontiers[2]			Arrivals at all means of accommodation[3]			Nights spent in all means of accommodation[4]		
	Volume 1992 (thousands)	% 92/91	% 91/90	Volume 1992 (thousands)	% 92/91	% 91/90	Volume 1992 (thousands)	% 92/91	% 91/90
Austria[5]				19 097.6	0.0	0.4	99 753.5	0.1	5.1
Belgium							12 880.0	5.8	− 5.6
Denmark							11 588.1	11.1	11.7
Finland							2 242.7	1.9	−10.8
France	59 590.0	8.3	3.5	59 589.0	8.3	3.5	428 381.0	8.2	2.3
Germany[7]				15 147.1	− 3.2	0.1	36 086.5	− 3.6	7.4
Greece	9 331.4	16.1	− 9.4				36 251.3	21.4	−14.7
Iceland	142.6	− 0.6	1.2						
Ireland	3 124.0	4.2	− 2.3	3 116.0	3.3	− 2.6	33 777.0	1.5	− 1.2
Italy	50 088.7	− 2.4	−14.9	20 425.0	0.9	− 2.9	83 642.6	− 3.6	2.4
Luxembourg									
Netherlands				6 082.9	4.1	0.8	18 099.0	5.2	4.5
Norway							4 275.2	9.2	10.7
Portugal	8 884.1	2.6	7.9	4 344.5	− 8.9	7.5	20 064.5	− 8.6	13.5
Spain	55 330.7	3.4	2.8	12 486.9	3.6	0.3	76 934.3	3.4	3.8
Sweden							5 814.5	3.8	−14.8
Switzerland[6]				10 265.4	1.5	− 3.9	36 995.7	− 0.1	0.4
Turkey[5]	7 076.1	28.2	2.4	3 720.6	55.1	−38.0	16 785.5	73.1	−26.9
United Kingdom	18 179.0	6.2	− 4.9				182 413.0	− 2.1	− 5.0
Canada	14 740.8	− 1.1	− 2.0				79 423.5	− 4.0	0.7
United States	44 627.5	3.9	8.5						
Australia	2 598.1	9.6	7.0				61 444.0	− 5.0	− 1.1
New Zealand	1 055.7	9.6	− 1.3				20 508.3	6.3	− 6.6
Japan	2 103.0	0.0	11.9						

1. Derived from tables by receiving country. See corresponding notes, except for the countries mentioned in notes 5 and 6 below.
2. *Tourist* or *visitor arrivals*. When both available: *tourist arrivals*.
3. Arrivals *in all means of accommodation* or *in hotels and similar establishments*. When both available: arrivals *in all means of accommodation*.
4. Nights spent *in all means of accommodation* or *in hotels and similar establishments*. When both available: nights spent *in all means of accommodation*.
5. *Traveller* arrivals at frontiers.
6. *Tourist* arrivals at frontiers: estimates.
7. The data relate to the territory of the Federal Republic of Germany prior to 3rd October 1990.

7. TOURISM FROM THE UNITED STATES
EXPENDITURE OF US RESIDENTS TRAVELLING ABROAD

In millions of dollars

	1988	1989	1990	1991	1992
Expenditure abroad[1]	32 114	33 418	37 349	35 322	39 872
Canada[2]	3 232	3 396	3 541	3 705	3 507
Mexico	3 622	4 276	4 879	5 111	5 229
Total overseas	25 260	25 746	28 929	26 506	31 136
Western Europe	11 086	11 668	13 615	11 073	13 221
United Kingdom	3 325	3 319	3 657	3 168	3 876
Germany	2 423	2 664	2 671	2 191	2 607
France	1 233	1 553	1 788	1 533	1 858
Italy	1 682	1 425	1 631	1 459	1 646
Eastern Europe	261	299	381	451	468
Caribbean, South and Central America	5 172	5 123	5 395	3 072	3 553
Japan	1 803	1 872	2 210	2 760	3 160
Australia, New Zealand and South Africa	1 019	1 049	1 249	1 124	1 186
Australia	694	726	867	783	816
Other	5 919	5 735	6 079	4 966	5 656
Fare payments					
Foreign-flag carriers	7 729	8 248	10 530	10 012	10 943

1.   Exclude travel by military personnel and other Government employees stationed abroad, their dependents and United States citizens residing abroad; includes shore expenditure of United States cruise travellers.
2.   Excluding fare payments and crew spending.
Source: US Department of Commerce, US Travel and tourism Administration and Bureau of Economic Analysis.

8. TOURISM FROM THE UNITED STATES
NUMBER AND EXPENDITURE OF US RESIDENTS TRAVELLING OVERSEAS

	Number of travellers			Total expenditure			Average expenditure		
	In thousands			Millions of dollars[1]			per traveller		
	1990[2]	1991	1992	1990[2]	1991	1992	1990[2]	1991	1992
Total overseas	15 990	14 521	15 945	28 929	26 506	31 136	1 809	1 925	1 950
Europe	8 043	6 316	7 136	13 996	11 524	13 689	1 740	1 825	1 918
Caribbean, South and Central America	4 749	5 155	5 285	5 395	3 072	3 553	1 136	596	672
Japan	1 103	897	1 017	2 210	2 760	3 160	2 004	3 078	3 107
Australia, New Zealand and South Africa	721	684	639	1 249	1 124	1 186	1 732	1 643	1 856
Other	1 374	1 469	1 888	6 079	4 966	5 656	4 424	3 381	2 996

n.d.: Non available
1.   Excludes travel by military personnel and other Government employees stationed abroad, their dependents and United States citizens residing abroad and cruise travellers.
2.   Includes shore expenditure of cruise travellers; excludes fares.
Source: US Department of Commerce, Bureau of Economic Analysis, based on data of the US Department of Justice, Immigration and Naturalization Service.

9. Average length of stay of foreign tourists

	Tourists from all foreign countries			Tourists from Europe (OECD)			Tourists from North America (OECD)			Tourists from Pacific (OECD)		
	1990	1991	1992	1990	1991	1992	1990	1991	1992	1990	1991	1992
	Average length of stay in tourist accommodation[1]											
Austria	5.0	5.2	5.2	5.4	5.5	5.6	2.4	2.5	2.4	2.1	2.2	2.2
Germany[3]	2.2	2.4	2.4	2.2	2.4	2.4	1.9	2.1	2.1	1.7	1.8	1.7
Italy	4.1	4.3	4.1	4.6	4.7	4.6	2.5	2.7	2.6	2.1	2.2	2.1
Netherlands	2.8	2.9	3.0	3.0	3.1	3.1	2.0	2.1	2.1	2.0	2.1	2.1
Portugal	4.4	4.6	4.6	4.6	4.8	4.8	2.9	3.1	2.9	2.3	2.4	2.2
Spain[2]	6.0	6.2	6.2	6.8	6.9	6.9	2.2	2.2	2.2	1.8	1.8	2.1
Switzerland	3.5	3.7	3.6	4.0	4.1	4.1	2.2	2.3	2.2	1.8	1.8	1.7
Turkey	3.4	4.0	4.5	3.8	5.1	5.4	2.2	3.1	2.4	1.8	1.9	1.8
Canada												

1. Unless otherwise stated below, the average length of stay in all means of accommodation is obtained by dividing the number of nights recorded in particular means of accommodation by the number of arrivals of tourists at the same means of accommodation (see country tables).
2. Hôtellerie.
3. The data relate to the territory of the Federal Republic of Germany prior to 3rd October 1990.

	Tourists from all foreign countries			Tourists from Europe (OECD)			Tourists from North America (OECD)			Tourists from Pacific (OECD)		
	1990	1991	1992	1990	1991	1992	1990	1991	1992	1990	1991	1992
	Average length of stay in the country visited[1]											
France												
Greece[2]												
Ireland[3]	9.2	9.9	9.5	9.3	9.9	9.5	10.5	11.4	10.7	14.4	16.3	13.5
Portugal[2]	7.4	7.6	7.3	7.4	7.6	7.3	11.3			8.0		
Turkey	8.3	6.9	8.4	10.7	11.8	12.3	8.0	12.9	13.4	9.8	12.3	18.2
United Kingdom	11.0	11.0	10.0				10.0	11.0	10.0	16.0	19.0	16.0
Canada	11.1	11.5	11.3	11.9	12.2	11.9	4.0	4.1	3.9	7.2	7.7	7.6
Australia	32.0	29.0	26.0	50.0	55.0	44.0	29.0	29.0	27.0	18.0	14.0	12.0
Japan	13.2	12.3	11.2									
New Zealand[2]	21.0	20.0	19.0				17.0	16.0	17.0	15.0	14.0	

1. Unless otherwise stated below, the average length of stay in the country visited is expressed in number of nights spent.
2. Greece, New Zealand and Portugal: number of days.
3. Ireland: visitors on overseas routes.

10. Nights spent by foreign and domestic tourists in all means of accommodation[1]

In thousands

	Nights spent by foreign tourists			Nights spent by domestic tourists			Total nights			Proportion spent by foreign tourists (%)	
	1991	1992	% 92/91	1991	1992	% 92/91	1991	1992	% 92/91	1991	1992
Austria	99 641.5	99 757.6	0.1	30 431.3	30 658.7	0.7	130 072.8	130 416.3	0.3	76.6	76.5
Belgium	12 170.1	7 694.1	−36.8	21 735.3	2 817.6	−87.0	33 905.4	10 511.6	−69.0	35.9	73.2
Denmark	10 430.3			13 436.5	14 054.9	4.6	23 866.8			43.7	
Finland	2 549.3	2 587.0	1.5	9 767.2	9 286.0	−4.9	12 316.5	11 873.0	−3.6	20.7	21.8
France	85 295.0	91 864.0	7.7	152 513.0	155 772.9	2.1	237 808.0	247 636.9	4.1	35.9	37.1
Germany[3]	37 426.4	36 086.5	−3.6	248 014.5	250 198.8	0.9	285 440.9	286 285.4	0.3	13.1	12.6
Greece	30 521.2	36 907.3	20.9	12 064.5	12 421.0	3.0	42 585.7	49 328.3	15.8	71.7	74.8
Italy	86 734.9			173 188.9			259 923.8			33.4	
Netherlands	17 205.9	18 023.4	4.8	39 140.4	40 554.3	3.6	56 346.3	58 577.7	4.0	30.5	30.8
Norway	6 304.8	7 062.6	12.0	11 921.8	11 909.8	−0.1	18 226.7	18 972.5	4.1	34.6	37.2
Portugal	21 957.3	20 064.5	−8.6	13 404.1	13 659.6	1.9	35 361.4	33 724.1	−4.6	62.1	59.5
Sweden	5 600.4	5 814.5	3.8	23 237.3	23 742.1	2.2	28 837.7	29 556.6	2.5	19.4	19.7
Switzerland	37 038.3	36 995.7	−0.1	39 817.6	39 203.5	−1.5	76 855.9	76 199.1	−0.9	48.2	48.6
Turkey[2]	9 699.1	16 785.5	73.1	8 011.4	9 170.5	14.5	17 710.5	25 956.0	46.6	54.8	64.7
Australia	64 644.8	61 448.0	−4.9	219 951.0	207 510.0	−5.7	284 595.8	268 958.0	−5.5	22.7	22.8

1. For the "Types of accommodation covered by the statistics" see Table C.
2. Turkey: figures based on a monthly sample survey carried out among establishments licenced by the Ministry of Tourism.
3. The data relate to the territory of the Federal Republic of Germany prior to 3rd October 1990; from the unification, tourists from the former German Democratic Republic are regarded as domestic tourists.

11. Nights spent by foreign and domestic tourists in hotels and similar establishments[1]

In thousands

	Nights spent by foreign tourists			Nights spent by domestic tourists			Total nights			Proportion spent by foreign tourists (%)	
	1991	1992	% 92/91	1991	1992	% 92/91	1991	1992	% 92/91	1991	1992
Austria	64 062.1	64 189.0	0.2	16 194.6	16 162.3	−0.2	80 256.7	80 351.3	0.1	79.8	79.9
Belgium	6 630.7	7 694.1	16.0	2 665.4	2 817.6	5.7	9 296.1	10 511.6	13.1	71.3	73.2
Denmark	5 962.9			5 267.9	5 378.2	2.1	11 230.8			53.1	
Finland	2 200.9	2 242.7	1.9	7 798.8	7 539.4	−3.3	9 999.7	9 782.1	−2.2	22.0	22.9
France[2]	53 044.9	59 635.5	12.4	88 012.7	91 603.8	4.1	141 057.6	151 239.3	7.2	37.6	39.4
Germany[4]	27 768.2	26 898.6	−3.1	132 688.9	130 787.3	−1.4	160 457.1	157 685.8	−1.7	17.3	17.1
Greece	29 873.0	36 260.3	21.4	11 594.5	11 943.1	3.0	41 467.5	48 203.4	16.2	72.0	75.2
Italy	65 842.8			129 864.1			195 706.9			33.6	
Netherlands	7 993.4	8 423.7	5.4	6 758.7	6 787.2	0.4	14 752.1	15 210.9	3.1	54.2	55.4
Norway	3 916.8	4 275.2	9.2	8 908.3	9 022.5	1.3	12 825.0	13 297.6	3.7	30.5	32.1
Portugal	19 088.9	17 877.0	−6.3	7 172.1	7 437.0	3.7	26 261.0	25 314.0	−3.6	72.7	70.6
Spain	73 978.4	76 934.3	4.0	59 628.7	54 469.1	−8.7	133 607.1	131 403.4	−1.6	55.4	58.5
Sweden	2 826.2	2 803.7	−0.8	11 668.1	11 344.6	−2.8	14 494.2	14 148.3	−2.4	19.5	19.8
Switzerland	20 365.5	20 235.9	−0.6	13 871.6	13 204.3	−4.8	34 237.1	33 440.3	−2.3	59.5	60.5
Turkey[3]	8 131.1	13 560.2	66.8	7 309.1	8 542.6	16.9	15 440.2	22 102.8	43.2	52.7	61.4
Australia	12 209.1	12 967.0	6.2	43 127.0	44 299.0	2.7	55 336.1	57 266.0	3.5	22.1	22.6

1. For the "Types of accommodation covered by the statistics" see Table C.
2. France: data covering all France except 2 regions (Pays de la Loire and Champagne-Ardennes in 1991; Champagne-Ardennes and Corse in 1992).
3. Turkey: does not include thermal hotels.
4. The data relate to the territory of the Federal Republic of Germany prior to 3rd October 1990; from the unification, tourists from the former German Democratic Republic are regarded as domestic tourists.

12. Nights spent by foreign and domestic tourists in supplementary means of accommodation[1]

In thousands

	Nights spent by foreign tourists			Nights spent by domestic tourists			Total nights			Proportion spent by foreign tourists (%)	
	1991	1992	% 92/91	1991	1992	% 92/91	1991	1992	% 92/91	1991	1992
Austria	35 579.4	35 568.6	0.0	14 236.7	14 496.4	1.8	49 816.1	50 065.0	0.5	71.4	71.0
Belgium	5 539.4			19 069.8			24 609.2			22.5	
Denmark	4 467.4			8 168.6	8 676.7	6.2	12 636.0			35.4	
Finland	348.4	344.3	−1.2	1 968.3	1 746.7	−11.3	2 316.8	2 091.0	−9.7	15.0	16.5
France[3]	32 250.1	32 228.5	−0.1	64 500.3	64 169.1	−0.5	96 750.4	96 397.6	−0.4	33.3	33.4
Germany[2]	9 658.2	9 188.0	−4.9	115 325.6	119 411.6	3.5	124 983.8	128 599.6	2.9	7.7	7.1
Greece	648.2	647.0	−0.2	470.1	477.9	1.7	1 118.2	1 124.9	0.6	58.0	57.5
Italy	20 892.1			43 324.8			64 216.9			32.5	
Netherlands	9 212.5	9 599.7	4.2	32 381.7	33 767.1	4.3	41 594.2	43 366.8	4.3	22.1	22.1
Norway	2 388.1	2 787.5	16.7	3 013.6	2 887.3	−4.2	5 401.6	5 674.8	5.1	44.2	49.1
Portugal	2 868.4	2 187.4	−23.7	6 232.0	6 222.6	−0.2	9 100.4	8 410.0	−7.6	31.5	26.0
Sweden	2 774.2	3 010.8	8.5	11 569.3	12 397.5	7.2	14 343.5	15 408.3	7.4	19.3	19.5
Switzerland	16 672.9	16 759.7	0.5	25 990.4	25 999.1	0.0	42 663.2	42 758.9	0.2	39.1	39.2
Turkey	1 568.0	3 225.3	105.7	702.3	627.9	−10.6	2 270.3	3 853.2	69.7	69.1	83.7
Australia	52 435.7	48 481.0	−7.5	176 824.0	163 211.0	−7.7	229 259.7	211 692.0	−7.7	22.9	22.9
Of which: **on camping sites**											
Austria	5 478.8	5 456.9	−0.4	1 385.1	1 432.8	3.4	6 863.9	6 889.7	0.4	79.8	79.2
Belgium	2 343.3	2 079.0	−11.3	8 728.1	4 982.4	−42.9	11 071.5	7 061.4	−36.2	21.2	29.4
Denmark	3 945.3			7 650.4	8 155.6	6.6	11 595.7			34.0	
Finland	348.4	344.3	−1.2	1 968.3	1 746.7	−11.3	2 316.8	2 091.0	−9.7	15.0	16.5
France[3]	32 250.1	32 228.5	−0.1	64 500.3	64 169.1	−0.5	96 750.4	96 397.6	−0.4	33.3	33.4
Germany[2]	4 180.3	4 133.2	−1.1	15 051.8	15 362.5	2.1	19 232.1	19 495.7	1.4	21.7	21.2
Greece	648.2	647.0	−0.2	470.1	477.9	1.7	1 118.2	1 124.9	0.6	58.0	57.5
Italy	15 552.9			29 254.9			44 807.8			34.7	
Netherlands	3 819.6	4 085.2	7.0	14 256.1	15 857.5	11.2	18 075.7	19 942.7	10.3	21.1	20.5
Norway	2 189.3	2 211.8	1.0	2 880.4	2 610.6	−9.4	5 069.7	4 822.4	−4.9	43.2	45.9
Portugal	2 784.2	2 123.1	−23.7	5 207.4	5 204.0	−0.1	7 991.7	7 327.1	−8.3	34.8	29.0
Sweden	2 066.2	2 323.8	12.5	8 332.3	9 150.0	9.8	10 398.6	11 473.8	10.3	19.9	20.3
Switzerland	2 702.5	2 707.7	0.2	5 579.0	5 603.7	0.4	8 281.5	8 311.4	0.4	32.6	32.6
Turkey	57.0	140.4	146.5	25.4	19.9	−21.3	82.3	160.4	94.8	69.2	87.6
Australia	2 440.6	1 954.0	−19.9	22 252.0	17 310.0	−22.2	24 692.6	19 264.0	−22.0	9.9	10.1
Of which: **in youth hostels**											
Austria	817.6	866.8	6.0	575.7	639.5	11.1	1 393.2	1 506.3	8.1	58.7	57.5
Denmark	522.1			518.2	521.1	0.6	1 040.3			50.2	
Germany[2]	1 139.8	1 060.7	−6.9	10 039.1	10 163.5	1.2	11 178.9	11 224.2	0.4	10.2	9.4
Italy	593.7			228.1			821.8			72.2	
Netherlands	761.7	755.5	−0.8	321.8	320.2	−0.5	1 083.5	1 075.7	−0.7	70.3	70.2
Norway	198.8	207.0	4.1	133.2	129.3	−2.9	331.9	336.3	1.3	59.9	61.6
Sweden	217.4	207.0	−4.7	790.4	761.0	−3.7	1 007.7	968.1	−3.9	21.6	21.4
Switzerland	553.6	543.0	−1.9	379.0	365.3	−3.6	932.6	908.3	−2.6	59.4	59.8
Australia	5 440.4	5 402.0	−0.7	2 530.0	1 641.0	−35.1	7 970.4	7 043.0	−11.6	68.3	76.7
Of which: **in private rooms, rented apartments and houses**											
Austria	16 237.7	15 574.3	−4.1	4 244.3	4 214.3	−0.7	20 482.0	19 788.6	−3.4	79.3	78.7
Belgium	482.5			5 281.0			5 763.4			8.4	
Germany[2]	1 777.2	1 561.3	−12.1	23 684.5	25 160.7	6.2	25 461.7	26 722.1	5.0	7.0	5.8
Italy	3 405.5			6 383.2			9 788.7			34.8	
Switzerland	11 000.0	11 055.0	0.5	13 500.0	13 500.0	0.0	24 500.0	24 555.0	0.2	44.9	45.0
Australia	9 009.9	8 083.0	−10.3	14 671.0	13 998.0	−4.6	23 680.9	22 081.0	−6.8	38.0	36.6

1. For the "Types of accommodatiom covered by the statistics" see Table C.
2. The data relate to the territory of the Federal Republic of Germany prior to 3rd October 1990; from the unification, tourists from the former German Democratic Republic are regarded as domestic tourists.
3. France: data covering all France except 3 regions (Basse Normandie, Corse and Ile de France).

13. Capacity in hotels and similar establishments[1]

In thousands

	Hotels			Motels			Boarding houses			Inns			Others			Total		
	1991	1992	% 92/91	1991	1992	% 92/91	1991	1992	% 92/91	1991	1992	% 92/91	1991	1992	% 92/91	1991	1992	% 92/91
Austria[2]																654.1	653.6	-0.1
Belgium	91.7	101.8	11.0													91.7	101.8	11.0
Denmark[3]																92.5	96.0	3.8
Finland[4]	85.5	94.7	10.8				15.4	12.4	-19.9							100.9	107.0	6.1
France[5]	1 094.6	1 198.3	9.5													1 094.6	1 198.3	9.5
Germany[6]	588.0	609.4	3.6				132.9	131.8	-0.9	239.5	240.2	0.3	239.4	240.9	0.6	1 199.7	1 222.3	1.9
Greece	379.7	389.5	2.6	3.2	3.2	-0.1	22.7	25.1	10.6	14.9	15.7	5.4	38.8	42.3	9.1	459.3	475.8	3.6
Netherlands																112.6	115.8	2.9
Norway[7]													116.9	120.5	3.0	116.9	120.5	3.0
Portugal[8]	94.3	100.8	6.9	1.5	1.4	-5.0	46.3	44.8	-3.2	3.9	4.0	2.7	42.5	39.8	-6.2	188.5	190.9	1.3
Spain[9]	781.6	818.0	4.7	191.2	185.2	-3.1	75.8						97.9			1 146.5	1 180.2	2.9
Sweden[13]	116.4	116.3	-0.1				49.7	49.8	0.4							166.1	166.2	0.1
Switzerland[10]	234.6	234.9	0.1	5.3	5.1	-2.1				27.2	26.1	-4.1				267.1	266.2	-0.3
Turkey[11]	147.6	164.2	11.2	3.6	3.4	-5.4	5.9	5.9	-0.6	1.7	1.2	-28.9	4.9	5.6	13.6	163.7	180.2	10.1
Australia[12]	163.8	169.7	3.6	300.8	306.4	1.9										464.6	476.1	2.5
Japan	119.9	124.2	3.6							97.1	99.0	2.0						
New Zealand																		

Notice : this table contains data on available bed capacity unless otherwise stated in the following notes by country.

1. For the ''Types of accommodation covered by the statistics'' see Table C.
2. Austria : position at 31st August.
3. Denmark : position at 31st July.
4. Finland : position at 31st December.
5. France : position at 1st January.
6. Germany : position at April; the data relate to the territory of the Federal Republic of Germany prior to 3rd October 1990.
7. Norway : position at 31st December.
8. Portugal : position at 31st July.
9. Spain : position at 31st December.
10. Switzerland : position at 31st December.
11. Turkey : position at 31st December of accommodation establishments approved by Ministry of Culture and Tourism.
12. Australia : position at 31st December.
13. Sweden : position at December.

14. Capacity in supplementary means of accommodation[1]

In thousands

	Youth hostels			Camping sites Places			Holiday villages			Rented rooms, houses and flats			Sanatoria and health establishments			Recreational camps			Others			Total		
	1991	1992	% 92/91	1991	1992	% 92/91	1991	1992	% 92/91	1991	1992	% 92/91	1991	1992	% 92/91	1991	1992	% 92/91	1991	1992	% 92/91	1991	1992	% 92/91
Austria	12.5	12.7	1.4				128.7	139.2	8.1	281.9	274.1	-2.8	15.6	15.7	0.4	28.4	26.6	-6.4	33.7	32.0	-5.0	500.9	500.3	-0.1
Belgium				347.5	360.1	3.6							4.8	1.5	-68.4	21.1	31.9	50.9	70.8	103.3	45.9	444.2	496.9	11.9
Denmark	10.4	10.5	0.5																			10.4	10.5	0.5
France	17.6			2 661.4	2 662.2	0.0	286.6												206.0	206.0	0.0	3 171.6	2 868.2	-9.6
Germany[4]	92.0	92.7	0.7				25.3	25.6	1.1	217.7	223.3	2.6	132.0	135.5	2.7				160.4	163.1	1.7	627.2	640.1	2.1
Greece																								
Italy	6.8	8.2	20.7	1 228.1	1 297.0	5.6				163.1	153.3	-6.1							159.3	159.7	0.2	1 557.4	1 548.1	-0.6
Norway	6.5																					6.5		
Portugal				265.6	267.4	0.7										10.8	9.2	-15.1				276.4	276.6	0.1
Spain				575.3	582.1	1.2				402.7	387.2	-3.9							6 629.9			7 607.9		
Sweden	14.8	15.1	1.5	395.0	350.0	-11.4	45.2	46.6	3.1													455.0	411.6	-9.5
Switzerland	7.9	8.0	1.0	264.9	261.7	-1.2				360.0	360.0	0.0	6.5	6.6	0.2				226.6	224.3	-1.0	865.9	860.5	-0.6
Turkey[2]				8.3	6.7	-18.8	28.7	32.7	14.0				0.0	0.0	0.0									
Australia[3]				190.6	181.6	-4.8																		
Japan	27.9	24.0	-14.0																			37.0	39.7	7.5

Notice: this table contains data on available bed capacity, unless otherwise stated in the following notes by country.

1. For the "Types of accommodation covered by the statistics" see Table C.
2. Turkey: the total doesn't include licenced yacht bed capacity (9 358) and beds registered by local municipalities in social tourism establishments (223 576).
3. Australia: assuming 3 beds per place.
4. The data relate to the territory of the Federal Republic of Germany prior to 3rd October 1990.

15. Monthly hotel occupancy rates

		Austria (B)	Belgium (B)	Finland[1] (R)	Germany[10] (B)	Italy (B)	Netherlands[11] (B)	Norway[2] (B)	Portugal[8] (B)	Spain (B)	Sweden[3] (B)	Switzerland[9] (B)	Turkey[4] (B)	United Kingdom[5] (B)	Australia[6] (B)	Japan[7] (R)
1990	January	27.2	19.1	42.0	27.4	26.3	15.6	28.8	31.9		24.5	28.7	25.3	29.0	38.6	65.0
	February	27.2	23.0	48.6	33.0	31.2	18.6	38.9	36.5		32.2	38.7	29.6	36.0	30.1	78.0
	March	27.2	25.4	52.5	33.6	33.8	16.9	39.7	46.6		33.5	40.0	32.7	38.0	31.3	79.1
	April	27.2	32.7	47.6	38.9	37.8	17.6	30.5	57.5		29.5	32.7	46.4	47.0	33.8	77.7
	May	31.8	33.3	48.6	45.9	34.3	22.5	27.8	52.8		31.3	29.5	52.8	48.0	28.1	79.6
	June	31.8	33.9	52.0	50.6	43.4	37.4	43.4	55.2		34.8	39.8	57.2	53.0	28.8	78.5
	July	31.8	41.2	53.0	55.7	55.7	43.9	51.1	60.4		45.4	50.9	69.0	58.0	32.1	78.5
	August	31.8	42.1	52.7	56.1	70.5	46.7	43.6	76.3		36.4	54.5	67.8	61.0	30.4	84.7
	September	31.8	35.1	51.9	54.4	48.4	19.9	33.0	69.4		30.6	47.6	56.0	57.0	35.5	80.5
	October	31.8	32.1	49.6	47.0	37.5	21.3	28.7	57.8		27.2	33.0	44.2	49.0	33.1	83.3
	November	29.0	27.2	48.5	33.2	25.5	20.8	27.6	40.1		25.6	18.0	31.7	40.0	30.2	82.0
	December	29.0	23.1	33.5	30.0	26.1	20.5	23.9	31.9		17.5	23.4	28.3	34.0	28.8	64.6
1991	January	29.0	12.3	38.1	28.9	26.0	16.3	26.5	30.2	38.3	20.5	29.4	21.5	24.0	35.4	62.7
	February	29.0	16.4	45.2	34.3	30.3	20.4	39.3	37.1	41.9	28.0	41.2	22.6	32.0	27.6	78.0
	March	29.0	11.8	45.9	37.3	35.7	28.0	40.1	44.6	45.9	29.0	42.4	25.8	40.0	31.0	79.9
	April	29.0	17.5	44.6	39.0	33.1	41.2	31.3	49.7	46.8	27.2	29.2	29.3	39.0	30.4	76.6
	May	33.9	19.8	43.0	47.1	35.3	45.3	27.8	57.3	49.1	25.1	28.7	31.1	46.0	26.4	77.2
	June	33.9	22.0	48.0	50.4	44.5	42.6	44.6	58.9	53.2	30.6	37.3	36.2	44.0	28.2	75.9
	July	33.9	47.3	48.8	56.7	58.5	47.3	54.8	63.7	62.4	39.9	49.4	46.3	53.0	31.6	75.8
	August	33.9	46.4	46.3	59.4	70.5	54.3	44.9	76.2	77.6	32.2	55.3	59.0	57.0	30.3	81.1
	September	33.9	19.5	44.4	55.7	48.1	46.5	32.5	70.0	64.1	25.3	46.8	54.2	54.0	34.7	76.2
	October	33.9	12.1	41.1	48.7	37.1	36.2	29.1	54.9	52.0	23.6	33.2	41.5	42.0	34.6	82.7
	November		12.8	41.1	33.5	25.0	27.7	28.6	43.1	44.8	22.7	17.6	30.5	31.0	31.2	82.6
	December		13.8	27.8	30.4	25.4	21.5	24.0	29.8	39.2	12.8	23.8	27.3	28.0	28.8	62.4
1992	January	29.7	11.2	31.6	29.4		19.7	28.0	29.2		19.4	32.1	24.6	21.0	34.8	
	February	29.7	14.2	39.5	34.7		22.1	38.3	35.1		26.0	40.3	30.5	28.0	28.0	
	March	29.7	14.2	42.7	35.2		26.7	37.0	42.4		26.1	40.5	26.6	31.0	29.5	
	April	29.7	14.5	38.8	40.5		44.7	29.1	50.9		23.1	30.8	39.0	36.0	32.8	
	May	33.6	15.2	37.9	46.3		48.7	29.6	55.4		25.2	28.4	55.4	41.0	27.4	
	June	33.6	15.0	43.9	50.0		45.5	44.1	50.3		29.7	37.0	65.0	44.0	27.3	
	July	33.6	27.9	48.6	55.8		48.7	57.6	51.0		41.5	48.3	63.1	52.0	31.6	
	August	33.6	33.0	43.4	57.0		55.1	46.1	67.4		32.0	52.7	70.9	51.0	29.9	
	September	33.6	20.0	41.3	54.4		42.9	33.6	58.4		24.9	44.9	64.0	48.0	34.5	
	October	33.6	17.5	38.5	46.9		33.4	28.8	48.3		21.7	29.2	54.7	42.0	34.5	
	November	29.7	16.9	38.8	32.0		24.2	26.9	30.7		21.1	15.9	30.8	32.0	31.2	
	December	29.7	15.0	28.3	29.5		20.1	23.6	28.9		18.5	24.0	29.4	27.0	30.2	

B = Beds.
R = Rooms.
Occupancy rates registered in hotels only, unless otherwise stated.
1. Finland: room occupancy rates in hotels and similar establishments.
2. Norway: Bed occupancy rates covers registered accommodation with 20 beds or more.
3. Sweden: occupancy rates in hotels, motels, resort hotels, holiday villages and youth hostels.
4. Turkey: bed occupancy rates in hotels, motels, boarding houses, inns, holiday villages, thermal resorts and campings.
5. United Kingdom: figures apply to England only.
6. Australia: quarterly figures in bed-places in hotels and motels with facilities in most rooms.
7. Japan: rates concerning hotels which are members of the "Japan Hotel Association".
8. Portugal: bed occupancy rates in hotels, studio-hotels, motels and state-owned inns.
9. Switzerland: bed occupancy rates in hotels, motels and inns.
10. Germany: bed occupancy rates cover registered accommodation with 9 beds or more; the data relate to the territory of the Federal Republic of Germany prior to 3rd October 1990.
11. Netherlands: bed occupancy rates in all means of accommodation.

16. International fare payments
Rail, air, sea and road transport
In million dollars

	Receipts			Expenditure		
	1990	1991	1992	1990	1991	1992
Germany[1]	5 117.5	5 117.0	5 933.1	5 282.8	5 566.1	6 257.7
Finland[2]	562.5	532.8	503.8	631.3	587.7	
Ireland[2]	435.0	442.4	476.6	276.2	291.2	318.3
Italy[2]	1.8	1.8		1.4	1.2	
Spain	878.9			378.6		
Sweden[3]	976.3	816.3		963.3	832.0	
Switzwerland	1 677.7	1 750.8	1 735.8	1 134.1	1 140.5	1 255.6
Turkey[4]	326.4	288.2	413.8	1.7	1.0	0.6
Canada	1 028.5	923.1	957.0	2 031.2	2 042.8	2 130.1
Australia	1 323.9	1 552.2	1 409.5	1 799.0	1 768.7	1 794.1

1. Germany: air, sea and rail transport. The data relate to the territory of the Federal Republic of Germany prior to 3rd October 1990.
2. Finland, Ireland and Italy: air and sea transport.
3. Sweden: sea and rail transport.
4. Turkey: air, sea and rail transport for receipts; rail transport only for expenditure.

17. Nominal exchange rates of national currencies against the dollar

	Exchange rates (units per dollar)			Per cent changes [1]	
	1990	1991	1992	91/90	92/91
Austria	11.37	11.67	10.99	2.7	−5.9
Belgium-Luxembourg	33.42	34.16	32.15	2.2	−5.9
Denmark	6.19	6.40	6.04	3.4	−5.6
Finland	3.82	4.04	4.49	5.8	10.9
France	5.45	5.64	5.29	3.6	−6.2
Germany	1.62	1.66	1.56	2.7	−5.8
Greece	158.23	182.06	190.47	15.1	4.6
Iceland	58.36	59.10	57.62	1.3	−2.5
Ireland	0.60	0.62	0.59	2.8	−5.5
Italy	1 198.37	1 240.65	1 232.03	3.5	−0.7
Netherlands	1.82	1.87	1.76	2.7	−6.0
Norway	6.26	6.48	6.21	3.6	−4.1
Portugal	142.31	144.35	134.82	1.4	−6.6
Spain	101.94	103.93	102.40	2.0	−1.5
Sweden	5.92	6.05	5.82	2.1	−3.7
Switzerland	1.39	1.43	1.41	3.2	−1.9
Turkey	2 606.48	4 168.91	6 860.59	59.9	64.6
United Kingdom	0.56	0.57	0.57	0.7	0.5
Canada	1.17	1.15	1.21	−1.8	5.5
United States	1.00	1.00	1.00	0.0	0.0
Australia	1.28	1.28	1.36	0.2	6.1
New Zealand	1.68	1.73	1.86	3.1	7.6
Japan	144.80	134.50	126.67	−7.1	−5.8

Source: OECD Balance of Payments Division.
. Minus signs indicate an appreciation of national currencies against the dollar.

Regional breakdown

In million

	R/E	Europe			North America			Australasia-Japan		
		1991	1992	% 92/91	1991	1992	% 92/91	1991	1992	% 92/91
Austria[1]	R	12 510.6	13 487.6	7.8	920.9	695.8	−24.4	96.1	100.5	4.6
	E	5 098.4	5 665.9	11.1	860.6	890.3	3.4	32.3	43.3	34.1
Belgium-Luxembourg	R									
	E									
Denmark	R	2 817.7	3 096.7	9.9	443.8	471.5	6.2	17.5	22.9	30.5
	E	2 594.4	2 886.4	11.3	563.5	657.1	16.6	4.7	7.9	69.5
Finland	R	887.7	1 063.4	19.8	175.4	154.3	−12.0	7.7	9.6	25.0
	E	2 005.6	1 731.7	−13.7	423.9	461.7	8.9	13.9	12.9	−6.6
France	R	16 229.6	18 624.2	14.8	2 769.6	3 430.9	23.9	651.9	774.7	18.8
	E	6 939.4	7 575.3	9.2	2 625.7	3 089.7	17.7	211.1	226.1	7.1
Germany[6]	R	7 982.9	8 378.1	5.0	929.6	1 160.7	24.9	472.0	478.3	1.3
	E	24 671.6	28 115.3	14.0	1 974.9	2 566.7	30.0	370.8	511.5	38.0
Greece	R									
	E									
Iceland	R									
	E									
Ireland[2]	R									
	E									
Italy[7]	R									
	E									
Netherlands	R	3 280.8			691.6			40.1		
	E	6 386.3			1 054.7			22.5		
Norway	R									
	E									
Portugal	R	2 770.6	2 770.2	0.0	914.3	859.2	−6.0	10.3	11.2	8.8
	E	700.4	770.8	10.0	302.1	361.8	19.8	3.2	4.0	23.3
Spain	R									
	E									
Sweden	R	1 974.6			308.8			17.9		
	E	4 650.0			1 012.8			35.6		
Switzerland	R									
	E									
Turkey	R									
	E									
United Kingdom[3]	R	6 132.1	6 015.7	−1.9	2 722.1	2 978.9	9.4	1 160.8	1 195.4	3.0
	E	11 200.5	12 235.0	9.2	2 716.8	2 950.8	8.6	681.0	639.0	−6.2
Canada[4]	R	1 102.9	1 103.9	0.1	3 652.5	3 498.2	−4.2	445.7	451.0	1.2
	E	1 390.3	1 547.8	11.3	8 415.4	8 056.0	−4.3	186.6	196.5	5.3
United States	R									
	E									
Australia	R									
	E									
New Zealand[5]	R									
	E									
Japan	R									
	E									

Important notice: the amounts, excluding those concerning Canada, United States, Ireland, Italy, United Kingdom and Switzerland, refer to receipts and expenditure registered in foreign currency grouped regionally according to the denomination of the currency.
1. Austria: including international fare payments.

18. International tourist receipts (R) and expenditure (E) in dollars (Continued)

Regional breakdown

In million

Total OECD countries			Non-Member countries			All countries			
1991	1992	% 92/91	1991	1992	% 92/91	1991	1992	% 92/91	
13 527.7	14 283.9	5.6	434.8	546.7	25.7	13 962.5	14 830.6	6.2	Austria[1]
5 991.3	6 599.5	10.2	1 461.0	1 771.2	21.2	7 452.3	8 370.7	12.3	
						3 632.7	4 053.4	11.6	Belgium-Luxembourg
						5 579.4	6 604.2	18.4	
3 278.9	3 591.1	9.5	194.6	191.3	-1.7	3 473.5	3 782.4	8.9	Denmark
3 162.6	3 551.5	12.3	212.1	226.2	6.7	3 374.8	3 777.7	11.9	
1 071.4	1 227.7	14.6	120.9	42.8	-64.6	1 192.4	1 270.5	6.5	Finland
2 446.6	2 222.8	-9.1	192.9	123.7	-35.9	2 639.5	2 346.5	-11.1	
19 651.1	22 829.8	16.2	1 712.7	2 223.0	29.8	21 363.8	25 052.8	17.3	France
9 776.2	10 891.1	11.4	2 497.7	2 975.3	19.1	12 273.9	13 866.4	13.0	
9 384.5	10 017.1	6.7	946.5	873.9	-7.7	10 331.0	10 891.0	5.4	Germany[6]
27 017.3	31 193.6	15.5	3 833.5	5 588.6	45.8	30 850.8	36 782.2	19.2	
						2 205.7	3 211.9	45.6	Greece
						901.1	1 156.7	28.4	
						136.0	128.5	-5.5	Iceland
						292.3	287.6	-1.6	
						1 510.7	1 615.3	6.9	Ireland[2]
						1 116.5	1 356.6	21.5	
						18 420.3	21 461.8	16.5	Italy[7]
						11 648.3	16 532.3	41.9	
4 025.4			50.3			4 275.7	5 193.8	21.5	Netherlands
7 605.2			282.4			8 195.7	9 527.5	16.3	
						1 658.5	1 973.5	19.0	Norway
						3 264.1	3 867.3	18.5	
3 701.9	3 642.1	-1.6	37.4	38.0	1.6	3 739.3	3 680.1	-1.6	Portugal
1 006.0	1 137.1	13.0	21.5	18.0	-16.2	1 027.5	1 155.1	12.4	
						19 157.6	20 734.5	8.2	Spain
						4 554.9	4 709.0	3.4	
2 302.1			431.1			2 732.2	3 041.4	11.3	Sweden
5 706.6			342.4			6 118.7	6 692.6	9.4	
						7 055.6	7 722.0	9.4	Switzerland
						5 705.8	6 125.0	7.3	
						2 654.0	3 639.0	37.1	Turkey
						592.0	776.0	31.1	
10 023.8	10 198.8	1.7	3 117.2	3 294.9	5.7	13 141.0	13 493.7	2.7	United Kingdom[3]
14 621.2	15 833.6	8.3	2 960.2	3 633.7	22.7	17 581.4	19 467.2	10.7	
5 201.1	5 053.1	-2.8	636.5	610.6	-4.1	5 837.6	5 663.7	-3.0	Canada[4]
9 992.3	9 800.2	-1.9	1 311.0	1 419.5	8.3	11 303.4	11 219.7	-0.7	
						48 384.0	53 861.0	11.3	United States
						35 322.0	39 872.0	12.9	
						3 953.3	4 089.6	3.4	Australia
						3 919.0	3 988.3	1.8	
						1 512.3	1 469.9	-2.8	New Zealand[5]
						994.7	979.0	-1.6	
						3 437.4	3 589.2	4.4	Japan
						23 964.2	26 809.7	11.9	

2. Ireland: expenditure include international fare payments.
3. United Kingdom: including estimates for the Channel Islands receipts and expenditure, and cruise expenditure.
4. Canada: excluding crew spending.
5. New Zealand: includes international airfares payments.
6. Germany: the data relate to the territory of the Federal Republic of Germany prior to 3rd October 1990. From July 1990, data include all transactions of the former German Democratic Republic with foreign countries.
7. Italy : change of methodology in 1990.

19. Foreign tourism by purpose of visit

	1991						1992					
	Business journeys (%)[1]	Private journeys (%)				Total volume in thousands	Business journeys (%)[1]	Private journeys (%)				Total volume in thousands
		Holidays	VFR[2]	Others	Total			Holidays	VFR[2]	Others	Total	
Greece[3]	9.4	81.0	4.0	5.6	90.6	8 036.1	9.9	80.5	4.3	5.4	90.1	9 331.4
Ireland[4]	14.8	48.9	30.3	5.9	85.2	2 997.0	14.6	49.9	28.9	6.6	85.4	3 129.0
Portugal[5]												
Spain[6]	13.0	56.0	12.0	19.0	87.0	35 306.7	17.9	67.0	5.0	10.1	82.1	35 068.0
Turkey[12]		76.6		23.4	100.0	5.5		79.6		20.4	100.0	7.1
United Kingdom[7]		55.6	27.8	16.6	100.0	12 905.0		54.3	26.3	19.4	100.0	14 413.0
Canada[8]	16.7	45.2	33.8	4.3	83.3	2 862.4	17.1	47.1	31.7	4.2	82.9	2 867.8
Australia[9]	11.2	59.7	20.0	9.2	88.8	2 370.5	10.3	61.3	18.8	9.6	89.7	2 603.2
New zealand[10]	12.1	51.7	24.6	11.7	87.9	963.5	12.3	53.0	24.8	9.8	87.7	1 055.7
Japan[11]	26.1	59.6		14.4	73.9	3 532.7	26.1	58.7		15.2	73.9	3 581.5

1. Includes : business, congresses, seminars, on missions, etc.
2. VFR : visits to friends and relatives.
3. Greece : number of tourists. "Others" includes journeys combining visiting relatives and holiday or business and holiday.
4. Ireland : number of visits on overseas routes.
5. Portugal : number of tourists. "Others" includes visits for cultural purposes and journeys for educational reasons.
6. Spain : number of tourists. "Others" includes journeys for educational reasons.
7. United Kingdom : number of visits. "Others" includes visits for religion, sports, health and visits of more than one purpose where none predominates.
8. Canada : number of tourists.
9. Australia : short-term visitors (less than one year). "Others" includes accompanying business traveller.
10. New Zealand : number of tourists. "Others" includes journeys for educational reasons.
11. Japan : number of visitors. "Others" includes journeys for educational reasons.
12. Turkey : "Others" includes journeys combining shopping and transit and journeys for study, health, religious and sports purposes.

20. Foreign tourism by mode of transport

	1991					1992				
	Breakdown of arrivals (%)				Total volume in thousands	Breakdown of arrivals (%)				Total volume in thousands
	Air	Sea	Rail	Road		Air	Sea	Rail	Road	
Belgium[1]					143.5					142.6
Iceland	94.5	5.5				95.0	5.0			
Ireland[8]	60.0	40.0		5.0	2 997.0	58.6	36.2		5.2	3 300.0
Italy[2]	12.1	2.3	8.9	76.8	51 317.2	13.6	2.8	8.2	75.5	50 088.7
Portugal[2]	89.7	6.6	3.8		3 910.9	90.9	6.1	3.1		4 059.2
Spain[3]	31.2	3.3	4.5	61.1	53 495.0	32.8	3.1	4.3	59.8	55 330.7
Turkey[4]	30.8	9.0	2.1	58.1	5 517.9	42.1	10.1	1.1	46.8	7 076.1
United Kingdom[2]	69.7	33.1			16 664.0	68.5	31.5			18 179.0
Canada[5]										
Australia[6]	99.6	0.4			2 370.4	99.5	0.5			2 603.3
New Zealand[5]	99.0	1.0			963.5	99.0	1.0			1 055.7
Japan[7]	97.3	2.7			3 856.0	97.3	2.7			3 926.3

1. Belgium: air and sea include both arrivals and departures of foreign and domestic visitors. Rail refers to international traffic only.
2. Italy, Portugal and United Kingdom : visitor arrivals.
3. Spain: visitor arrivals, including Spaniards living abroad.
4. Turkey: traveller arrivals.
5. Canada and New Zealand: tourist arrivals.
6. Australia: arrivals of short-term visitors (less than one year).
7. Japan: visitor arrivals, including those of returning residents and excluding crew members.
8. Ireland: visitors on overseas routes (average of arrivals and departure).

21. Staff employed in tourism

		1990			1991			1992		
		Total	Men %	Women %	Total	Men %	Women %	Total	Men %	Women %
Austria [1]										
	HR	126 034	38.7	61.3	131 240	39.4	60.6	136 543	40.1	59.9
Belgium [2]										
	H	14 293	46.5	53.4	14 666	46.1	53.9			
	R	60 230	48.4	51.6	59 485	48.8	51.2			
	HR	74 523	48.1	51.9	74 151	48.3	51.7			
	V	4 133	33.2	66.8	4 086	33.3	66.7			
	A	10 832	48.0	52.0	10 541	46.3	53.7			
	O	5 871	35.1	64.9	5 727	34.3	65.7			
Finland [3]										
	HR	75 000	24.0	76.0	69 000	23.2	76.8	63 000	23.8	76.2
Germany [4]										
	HR	774 400	41.5	58.5	774 800	41.0	59.0			
Norway [5]										
	HR	57 000			57 000			59 000		
Sweden										
	HR	98 000	37.8	62.2	98 000	36.7	63.3	91 000	39.6	60.4
Turkey [6]										
	HR	140 363			145 530			153 168		
	V	3 249			11 000			17 150		
	A	2 368	70.7	29.3	1 985	65.4	34.6	1 990	63.4	35.2
	O	1 455			2 420			3 874		
United Kingdom [7]										
	H	303 100	39.1	60.9	296 000	39.3	60.7	289 200	40.7	59.3
	R	306 000	41.3	58.7	291 900	41.0	59.0	295 500	41.6	58.4
	HR	1 463 700	39.7	60.3	1 442 700	40.0	60.0	1 442 500	40.7	59.3
	O	854 600	39.4	60.6	854 800	39.9	60.1	857 800	40.4	59.6
Canada										

H: staff employed in hotels.
R: staff employed in restaurants.
HR: staff employed in hotels and restaurants.
V: staff employed in travel agencies.A staff employed in national tourism administrations.
O staff employed in other sectors of tourist industry.
1. Austria weighted average of peak season (August) and low season (November).
2. Belgium A = tourist offices libraries public archives museums botanical gardens and zoos. O = sleeper trains and restaurantcars youth hostels camping sites holiday centers and holiday homesrecreation homes for children and furnished appartments.
3. Finland weighted average of peak season (July) and lowseason (January).
4. The data relate to the territory of the Federal Republicof Germany prior to rd October .
5. Norway average of st and th quarters.
6. Turkey data registered at December of each year except for O registered at March and V registered at October. V = total number of persons (new series from) which travel agencies (central and local offices) have to employ. A includes regional tourism administrations and staff working at the Ministry of Tourism. O = tourist guides whose licences have been renewed.
7. United Kingdom data registered at September. O = ''pubs'' bars night clubs clubs librairies museums art galleries sports and other recreational services.

22. Trends in tourism prices

		%87/86	%88/87	%89/88	%90/89	%91/90	%92/91
Austria	H	3.0	3.8	2.2	3.3	4.0	
	R	4.0	2.8	2.2	3.3	4.0	
	T	2.2	2.5	2.5	3.5	4.1	4.4
	C	1.4	1.9	2.6	3.3	3.3	4.0
Belgium[1]	H	9.3	6.3	3.8	5.7	6.7	10.3
	R	3.7	2.4	3.4	4.7	6.5	8.9
	T	4.0	2.6	3.4	4.1	7.1	7.0
	C	1.6	1.2	3.1	3.4	3.2	2.4
Finland[2]	H	5.0	6.0	6.0	7.0	1.0	−6.0
	R	7.0	7.0	8.0	8.0	6.0	2.0
	T						
	C	4.1	5.1	6.6	6.1	4.1	2.9
France	H	9.2	7.8	6.3	6.6	6.8	5.1
	R	7.1	5.4	5.0	6.1	4.7	4.0
	T		5.1	5.7	5.7	4.6	4.3
	C	3.3	2.7	3.5	3.4	3.1	2.4
Germany	H	3.4	4.3	4.4	4.8	5.3	5.8
	R	1.7	1.5	1.9	2.8	3.8	4.2
	T	1.3	1.0	1.8	0.5	1.6	2.5
	C	0.2	1.3	2.8	2.7	3.5	3.8
Greece	H	40.0	10.0				
	R						
	T						
	C	16.4	13.5	13.7	20.4	18.9	15.9
Italy[3]	H	9.0	7.3	8.3	7.8	8.8	
	R	5.8	7.2	7.9	7.8	7.9	
	T	6.4	7.1	7.9	7.8	6.1	
	C	4.6	5.0	6.6	6.1	6.5	5.3
Netherlands[4]	H	2.0	2.0	2.0	3.0	3.0	
	R	2.0	1.0	2.0	3.0	3.0	
	T						
	C	−0.7	0.7	1.1	2.5	3.9	3.7
Norway[5]	H	12.0	11.5	9.0	6.0	5.0	5.6
	R	8.6	5.7	3.9	3.0	4.7	3.4
	T						
	C	8.7	6.7	4.6	4.1	3.4	2.3
Portugal[6]	H	23.0	12.0	14.0	17.0	15.0	13.0
	R	14.0	17.0	17.0	11.0	12.0	13.0
	T						
	C	9.4	9.7	12.6	13.4	11.4	8.9
Spain[7]	H	13.1	10.9	10.6	13.6	7.5	17.5
	R	5.1	8.7	10.9	10.5	4.9	9.3
	T	4.8	6.9	8.6	9.7	6.9	9.7
	C	5.2	4.8	6.8	6.7	5.9	5.9
Sweden[8]	H	−1.4	5.8	6.0	14.4	9.2	2.3
	R	6.6	9.5	9.3	18.8	6.6	−2.2
	T						
	C	4.2	5.8	6.4	10.5	9.3	2.3
Switzerland[9]	H	5.6	5.5	6.6	9.2	8.8	6.5
	R	2.2	3.0	4.3	5.1	5.8	4.9
	T						
	C	1.4	1.9	3.2	5.4	5.8	4.0
Turkey[10]	H						
	R						
	T						
	C	38.9	75.4	69.6	60.3	66.0	70.1
United Kingdom[11]	H	9.9	10.9	8.7	11.8	11.6	4.8
	R	7.0	6.8	6.8	8.0	9.6	6.0
	T	6.3	8.1	7.5	8.7	8.5	5.6
	C	4.1	4.9	7.8	9.5	5.9	3.7
Canada[12]	H	3.0	7.2	5.3	2.8	2.4	−0.8
	R	4.0	4.6	5.3	4.9	10.9	1.5
	T	4.2	1.4	5.7	7.2	7.6	0.8
	C	4.4	4.0	5.0	4.8	5.6	1.5
Australia[13]	H	16.2	16.6				
	R	6.7	7.3				
	T	6.6	13.5	7.6	7.6	−5.6	−0.5
	C	8.6	7.2	7.6	7.3	3.2	1.0

NOTE TO TABLE 22

H: average increase in hotel prices.

R: average increase in restaurant prices.

T: average increase in travel prices.

C: average increase in consumer prices (CPI). Source: OECD Balance of Payments Division.

 1. Belgium : H = hotels and campings, R = cafés, restaurants and bars, T = hotels, campings, cafés, restaurants, bars and package tours.

 2. Finland: H = hotels, R = food and alcoholic beverages, T = transports and communications.

 3. Italy: T = hotels, restaurants and public establishments (bars, night club, sea-side resorts....).

 4. Netherlands: H = price of a night spent in an hotel, R = price of a certain number of typical expenses made in bars and restaurants (cup of coffee, fruit drinks, beer, jenever, croquette, fried potatoes, several hot meals, ham roll, ice cream).

 5. Norway: H = approved hotels and boarding houses, R = restaurants and cafés.

 6. Portugal: H = hotels of from 1 to 5 stars, R concerns Lisbon only.

 7. Spain H takes into account the types of accommodation presented in the official guide R = hotels restaurants cafeteriaand bars.

 8. Sweden: position at December of each year H = hotel room, R = meals not taken at home (lunch, dinner, coffee with bread, hot sausage with bread).

 9. Switzerland: H = hotels and similar establishments. R is estimated.

10. Turkey: H = hotels, motels, inns, boarding houses, holiday villages, health resorts. R = 1st and 2nd class restaurants. In 1985 H and R = freely determined prices approved by the Ministry of Culture and Tourism. C concerns the city of Ankara only.

11. United Kingdom: H = all holiday accommodation. R = meals and snacks including take-away. T = accommodation, meals, food, alcohol, tobacco, durable household goods, clothes, footwear, motoring and cycling fares, entertainment and other services.

12. Canada: H = hotels and motels. R = food purchases for restaurants, T is calculated from domestic tourist spending patterns only.

13. Australia: position every fourth quarter of each year. H = change in the price of a room in hotels, motels, and similar establishments. R = change in the price of meals taken outside home and take-away food (one component of the CPI). C = weighted average of eight State capital cities. T = air, bus and rail fares, hotel, motel and caravan park charges, package tours.

International tourist flows from main generating countries

Tables 23 to 49 gather data available for the period 1981 to 1992 concerning physical flows to OECD Member countries.

These tables contain data on arrivals at frontiers and arrivals and nights spent at/in accommodation:

-- from all the foreign countries;

-- from the eight main generators of tourism to the OECD area (Canada, France, Germany, Italy, Japan, the Netherlands, the United Kingdom and the United States).

Data used in the synthesis tables are derived from data broken down by country of origin; when these data are not available, the tables are derived from monthly or quarterly statistics.

Methodological notes

These notes present on a country-by-country basis, and where appropriate, the main methodological and statistical changes affecting the series available between 1981 and 1992.

France. Arrivals and nights spent at/in hotels and similar establishments: change of series in 1986. Change of series in 1991; the new frontiers' survey covers autocarists and introduces a better breakdown between visitors, tourists and same-day visitors.

Germany. The data relate to the territory of the Federal Republic of Germany prior to 3rd October 1990. Arrivals and nights spent at/in hotels and similar establishments and in all means of accommodation: changes of series in 1981 and in 1984. Arrivals and nights spent at/in all means of accommodations: from 1988, includes camping sites.

Ireland. Arrivals and nights spent at/in hotels and similar establishments: series available from 1985.

Japan. Arrivals and nights spent at/in hotels and similar establishments: series discontinued from 1986.

Netherlands. Arrivals and nights spent at/in hotels and similar establishments: change of series in 1986. Arrivals and nights spent at/in all means of accommodations: new series from 1988.

Norway. Arrivals of foreign visitors at frontiers: series discontinued from 1984.

Sweden. Nights spent in all means of accommodation: change of series in 1985.

Switzerland. Arrivals of foreign tourists/visitors at frontiers: annual estimates.

United States. Arrivals of foreign tourists at frontiers: change of series in 1984.

Conventional signs

/ Break of series

ARRIVALS OF FOREIGN TOURISTS/VISITORS AT FRONTIERS
ARRIVÉES DE TOURISTES/VISITEURS ÉTRANGERS AUX FRONTIÈRES

1987=100

Country	T/V	Volume 1981	1982	1983	1984	1985	1986	Volume 1987	1988	1989	1990	1991	1992	Volume 1992	T/V	Pays
France (R)	T	30 476 000	90.5	92.0	95.7	99.4	97.6	36 974 000	103.6	134.0	143.9	148.9	161.2	59 590 000	T	France (R)
Greece (N)	T	5 094 349	66.4	63.1	72.9	86.8	93.6	7 576 000	102.7	106.7	117.1	106.1	123.2	9 331 360	T	Grèce (N)
Greece (N)	V	5 577 109	68.3	65.7	75.3	87.9	91.7	8 004 000	102.8	101.0	110.9	100.4	116.6	9 331 360	V	Grèce (N)
Iceland (N)	T	71 898	56.0	59.9	65.9	75.2	87.6	129 565	99.4	99.0	109.4	110.7	110.0	142 559	T	Islande (N)
Ireland (R)	V	1 668 000	86.1	86.9	91.8	93.6	88.9	2 040 000	115.0	133.9	150.4	147.0	153.1	3 124 000	V	Irlande (R)
Italy (N)	T	19 701 343	85.0	86.0	89.5	97.3		25 749 422	101.6						T	Italie (N)
Italy (N)	V	43 526 584	91.6	88.3	93.2	101.7	101.1	52 724 941	105.6	104.6	114.4	97.3	95.0	50 088 710	V	Italie (N)
Norway (N)	V	3 021 047	51.9	60.9	67.5	81.8	88.7	6 101 712	108.6	116.6	131.4	141.9	145.6	8 884 125	V	Norvège (N)
Portugal (N)	V	7 277 002	45.1	54.9	60.7	72.3	80.7	16 173 277	99.4	101.9	113.9	121.4	128.2	20 741 879	V	Portugal (N)
Spain (N)	V	40 129 323	83.1	81.6	84.5	85.1	93.8	50 544 874	107.2	106.9	103.0	105.8	109.5	55 330 716	V	Espagne (N)
Switzerland (R) [1]	T	11 250 000	98.3	98.3	101.3	101.7	98.3	11 700 000	100.0	107.7	112.8	107.7	109.4	12 800 000	T	Suisse (R) [1]
Switzerland (R) [1]	V	89 750 000	79.7	84.3	91.7	90.8	99.7	111 790 000	100.4	109.9	115.6	12.3	130.6	146 000 000	V	Suisse (R) [1]
Turkey (N)	V	1 405 311	48.7	56.9	74.1	91.6	83.7	2 855 546	146.1	156.2	188.7	193.2	247.8	7 076 096	V	Turquie (N)
United Kingdom (R)	V	11 452 200	74.8	80.1	87.7	92.8	89.3	15 566 000	101.5	111.4	115.7	110.0	116.8	18 179 000	V	Royaume-Uni (R)
Canada (R)	T	12 811 200	81.1	83.2	86.4	87.7	104.0	15 016 600	103.1	100.9	101.3	99.3	98.2	14 740 800	T	Canada (R)
Canada (R)	V	41 953 400	86.9	86.5	88.1	90.7	102.2	39 595 200	99.1	95.9	95.9	93.0	91.4	36 186 300	V	Canada (R)
United States (R)	T	23 567 227	75.3	75.3	93.6	88.4	85.5	28 766 071	95.4	127.3	137.6	149.3	155.1	44 627 461	T	États-Unis (R)
Australia (R)	V	936 726	53.5	52.9	57.0	64.0	80.1	1 784 900	126.0	116.5	124.1	132.8	145.6	2 598 100	V	Australie (R)
Japan (N)	T	1 583 043	83.2	91.3	97.9	108.0	95.7	2 154 864	109.3	131.6	150.2	164.0	166.3	3 582 765	T	Japon (N)
New Zealand (R)	T	478 037	57.1	60.2	67.2	79.3	86.9	844 313	102.4	106.7	115.6	114.1	125.0	1 055 681	T	Nouvelle-Zélande (R)

V   Visitors (travellers in Austria, Germany and Turkey)
T   Tourists
(R) Tourist count by country of residence
(N) Tourist count by country of nationality
1. Estimates

V   Visiteurs (voyageurs en Allemagne, en Autriche et en Turquie)
T   Touristes
(R) Recensement des touristes par pays de résidence
(N) Recensement des touristes par pays de nationalité
1. Estimations

Table/Tableau 24

ARRIVALS AND NIGHTS OF FOREIGN TOURISTS AT/IN HOTELS
ARRIVÉES ET NUITÉES DE TOURISTES ÉTRANGERS DANS L'HÔTELLERIE

	AH/NH	Volume 1981	1982	1983	1984	1985	1986	Volume 1987	1988	1989	1990	1991	1992	Volume 1992	AH/NH	
Austria (R)	NH	56 848 502	101.0	99.3	100.2	98.5	98.4	55 401 204	101.7	110.9	111.7	115.9	115.9	64 188 976	NH	Autriche (R)
	AH	9 868 572	87.6	89.9	95.5	96.2	94.6	11 382 846	104.7	115.6	121.5	120.2	119.9	13 647 177	AH	
Belgium (R)	NH	4 369 987	89.0	92.7	98.9	104.1	100.1	5 315 921	102.0	123.7	129.3	123.7	144.7	7 694 055	NH	Belgique (R)
Denmark (N)	NH	4 477 400	99.3	100.5	102.9	102.5	96.8	4 480 300	97.7	109.1	121.2	133.1	137.9	6 177 700	NH	Danemark (N)
Finland (R)	NH	2 054 248	91.7	93.3	95.7	95.0	91.6	2 207 484	104.1	114.0	111.8	99.7	101.6	2 242 741	NH	Finlande (R)
	AH							2 290 000							AH	
France (R)¹	NH	16 589 740	43.9	45.7	49.3	49.9	100.0	36 407 821	114.1	142.0	149.9	145.7	163.6	59 575 470	NH	France (R)¹
	AH	6 080 559	35.5	35.6	38.0	40.4	99.4	17 168 413	113.6	141.6	147.0	147.0	165.4	28 390 452	AH	
Germany (R)	NH	19 444 557	77.6	78.5	91.2	98.0	96.3	24 385 740	103.4	116.4	122.1	113.9	110.3	26 898 563	NH	Allemagne (R)
	AH	9 201 230	78.2	80.8	94.1	100.2	95.9	11 778 277	102.4	114.3	122.4	110.8	107.7	12 688 994	AH	
Greece (N)	NH	27 108 295	78.3	74.7	85.9	100.9	99.9	33 757 566	98.8	97.6	103.7	88.5	107.4	36 251 299	NH	Grèce (N)
	AH	5 353 636	85.5	81.2	98.9	106.1	95.5	6 166 658	97.4						AH	
Iceland (N)	NH					95.5	95.4		111.9	138.1	149.8	170.5	168.9	431 455	NH	Islande (N)
Ireland (R)	NH					97.5	94.4	5 526 000	110.4	138.2	147.6	153.1	160.7	9 333 000	NH	Irlande (R)
	AH							1 119 000						1 798 000	AH	
Italy (N)	NH	58 958 045	91.4	89.7	89.2	90.5	92.2	70 694 834	99.6	96.4	93.4	93.1	89.7	63 415 459	NH	Italie (N)
	AH	13 273 414	87.0	87.8	92.8	94.5	89.1	17 025 545	102.4	103.9	105.3	100.2	102.0	17 365 849	AH	
Luxembourg (R)	NH	6 098 551	98.9	96.9	94.1	99.0	96.4	941 163	102.9	108.1	114.4	113.9	107.0	1 007 191	NH	Luxembourg (R)
	AH	2 812 359	96.9	87.5	88.5	96.5	97.1	463 776	104.7	108.1	113.7	112.2	106.0	491 501	AH	
Netherlands (R)	NH	2 488 548	89.3	85.4	92.9	95.8	100.9	7 040 800	96.0	102.0	115.1	113.5	120.7	8 496 000	NH	Pays-Bas (R)
	AH	1 279 766	88.4	86.4	96.0	99.3	100.1	3 353 300	99.1	104.0	116.4	109.9	117.3	3 931 900	AH	
Norway (N)	NH	9 359 161	59.3	60.5	89.5	96.0	85.3	3 865 930	86.8	88.8	91.5	101.3	110.6	4 275 163	NH	Norvège (N)
	AH	1 849 101	68.0	71.4	97.9	108.5	91.9	1 781 737	95.6	104.8	109.7	118.6	133.3	2 375 452	AH	
Portugal (N)	NH	1 849 101	65.8	68.1	75.9	89.1	98.4	14 522 410	103.3	106.5	115.1	131.4	123.1	17 877 031	NH	Portugal (N)
	AH		61.6	67.5	77.4	89.0	92.3	3 071 118	104.0	109.2	118.3	127.4	119.6	3 671 539	AH	
Spain (N)	NH	70 811 003	83.0	86.2	96.3	85.4	94.9	92 444 337	95.6	84.7	77.6	80.5	83.2	76 934 318	NH	Espagne (N)
	AH	10 585 851	79.3	81.7	92.2	88.1	96.3	14 115 641	96.6	93.4	85.1	85.4	88.5	12 486 880	AH	
Sweden (N)	NH	2 734 153	84.6	93.3	101.0	109.4	102.0	3 243 324	98.4	104.9	98.5	87.1	86.4	2 803 711	NH	Suède (N)
Switzerland (R)	NH	21 185 856	102.3	101.6	103.3	104.0	100.1	19 534 253	97.8	104.9	107.7	104.3	103.6	20 235 938	NH	Suisse (R)
	AH	6 931 214	96.4	97.5	103.1	103.8	97.4	7 062 251	99.2	108.6	112.8	104.8	106.6	7 527 998	AH	
Turkey (N)	NH	1 496 772	27.5	40.0	53.4	68.2	77.3	6 517 988	144.6	149.5	158.0	124.7	208.0	13 560 159	NH	Turquie (N)
	AH	617 602	30.7	44.3	55.7	70.0	79.7	2 400 284	129.2	144.5	145.6	92.3	142.1	3 410 189	AH	
United Kingdom (R)	AH													9 531 000	AH	Royaume-Uni (R)
Australia (R)	NH	6 264 600		53.5	55.7	64.0	80.3	11 048 100	128.1	95.5	113.6	104.1	112.8	12 460 800	NH	Australie (R)
Japan (N)	NH	4 868 581													NH	Japon (N)
	AH	2 204 683													AH	

AH Arrivals at hotels and similar establishments
NH Nights in hotels and similar establishments
(R) Tourist count by country of residence
(N) Tourist count by country of nationality
1. Ile de France only

AH Arrivées dans les hôtels et les établissements assimilés
NH Nuitées dans les hôtels et établissements assimilés
(R) Recensement des touristes par pays de résidence
(N) Recensement des touristes par pays de nationalité
1. Ile de France seulement

Table/Tableau 25

ARRIVALS AND NIGHTS OF FOREIGN TOURISTS AT/IN ALL MEANS OF ACCOMMODATION
ARRIVÉES ET NUITÉES DE TOURISTES ÉTRANGERS DANS L'ENSEMBLE DES MOYENS D'HÉBERGEMENT

1987=100 ... 1987=100

	AAA/NAA	Volume 1981	1982	1983	1984	1985	1986	Volume 1987	1988	1989	1990	1991	1992	Volume 1992	AEH/NEH	
Austria (R)	NAA	92 520 201	105.0	102.0	101.2	99.3	99.7	85 692 004	102.2	110.8	110.6	116.3	116.4	99 753 475	NEH	Autriche (R)
	AAA	14 241 392	90.4	91.9	95.9	96.7	95.8	15 761 399	105.1	115.5	120.6	121.1	121.2	19 097 640	AEH	
Belgium (R)	NAA	7 203 688	85.0	88.8	92.8	97.7	97.9	10 064 504	105.1	120.9	128.0	120.9	128.0	12 879 982	NEH	Belgique (R)
	AAA														AEH	
Denmark (N)	NAA	8 922 642	112.5	116.2	111.1	109.4	103.8	8 199 861	99.0	104.6	113.9	127.2	141.3	11 588 100	NEH	Danemark (N)
France (R)	NAA	254 718 000	87.9	90.6	94.1	97.0	97.7	339 922 000	89.8	103.1	113.9	116.5	126.0	428 381 000	NEH	France (R)
	AAA	30 476 000	90.5	92.0	95.7	99.4	97.6	36 974 000	103.6		143.9	148.9	161.2	59 589 000	AEH	
Germany (R)	NAA	21 331 330	71.7	74.1	89.9	96.5	95.6	29 093 709	103.5	115.4	119.8	128.6	124.0	36 086 535	NEH	Allemagne (R)
	AAA	9 445 563	74.0	76.9	93.4	99.3	95.6	12 779 904	102.6	114.7	122.3	122.4	118.5	15 147 075	AEH	
Greece (N)	NAA	30 623 057	83.8	76.5	92.8	99.9	99.1	35 755 308	97.3	95.5	101.5	85.4	103.2	36 907 308	NEH	Grèce (N)
	AAA	6 143 428	90.8	85.6	102.6	105.4	95.9	6 690 675							AEH	
Ireland (R)	NAA	17 311 000	76.1	82.7	85.1	83.2	83.9	22 623 800	115.8	138.6	148.9	147.1	149.3	33 777 000	NEH	Irlande (R)
	AAA	1 680 000												3 116 000	AEH	
Italy (N)	NAA	92 383 478	108.5	104.7	102.4	103.9	106.9	92 907 913	99.3	93.5	91.2	93.4	90.0	83 642 567	NEH	Italie (N)
	AAA	16 580 348	91.5	91.6	95.5	98.1	94.6	20 177 321	102.1	102.0	103.3	100.3	107.6	20 424 982	AEH	
Luxembourg (R)	NAA		93.7	95.0	112.9	101.1	108.6	2 170 698	98.6	101.5	111.3	117.9	106.8	2 335 043	NEH	Luxembourg (R)
	AAA							710 840						759 496	AEH	
Netherlands (R)	NAA	11 783 255		82.4	96.7	96.9	100.0		102.5	106.5	114.8	116.3	129.4	18 099 000	NEH	Pays-Bas (R)
	AAA	4 311 131												6 082 900	AEH	
Norway (N)	NAA	4 398 000	65.8	90.0	94.5	96.3	97.5	5 456 803	98.7	108.7	107.0	115.5	117.3	7 062 635	NEH	Norvège (N)
	AAA														AEH	
Portugal (N)	NAA	11 780 397	69.3	69.7	74.5	87.3	92.8	17 109 866	104.0	93.4	113.1	128.3	113.5	20 064 465	NEH	Portugal (N)
	AAA	2 346 625	62.5	66.8	74.9	86.4		3 828 604	104.2	107.0	115.8	124.6		4 344 547	AEH	
Spain (N)	NAA	72 985 596	80.3	84.3	93.1	89.2	101.2	14 115 641	96.6	104.0	92.8	79.0	82.0		NEH	Espagne (N)
	AAA	10 732 087	86.7	102.5	103.7	105.6	101.0	7 089 246	100.3		106.7	107.1	107.0		AEH	
Sweden (N)	NAA	6 055 105												5 814 522	NEH	Suède (N)
	AAA														AEH	
Switzerland (R)	NAA	39 192 600	106.2	104.0	101.1	101.7	98.2	34 581 000	99.6	108.3	112.8	108.4	110.1	36 995 680	NEH	Suisse (R)
	AAA	9 383 300	98.5	98.7	101.7	102.2		9 323 800	100.2					10 265 423	AEH	
Turkey (N)	NAA	1 578 011	22.7	34.1	44.7	58.6	71.3	8 325 001	140.0	142.5	159.4	116.5	201.6	16 785 455	NEH	Turquie (N)
	AAA	627 696	28.2	41.1	51.4	65.1	75.5	2 661 890	128.2	142.2	145.4	90.1	139.8	3 720 627	AEH	
United Kingdom (R)	NAA	135 450 000	76.5	81.3	86.7	93.7	88.7	178 244 000	97.0	105.1	110.0	104.6	102.3	182 413 000	NEH	Royaume-Uni (R)
	AAA													15 727 000	AEH	
Canada (R)	NAA	76 770 600	85.5	82.9	90.6	90.9	107.8	84 860 500	108.3	106.1	96.8	97.5	93.6	79 423 500	NEH	Canada (R)
	AAA	12 811 300	81.4	83.4	86.6	88.0	104.3	14 974 500	103.4	100.9	101.6	99.6	98.4	14 740 800	AEH	
Australia (R)	NAA	12 769 100	62.5	62.5	67.1	64.5	80.1	22 571 100		247.7	289.5	286.4	272.2	61 444 000	NEH	Australie (R)
New Zealand (R)	NAA				69.5	81.1	88.9	18 156 290	102.0	103.9	113.8	106.2	113.0	20 508 284	NEH	Nouvelle-Zélande (R)

AAA Arrivals in all means of accommodation
NAA Nights in all means of accommodation
(R) Tourist count by country of residence
(N) Tourist count by country of nationality

AEH Arrivées dans l'ensemble des moyens d'hébergement
NEH Nuitées dans l'ensemble des moyens d'hébergement
(R) Recensement des touristes par pays de résidence
(N) Recensement des touristes par pays de nationalité

Table/Tableau 26

ARRIVALS OF FOREIGN TOURISTS/VISITORS AT FRONTIERS
ARRIVÉES DE TOURISTES/VISITEURS ÉTRANGERS AUX FRONTIÈRES

From Germany / *En provenance de l'Allemagne*

1987=100

Country (EN)	T/V	Volume 1981	1982	1983	1984	1985	1986	Volume 1987	1988	1989	1990	1991	1992	Volume 1992	T/V	Country (FR)
France (R)	T V	7 730 000	94.3	90.4	93.0	97.8	94.4	8 915 000	102.2	118.8	118.5	131.3	140.8	12 553 000	T V	France (R)
Greece (N)	T	625 121	50.3	60.5	71.7	87.1	95.0	1 205 000	114.7	137.3	159.5	129.6	161.4	1 944 704	T	Grèce (N)
Iceland (N)	T	9 091	60.8	62.6	68.6	67.2	97.1	14 011	113.4	132.0	147.3	160.4	175.0	24 520	T	Islande (N)
Ireland (R)	V	83 509	80.9	92.1	90.1	95.0	96.0	101 000	110.9	149.5	170.3	192.1	218.8	221 000	V	Irlande (R)
Italy (N)	V	9 340 392	108.0	107.8	112.4	121.8	99.4	9 617 677	109.0	105.4	111.0	95.7	91.3	8 782 614	V	Italie (N)
Norway (N)	V	98 594													V	Norvège (N)
Portugal (N)	T	267 895	50.4	64.7	61.1	76.5	79.3	482 337	109.8	117.1	128.8	163.1	168.4	812 310	T	Portugal (N)
Portugal (N)	V	306 606	55.0	67.5	65.4	78.5	81.8	526 038	108.1	116.2	129.5	161.9	166.8	877 456	V	Portugal (N)
Spain (N)	V	4 561 103	72.4	75.3	79.6	85.6	90.0	6 596 400	104.7	102.8	104.3	116.2	117.7	7 762 127	V	Espagne (N)
Turkey (N)	V	155 054	32.3	33.4	46.2	57.2	74.1	523 675	146.6	171.3	186.0	148.9	222.5	1 165 164	V	Turquie (N)
United Kingdom (R)	T	1 468 400	87.7	83.6	90.3	90.3	97.3	1 644 200	111.3	123.3	115.3	129.8	137.3	2 116 000	T	Royaume-Uni (R)
United Kingdom (R)	V													2 257 000	V	Royaume-Uni (R)
Canada (R)	T	200 000	76.7	68.1	70.9	65.3	82.8	239 500	109.8	112.7	105.0	113.9	121.2	290 300	T	Canada (R)
Canada (R)	V	241 000	73.6	64.0	67.0	60.9	79.0	298 700	107.7	103.3	97.3	104.6	113.8	339 900	V	Canada (R)
United States (R)	T	699 750	69.9	59.1	57.3	53.5	70.4	952 119	121.1	113.1	126.3	150.2	177.7	1 691 663	T	États-Unis (R)
Australia (R)	V	39 055	73.0	64.9	64.2	70.0	78.6	53 300	123.6	127.8	139.2	145.8	168.7	89 900	V	Australie (R)
Japan (N)	T	40 888	77.2	81.1	91.5	90.8	91.8	53 543	106.3	115.0	122.9	114.4	119.4	27 640	T	Japon (N)
Japan (N)	V	8 725	54.6	58.0	57.9	64.8	73.2	16 438	122.3	144.6	182.5	208.7	278.0	63 930	V	Japon (N)
New Zealand (R)	T													45 705	T	Nouvelle-Zélande (R)

V Visitors (travellers in Turkey) / Visiteurs (voyageurs en Turquie)
T Tourists / Touristes
(R) Tourist count by country of residence / Recensement des touristes par pays de résidence
(N) Tourist count by country of nationality / Recensement des touristes par pays de nationalité

Table/Tableau 27

ARRIVALS AND NIGHTS OF FOREIGN TOURISTS AT/IN HOTELS
ARRIVÉES ET NUITÉES DE TOURISTES ÉTRANGERS DANS L'HÔTELLERIE

From Germany
1987=100

En provenance de l'Allemagne
1987=100

	AH/NH	Volume 1981	1982	1983	1984	1985	1986	Volume 1987	1988	1989	1990	1991	1992	Volume 1992	AH/NH	
Austria (R)	NH	38 192 578	110.7	107.3	103.0	99.7	100.8	32 903 694	101.6	108.3	103.4	116.0	117.1	38 519 615	NH	Autriche (R)
	AH		95.1	96.2	94.6	93.4	96.5	5 678 873	104.7	112.0	110.0	122.1	122.9	6 978 329	AH	
Belgium (R)	NH	5 509 487	90.7	92.5	95.6	95.9	97.7	779 167	102.9	119.7	115.3	123.7	145.1	1 130 757	NH	Belgique (R)
	AH	649 533												1 130 757	AH	
Denmark (N)	NH	1 481 000	130.9	122.6	113.5	102.5	98.7	943 400	98.5	113.7	136.5	168.2	180.6	1 703 900	NH	Danemark (N)
Finland (R)	NH	332 299	96.0	90.8	98.9	97.3	89.0	280 953	114.5	125.8	120.4	124.9	134.1	376 700	NH	Finlande (R)
	AH							323 000							AH	
France (R)[1]	NH	2 302 350	31.7	33.9	31.6	31.9	94.3	6 173 451	108.6	123.0	128.8	137.7	134.6	8 308 398	NH	France (R)[1]
	AH	860 005	25.1	26.7	24.3	26.2	93.8	3 046 444	110.1	124.8	129.5	134.7	135.4	4 124 757	AH	
Greece (N)	NH	5 324 697	67.1	63.6	75.9	95.6	99.0	7 201 113	109.3						NH	Grèce (N)
	AH	869 252	80.9	75.5	85.9	99.1	98.3	1 032 837	102.8						AH	
Iceland (N)	NH													94 483	NH	Islande (N)
Ireland (R)	NH					90.9	97.4	352 000	146.0	160.2	225.9	232.1	229.5	808 000	NH	Irlande (R)
	AH					86.2	93.1	58 000	115.5	150.0	165.5	189.7	215.5	125 000	AH	
Italy (N)	NH	23 694 679	91.8	89.8	87.0	88.0	94.8	28 309 774	100.3	91.8	84.5	92.4	84.7	23 979 885	NH	Italie (N)
	AH	3 535 565	81.2	81.7	82.4	84.4	91.2	4 933 170	102.3	98.9	95.6	103.7	96.9	4 780 006	AH	
Luxembourg (R)	NH		80.1	79.7	84.1	88.0	90.2	123 735	100.1	96.8	102.0	108.8	115.8	143 329	NH	Luxembourg (R)
	AH				85.9	91.4	93.5	67 740	104.5				117.7	79 722	AH	
Netherlands (R)	NH	1 439 045	89.6	82.3	90.0	87.5	103.5	1 573 700	93.7	101.3	105.3	118.1	123.0	1 935 200	NH	Pays-Bas (R)
	AH	599 265	88.0	88.0	92.2	91.4	103.7	666 100	99.8	114.9	109.8	119.9	122.2	813 900	AH	
Norway (N)	NH	465 951	73.3	69.6	98.3	101.0	98.2	505 168	106.8	114.8	114.8	141.2	168.4	850 587	NH	Norvège (N)
Portugal (N)	NH	1 306 443	57.0	55.7	60.3	82.9	92.2	2 051 812	100.2	101.5	115.0	157.6	160.7	3 297 973	NH	Portugal (N)
	AH	192 042	50.7	54.6	57.8	77.9	82.8	370 153	101.5	101.7		144.3	148.5	549 600	AH	
Spain (N)	NH	20 980 930	83.2	85.9	88.8	90.6	90.5	26 071 478	94.5	83.6	113.2	99.6	96.7	25 216 078	NH	Espagne (N)
	AH	2 120 081	77.8	82.5	85.4	88.1	91.7	2 836 075	87.5	87.5	87.2	102.9	100.9	2 862 211	AH	
Sweden (N)	NH	426 677	90.6	90.0	97.6	99.2	106.8	424 004	112.2	120.4	109.5	102.9	114.7	486 464	NH	Suède (N)
Switzerland (R)	NH	7 646 051	107.2	104.4	97.7	97.0	100.2	6 186 669	100.6	104.9	103.7	112.5	110.5	6 838 980	NH	Suisse (R)
	AH		99.1	98.6	94.4	93.1	97.4	1 969 802	102.3	108.1	106.7	113.9	111.2	2 190 223	AH	
Turkey (N)	NH	2 116 141	14.6	21.4	30.1	46.4	70.6	2 278 079	154.5	162.0	135.5	151.8	250.2	5 699 323	NH	Turquie (N)
	AH		17.3	26.9	34.2	49.9	73.3	708 723	126.6	134.0		79.6	125.5	889 630	AH	
Australia (R)	NH	310 500		61.3	56.5	71.3	78.6	424 800	123.6	120.4	122.4	137.0	178.5	758 300	NH	Australie (R)
Japan (N)	NH	187 070													NH	Japon (N)
	AH	67 653													AH	

AH Arrivals at hotels and similar establishments
NH Nights in hotels and similar establishments
(R) Tourist count by country of residence
(N) Tourist count by country of nationality
1. Ile de France only

AH Arrivées dans les hôtels et les établissements assimilés
NH Nuitées dans les hôtels et établissements assimilés
(R) Recensement des touristes par pays de résidence
(N) Recensement des touristes par pays de nationalité
1. Ile de France seulement

Table/Tableau 28

ARRIVALS AND NIGHTS OF FOREIGN TOURISTS AT/IN ALL MEANS OF ACCOMMODATION
ARRIVÉES ET NUITÉES DE TOURISTES ÉTRANGERS DANS L'ENSEMBLE DES MOYENS D'HÉBERGEMENT

From Germany
En provenance de l'Allemagne
1987=100

Country	AAA/NAA	Volume 1981	1982	1983	1984	1985	1986	Volume 1987	1988	1989	1990	1991	1992	Volume 1992	AEH/NEH	
Austria (R)	NAA	65 989 261	114.2	110.1	104.5	100.9	102.0	54 937 062	102.0	109.1	103.4	117.0	117.8	64 715 088	NEH	Autriche (R)
	AAA	8 631 994	98.2	98.7	96.3	94.8	97.7	8 588 795	104.8	112.5	109.7	123.6	124.2	10 664 269	AEH	
Belgium (R)	NAA	1 165 074	84.9	84.9	90.1	97.2	96.9	1 561 267	108.3	125.5	124.3	132.2	145.0	2 263 102	NEH	Belgique (R)
	AAA													2 263 102	AEH	
Denmark (N)	NAA	4 101 963	137.3	140.9	125.9	119.1	112.1	2 921 015	96.5	103.0	114.8	134.5	156.6	4 573 000	NEH	Danemark (N)
France (R)	NAA	61 840 000	95.2	92.1	93.6	96.9	96.9	78 836 000	101.7	87.2	93.0	101.9	108.0	85 167 000	NEH	France (R)
	AAA	7 730 000	94.3	90.4	93.0	97.8	94.4	8 915 000	102.2		118.5	131.3	140.8	12 553 000	AEH	
Greece (N)	NAA	6 122 776	72.5	68.3	80.8	95.4	98.4	7 715 105	107.8					3 420 000	NEH	Grèce (N)
	AAA	1 075 715												23 000	AEH	
Ireland (R)	NAA	1 038 000	87.4	79.8	89.9	97.5	97.6	1 193 510	115.9	146.4	182.2	211.2	224.4		NEH	Irlande (R)
	AAA	90 000	77.2	86.4	80.2	82.9	87.4	1 524 000							AEH	
Italy (N)	NAA	39 745 499	111.6	108.8	105.4	106.4	114.2	39 242 604	100.7	89.5	83.5	91.8	84.6	33 205 307	NEH	Italie (N)
	AAA	5 031 807	90.2	90.9	90.9	93.5	100.9	6 362 305	102.0	96.2	93.2	101.4	95.0	6 046 075	AEH	
Luxembourg (R)	NAA		74.7	73.0	93.0	93.9	89.5	175 901	99.9		95.1	117.4	118.6	208 583	NEH	Luxembourg (R)
	AAA			76.1	92.3	94.7	94.1	85 340	104.0		100.6	114.1	119.3	101 787	AEH	
Netherlands (R)	NAA	5 449 619												9 067 700	NEH	Pays-Bas (R)
	AAA	1 459 141												2 146 700	AEH	
Portugal (N)	NAA	1 988 190	64.0	59.6	59.7	80.4	90.8	2 789 466	99.7	98.7	106.2	142.2	137.1	3 825 534	NEH	Portugal (N)
	AAA	322 725	54.1	56.0	58.4	75.6	85.1	567 926	101.0	98.9	105.9	132.1	123.3	700 490	AEH	
Spain (N)	NAA	21 925 030													NEH	Espagne (N)
	AAA	2 251 577													AEH	
Sweden (N)	NAA	1 449 008	108.8	122.3	112.2	111.9	107.7	1 194 293	115.3	126.8	117.4	110.5	126.6	1 512 494	NEH	Suède (N)
Switzerland (R)	NAA	17 538 600	110.8	108.9	99.8	100.3	102.3	14 436 300	102.4	103.5	102.0	111.8	110.6	15 964 680	NEH	Suisse (R)
	AAA	3 245 700	101.2	101.4	95.7	95.4	99.1	3 020 200	103.6	107.7	107.2	116.6	115.4	3 485 649	AEH	
Turkey (N)	NAA	289 357	10.6	17.1	22.7	36.4	63.2	3 243 670	141.6	145.2	167.3	137.1	233.5	7 573 318	NEH	Turquie (N)
	AAA	100 163	14.9	23.7	29.8	44.0	67.2	832 863	123.5	129.9	133.7	79.4	124.6	1 038 062	AEH	
United Kingdom (R)	NAA	15 272 000	99.1	89.8	91.4	93.2	104.7	15 655 000	110.0	113.2	112.1	124.3	122.7	19 212 000	NEH	Royaume-Uni (R)
	AAA													2 116 000	AEH	
Canada (R)	NAA	2 908 800	92.9	80.1	83.0	74.4	89.7	3 038 700	117.8	106.9	105.9	119.6	118.1	3 589 400	NEH	Canada (R)
	AAA	200 000	78.4	69.6	72.5	66.8	84.7	234 200	112.3	112.2	107.3	116.5	124.0	290 300	AEH	
Australia (R)	NAA	737 000			50.4	55.6	71.4	575 025	108.8	128.8	153.8	197.1	239.3	3 245 200	NEH	Australie (R)
New Zealand (R)	NAA													1 375 924	NEH	Nouvelle-Zélande (R)

AAA Arrivals in all means of accommodation
NAA Nights in all means of accommodation
(R) Tourist count by country of residence
(N) Tourist count by country of nationality

AEH Arrivées dans l'ensemble des moyens d'hébergement
NEH Nuitées dans l'ensemble des moyens d'hébergement
(R) Recensement des touristes par pays de résidence
(N) Recensement des touristes par pays de nationalité

Table/Tableau 29

ARRIVALS OF FOREIGN TOURISTS/VISITORS AT FRONTIERS
ARRIVÉES DE TOURISTES/VISITEURS ÉTRANGERS AUX FRONTIÈRES

From Canada — 1987=100 | En provenance du Canada — 1987=100

Country	T/V	Volume 1981	1982	1983	1984	1985	1986	Volume 1987	1988	1989	1990	1991	1992	Volume 1992	T/V	Pays
France (R)	T	357 000	71.6	81.1	108.0	136.7	110.6	349 000	98.6	142.0	158.2	141.3	166.5	581 000	T	France (R)
Greece (N)	T	65 732	71.3	79.7	90.4	112.7	82.0	91 000	117.6	86.8	81.6	51.8	65.7	59 807	V	Grèce (N)
Iceland (N)	T	891	78.0	80.7	77.8	100.0	92.9	1 286	99.3	100.5	88.6	73.3	89.7	1 153	T	Islande (N)
Ireland (R)	V	25 552	65.0	84.0	84.0	100.0	112.0	25 000	112.0	148.0	152.0	120.0	156.0	39 000	T	Irlande (R)
Italy (N)	V	308 847	80.2	86.2	87.5	90.7	87.9	384 453	92.1	110.0	123.6	91.1	93.0	357 692	V	Italie (N)
Norway (N)	V	9 375	52.2	57.1	72.1	94.9	99.4	72 626	104.7	114.4	114.6	86.6	91.3	66 276	V	Norvège (N)
Portugal (N)	T	41 473	54.2	60.3	72.4	90.6	95.2	77 543	102.0	117.5	117.1	89.4	95.4	73 955	V	Portugal (N)
Spain (N)	V	135 795	74.7	77.5	87.1	106.9	99.0	178 691	94.0	96.5	88.3	77.2	81.9	146 429	V	Espagne (N)
Turkey (N)	V	11 529	41.1	69.2	86.7	103.4	62.9	20 825	140.3	151.7	166.0	84.9	126.6	26 355	V	Turquie (N)
United Kingdom (R)	V	389 400	68.8	87.4	95.4	106.3	93.5	593 900	109.7	107.5	116.9	92.1	103.2	613 000	V	Royaume-Uni (R)
United States (R)	T	10 930 203	84.0	96.3	88.4	87.6	88.1	12 417 999	111.5	123.7	139.0	153.9	149.6	18 578 461	T	États-Unis (R)
Australia (R)	V	30 948	61.6	62.6	65.5	77.6	89.2	52 700	126.6	102.8	101.9	101.3	92.8	48 900	V	Australie (R)
Japan (N)	T	44 869	82.8	92.0	90.9	104.7	94.7	58 286	99.8	102.5	109.5	106.9	119.4	69 620	T	Japon (N)
New Zealand (R)	V	18 332	50.7	57.6	64.8	83.9	96.5	35 553	104.5	87.0	95.6	85.2	72.7	25 849	V	Nouvelle-Zélande (R)

V   Visitors (travellers in Turkey)
T   Tourists
(R) Tourist count by country of residence
(N) Tourist count by country of nationality

V   Visiteurs (voyageurs en Turquie)
T   Touristes
(R) Recensement des touristes par pays de résidence
(N) Recensement des touristes par pays de nationalité

Table/Tableau 30

ARRIVALS AND NIGHTS OF FOREIGN TOURISTS AT/IN HOTELS
ARRIVÉES ET NUITÉES DE TOURISTES ÉTRANGERS DANS L'HÔTELLERIE

From Canada / En provenance du Canada
1987=100

	AH/NH	Volume 1981	1982	1983	1984	1985	1986	Volume 1987	1988	1989	1990	1991	1992	Volume 1992	
Austria (R)	NH	117 841	70.5	74.6	90.2	110.1	90.9	181 738	92.6	95.6	106.9	85.3	87.2	158 559	Autriche (R)
	AH	41 327	65.9	77.5	96.2	114.8	89.2	68 999	97.6	104.8	121.4	90.8	95.6	65 933	
Belgium (R)	NH	48 099	64.9	74.8	98.3	121.8	95.5	76 131	104.3	122.8	129.8	100.7	102.3	77 901	Belgique (R)
Finland (R)	NH	18 617	73.6	91.4	94.9	103.0	87.6	29 051	104.7	114.4	110.3	85.7	72.4	21 033	Finlande (R)
France (R)[1]	NH	301 094	44.3	53.2	62.4	75.3	108.4	745 526	101.0	128.2	138.5	101.5	107.2	799 555	France (R)[1]
	AH	108 746	35.8	40.2	49.6	63.6	115.6	330 070	101.0	130.6	143.2	109.3	121.0	399 387	
Germany (R)	NH	205 613	74.6	83.0	108.0	117.4	103.3	289 780	106.6	122.9	130.7	102.8	99.9	289 426	Allemagne (R)
	AH	105 642	76.6	86.6	116.6	124.6	103.7	148 085	100.6	115.5	126.3	95.4	94.9	140 589	
Greece (N)	NH	209 429	82.3	91.3	112.4	158.4	85.4	229 838	102.9							Grèce (N)
	AH	74 164	79.3	87.1	113.9	155.4	85.3	88 682	103.0							
Ireland (R)	NH						145.8	107 000	107.5	237.4	100.9	153.3	195.3	209 000	Irlande (R)
	AH						121.7	23 000	104.3	160.9	91.3	126.1	121.7	28 000	
Italy (N)	NH	372 017	73.5	86.8	96.9	110.5	86.2	606 738	94.5	103.7	104.5	80.1	84.2	510 908	Italie (N)
	AH	137 099	70.5	87.0	102.0	112.8	86.4	237 070	97.9	102.7	106.7	79.8	87.0	206 297	
Luxembourg (R)	NH														Luxembourg (R)
	AH														
Netherlands (R)	NH	113 933	68.4	86.6	98.8	111.5	94.3	174 300	100.6	103.4	106.5	77.0	75.7	132 000	Pays-Bas (R)
	AH	60 831	63.6	87.6	100.0	115.2	95.0	98 800	104.1	95.0	92.9	63.9	65.0	64 200	
Portugal (N)	NH	201 718	50.2	62.1	74.6	111.9	104.9	346 747	90.0	98.2	108.4	80.4	62.5	216 555	Portugal (N)
	AH	53 999	51.1	60.9	74.7	97.5	91.6	100 886	90.9	98.7	100.0	62.8	54.0	54 444	
Spain (N)	NH	278 397	128.4	156.9	181.7	213.3	150.7	226 696	80.7	78.5	73.1	54.0	62.9	142 662	Espagne (N)
	AH	110 600	131.0					87 870	89.1	85.7	74.0	58.1	57.0	50 116	
Sweden (N)	NH	27 477	76.3	82.4	102.5	100.0	78.3	28 077	81.4	89.3	92.5	56.8	56.9	15 967	Suède (N)
Switzerland (R)	NH	185 055	82.4	96.6	109.6	132.4	109.0	240 013	87.3	90.8	97.9	73.9	72.7	174 388	Suisse (R)
	AH	76 810	79.8	99.3	120.1	135.8	108.5	104 816	89.1	95.4	103.5	73.5	74.9	78 549	
Turkey (N)	NH		50.8	55.3	72.4	73.5	86.3	19 005	155.8	162.1	147.6	102.7	155.5	29 546	Turquie (N)
	AH		36.6	57.3	65.5	72.2	91.0	7 693	137.1	205.4	169.6	103.3	189.1	14 544	
Australia (R)	NH	257 100		80.3	55.9	75.6	89.2	470 300	126.6	82.4	103.1	77.8	59.9	281 500	Australie (R)
Japan (N)	NH	101 330													Japon (N)
	AH	46 758													

AH Arrivals at hotels and similar establishments — Arrivées dans les hôtels et les établissements assimilés
NH Nights in hotels and similar establishments — Nuitées dans les hôtels et établissements assimilés
(R) Tourist count by country of residence — Recensement des touristes par pays de résidence
(N) Tourist count by country of nationality — Recensement des touristes par pays de nationalité
1. Ile de France only — Ile de France seulement

144

Table/Tableau 31

ARRIVALS AND NIGHTS OF FOREIGN TOURISTS AT/IN ALL MEANS OF ACCOMMODATION
ARRIVÉES ET NUITÉES DE TOURISTES ÉTRANGERS DANS L'ENSEMBLE DES MOYENS D'HÉBERGEMENT

From Canada — En provenance du Canada
1987=100

	AAA/NAA	Volume 1981	1982	1983	1984	1985	1986	Volume 1987	1988	1989	1990	1991	1992	Volume 1992	AEH/NEH	
Austria (R)	NAA	150 586	74.4	77.7	92.2	108.1	92.2	227 475	98.2	97.0	109.4	86.3	91.3	207 787	NEH	Autriche (R)
	AAA	50 639	66.8	76.2	95.5	112.2	90.6	84 485	100.2	106.5	122.9	92.1	97.8	82 638	AEH	
Belgium (R)	NAA	55 565	68.6	77.0	100.2	123.3	102.1	85 920	105.6	122.5	132.2	104.4	100.3	86 204	NEH	Belgique (R)
France (R)	NAA	3 570 000	62.6	75.1	94.6	117.0	103.5	5 683 000	100.1	95.4	97.0	81.8	93.9	5 336 000	NEH	France (R)
Germany (R)	NAA	357 000	71.6	81.1	108.0	136.7	110.6	349 000	98.6	123.6	158.2	141.3	166.5	581 000	NEH	Allemagne (R)
	AAA	210 104	67.5	75.3	107.0	116.1	103.7	327 469	107.1	116.3	130.9	106.5	103.7	339 536	AEH	
Greece (N)	NAA	106 336	68.0	76.9	115.2	122.1	104.7	167 937	101.2		127.5	99.8	99.3	166 685	NEH	Grèce (N)
Ireland (R)	NAA	229 322	88.5	96.5	163.8	158.4	86.1	235 251	102.4					569 000	NEH	Irlande (R)
	AAA	81 879	85.8	93.1	122.3	154.7	85.8	91 022	102.4					43 000	AEH	
Italy (N)	NAA	532 348	87.6	95.8	104.2	115.0	93.4	704 207	95.9	104.4	105.5	85.2	89.8	632 043	NEH	Italie (N)
	AAA	158 272	72.2	87.8	102.3	111.8	88.4	261 245	99.2	103.3	107.5	82.4	89.6	234 163	AEH	
Luxembourg (R)	NAA														NEH	Luxembourg (R)
Netherlands (R)	NAA	142 653												161 700	NEH	Pays-Bas (R)
	AAA	77 290												79 300	AEH	
Portugal (N)	NAA	214 213	51.6	63.3	75.8	112.1	104.5	357 996	90.4	98.2	108.4	80.4	62.7	224 440	NEH	Portugal (N)
	AAA	57 908	52.3	62.0	75.5	97.8	91.5	105 055	91.3	99.2	101.1	63.8	55.0	57 814	AEH	
Sweden (N)	NAA	30 113	78.3	85.6	103.7	101.4	81.8	30 786	83.8	91.3	94.7	59.7	60.0	18 463	NEH	Suède (N)
Switzerland (R)	NAA	229 200	83.9	95.9	108.2	128.9	107.9	291 600	87.7	92.1	97.9	76.5	74.9	218 355	NEH	Suisse (R)
	AAA	96 900	83.2	100.4	118.7	134.9	109.2	125 600	90.9	97.4	104.4	76.9	78.6	98 698	AEH	
Turkey (N)	NAA	5 691	48.6	53.3	70.4	71.7	84.1	19 967	155.6	158.4	146.6	101.1	152.6	30 466	NEH	Turquie (N)
	AAA	2 520	35.3	55.5	63.5	71.0	88.4	8 017	139.2	201.2	167.8	103.4	185.0	14 829	AEH	
United Kingdom (R)	NAA	6 583 000	86.4	97.9	102.4	110.7	103.9	8 234 000	107.5	104.2	112.7	92.6	89.7	7 385 000	NEH	Royaume-Uni (R)
Australia (R)	NAA	688 500		137.1	82.3	79.8	89.2	967 000	126.6	185.8	276.4	236.7	178.3	1 724 400	NEH	Australie (R)
New Zealand (R)	NAA								185.8					620 000	NEH	Nouvelle-Zélande (R)

AAA Arrivals in all means of accommodation
NAA Nights in all means of accommodation
(R) Tourist count by country of residence
(N) Tourist count by country of nationality

AEH Arrivées dans l'ensemble des moyens d'hébergement
NEH Nuitées dans l'ensemble des moyens d'hébergement
(R) Recensement des touristes par pays de résidence
(N) Recensement des touristes par pays de nationalité

145

Table/Tableau 32

ARRIVALS OF FOREIGN TOURISTS/VISITORS AT FRONTIERS
ARRIVÉES DE TOURISTES/VISITEURS ÉTRANGERS AUX FRONTIÈRES

From the United States 1987=100

En provenance des États-Unis 1987=100

	T/V	Volume 1981	1982	1983	1984	1985	1986	Volume 1987	1988	1989	1990	1991	1992	Volume 1992	T/V	
France (R)	T	1 370 000	75.2	113.8	140.9	154.2	92.6	1 802 000	108.2	120.3	111.2	91.2	111.4	2 008 000	T	France (R)
	V														V	
Greece (N)	T	321 081	128.1	156.5	182.6	179.3	78.7	260 000	113.5	107.3	105.3	69.4	107.3	278 941	T	Grèce (N)
Iceland (N)	T	17 904	58.4	69.9	76.5	88.7	91.7	35 669	80.5	64.3	63.4	63.1	60.9	21 706	T	Islande (N)
Ireland (R)	V	243 110	84.3	74.9	84.6	105.6	83.2	358 000	104.2	106.1	110.6	87.4	102.2	366 000	V	Irlande (R)
Italy (N)	V	1 443 556	108.1	115.8	119.7	123.7	107.3	1 482 607	91.1	91.5	95.8	76.7	87.3	1 294 423	V	Italie (N)
Norway (N)	V	77 403													V	Norvège (N)
Portugal (N)	T	109 008	84.1	75.8	109.1	108.8	75.5	151 601	128.1	123.2	121.3	94.6	103.3	156 583	T	Portugal (N)
	V	141 698	79.0	95.8	107.3	117.6	76.8	195 117	114.4	120.7	129.2	91.3	113.0	220 452	V	
Spain (N)	V	772 441	87.6	93.8	108.1	115.3	88.9	865 592	99.2	110.2	96.6	75.4	95.4	825 387	V	Espagne (N)
Turkey (N)	V	103 640	80.2	144.7	163.4	150.3	61.0	130 557	126.7	156.6	157.7	60.7	139.7	182 429	V	Turquie (N)
United Kingdom (R)	T	1 715 900	61.6	82.8	98.7	113.1	81.7	2 800 100	93.6	101.5	106.8	82.9	96.1	2 668 000	T	Royaume-Uni (R)
	V													2 690 000	V	
Canada (R)	T	10 968 200	82.3	85.8	88.8	90.9	107.0	12 719 800	100.3	95.8	96.3	94.4	92.9	11 818 700	T	Canada (R)
	V	39 808 700	87.8	87.9	89.2	92.3	103.4	36 952 600	97.8	93.9	94.0	90.9	87.8	32 427 300	V	
Australia (R)	V	113 964	40.6	45.2	51.9	63.6	79.4	309 000	104.3	84.4	81.1	88.0	85.1	262 900	V	Australie (R)
Japan (N)	T	353 151	74.7	83.8	92.9	101.4	100.3	550 261	93.8	96.6	100.8	98.7	101.9	298 049	T	Japon (N)
	V	76 798	42.3	48.1	56.0	68.2	85.4	180 354	92.9	76.2	77.4	73.6	72.8	560 940	V	
New Zealand (R)	T													131 357	T	Nouvelle-Zélande (R)

V Visitors (travellers in Turkey)
T Tourists
(R) Tourist count by country of residence
(N) Tourist count by country of nationality

V Visiteurs (voyageurs en Turquie)
T Touristes
(R) Recensement des touristes par pays de résidence
(N) Recensement des touristes par pays de nationalité

Table/Tableau 33

ARRIVALS AND NIGHTS OF FOREIGN TOURISTS AT/IN HOTELS
ARRIVÉES ET NUITÉES DE TOURISTES ÉTRANGERS DANS L'HÔTELLERIE

From the United States — En provenance des États-Unis

1987=100

Country	AH/NH	Volume 1981	1982	1983	1984	1985	1986	Volume 1987	1988	1989	1990	1991	1992	Volume 1992	AH/NH	
Austria (R)	NH	1 025 779	83.6	102.2	130.5	140.7	80.9	1 551 294	92.1	98.7	126.3	68.5	88.3	1 369 969	NH	Autriche (R)
Belgium (R)	AH	401 197	80.7	104.6	143.3	151.3	74.9	611 918	91.9	100.3	133.3	68.4	92.6	566 756	AH	Belgique (R)
	NH	464 519	100.9	107.9	127.8	143.2	111.4	538 924	86.1	102.8	108.8	90.3	111.9	602 921	NH	
Denmark (N)	NH	337 700	93.1	113.1	119.5	129.0	93.2	444 200	85.1	93.4	89.9	65.6	68.7	305 200	NH	Danemark (N)
Finland (R)	NH	97 744	57.5	75.1	78.9	92.6	79.9	199 655	101.8	101.4	98.8	72.2	75.7	151 137	NH	Finlande (R)
	AH							200 000							AH	
France (R) [1]	NH	2 009 624	57.9	72.1	94.6	107.2	90.9	3 593 735	110.1	145.7	157.8	109.0	138.5	4 976 852	NH	France (R) [1]
	AH	722 553	53.0	62.3	84.0	93.2	92.3	1 528 579	115.2	151.1	161.5	114.7	147.5	2 254 545	AH	
Germany (R)	NH	2 436 048	69.1	85.5	110.8	120.0	88.8	4 037 744	90.5	98.6	110.1	78.8	81.1	3 275 901	NH	Allemagne (R)
	AH	1 255 015	73.1	91.8	121.5	128.4	89.5	1 976 750	90.3	99.3	116.8	77.8	81.3	1 607 951	AH	
Greece (N)	NH	1 244 984	163.9	206.6	247.3	211.4	64.4	790 346	104.8					30 809	NH	Grèce (N)
	AH	486 148	156.3	202.2	253.8	222.5	57.4	323 903	110.3						AH	
Iceland (N)	NH					106.4	80.2	2 012 000	106.0	96.8	101.4	89.1	93.9	1 890 000	NH	Islande (N)
Ireland (R)	NH					105.8	81.9	381 000	99.7	99.2	98.2	75.6	89.5	341 000	NH	Irlande (R)
Italy (N)	NH	3 442 564	87.5	109.7	129.3	138.2	71.2	4 760 100	96.4	101.9	104.8	76.2	95.6	4 550 965	NH	Italie (N)
	AH	1 369 335	89.3	115.6	140.9	149.6	68.0	1 885 168	98.9	103.0	108.4	75.3	97.9	1 846 323	AH	
Luxembourg (R)	NH		66.2	91.4	111.8	129.2	96.6	77 175	82.1	77.3	77.3	57.5	60.6	46 771	NH	Luxembourg (R)
	AH		67.2	89.3	108.5	128.9	96.0	44 692	74.4	74.1	74.1	52.4	55.3	24 728	AH	
Netherlands (R)	NH	667 567	98.0	104.6	128.1	135.0	99.6	836 200	90.4	98.0	109.3	91.4	103.0	861 200	NH	Pays-Bas (R)
	AH	316 813	96.0	106.5	134.6	140.6	98.5	426 900	89.2	96.6	106.7	85.8	95.8	408 800	AH	
Norway (N)	NH	335 282	82.0	98.0	122.7	140.6	89.9	457 414	76.1	75.9	79.7	61.3	76.9	351 528	NH	Norvège (N)
Portugal (N)	NH	460 037	74.3	95.6	113.2	125.8	79.1	627 198	103.6	108.0	107.2	77.4	85.9	538 840	NH	Portugal (N)
	AH	167 609	73.2	98.0	116.4	126.0	74.3	231 624	103.5	109.7	108.9	80.3	87.6	202 938	AH	
Spain (N)	NH	1 577 582	86.5	109.1	129.5	133.2	77.9	1 906 206	92.2	96.3	92.0	67.9	78.7	1 499 247	NH	Espagne (N)
	AH	626 736	81.0	120.4	144.0	154.0	88.2	805 661	96.2	102.6	98.3	71.9	84.4	679 834	AH	
Sweden (N)	NH	272 925	84.4	113.4	119.2	138.4	93.4	348 593	93.4	95.1	93.8	68.4	76.7	267 328	NH	Suède (N)
Switzerland (R)	NH	1 760 155	88.8	102.3	131.3	139.9	89.1	2 332 231	87.4	95.4	107.6	67.6	81.0	1 889 289	NH	Suisse (R)
	AH	777 682	90.1	106.9	140.2	146.5	86.1	1 037 368	89.5	99.5	116.1	69.0	85.5	887 431	AH	
Turkey (N)	NH		55.8	71.5	95.1	100.1	81.7	267 680	117.6	142.3	130.3	105.5	144.5	386 880	NH	Turquie (N)
	AH		53.8	77.0	85.3	95.2	82.0	92 831	127.2	180.5	170.7	98.3	170.3	158 048	AH	
Australia (R)	NH	922 000		45.8	39.8	61.1	79.4	2 716 500	104.3	75.4	77.2	77.7	70.7	1 920 100	NH	Australie (R)
Japan (N)	NH	1 317 494													NH	Japon (N)
	AH	578 483													AH	

AH Arrivals at hotels and similar establishments — Arrivées dans les hôtels et les établissements assimilés
NH Nights in hotels and similar establishments — Nuitées dans les hôtels et établissements assimilés
(R) Tourist count by country of residence — Recensement des touristes par pays de résidence
(N) Tourist count by country of nationality — Recensement des touristes par pays de nationalité
1. Ile de France only — Ile de France seulement

Table/Tableau 34

ARRIVALS AND NIGHTS OF FOREIGN TOURISTS AT/IN ALL MEANS OF ACCOMMODATION
ARRIVÉES ET NUITÉES DE TOURISTES ÉTRANGERS DANS L'ENSEMBLE DES MOYENS D'HÉBERGEMENT

From the United States / *En provenance des États-Unis*

1987=100

Country	AAA/NAA	Volume 1981	1982	1983	1984	1985	1986	Volume 1987	1988	1989	1990	1991	1992	Volume 1992	AEH/NEH	
Austria (R)	NAA	1 170 124	83.6	101.2	128.1	138.2	81.9	1 719 816	92.5	98.7	124.4	69.3	88.8	1 526 478	NEH	Autriche (R)
Belgium (R)	NAA	440 965	79.7	102.3	138.7	147.1	75.9	671 474	92.3	100.7	131.8	69.8	93.5	627 632	NEH	Belgique (R)
	AAA	490 742	77.3	82.6	101.1	121.8	109.2	732 728	78.2	80.6	86.6	69.6	84.5	619 092	AEH	
Denmark (N)	NAA	362 935	94.2	112.3	118.4	127.5	93.4	467 349	85.3	93.4	90.1	66.5	69.4	324 200	NEH	Danemark (N)
France (R)	NAA	10 960 000	59.1	89.3	107.2	121.4	91.1	25 477 000	103.2	69.8	67.8	56.0	69.0	17 569 000	NEH	France (R)
	AAA	1 370 000	75.2	113.8	140.9	154.2	92.6	1 802 000	108.2		111.2	91.2	111.4	2 008 000	AEH	
Germany (R)	NAA	2 469 301	66.3	82.6	110.1	119.3	88.9	4 269 863	90.7	99.1	110.4	80.0	82.5	3 523 534	NEH	Allemagne (R)
	AAA	1 260 557	70.0	88.2	120.6	127.0	89.4	2 071 647	90.7	99.8	117.2	78.9	82.5	1 709 312	AEH	
Greece (N)	NAA	1 335 728	172.0	215.3	260.0	210.5	65.3	799 545	104.6						NEH	Grèce (N)
	AAA	508 588	161.5	207.6	262.4	221.4	57.9	327 799							AEH	
Ireland (R)	NAA	2 607 000	77.0	89.3	83.9	102.3	82.2	4 001 500	102.7	113.6	110.8	96.8	106.4	4 256 000	NEH	Irlande (R)
	AAA	249 000												374 000	AEH	
Italy (N)	NAA	4 181 985	97.0	118.2	135.7	144.0	79.0	5 104 996	96.4	101.3	104.7	77.5	96.7	4 936 644	NEH	Italie (N)
	AAA	1 442 963	89.9	115.6	139.9	148.6	69.2	1 956 153	101.9	103.0	108.6	76.1	98.5	1 926 351	AEH	
Luxembourg (R)	NAA		62.4	84.8	109.4	124.9	94.8	84 936	82.6		78.3	61.7	68.9	58 542	NEH	Luxembourg (R)
	AAA			81.1	106.3	124.6	94.4	50 046	76.8		74.4	55.0	59.3	29 700	AEH	
Netherlands (R)	NAA	755 437												944 000	NEH	Pays-Bas (R)
	AAA	365 860												451 200	AEH	
Portugal (N)	NAA	479 506	74.5	94.7	111.1	123.8	78.3	651 637	102.4	106.3	105.5	76.7	84.5	550 449	NEH	Portugal (N)
	AAA	173 370	73.4	97.5	115.3	125.1	74.6	237 985	103.4	109.3	108.8	80.3	87.3	207 664	AEH	
Spain (N)	NAA	1 887 258													NEH	Espagne (N)
	AAA	744 353													AEH	
Sweden (N)	NAA	285 581	84.3	112.1	118.5	137.2	93.6	364 304	93.3	95.4	93.9	69.3	77.3	281 476	NEH	Suède (N)
Switzerland (R)	NAA	1 978 900	89.8	101.6	129.0	138.1	90.5	2 572 800	88.6	96.3	108.6	70.1	82.2	2 114 320	NEH	Suisse (R)
	AAA	855 700	91.2	106.7	137.6	144.3	86.6	1 116 900	90.0	99.7	115.6	70.1	86.1	961 355	AEH	
Turkey (N)	NAA	103 644	55.1	70.6	94.4	99.0	81.4	273 805	117.6	142.1	130.5	105.0	113.6	393 281	NEH	Turquie (N)
	AAA	36 275	53.1	75.8	84.5	94.2	81.1	95 073	127.1	178.7	169.4	97.3	168.1	159 848	AEH	
United Kingdom (R)	NAA	18 067 000	66.3	79.9	92.2	107.8	85.0	28 940 000	88.2	95.4	97.2	86.2	91.4	26 448 000	NEH	Royaume-Uni (R)
	AAA													2 668 000	AEH	
Canada (R)	NAA	51 503 100	85.5	87.3	95.7	97.2	114.4	55 367 000	101.5	96.8	88.9	89.2	83.6	46 289 400	NEH	Canada (R)
	AAA	10 968 200	82.3	85.8	88.8	90.9	107.0	12 719 800	100.3	95.8	96.3	94.4	92.9	11 818 700	AEH	
Australia (R)	NAA	1 696 300												6 196 000	NEH	Australie (R)
New Zealand (R)	NAA				63.7	80.5	93.3	2 448 551	92.2	82.5	86.9	77.7	80.6	1 973 664	NEH	Nouvelle-Zélande (R)

AAA Arrivals in all means of accommodation
NAA Nights in all means of accommodation
(R) Tourist count by country of residence
(N) Tourist count by country of nationality

AEH Arrivées dans l'ensemble des moyens d'hébergement
NEH Nuitées dans l'ensemble des moyens d'hébergement
(R) Recensement des touristes par pays de résidence
(N) Recensement des touristes par pays de nationalité

Table/Tableau 35

ARRIVALS OF FOREIGN TOURISTS/VISITORS AT FRONTIERS
ARRIVÉES DE TOURISTES/VISITEURS ÉTRANGERS AUX FRONTIÈRES

From France / En provenance de la France
1987=100

	T/V	Volume 1981	1982	1983	1984	1985	1986	Volume 1987	1988	1989	1990	1991	1992	Volume 1992	T/V	
Greece (N)	T	296 499	65.8	58.7	79.6	86.5	91.9	510 000	92.0	93.7	110.9	92.3	106.3	542 222	T	Grèce (N)
Iceland (N)	T	4 251	83.4	73.8	91.2	84.4	105.8	5 311	115.6	154.2	188.7	189.6	149.2	7 925	T	Islande (N)
Ireland (R)	V	86 422	84.5	73.0	73.0	83.8	77.5	111 000	96.4	122.5	176.6	197.3	195.5	217 000	V	Irlande (R)
Italy (N)	V	7 465 870	93.7	87.3	93.6	96.3	94.8	9 042 482	99.3	103.8	102.0	100.8	97.3	8 798 740	V	Italie (N)
Norway (N)	V	25 717	67.5	76.3	75.6	77.4	82.3	413 672	136.7	147.7	149.4	161.3	156.6	647 807	V	Norvège (N)
Portugal (N)	T	228 578	66.3	75.4	75.1	79.9	80.5	434 767	136.5	148.8	151.4	163.6	157.7	685 682	T	Portugal (N)
Spain (N)	V	10 659 443	93.2	88.5	85.5	94.3	96.6	11 671 357	103.5	102.8	99.6	103.3	101.0	11 792 108	V	Espagne (N)
Turkey (N)	V	96 694	58.9	52.3	61.3	89.0	85.4	168 566	146.4	168.2	184.4	69.5	146.9	247 603	V	Turquie (N)
United Kingdom (R)	V	1 413 400	75.6	75.5	81.2	80.7	87.4	2 008 400	98.1	112.6	114.4	114.0	123.3	2 477 000	V	Royaume-Uni (R)
Canada (R)	T	118 800	62.2	47.8	58.4	56.5	73.9	189 800	121.0	128.9	136.3	161.5	163.3	310 000	T	Canada (R)
Canada (R)	V	137 100	62.9	47.4	57.8	55.6	74.0	210 800	118.8	124.2	131.3	154.1	155.7	328 300	V	
United States (R)	T	411 096	77.8	56.0	60.7	61.6	80.7	544 435	113.6	120.1	131.5	141.5	146.1	795 444	T	États-Unis (R)
Australia (R)	V	8 376	59.9	58.5	65.5	70.2	81.3	17 100	122.8	117.5	123.4	132.7	148.5	25 400	V	Australie (R)
Japan (N)	T													20 490	T	Japon (N)
Japan (N)	V	27 624	79.6	77.5	91.7	106.7	95.0	37 185	108.8	127.1	137.2	134.8	130.7	48 605	V	
New Zealand (R)	T	1 872	48.0	50.6	58.1	63.7	69.5	3 812	90.2	106.9	90.0	121.8	139.7	5 325	T	Nouvelle-Zélande (R)

V Visitors (travellers in Turkey)
T Tourists
(R) Tourist count by country of residence
(N) Tourist count by country of nationality

V Visiteurs (voyageurs en Turquie)
T Touristes
(R) Recensement des touristes par pays de résidence
(N) Recensement des touristes par pays de nationalité

Table/Tableau 36

ARRIVALS AND NIGHTS OF FOREIGN TOURISTS AT/IN HOTELS
ARRIVÉES ET NUITÉES DE TOURISTES ÉTRANGERS DANS L'HÔTELLERIE

From France / En provenance de la France — 1987=100

Country	AH/NH	Volume 1981	1982	1983	1984	1985	1986	Volume 1987	1988	1989	1990	1991	1992	Volume 1992	AH/NH	
Austria (R)	NH	1 402 410	75.6	66.6	85.8	91.6	101.7	2 086 666	99.4	108.7	113.7	118.7	104.9	2 189 896	NH	Autriche (R)
	AH	432 018	82.1	70.9	90.0	94.9	103.6	554 447	101.0	111.9	118.2	120.2	104.0	576 589	AH	
Belgium (R)	NH	527 133	93.9	79.8	87.4	95.2	97.8	605 911	108.5	129.4	136.0	136.6	166.6	1 009 516	NH	Belgique (R)
	AH													1 009 516	AH	
Denmark (N)	NH	85 900	117.2	94.1	105.5	109.8	99.9	76 700	98.8	103.0	107.6	111.1	105.9	81 200	NH	Danemark (N)
Finland (R)	NH	46 906	82.0	75.1	95.1	93.5	87.9	61 888	107.3	115.2	135.2	130.6	135.2	83 679	NH	Finlande (R)
	AH							65 000							AH	
Germany (R)	NH	1 146 197	90.2	78.4	88.6	93.9	98.0	1 186 669	103.0	117.4	123.6	118.3	111.4	1 322 317	NH	Allemagne (R)
	AH	606 546	92.3	80.4	90.6	95.5	98.5	622 464	102.8	116.6	122.2	117.2	110.9	690 102	AH	
Greece (N)	NH	1 876 098	79.7	66.6	90.9	103.4	94.7	2 550 897	95.9						NH	Grèce (N)
	AH	624 927	87.7	71.2	97.5	103.4	98.0	778 404	92.8						AH	
Iceland (N)	NH		102.5	83.1	88.0	102.0	97.4	353 000	126.6	133.1	267.1	252.7	252.1	890 000	NH	Islande (N)
Ireland (R)	NH		99.4	81.3	90.2	81.2	96.1	69 000	97.1	111.6	188.4	200.0	201.4	139 000	NH	Irlande (R)
	AH													26 778	AH	
Italy (N)	NH	5 163 744	90.0	72.2	78.3	91.6	90.5	5 743 428	96.3	89.4	87.4	88.8	79.5	4 564 715	NH	Italie (N)
	AH	1 557 879	102.9	72.6	77.9	91.6	91.9	1 802 788	99.6	97.6	97.6	95.0	87.9	1 585 031	AH	
Luxembourg (R)	NH							75 937	112.0		142.3	130.8	126.3	95 931	NH	Luxembourg (R)
	AH							42 232	113.8		129.9	121.2	119.5	50 463	AH	
Netherlands (R)	NH	420 571	96.4	75.0	86.0	87.4	96.9	459 800	96.7	101.1	118.7	107.8	119.6	549 900	NH	Pays-Bas (R)
	AH	229 629	94.7	75.7	88.3	88.6	97.0	263 800	97.7	98.2	115.4	98.5	109.1	287 800	AH	
Norway (N)	NH	87 715	74.9	61.6	85.6	85.3	91.8	119 521	100.3	117.1	142.8	174.4	202.9	242 475	NH	Norvège (N)
Portugal (N)	NH	536 732	86.0	76.0	96.1	99.1	110.3	678 825	109.1	117.8	121.6	144.4	115.6	784 594	NH	Portugal (N)
	AH	167 621	74.1	66.7	83.8	86.9	98.8	253 573	110.5	117.2	122.2	138.2	119.1	301 913	AH	
Spain (N)	NH	6 092 087	91.3	88.4	93.5	88.0	91.1	6 809 646	104.5	103.5	96.2	98.8	89.1	6 064 101	NH	Espagne (N)
	AH	1 381 252	82.7	82.9	82.2	80.4	93.0	1 675 372	103.2	104.2	90.4	94.5	95.1	1 592 851	AH	
Sweden (N)	NH	84 559	100.1	86.7	98.8	100.0	104.7	84 236	107.9	114.1	116.7	109.8	109.9	92 599	NH	Suède (N)
Switzerland (R)	NH	1 924 715	107.8	93.5	100.0	100.0	105.1	1 612 186	96.7	97.8	95.2	95.9	89.5	1 442 258	NH	Suisse (R)
	AH	632 477	107.0	89.0	97.5	97.3	103.5	544 954	99.0	102.9	103.2	102.6	96.8	527 755	AH	
Turkey (N)	NH		30.0	35.9	41.4	64.1	74.4	847 620	132.3	133.8	142.1	55.2	121.6	1 030 526	NH	Turquie (N)
	AH		28.6	35.8	42.3	65.4	76.0	454 878	119.2	144.2	138.9	40.4	95.5	434 260	AH	
Australia (R)	NH	69 000													NH	Australie (R)
Japan (N)	NH	132 402													NH	Japon (N)
	AH	49 758													AH	

AH Arrivals at hotels and similar establishments — Arrivées dans les hôtels et les établissements assimilés
NH Nights in hotels and similar establishments — Nuitées dans les hôtels et établissements assimilés
(R) Tourist count by country of residence — Recensement des touristes par pays de résidence
(N) Tourist count by country of nationality — Recensement des touristes par pays de nationalité

Table/Tableau 37

ARRIVALS AND NIGHTS OF FOREIGN TOURISTS AT/IN ALL MEANS OF ACCOMMODATION
ARRIVÉES ET NUITÉES DE TOURISTES ÉTRANGERS DANS L'ENSEMBLE DES MOYENS D'HÉBERGEMENT

From France / En provenance de la France
1987=100

Country	AAA/NAA	Volume 1981	1982	1983	1984	1985	1986	Volume 1987	1988	1989	1990	1991	1992	Volume 1992	AEH/NEH	
Austria (R)	NAA	1 919 737	80.7	68.8	88.6	93.0	101.4	2 666 491	99.4	108.6	115.4	118.9	106.7	2 845 545	NEH	Autriche (R)
	AAA	552 784	85.1	70.9	92.2	95.9	104.3	693 199	101.2	112.3	120.8	122.0	106.4	737 709	AEH	
Belgium (R)	NAA	883 244	103.4	92.1	98.3	97.2	100.0	972 359	104.0	124.5	129.9	124.8	134.5	1 307 776	NEH	Belgique (R)
	AAA													1 307 776	AEH	
Denmark (N)	NAA	147 335	112.5	83.0	109.0	105.0	96.0	137 030	101.3	104.5	108.3	111.1	109.8	150 400	NEH	Danemark (N)
Germany (R)	NAA	1 198 430	80.6	70.2	86.6	92.6	96.3	1 396 948	105.0	118.7	125.5	130.3	122.7	1 714 516	NEH	Allemagne (R)
	AAA	615 837	84.9	74.0	89.8	94.7	97.8	687 899	103.9	117.5	123.5	127.9	120.6	829 439	AEH	
Greece (N)	NAA	2 351 936	92.9	77.4	101.8	102.4	94.5	2 729 910	95.0						NEH	Grèce (N)
	AAA	743 501	95.7	78.1	104.2	103.0	98.8	851 363							AEH	
Ireland (R)	NAA	1 021 000	75.5	74.3	59.8	75.2	72.2	1 451 500	107.9	148.7	215.0	208.7	229.0	3 324 000	NEH	Irlande (R)
	AAA	91 980												220 000	AEH	
Italy (N)	NAA	7 470 302	117.5	94.1	97.9	101.0	106.0	7 162 935	95.5	88.1	85.9	87.3	77.8	5 571 214	NEH	Italie (N)
	AAA	1 875 195	102.3	83.6	92.5	94.3	98.0	2 104 321	99.1	96.6	94.5	93.4	85.6	1 801 753	AEH	
Luxembourg (R)	NAA		90.6	70.0	86.2	90.8	92.2	95 753	113.3	139.3	133.0	136.8	126.9	121 542	NEH	Luxembourg (R)
Netherlands (R)	NAA	604 420		69.9	83.9	88.3	93.4	48 141	115.2	133.0	139.7	126.0	122.3	58 869	NEH	Pays-Bas (R)
	AAA	325 696												791 600	AEH	
Portugal (N)	NAA	1 034 395	95.6	82.6	87.9	90.2	104.7	1 134 837	110.5	117.2	116.0	130.8	105.3	1 195 064	NEH	Portugal (N)
	AAA	284 842	75.8	67.1	78.2	80.1	98.1	421 060	108.6	114.6	116.9	127.2	109.1	459 327	AEH	
Spain (N)	NAA	6 910 530												396 000	NEH	Espagne (N)
	AAA	1 515 432													AEH	
Sweden (N)	NAA	143 925	99.0	80.9	102.6	97.2	106.8	146 823	103.1	113.5	124.2	112.2	113.8	167 108	NEH	Suède (N)
Switzerland (R)	NAA	3 039 000	111.3	93.5	95.7	96.2	102.2	2 607 400	95.6	94.8	93.6	95.7	90.0	2 346 388	NEH	Suisse (R)
	AAA	819 200	107.1	88.5	96.5	96.2	103.0	725 300	99.2	102.0	103.5	103.8	98.7	715 778	AEH	
Turkey (N)	NAA	223 853	26.5	34.2	39.2	59.9	75.7	1 091 517	140.1	135.3	145.3	57.8	132.6	1 447 251	NEH	Turquie (N)
	AAA	109 124	27.3	35.0	41.0	64.4	75.8	491 599	120.9	144.4	141.3	42.0	99.1	487 120	AEH	
United Kingdom (R)	NAA	10 439 000	66.9	67.5	78.1	76.6	73.1	16 709 000	84.1	97.1	101.1	88.5	89.4	14 936 000	NEH	Royaume-Uni (R)
	AAA													1 992 000	AEH	
Canada (R)	NAA	1 602 000	65.0	52.0	61.0	59.1	77.8	2 322 400	122.4	125.8	132.3	163.2	164.5	3 819 600	NEH	Canada (R)
	AAA	118 800	63.0	48.3	59.1	57.2	74.8	187 600	122.4	129.5	137.9	163.4	165.2	310 000	AEH	
Australia (R)	NAA	166 300													NEH	Australie (R)
New Zealand (R)	NAA													103 560	NEH	Nouvelle-Zélande (R)

AAA Arrivals in all means of accommodation — AEH Arrivées dans l'ensemble des moyens d'hébergement
NAA Nights in all means of accommodation — NEH Nuitées dans l'ensemble des moyens d'hébergement
(R) Tourist count by country of residence — (R) Recensement des touristes par pays de résidence
(N) Tourist count by country of nationality — (N) Recensement des touristes par pays de nationalité

Table/Tableau 38

ARRIVALS OF FOREIGN TOURISTS/VISITORS AT FRONTIERS
ARRIVÉES DE TOURISTES/VISITEURS ÉTRANGERS AUX FRONTIÈRES

From Italy
1987=100

En provenance de l'Italie
1987=100

From Italy	T/V	Volume 1981	1982	1983	1984	1985	1986	Volume 1987	1988	1989	1990	1991	1992	Volume 1992	T/V	En provenance de l'Italie
France (R)	T / V	1 390 000	63.4	69.5	80.6	83.8	88.6	3 157 000	109.0	166.0	179.2	186.8	227.2	7 174 000	T / V	France (R)
Greece (N)	T	225 479	48.2	70.5	70.7	78.3	94.6	465 000	117.0	122.4	133.5	111.2	133.9	622 619	T	Grèce (N)
Iceland (N)	T	821	33.5	39.0	38.4	43.3	78.5	2 699	104.6	110.4	133.9	178.1	154.1	4 158	T	Islande (N)
Norway (N)	V	9 301													V	Norvège (N)
Portugal (N)	T	46 967	45.3	44.8	49.4	68.8	75.3	120 317	115.4	138.9	157.4	208.2	214.8	258 443	T	Portugal (N)
Portugal (N)	V	68 288	53.9	49.2	53.4	69.5	80.8	134 377	115.1	137.8	164.5	216.5	210.6	283 063	V	Portugal (N)
Spain (N)	V	558 863	55.2	56.1	68.3	85.7	91.4	1 192 578	111.8	126.8	138.9	148.2	155.3	1 852 567	V	Espagne (N)
Turkey (N)	V	67 707	43.5	56.3	64.3	73.1	85.6	102 358	141.0	150.5	152.7	62.7	154.5	158 185	V	Turquie (N)
United Kingdom (R)	V	409 200	58.2	67.1	69.6	72.4	72.3	682 800	96.8	103.7	104.4	105.7	113.8	777 000	V	Royaume-Uni (R)
Canada (R)	T	51 000	61.1	59.3	69.0	71.6	84.6	77 100	111.9	120.4	117.9	113.2	123.0	94 800	T	Canada (R)
United States (R)	V	65 800	60.1	55.7	63.4	63.0	77.8	103 500	104.0	103.8	97.7	96.6	107.3	111 100	V	États-Unis (R)
United States (R)	T	229 250	72.9	62.3	68.5	69.1	84.1	318 815	111.8	111.3	124.2	150.2	185.0	589 837	T	États-Unis (R)
Australia (R)	V	12 154	62.7	62.2	69.4	75.1	89.6	19 300	130.6	106.2	126.4	125.9	142.0	27 400	V	Australie (R)
Japan (N)	T	14 657	65.6	68.2	75.2	103.3	90.1	20 880	112.4	132.5	142.7	144.6	128.7	26 866	T	Japon (N)
New Zealand (R)	V	1 004												11 038	V	Nouvelle-Zélande (R)
New Zealand (R)	T		35.1	33.1	36.6	48.3	65.6	2 611	107.8	100.7	120.7	137.1	144.2	3 766	T	Nouvelle-Zélande (R)

V   Visitors (travellers in Turkey)
T   Tourists
(R)   Tourist count by country of residence
(N)   Tourist count by country of nationality

V   Visiteurs (voyageurs en Turquie)
T   Touristes
(R)   Recensement des touristes par pays de résidence
(N)   Recensement des touristes par pays de nationalité

Table/Tableau 39

ARRIVALS AND NIGHTS OF FOREIGN TOURISTS AT/IN HOTELS
ARRIVÉES ET NUITÉES DE TOURISTES ÉTRANGERS DANS L'HÔTELLERIE

From Italy — 1987=100 / En provenance de l'Italie — 1987=100

Country	AH/NH	Volume 1981	1982	1983	1984	1985	1986	Volume 1987	1988	1989	1990	1991	1992	Volume 1992	AH/NH	
Austria (R)	NH	697 087	53.7	58.1	69.7	74.2	90.3	1 461 837	126.2	166.9	184.0	192.0	207.8	3 037 178	NH	Autriche (R)
	AH	321 254	55.3	59.2	71.2	74.5	90.5	633 896	123.7	156.8	168.2	164.7	169.5	1 074 544	AH	
Belgium (R)	NH	184 815	77.2	83.2	87.1	91.8	90.9	239 610	111.1	134.4	143.8	141.5	163.8	392 560	NH	Belgique (R)
Denmark (N)	NH	87 100	95.0	92.7	91.6	88.7	88.5	88 600	117.3	122.8	143.5	160.6	178.0	157 700	NH	Danemark (N)
Finland (R)	NH	30 841	56.2	59.0	66.8	69.9	75.2	67 284	121.6	129.2	117.8	121.6	113.8	76 557	NH	Finlande (R)
France (R)[1]	NH	1 308 446	31.5	32.5	34.5	33.8	91.5	3 957 665	132.9	172.2	177.1	176.9	211.8	8 380 527	NH	France (R)[1]
	AH	476 045	25.4	25.2	27.0	27.6	91.5	1 764 895	124.7	167.6	176.4	177.8	210.9	3 722 894	AH	
Germany (R)	NH	792 917	70.9	74.2	81.3	85.5	93.5	1 176 523	113.1	133.9	143.6	147.5	139.2	1 637 150	NH	Allemagne (R)
	AH	406 778	70.9	74.1	81.5	85.9	92.8	610 703	113.9	134.0	143.7	147.2	137.6	840 586	AH	
Greece (N)	NH	860 681	65.5	71.2	81.2	99.7	97.1	1 386 069	119.0						NH	Grèce (N)
Ireland (R)	NH	282 598	61.0	69.8	77.8	88.5	87.0	499 607	99.6					509 000	NH	Irlande (R)
	AH													80 000	AH	
Luxembourg (R)	NH														NH	Luxembourg (R)
	AH														AH	
Netherlands (R)	NH	206 372	67.8	61.7	68.2	71.6	86.4	311 200	116.2	132.1	196.0	173.1	166.2	517 100	NH	Pays-Bas (R)
	AH	91 063	66.3	62.8	70.6	76.3	87.9	142 700	115.6	146.4	209.7	173.0	171.1	244 200	AH	
Norway (N)	NH	128 971	48.7	49.8	55.6	69.9	81.1	303 809	115.5	124.7	151.3	197.1	188.6	573 061	NH	Norvège (N)
Portugal (N)	NH	45 107	44.2	48.4	54.2	68.3	79.9	118 628	113.6	124.2	147.8	195.9	195.9	232 420	NH	Portugal (N)
	AH														AH	
Spain (N)	NH	1 437 881	52.1	55.0	83.1	94.9	90.3	4 312 615	107.8	106.4	99.3	107.4	122.0	5 261 600	NH	Espagne (N)
	AH	456 463	68.5	62.9	87.6	98.1	101.8	1 086 117	103.6	110.3	97.3	103.0	102.6	1 114 892	AH	
Sweden (N)	NH	60 558	83.5	65.4	73.2	79.4	82.4	95 809	100.1	123.0	128.9	123.5	120.7	115 680	NH	Suède (N)
Switzerland (R)	NH	878 348	82.0	81.1	86.0	88.0	94.3	1 037 179	105.7	122.3	131.6	135.7	134.7	1 397 301	NH	Suisse (R)
	AH	425 596	33.7	56.7	86.6	88.7	95.3	510 844	104.8	120.2	124.8	129.1	127.5	651 364	AH	
Turkey (N)	NH		32.8	53.6	60.5	69.0	76.2	314 344	124.5	120.4	127.5	93.3	161.6	507 873	NH	Turquie (N)
	AH				58.6	69.6	75.0	152 543	122.8	129.4	135.9	75.4	142.3	217 119	AH	
Australia (R)	NH	74 400		32.7	49.3	64.2	89.6	145 500	130.5						NH	Australie (R)
Japan (N)	NH	89 831													NH	Japon (N)
	AH	25 110													AH	

AH Arrivals at hotels and similar establishments — Arrivées dans les hôtels et les établissements assimilés
NH Nights in hotels and similar establishments — Nuitées dans les hôtels et établissements assimilés
(R) Tourist count by country of residence — Recensement des touristes par pays de résidence
(N) Tourist count by country of nationality — Recensement des touristes par pays de nationalité

Table/Tableau 40

ARRIVALS AND NIGHTS OF FOREIGN TOURISTS AT/IN ALL MEANS OF ACCOMMODATION
ARRIVÉES ET NUITÉES DE TOURISTES ÉTRANGERS DANS L'ENSEMBLE DES MOYENS D'HÉBERGEMENT

From Italy / En provenance de l'Italie
1987=100

Country / Pays	AAA/NAA	Volume 1981	1982	1983	1984	1985	1986	Volume 1987	1988	1989	1990	1991	1992	Volume 1992	AEH/NEH
Austria (R) / Autriche (R)	NAA	831 050	54.9	62.2	73.7	74.8	89.8	1 690 820	123.7	164.8	182.8	195.6	213.5	3 609 209	NEH
	AAA	361 153	56.3	61.4	76.4	75.6	90.6	707 581	122.4	155.7	167.4	167.7	172.3	1 219 512	AEH
Belgium (R) / Belgique (R)	NAA	214 313	79.0	84.6	88.9	92.7	92.0	269 549	112.9	134.0	143.7	138.9	159.6	430 160	NEH
Denmark (N) / Danemark (N)	NAA	117 736	86.2	87.8	87.1	87.7	85.4	137 726	111.4	121.0	136.2	132.6	169.4	233 300	NEH
France (R) / France (R)	NAA	8 340 000	63.4	67.8	76.0	77.7	86.8	26 655 000	105.8	109.8	114.4	132.6	159.2	42 441 000	NEH
	AAA	1 390 000	69.5	69.5	80.6	83.8	88.6	3 157 000	109.0		179.2	186.8	227.2	7 174 000	AEH
Germany (R) / Allemagne (R)	NAA	809 003	68.3	71.3	80.1	84.9	93.4	1 247 018	113.3	133.5	142.9	155.8	146.6	1 827 793	NEH
	AAA	408 903	68.5	71.5	80.7	85.3	92.6	635 888	113.9	133.7	143.4	155.9	145.7	926 256	AEH
Greece (N) / Grèce (N)	NAA	1 103 421	65.8	69.4	83.7	89.5	86.4	1 756 643	102.1						NEH
	AAA	353 044	69.4	83.7	89.5			358 261	153.0						AEH
Ireland (R) / Irlande (R)	NAA		107.0	120.8	133.7	141.9	138.3								NEH
	AAA		120.8	133.7	141.9										AEH
Luxembourg (R) / Luxembourg (R)	NAA													1 340 000	NEH
	AAA													101 000	AEH
Netherlands (R) / Pays-Bas (R)	NAA	264 611												644 500	NEH
	AAA	118 447												301 800	AEH
Portugal (N) / Portugal (N)	NAA	194 800	57.9	53.2	54.3	72.2	86.4	372 162	114.7	124.6	143.9	190.6	173.6	646 027	NEH
	AAA	57 111	45.7	49.6	53.2	70.9	85.0	143 687	112.5	123.9	141.5	188.3	181.4	260 621	AEH
Spain (N) / Espagne (N)	NAA	1 437 881													NEH
	AAA	456 463													AEH
Sweden (N) / Suède (N)	NAA	65 949	66.0	64.0	72.5	76.7	81.1	108 185	101.9	125.6	130.3	124.0	120.3	130 178	NEH
Switzerland (R) / Suisse (R)	NAA	1 130 200	80.7	80.9	85.6	87.1	93.8	1 408 900	107.6	122.7	135.0	140.3	144.0	2 028 631	NEH
	AAA	483 300	81.0	81.5	86.8	89.0	95.7	595 300	105.3	119.6	125.5	130.3	129.7	772 149	AEH
Turkey (N) / Turquie (N)	NAA	109 066	28.8	50.3	67.3	75.4	69.7	379 061	129.8	129.2	140.8	96.8	169.4	642 069	NEH
United Kingdom (R) / Royaume-Uni (R)	AAA	45 436	29.3	48.3	53.4	63.1	68.0	172 226	123.9	130.8	136.5	72.5	135.8	233 962	AEH
	NAA	5 654 000	56.6	68.9	67.3	75.4	66.4	9 235 000	92.1	89.6	90.5	98.3	95.4	8 807 000	NEH
Canada (R) / Canada (R)	NAA	674 000	73.4	54.3	73.1	75.5	83.6	999 900	107.1	100.7	89.5	88.9	90.7	907 000	NEH
Australia (R) / Australie (R)	NAA	144 100	39.4	39.4	39.3	42.6	89.6	336 900	130.6						NEH
New Zealand (R) / Nouvelle-Zélande (R)	NAA													57 817	NEH

AAA Arrivals in all means of accommodation
NAA Nights in all means of accommodation
(R) Tourist count by country of residence
(N) Tourist count by country of nationality

AEH Arrivées dans l'ensemble des moyens d'hébergement
NEH Nuitées dans l'ensemble des moyens d'hébergement
(R) Recensement des touristes par pays de résidence
(N) Recensement des touristes par pays de nationalité

Table/Tableau 41

ARRIVALS OF FOREIGN TOURISTS/VISITORS AT FRONTIERS
ARRIVÉES DE TOURISTES/VISITEURS ÉTRANGERS AUX FRONTIÈRES

From Japan — 1987=100 / En provenance du Japon — 1987=100

Country	T/V	Volume 1981	1982	1983	1984	1985	1986	Volume 1987	1988	1989	1990	1991	1992	Volume 1992	T/V
France (R)	T	445 000	81.3	89.2	89.2	92.3	88.8	572 000	115.7	134.8	131.1	73.8	76.0	435 000	T
Greece (N) / Grèce (N)	T	75 154	38.6	45.3	94.0	100.9	92.5	92 000	114.1	113.0	117.1	62.9	119.2	109 680	T
Iceland (N) / Islande (N)	T	339			53.9	71.6	85.7	1 000	99.3	125.4	116.4	125.4	143.1	1 431	T
Italy (N) / Italie (N)	V	263 041	78.9	85.0	88.4	87.1	104.3	384 837	100.0	118.7	165.5	145.4	192.8	741 984	V
Norway (N) / Norvège (N)	V	9 966	42.7	47.6	58.4	66.7	79.8	27 574	102.2	109.2	118.5	96.4	92.7	25 569	T
Portugal (N)	T	12 996	48.4	50.2	68.2	69.9	81.3	28 596	103.7	112.3	123.9	99.4	95.2	27 234	T
Spain (N) / Espagne (N)	V	86 731	61.5	72.8	83.2	97.1	92.8	130 487	130.5	165.9	186.8	142.9	170.3	222 243	V
Turkey (N) / Turquie (N)	V	6 944	29.8	36.9	62.0	79.8	79.5	21 067	132.9	153.3	167.8	87.7	172.8	36 398	V
United Kingdom (R) / Royaume-Uni (R)	V	163 800	53.7	57.3	67.5	70.9	69.1	297 200	130.6	169.9	189.4	154.1	179.7	534 000	V
Canada (R)	T	113 600	46.1	46.8	54.3	58.5	79.1	249 200	130.1	156.4	164.8	157.7	157.4	392 300	T
		146 500	44.8	44.5	52.1	56.0	75.5	311 700	129.8	148.4	152.1	154.1	159.1	495 800	
United States (R) / États-Unis (R)	V	1 353 801	67.5	60.3	66.5	70.3	79.0	2 128 481	119.1	144.7	151.8	156.0	171.6	3 652 828	T
Australia (R) / Australie (R)	V	53 699	28.0	33.3	40.8	49.9	67.5	215 600	163.4	162.1	222.6	245.1	292.2	629 900	V
New Zealand (R) / Nouvelle-Zélande (R)	T	25 736	35.9	42.7	55.0	66.0	82.3	76 150	123.2	127.8	141.6	150.6	169.4	128 962	T

V   Visitors (travellers in Austria, Germany and Turkey) / Visiteurs (voyageurs en Allemagne, en Autriche et en Turquie)
T   Tourists / Touristes
(R) Tourist count by country of residence / Recensement des touristes par pays de résidence
(N) Tourist count by country of nationality / Recensement des touristes par pays de nationalité
1.   Estimates / Estimations

Table/Tableau 42

ARRIVALS AND NIGHTS OF FOREIGN TOURISTS AT/IN HOTELS
ARRIVÉES ET NUITÉES DE TOURISTES ÉTRANGERS DANS L'HÔTELLERIE

From Japan — En provenance du Japon
1987=100

	AH/NH	Volume 1981	1982	1983	1984	1985	1986	Volume 1987	1988	1989	1990	1991	1992	Volume 1992
Austria (R)	NH	155 788	53.9	58.9	64.1	75.9	74.7	308 291	104.0	120.2	152.1	134.0	147.0	453 099
	AH	73 116	51.6	55.7	65.3	77.1	72.8	162 976	102.0	117.8	144.6	116.6	134.6	219 337
Belgium (R)	NH	81 467	74.4	68.0	80.0	88.5	89.6	106 398	113.3	157.4	145.8	144.0	215.7	229 517
Denmark (N)	NH	79 700	89.6	99.0	95.9	94.1	84.6	82 900	129.9	141.6	130.3	112.7	133.8	110 900
Finland (R)	NH	22 782	46.9	71.7	81.6	86.1	75.1	51 318	108.7	118.6	124.1	111.6	111.4	57 170
France (R)[1]	NH	1 157 021	82.0	83.7	78.4	75.2	87.3	1 369 013	124.6	209.9	195.4	160.0	255.8	3 501 848
	AH	445 007	76.7	74.7	73.2	76.8	88.8	612 077	126.5	205.3	206.7	166.1	253.4	1 551 074
Germany (R)	NH	600 884	67.0	67.9	74.0	87.8	89.2	940 372	107.4	129.4	140.5	118.2	123.6	1 162 290
	AH	326 400	61.1	62.2	69.9	83.3	84.1	569 186	105.2	129.2	141.5	112.3	122.4	696 937
Greece (N)	NH	203 462	90.3	92.1	99.5	107.9	87.0	238 414	109.6					
	AH	86 342	83.6	87.2	93.4	105.3	87.0		113.5					
Italy (N)	NH	474 846	57.4	61.4	62.8	61.9	69.6	941 896	122.1	152.8	166.8	145.2	196.8	1 853 210
	AH	221 108	52.6	55.4	59.6	58.7	68.2	473 362	120.9	149.4	160.3	138.9	191.4	905 784
Luxembourg (R)	NH													
	AH													
Netherlands (R)	NH	129 386	100.3	89.5	85.0	102.9	104.7	148 800	107.6	109.3	124.9	117.1	148.2	220 500
	AH	65 428	97.5	83.5	89.4	97.2	93.1	79 200	105.9	106.6	121.0	110.2	141.0	111 700
Norway (N)	NH	39 474	55.4	70.5	83.8	85.7	61.3	75 131	88.8	106.6	112.5	113.1	132.9	99 840
Portugal (N)	NH	34 014	51.2	55.9	77.3	76.7	82.2	64 669	111.6	113.4	118.7	112.4	115.5	74 686
	AH	13 335	45.2	52.3	75.6	75.9	80.7	30 421	106.2	109.0	112.4	104.9	113.9	34 663
Spain (N)	NH	310 740	52.2	53.1	57.4	66.2	71.5	590 336	108.3	145.2	148.6	104.5	119.0	702 352
	AH	139 292	41.3	43.7	52.1	62.7	70.9	327 559	108.8	144.0	152.0	104.3	104.0	340 567
Sweden (N)	NH	50 580	89.5	83.8	94.0	92.9	85.9	62 181	119.5	131.2	151.7	135.3	131.1	81 528
Switzerland (R)	NH	421 322	72.1	77.9	79.6	82.6	86.0	624 387	104.6	125.3	131.1	116.1	130.6	815 392
	AH	226 869	66.2	72.5	76.1	79.9	84.9	369 008	107.8	128.0	134.9	112.5	136.3	502 796
Turkey (N)	NH		33.2	47.8	45.5	72.9	90.7	98 324	119.0	137.0	136.6	92.4	218.2	214 535
	AH		26.7	43.8	42.3	63.2	82.7	52 106	121.0	142.3	147.9	95.2	236.8	123 402
Australia (R)	NH	199 800		35.1	50.8	59.2	67.5	1 073 700	163.4	176.0	236.8	249.1	294.2	3 158 900

AH — Arrivals at hotels and similar establishments — Arrivées dans les hôtels et les établissements assimilés
NH — Nights in hotels and similar establishments — Nuitées dans les hôtels et établissements assimilés
(R) — Tourist count by country of residence — Recensement des touristes par pays de résidence
(N) — Tourist count by country of nationality — Recensement des touristes par pays de nationalité
1. Ile de France only — Ile de France seulement

Table/Tableau 43

ARRIVALS AND NIGHTS OF FOREIGN TOURISTS AT/IN ALL MEANS OF ACCOMMODATION
ARRIVÉES ET NUITÉES DE TOURISTES ÉTRANGERS DANS L'ENSEMBLE DES MOYENS D'HÉBERGEMENT

From Japan / *En provenance du Japon*
1987=100

	AAA/NAA	Volume 1981	1982	1983	1984	1985	1986	Volume 1987	1988	1989	1990	1991	1992	Volume 1992	AEH/NEH	
Austria (R)	NAA	155 788	53.9	58.9	64.1	75.9	74.7	308 291	104.0	120.2	152.1	134.0	147.0	453 099	NEH	Autriche (R)
	AAA	73 116	51.6	55.7	65.3	77.1	72.8	162 976	102.0	117.8	144.6	116.6	134.6	219 337	AEH	
Belgium (R)	NAA	84 039	73.5	68.0	80.5	89.2	89.8	110 142	113.8	157.2	147.3	143.4	211.9	233 368	NEH	Belgique (R)
Denmark (N)	NAA													110 900	NEH	Danemark (N)
France (R)	NAA	3 130 000			84.9	87.4	87.0	4 248 000	74.6	105.8	65.8	46.5	46.1	1 959 000	NEH	France (R)
	AAA	445 000			89.2	92.3	88.8	572 000	115.7		131.1	73.8	76.0	435 000	AEH	
Germany (R)	NAA	604 634	64.9	66.0	73.9	87.3	88.9	977 349	107.9	129.4	141.3	118.6	124.6	1 217 620	NEH	Allemagne (R)
	AAA	327 124	59.2	60.3	69.7	83.0	84.0	588 615	105.8	129.6	143.0	113.2	123.7	728 195	AEH	
Greece (N)	NAA	206 912	93.2	93.5	100.8	107.9	87.0	238 613	109.6						NEH	Grèce (N)
	AAA	87 868	85.6	88.2	94.8	105.4	87.1	105 671	113.5						AEH	
Ireland (R)	NAA													14 000	NEH	Irlande (R)
	AAA														AEH	
Italy (N)	NAA	520 066	60.1	63.3	65.0	64.3	72.7	977 382	121.7	151.3	165.5	144.8	195.6	1 911 799	NEH	Italie (N)
	AAA	226 322	52.8	55.6	59.8	59.1	68.8	482 629	120.8	149.0	160.1	138.8	190.9	921 431	AEH	
Luxembourg (R)	NAA														NEH	Luxembourg (R)
	AAA														AEH	
Netherlands (R)	NAA	134 876												228 400	NEH	Pays-Bas (R)
	AAA	69 018												116 100	AEH	
Portugal (N)	NAA	35 113	52.5	56.4	77.4	77.0	82.2	65 706	112.3	113.7	120.8	112.9	115.1	75 595	NEH	Portugal (N)
	AAA	13 798	46.0	52.8	75.8	76.1	80.8	30 866	107.5	109.6	114.8	105.5	113.8	35 127	AEH	
Spain (N)	NAA	310 740													NEH	Espagne (N)
	AAA	139 292													AEH	
Sweden (N)	NAA	51 935	88.7	84.5	93.6	93.2	85.1	64 286	119.1	130.4	151.1	139.8	133.6	85 901	NEH	Suède (N)
	AAA														AEH	
Switzerland (R)	NAA	442 400	71.8	77.4	79.3	82.6	86.2	651 500	104.3	124.8	130.5	115.9	130.1	847 811	NEH	Suisse (R)
	AAA	237 100	66.1	72.4	76.1	80.2	85.2	382 800	107.9	127.9	134.6	112.2	135.7	519 525	AEH	
Turkey (N)	NAA	21 135	32.7	47.0	44.9	71.7	89.2	100 307	117.2	134.9	134.7	90.8	214.1	214 770	NEH	Turquie (N)
	AAA	8 652	26.3	43.1	41.7	62.4	81.5	53 028	119.2	140.3	146.1	93.7	232.9	123 504	AEH	
United Kingdom (R)	NAA	1 219 000	47.1	42.3	65.8	102.9	75.2	2 331 000	126.3	141.1	167.3	180.9	173.5	4 045 000	NEH	Royaume-Uni (R)
Canada (R)	NAA	904 300	48.7	42.1	57.6	52.7	86.7	1 761 100	126.6	144.1	139.2	149.8	141.7	2 495 400	NEH	Canada (R)
Australia (R)	NAA	328 200		35.1	45.7	64.7	67.5	1 416 500	163.4	303.2	411.9	300.9	369.4	5 232 000	NEH	Australie (R)
New Zealand (R)	NAA													1 456 413	NEH	Nouvelle-Zélande (R)

AAA Arrivals in all means of accommodation
NAA Nights in all means of accommodation
(R)   Tourist count by country of residence
(N)   Tourist count by country of nationality

AEH Arrivées dans l'ensemble des moyens d'hébergement
NEH Nuitées dans l'ensemble des moyens d'hébergement
(R)   Recensement des touristes par pays de résidence
(N)   Recensement des touristes par pays de nationalité

Table/Tableau 44

ARRIVALS OF FOREIGN TOURISTS/VISITORS AT FRONTIERS
ARRIVÉES DE TOURISTES/VISITEURS ÉTRANGERS AUX FRONTIÈRES

From the Netherlands
1987=100

En provenance des Pays-Bas
1987=100

Country	T/V	Volume 1981	1982	1983	1984	1985	1986	Volume 1987	1988	1989	1990	1991	1992	Volume 1992	T/V	Pays
France (R)	T / V	2 930 000	98.8	96.7	95.7	92.9	101.9	3 936 000	102.8	101.5	101.3	150.7	157.4	6 197 000	T / V	France (R)
Greece (N)	T	170 002	40.4	44.5	55.9	81.2	95.7	345 000	112.8	124.1	143.7	130.5	158.3	546 187	T	Grèce (N)
Iceland (N)	T	1 569	70.6	62.3	66.6	68.3	95.5	2 419	117.1	104.0	123.8	122.0	157.4	3 808	T	Islande (N)
Ireland (R)	V	126 684													V	Irlande (R)
Italy (N)	V	1 541 780	127.8	122.7	127.0	119.6	125.5	1 388 693	129.8	132.6	152.8	110.4	86.8	1 205 676	V	Italie (N)
Norway (N)	V	36 693													V	Norvège (N)
Portugal (N)	T	117 985	55.6	71.3	69.5	73.8	79.6	205 088	134.3	154.4	145.8	158.8	164.5	337 427	T	Portugal (N)
Portugal (N)	V	128 719	58.2	72.9	70.9	76.5	80.2	214 192	133.2	155.4	153.8	168.3	171.2	366 674	V	Portugal (N)
Spain (N)	V	1 381 271	80.5	78.1	82.2	84.1	92.4	1 684 571	119.0	120.8	116.0	128.0	125.7	2 117 030	V	Espagne (N)
Turkey (N)	V	23 033	44.6	52.7	54.3	62.5	79.0	49 915	162.4	213.8	301.2	214.4	410.3	204 802	V	Turquie (N)
United Kingdom (R)	V	745 000	82.0	85.9	86.6	89.1	89.9	855 300	103.0	110.0	116.5	130.7	116.2	994 000	V	Royaume-Uni (R)
Canada (R)	T	79 100	91.9	81.3	78.0	75.0	88.1	77 900	113.0	115.1	109.0	112.6	109.4	85 200	T	Canada (R)
Canada (R)	V	87 900	89.5	78.0	75.5	72.2	85.5	88 500	111.8	109.4	105.4	107.6	104.1	92 100	V	Canada (R)
United States (R)	T	197 436	94.1	71.9	66.5	65.1	80.7	201 692	122.9	129.3	140.8	157.0	169.6	342 034	T	États-Unis (R)
Australia (R)	V	18 010	96.9	86.1	81.5	89.0	91.9	17 300	129.5	116.2	122.0	123.7	135.8	23 500	V	Australie (R)
Japan (N)	T													6 229	T	Japon (N)
Japan (N)	V	12 120	72.0	80.6	89.1	96.9	91.1	15 902	99.7	103.3	110.5	113.5	114.8	18 253	V	Japon (N)
New Zealand (R)	T	5 182	81.4	76.3	81.7	85.6	91.6	6 322	111.7	112.7	123.1	120.0	154.0	9 734	T	Nouvelle-Zélande (R)

V Visitors (travellers in Turkey)
T Tourists
(R) Tourist count by country of residence
(N) Tourist count by country of nationality

V Visiteurs (voyageurs en Turquie)
T Touristes
(R) Recensement des touristes par pays de résidence
(N) Recensement des touristes par pays de nationalité

Table/Tableau 45

ARRIVALS AND NIGHTS OF FOREIGN TOURISTS AT/IN HOTELS
ARRIVÉES ET NUITÉES DE TOURISTES ÉTRANGERS DANS L'HÔTELLERIE

From the Netherlands / En provenance des Pays-Bas

1987=100

Country	AH/NH	Volume 1981	1982	1983	1984	1985	1986	Volume 1987	1988	1989	1990	1991	1992	Volume 1992	AH/NH	
Austria (R)	NH	5 916 275	108.7	101.2	103.9	99.4	98.6	5 108 486	97.9	102.9	97.7	100.9	97.8	4 998 214	NH	Autriche (R)
	AH	814 078	100.8	96.0	98.8	96.7	96.0	763 629	101.7	107.2	104.2	104.2	101.5	775 249	AH	
Belgium (R)	NH	456 186	73.1	85.6	92.8	92.3	94.9	713 346	103.9	129.4	132.6	130.7	141.6	1 010 282	NH	Belgique (R)
Denmark (N)	NH	119 500	114.3	119.9	107.8	97.5	93.3	100 500	101.6	107.4	113.2	155.9	193.7	194 700	NH	Danemark (N)
Finland (R)	NH	42 326	86.4	88.1	105.7	96.8	88.6	41 743	110.8	125.0	132.1	126.5	148.2	61 863	NH	Finlande (R)
France (R)[1]	NH	920 511	39.5	39.0	41.2	36.9	94.4	2 047 829	111.3	118.4	114.0	118.2	118.4	2 424 585	NH	France (R)[1]
	AH	362 684	29.3	28.7	28.3	26.9	93.6	1 105 918	114.5	114.6	113.4	120.9	117.0	1 293 800	AH	
Germany (R)	NH	3 399 336	93.8	86.9	90.7	91.5	96.3	3 443 653	99.8	105.2	102.6	101.5	92.3	3 178 529	NH	Allemagne (R)
	AH	1 513 847	93.4	89.1	93.3	93.8	95.0	1 538 102	101.3	104.5	103.9	100.9	93.9	1 444 564	AH	
Greece (N)	NH	1 062 546	59.6	55.1	77.3	114.4	118.3	1 648 814	100.5						NH	Grèce (N)
	AH	184 911	67.0	63.1	82.6	108.8	105.9	259 145	99.4						AH	
Ireland (R)	NH						121.3	108 000	115.7	185.2	201.9	279.6	252.8	273 000	NH	Irlande (R)
	AH						110.0	20 000	125.0	165.0	200.0	250.0	225.0	45 000	AH	
Italy (N)	NH	1 367 808	76.3	69.3	56.5	61.3	69.7	1 840 833	81.8	74.9	73.9	76.5	68.8	1 265 965	NH	Italie (N)
	AH	262 297	93.2	88.1	78.3	85.3	90.3	307 468	110.8	108.7	112.2	112.0	104.8	322 190	AH	
Luxembourg (R)	NH														NH	Luxembourg (R)
	AH														AH	
Norway (N)	NH	167 320	97.3	90.4	114.1	110.2	91.8	120 646	89.4	98.0	104.5	124.7	144.4	174 272	NH	Norvège (N)
Portugal (N)	NH	814 676	87.6	73.5	82.8	85.0	93.0	876 750	136.3	147.1	163.0	193.1	170.5	1 494 667	NH	Portugal (N)
	AH	94 352	73.2	73.3	79.3	82.2	85.0	129 531	130.9	141.8	160.1	176.0	158.1	204 772	AH	
Spain (N)	NH	3 601 552	106.7	100.6	115.6	101.0	114.9	3 391 716	98.0	82.9	61.6	71.8	69.5	2 357 636	NH	Espagne (N)
	AH	441 444	96.7	93.2	96.4	97.5		446 457	99.8	91.9	72.8	80.0	79.0		AH	
Sweden (N)	NH	126 760	147.6	172.1	119.8	110.1	104.7	70 017	98.9	108.6	111.3	98.2	119.7	83 804	NH	Suède (N)
Switzerland (R)	NH	1 259 211	125.8	114.2	99.6	96.9	102.5	826 063	97.0	104.1	104.3	108.1	106.7	881 383	NH	Suisse (R)
	AH	335 318	119.3	111.3	100.2	96.1	102.0	248 393	99.6	107.3	106.4	110.0	106.5	264 555	AH	
Australia (R)	NH	71 800		83.1	81.1	110.1	91.8	66 100	129.3						NH	Australie (R)
Japan (N)	NH	49 545													NH	Japon (N)
	AH	17 620													AH	

AH   Arrivals at hotels and similar establishments — Arrivées dans les hôtels et les établissements assimilés
NH   Nights in hotels and similar establishments — Nuitées dans les hôtels et établissements assimilés
(R)   Tourist count by country of residence — Recensement des touristes par pays de résidence
(N)   Tourist count by country of nationality — Recensement des touristes par pays de nationalité
1.   Ile de France only — Ile de France seulement

159

Table/Tableau 46

ARRIVALS AND NIGHTS OF FOREIGN TOURISTS AT/IN ALL MEANS OF ACCOMMODATION
ARRIVÉES ET NUITÉES DE TOURISTES ÉTRANGERS DANS L'ENSEMBLE DES MOYENS D'HÉBERGEMENT

From the Netherlands / *En provenance des Pays-Bas*

1987=100

	AAA/NAA	Volume 1981	1982	1983	1984	1985	1986	Volume 1987	1988	1989	1990	1991	1992	Volume 1992	AEH/NEH	
Austria (R)	NAA	10 338 094	104.3	97.1	100.4	98.5	98.5	9 320 245	99.4	103.6	97.8	99.2	96.6	8 998 720	NEH	Autriche (R)
	AAA	1 344 649	97.5	92.6	96.3	96.0	95.7	1 299 660	102.4	108.0	103.5	101.8	99.3	1 291 134	AEH	
Belgium (R)	NAA	1 914 982	77.6	85.6	85.7	88.1	92.5	3 592 857	113.3	124.8	133.7	121.8	117.5	4 220 802	NEH	Belgique (R)
Denmark (N)	NAA	686 352	143.0	164.4	134.1	124.1	110.7	540 301	94.3	97.4	94.5	116.7	185.7	1 003 300	NEH	Danemark (N)
France (R)	NAA	20 510 000	101.8	99.9	101.9	95.0	105.0	32 923 000	101.5	105.6	102.1	169.7	180.3	59 351 000	NEH	France (R)
	AAA	2 930 000	98.8	96.7	95.7	92.9	101.9	3 936 000	102.8	101.5	101.5	150.7	157.4	6 197 000	AEH	
Germany (R)	NAA	4 620 773	78.4	79.3	88.3	89.6	94.6	5 641 001	100.9	105.7	102.1	147.7	138.8	7 831 158	NEH	Allemagne (R)
	AAA	1 654 275	84.8	84.0	91.6	91.9	94.2	1 856 538	101.2	105.3	103.2	132.8	126.3	2 345 133	AEH	
Greece (N)	NAA	1 261 668	67.0	61.1	87.9	114.0	117.3	1 756 987	99.7						NEH	Grèce (N)
	AAA	231 365	76.0	69.5	92.0	109.3	106.8	292 234	98.9						AEH	
Ireland (R)	NAA													827 000	NEH	Irlande (R)
	AAA													73 000	AEH	
Italy (N)	NAA	4 265 067	127.5	104.7	90.6	97.6	107.6	3 403 175	104.5	94.9	89.9	94.2	84.2	2 864 264	NEH	Italie (N)
	AAA	515 678	99.2	88.5	80.5	87.3	94.7	554 293	106.0	101.1	99.7	103.2	95.1	527 305	AEH	
Luxembourg (R)	NAA															Luxembourg (R)
	AAA															
Portugal (N)	NAA	1 109 112	86.2	72.0	77.8	82.9	92.7	1 221 306	135.1	142.8	151.5	176.3	151.0	1 844 244	NEH	Portugal (N)
	AAA	148 065	69.3	66.4	70.6	80.8	89.8	218 171	128.2	135.3	142.0	156.8	133.5	291 256	AEH	
Sweden (N)	NAA	554 696	126.2	191.1	138.8	125.6	100.8	375 045	91.7	106.5	101.4	85.6	90.0	337 636	NEH	Suède (N)
Switzerland (R)	NAA	4 356 800	123.7	112.5	99.4	93.3	102.7	2 978 300	100.2	106.1	112.3	114.0	114.3	3 405 046	NEH	Suisse (R)
	AAA	694 200	120.6	112.4	101.5	92.9	101.5	511 900	101.3	108.6	112.6	115.9	116.0	593 752	AEH	
United Kingdom (R)	NAA	5 339 000	85.5	91.9	88.4	104.1	84.7	5 162 000	107.8	100.5	108.4	125.8	111.8	5 770 000	NEH	Royaume-Uni (R)
Canada (R)	NAA	1 231 100	105.6	91.7	87.5	83.5	88.3	1 097 700	109.9	104.7	102.0	96.4	96.4	1 058 700	NEH	Canada (R)
Australia (R)	NAA	175 400		145.1	100.2	91.0	92.0	161 500	129.5					367 003	NEH	Australie (R)
New Zealand (R)	NAA														NEH	Nouvelle-Zélande (R)

AAA Arrivals in all means of accommodation
NAA Nights in all means of accommodation
(R) Tourist count by country of residence
(N) Tourist count by country of nationality

AEH Arrivées dans l'ensemble des moyens d'hébergement
NEH Nuitées dans l'ensemble des moyens d'hébergement
(R) Recensement des touristes par pays de résidence
(N) Recensement des touristes par pays de nationalité

Table/Tableau 47

ARRIVALS OF FOREIGN TOURISTS/VISITORS AT FRONTIERS
ARRIVÉES DE TOURISTES/VISITEURS ÉTRANGERS AUX FRONTIÈRES

From the United Kingdom — En provenance du Royaume-Uni

1987=100

	T/V	Volume 1981	1982	1983	1984	1985	1986	Volume 1987	1988	1989	1990	1991	1992	Volume 1992	T/V	
France (R)	T	3 620 000	94.5	93.2	86.1	92.1	98.9	6 368 000	104.3	111.4	127.1	127.2	128.7	8 196 000	T	France (R)
	V														V	
Greece (N)	T	964 707	51.7	44.9	52.7	67.1	86.4	1 980 000	90.4	82.4	83.2	84.6	108.8	2 154 850	T	Grèce (N)
Iceland (N)	T	7 880	68.8	83.8	88.8	91.9	97.0	10 579	99.5	113.3	129.9	138.6	131.4	13 900	T	Islande (N)
Ireland (R)	V	1 026 439	89.1	93.4	98.3	91.3	89.7	1 209 000	121.2	138.0	147.7	143.0	145.4	1 758 000	V	Irlande (R)
Italy (N)	V	1 806 680	92.3	94.5	89.4	88.6	102.4	1 999 353	91.0	95.3	102.4	85.6	80.7	1 612 803	V	Italie (N)
Norway (N)	V	134 557													V	Norvège (N)
Portugal (N)	T	444 267	44.7	48.7	56.1	66.4	87.3	1 137 560	93.6	90.3	93.3	102.1	112.2	1 276 001	T	Portugal (N)
	V	548 541	47.4	52.3	58.9	73.1	88.8	1 204 263	94.6	94.5	99.9	108.6	119.2	1 435 346	V	
Spain (N)	V	4 064 326	64.2	68.7	79.8	66.7	85.2	7 550 198	101.3	97.3	83.3	81.4	86.3	6 515 540	V	Espagne (N)
Turkey (N)	V	60 294	22.3	31.6	33.6	46.7	57.8	266 900	174.3	152.1	131.7	75.2	117.9	314 608	V	Turquie (N)
Canada (R)	T	485 000	95.4	81.4	78.4	70.3	89.5	446 400	118.1	127.7	123.9	118.8	120.2	536 400	T	Canada (R)
	V	540 600	93.6	79.1	76.1	68.1	86.7	506 600	115.6	121.4	118.9	114.6	117.6	595 600	V	
United States (R)	T	1 574 837	95.0	74.6	68.1	63.2	83.2	1 362 479	133.4	163.1	164.7	183.1	207.3	2 823 983	T	États-Unis (R)
Australia (R)	V	142 171	87.0	74.3	73.2	77.1	88.5	198 900	130.9	137.2	139.7	132.6	145.8	289 900	V	Australie (R)
Japan (N)	T	121 525	103.0	117.7	112.7	123.3	95.8	148 302	104.2	119.5	144.6	148.0	163.1	143 341	T	Japon (N)
	V													241 893	V	
New Zealand (R)	T	38 072	62.1	64.0	65.9	71.4	81.4	61 048	119.1	121.8	142.9	144.1	158.1	96 523	T	Nouvelle-Zélande (R)

V   Visitors (travellers in Turkey)
T   Tourists
(R)   Tourist count by country of residence
(N)   Tourist count by country of nationality

V   Visiteurs (voyageurs en Turquie)
T   Touristes
(R)   Recensement des touristes par pays de résidence
(N)   Recensement des touristes par pays de nationalité

161

Table/Tableau 48

ARRIVALS AND NIGHTS OF FOREIGN TOURISTS AT/IN HOTELS
ARRIVÉES ET NUITÉES DE TOURISTES ÉTRANGERS DANS L'HÔTELLERIE

From the United Kingdom *En provenance du Royaume-Uni*

1987=100   1987=100

	AH/NH	Volume 1981	1982	1983	1984	1985	1986	Volume 1987	1988	1989	1990	1991	1992	Volume 1992	AH/NH	
Austria (R)	NH	2 356 131	84.0	95.7	103.5	99.2	101.3	3 774 576	98.6	110.7	116.3	97.1	94.4	3 563 269	NH	Autriche (R)
	AH	476 853	89.5	99.2	109.7	104.4	100.9	667 867	98.1	112.5	122.9	101.1	97.7	652 332	AH	
Belgium (R)	NH	896 910	106.3	117.1	115.9	116.0	107.7	906 235	94.5	116.5	132.4	122.4	146.5	1 327 547	NH	Belgique (R)
	AH													1 327 547	AH	
Denmark (N)	NH	336 500	119.3	112.0	98.7	109.5	102.4	304 400	95.3	100.3	109.6	104.0	105.3	320 400	NH	Danemark (N)
Finland (R)	NH	93 597	82.4	89.3	92.7	92.9	88.7	116 553	113.0	121.2	121.9	113.0	108.9	126 885	NH	Finlande (R)
	AH							128 000							AH	
France (R)[1]	NH	1 849 165	32.8	33.9	36.7	38.0	103.1	5 719 861	118.1	155.6	191.6	177.5	194.5	11 123 432	NH	France (R)[1]
	AH	779 837	25.4	25.7	26.4	28.6	100.8	3 078 144	113.8	150.1	158.3	166.9	180.5	5 556 868	AH	
Germany (R)	NH	1 907 464	82.3	83.4	95.3	99.5	103.9	2 290 247	101.3	117.9	131.7	118.4	116.2	2 661 220	NH	Allemagne (R)
	AH	910 540	86.5	87.4	98.2	101.0	102.1	1 098 918	101.6	116.1	131.5	111.2	110.4	1 213 410	AH	
Greece (N)	NH	6 838 110	74.0	61.4	74.0	89.6	102.1	8 423 975	85.7							NH	Grèce (N)
	AH	888 442	81.3	68.1	78.8	93.4	99.8	985 904	89.0							AH	
Iceland (N)	NH														45 519	NH	Islande (N)
Ireland (R)	NH					88.9	102.7	1 845 000	113.7	157.2	143.2	193.1	179.7	3 316 000	NH	Irlande (R)
	AH					95.6	103.7	428 000	123.6	158.4	166.6	185.7	184.3	789 000	AH	
Italy (N)	NH	5 283 498	105.1	106.4	92.6	88.7	104.8	5 537 159	93.6	100.7	92.6	82.1	82.6	4 571 866	NH	Italie (N)
	AH	1 066 821	98.0	99.6	91.8	89.4	99.0	1 180 489	98.4	107.2	104.0	93.0	97.6	1 151 684	AH	
Luxembourg (R)	NH				82.8	88.8	104.8	51 472	108.2	108.0	123.1	122.3	142.2	73 194	NH	Luxembourg (R)
	AH				88.8	102.6	104.9	25 632	109.9	108.0	124.9	124.7	132.4	33 944	AH	
Netherlands (R)	NH	1 136 957	98.5	89.3	97.1	103.3	106.8	1 250 700	98.3	108.6	121.5	121.5	130.6	1 633 300	NH	Pays-Bas (R)
	AH	519 796	94.2	86.8	93.2	98.8	103.1	600 800	100.5	108.0	119.2	117.1	124.1	745 500	AH	
Norway (N)	NH	338 144	92.8	86.2	123.2	129.6	105.2	346 954	96.0	97.2	98.3	100.1	123.5	428 593	NH	Norvège (N)
Portugal (N)	NH	2 997 848	59.0	64.3	70.3	88.9	104.7	5 571 625	94.6	91.5	94.4	100.8	102.2	5 696 672	NH	Portugal (N)
	AH	362 142	56.6	64.8	73.8	93.1	100.2	691 124	94.7	93.7	100.7	104.0	101.6	702 502	AH	
Spain (N)	NH	23 806 844	82.9	88.9	104.2	74.1	100.2	33 757 650	92.7	79.8	58.0	56.4	57.3	19 331 397	NH	Espagne (N)
	AH	2 682 881	83.8	86.8	99.2	74.3	100.4	3 741 361	92.4	74.8	59.2	62.5	63.2	2 365 488	AH	
Sweden (N)	NH	246 530	108.8	112.8	113.3	114.8	109.2	225 696	106.1	117.8	120.0	101.1	105.7	238 579	NH	Suède (N)
Switzerland (R)	NH	1 755 838	108.2	110.9	107.4	106.2	110.8	1 820 526	97.5	105.7	111.1	101.5	101.5	1 847 948	NH	Suisse (R)
	AH	515 663	104.6	105.6	105.5	102.2	103.7	520 279	100.8	108.6	116.2	103.1	105.3	548 076	AH	
Turkey (N)	NH		17.0	29.6	32.5	49.9	64.5	508 541	175.2	152.2	124.9	74.5	154.9	787 486	NH	Turquie (N)
	AH		24.2	36.5	44.8	59.4	72.5	142 408	154.9	143.1	122.6	66.1	111.3	158 533	AH	
Australia (R)	NH	340 200		46.7	46.8	59.3	88.5	1 262 500	130.9	113.6	174.0	106.9	118.4	1 494 700	NH	Australie (R)
Japan (N)	NH	239 763														NH	Japon (N)
	AH	86 158														AH	

AH   Arrivals at hotels and similar establishments
NH   Nights in hotels and similar establishments
(R)   Tourist count by country of residence
(N)   Tourist count by country of nationality
1.   Ile de France only

AH   Arrivées dans les hôtels et les établissements assimilés
NH   Nuitées dans les hôtels et établissements assimilés
(R)   Recensement des touristes par pays de résidence
(N)   Recensement des touristes par pays de nationalité
1.   Ile de France seulement

Table/Tableau 49

ARRIVALS AND NIGHTS OF FOREIGN TOURISTS AT/IN ALL MEANS OF ACCOMMODATION
ARRIVÉES ET NUITÉES DE TOURISTES ÉTRANGERS DANS L'ENSEMBLE DES MOYENS D'HÉBERGEMENT

From the United Kingdom
En provenance du Royaume-Uni

1987=100

Country	AAA/NAA	Volume 1981	1982	1983	1984	1985	1986	Volume 1987	1988	1989	1990	1991	1992	Volume 1992	AEH/NEH	Pays
Austria (R)	NAA	2 681 843	83.8	95.5	102.1	99.6	101.1	4 249 774	99.1	111.1	116.0	98.9	95.7	4 068 302	NEH	Autriche (R)
	AAA	552 764	88.8	98.7	107.4	104.0	101.0	765 150	98.4	112.9	122.3	102.8	98.4	752 918	AEH	
Belgium (R)	NAA	1 114 074	107.7	117.0	116.3	114.3	106.4	1 080 624	90.2	109.5	125.0	116.0	139.4	1 506 260	NEH	Belgique (R)
	AAA													1 506 259	AEH	
Denmark (N)	NAA	425 443	126.3	119.8	106.2	113.6	104.6	358 521	97.1	100.6	110.3	102.3	106.5	381 800	NEH	Danemark (N)
France (R)	NAA	32 580 000	85.1	85.9	82.6	87.6	96.8	60 553 000	70.7	83.7	100.4	99.7	100.2	60 695 000	NEH	France (R)
	AAA	3 620 000	94.5	93.2	86.1	92.1	98.9	6 368 000	104.3		127.1	127.2	128.7	8 196 000	AEH	
Germany (R)	NAA	1 954 482	76.2	77.4	92.6	97.3	101.2	2 547 039	100.5	116.4	128.1	129.6	125.8	3 205 018	NEH	Allemagne (R)
	AAA	917 809	81.6	82.6	97.2	100.4	100.8	1 174 602	101.0	115.4	129.9	120.6	118.2	1 388 045	AEH	
Greece (N)	NAA	7 274 704	77.5	64.6	80.0	89.7	102.2	8 507 877	85.6							Grèce (N)
	AAA	957 640	85.7	72.1	85.9	93.5	100.0	1 006 878								
Ireland (R)	NAA	9 443 000	78.2	83.4	89.9	79.5	80.9	12 049 400	114.6	133.9	129.3	122.2	119.3	14 373 000	NEH	Irlande (R)
	AAA	1 008 000												1 707 000	AEH	
Italy (N)	NAA	6 665 903	81.1	81.5	70.2	67.7	80.4	8 854 692	69.3	73.4	67.9	60.8	61.0	5 398 815	NEH	Italie (N)
	AAA	1 239 674	98.5	99.8	91.6	89.0	100.0	1 340 781	98.6	106.5	103.1	93.0	96.4	1 292 347	AEH	
Luxembourg (R)	NAA			89.1	97.1	92.8	99.3	72 930	106.2		123.1	119.2	137.8	100 505	NEH	Luxembourg (R)
	AAA			96.1	100.2	99.6	101.0	34 731	107.2		126.3	124.4	131.1	45 540	AEH	
Netherlands (R)	NAA	1 394 589												2 061 200	NEH	Pays-Bas (R)
	AAA	634 003												871 200	AEH	
Portugal (N)	NAA	3 159 510	60.1	64.9	70.5	88.6	104.4	5 742 461	94.3	91.2	94.5	100.7	101.4	5 824 570	NEH	Portugal (N)
	AAA	392 421	58.1	65.6	74.0	92.7	102.0	725 023	94.2	93.5	100.2	103.5	100.6	729 221	AEH	
Spain (N)	NAA	24 179 815														Espagne (N)
	AAA	2 739 498														
Sweden (N)	NAA	414 399	117.9	117.1	115.5	114.7	110.5	301 565	103.4	113.1	111.5	91.2	95.6	288 183	NEH	Suède (N)
Switzerland (R)	NAA	2 466 900	100.0	105.3	102.5	102.5	108.8	2 667 700	97.0	102.1	105.0	95.6	97.8	2 608 563	NEH	Suisse (R)
	AAA	681 200	104.8	106.0	104.6	101.1	103.8	668 100	99.2	107.1	112.3	100.4	102.1	681 851	AEH	
Turkey (N)	NAA	84 866	14.9	26.6	28.6	44.7	59.4	594 637	164.9	141.6	113.5	70.5	146.4	870 592	NEH	Turquie (N)
	AAA	33 008	22.8	34.8	42.6	56.7	70.3	152 010	152.5	140.8	119.7	67.3	111.0	168 803	AEH	
Canada (R)	NAA	6 734 300	108.5	94.2	91.0	80.9	100.7	5 699 200	119.6	119.9	116.1	110.8	107.4	6 118 700	NEH	Canada (R)
	AAA	485 000	96.9	82.7	79.7	71.5	90.9	439 300	120.0	127.6	125.9	120.7	122.1	536 400	AEH	
Australia (R)	NAA	903 900												13 083 900	NEH	Australie (R)
New Zealand (R)	NAA				67.7	73.6	83.2	2 569 100	113.2	111.3	124.3	122.1	123.4	3 169 126	NEH	Nouvelle-Zélande (R)

AAA   Arrivals in all means of accommodation
NAA   Nights in all means of accommodation
(R)   Tourist count by country of residence
(N)   Tourist count by country of nationality

AEH   Arrivées dans l'ensemble des moyens d'hébergement
NEH   Nuitées dans l'ensemble des moyens d'hébergement
(R)   Recensement des touristes par pays de résidence
(N)   Recensement des touristes par pays de nationalité

163

AUSTRALIA

ARRIVALS OF FOREIGN VISITORS AT FRONTIERS[1]

(by country of residence)

	1991	Relative share	1992	Relative share	% Variation over 1991
Austria	10 300	0.4	10 800	0.4	4.9
Belgium	4 100	0.2	4 200	0.2	2.4
Denmark	9 900	0.4	10 300	0.4	4.0
Finland	5 700	0.2	5 100	0.2	−10.5
France	22 700	1.0	25 400	1.0	11.9
Germany[2]	77 700	3.3	89 900	3.5	15.7
Greece	5 800	0.2	6 100	0.2	5.2
Iceland	100	0.0	100	0.0	0.0
Ireland	9 600	0.4	8 800	0.3	−8.3
Italy	24 300	1.0	27 400	1.1	12.8
Luxembourg	300	0.0	500	0.0	66.7
Netherlands	21 400	0.9	23 500	0.9	9.8
Norway	4 100	0.2	4 500	0.2	9.8
Portugal	1 200	0.1	1 600	0.1	33.3
Spain	4 000	0.2	4 900	0.2	22.5
Sweden	19 100	0.8	19 100	0.7	0.0
Switzerland	29 600	1.2	29 000	1.1	−2.0
Turkey	1 500	0.1	1 400	0.1	−6.7
United Kingdom	263 800	11.1	289 900	11.2	9.9
Other OECD-Europe	..	..	..	..	..
Total Europe	515 200	21.7	562 500	21.7	9.2
Canada	53 400	2.3	48 900	1.9	−8.4
United States	271 800	11.5	262 900	10.1	−3.3
Total North America	325 200	13.7	311 800	12.0	−4.1
Australia	..	..	..	..	..
New Zealand	480 600	20.3	447 500	17.2	−6.9
Japan	528 500	22.3	629 900	24.2	19.2
Total Australasia and Japan	1 009 100	42.6	1 077 400	41.5	6.8
Total OECD Countries	**1 849 500**	**78.0**	**1 951 700**	**75.1**	**5.5**
Ex-Yugoslavia	4 900	0.2	3 200	0.1	−34.7
Other European countries	10 700	0.5	12 700	0.5	18.7
Bulgaria	300	0.0	200	0.0	−33.3
Ex-Czechoslovakia	1 300	0.1	1 500	0.1	15.4
Hungary	1 400	0.1	1 700	0.1	21.4
Poland	2 200	0.1	2 000	0.1	−9.1
Rumania	500	0.0	400	0.0	−20.0
Ex-USSR	4 300	0.2	4 500	0.2	4.7
Latin America	10 800	0.5	11 700	0.5	8.3
Argentina	2 600	0.1	3 100	0.1	19.2
Brazil	2 500	0.1	2 500	0.1	0.0
Chile	1 300	0.1	1 400	0.1	7.7
Colombia	500	0.0	500	0.0	0.0
Mexico	1 600	0.1	1 900	0.1	18.8
Venezuela	300	0.0	400	0.0	33.3
Asia-Oceania	472 560	19.9	589 700	22.7	24.8
China	16 400	0.7	18 700	0.7	14.0
Hong Kong	62 800	2.6	74 700	2.9	18.9
India	9 800	0.4	9 600	0.4	−2.0
Iran	1 300	0.1	1 200	0.0	−7.7
Israel	4 900	0.2	4 600	0.2	−6.1
Republic of Korea	23 600	1.0	33 600	1.3	42.4
Lebanon	1 300	0.1	1 800	0.1	38.5
Malaysia	48 000	2.0	60 400	2.3	25.8
Pakistan	1 300	0.1	1 600	0.1	23.1
Philippines	15 700	0.7	16 100	0.6	2.5
Saudi Arabia	2 000	0.1	2 600	0.1	30.0
Singapore	87 500	3.7	116 800	4.5	33.5
Taiwan	34 700	1.5	63 500	2.4	83.0
Thailand	24 700	1.0	33 600	1.3	36.0
Africa	18 300	0.8	23 800	0.9	30.1
Egypt	900	0.0	1 000	0.0	11.1
South Africa	9 200	0.4	15 300	0.6	66.3
Origin country undetermined	3 500	0.1	5 300	0.2	51.4
Total non-OECD Countries	**520 760**	**22.0**	**646 400**	**24.9**	**24.1**
TOTAL	**2 370 260**	**100.0**	**2 598 100**	**100.0**	**9.6**

1. Includes a small number of "in transit" passengers who leave the port or airport, but do not necessarily stay overnight in Australia.
2. Germany includes Federal and Democratic Republics.

AUSTRALIA

NIGHTS SPENT BY FOREIGN TOURISTS IN HOTELS[1]

(by country of residence)

	1991	Relative share	1992	Relative share	% Variation over 1991
Austria	..	..	..	..	..
Belgium	..	..	..	..	..
Denmark	..	..	..	..	..
Finland	..	..	..	..	..
France	..	..	..	..	..
Germany	581 800	5.1	758 300	6.1	30.3
Greece	..	..	..	..	..
Iceland	..	..	..	..	..
Ireland	..	..	..	..	..
Italy	..	..	..	..	..
Luxembourg	..	..	..	..	..
Netherlands	..	..	..	..	..
Norway	..	..	..	..	..
Portugal	..	..	..	..	..
Spain	..	..	..	..	..
Sweden	..	..	..	..	..
Switzerland	..	..	..	..	..
Turkey	..	..	..	..	..
United Kingdom[2]	1 349 700	11.7	1 494 700	12.0	10.7
Other OECD-Europe	1 086 800	9.4	1 178 200	9.5	8.4
Total Europe	3 018 300	26.2	3 431 200	27.5	13.7
Canada	365 700	3.2	281 500	2.3	−23.0
United States	2 110 400	18.3	1 920 100	15.4	−9.0
Total North America	2 476 100	21.5	2 201 600	17.7	−11.1
Australia	..	..	..	..	..
New Zealand	1 568 700	13.6	1 314 300	10.5	−16.2
Japan	2 674 800	23.3	3 158 900	25.4	18.1
Total Australasia and Japan	4 243 500	36.9	4 473 200	35.9	5.4
Total OECD Countries	**9 737 900**	**84.7**	**10 106 000**	**81.1**	**3.8**
Ex-Yugoslavia	..	..	..	..	..
Origin country undetermined	1 765 100	15.3	2 354 800	18.9	33.4
Total non-OECD Countries	**1 765 100**	**15.3**	**2 354 800**	**18.9**	**33.4**
TOTAL	**11 503 000**	**100.0**	**12 460 800**	**100.0**	**8.3**

1. Includes nights spent by tourists aged 15 years and above.
2. United Kingdom includes Ireland.

AUSTRALIA

NIGHTS SPENT BY FOREIGN TOURISTS IN REGISTERED TOURIST ACCOMMODATION[1]

(by country of residence)

	1991	Relative share	1992	Relative share	% Variation over 1991
Austria	..	..	..	..	..
Belgium	..	..	..	..	..
Denmark	..	..	..	..	..
Finland	..	..	..	..	..
France	..	..	..	..	..
Germany	3 096 900	4.8	3 245 200	5.3	4.8
Greece	..	..	..	..	..
Iceland	..	..	..	..	..
Ireland	..	..	..	..	..
Italy	..	..	..	..	..
Luxembourg	..	..	..	..	..
Netherlands	..	..	..	..	..
Norway	..	..	..	..	..
Portugal	..	..	..	..	..
Spain	..	..	..	..	..
Sweden	..	..	..	..	..
Switzerland	..	..	..	..	..
Turkey	..	..	..	..	..
United Kingdom[2]	15 082 100	23.3	13 083 900	21.3	−13.2
Other OECD-Europe	8 234 400	12.7	7 374 800	12.0	−10.4
Total Europe	26 413 400	40.9	23 703 900	38.6	−10.3
Canada	2 288 900	3.5	1 724 400	2.8	−24.7
United States	6 638 200	10.3	6 196 000	10.1	−6.7
Total North America	8 927 100	13.8	7 920 400	12.9	−11.3
Australia	..	..	..	..	..
New Zealand	8 966 300	13.9	7 199 600	11.7	−19.7
Japan	4 262 000	6.6	5 232 000	8.5	22.8
Total Australasia and Japan	13 228 300	20.5	12 431 600	20.2	−6.0
Total OECD Countries	**48 568 800**	**75.1**	**44 055 900**	**71.7**	**−9.3**
Ex-Yugoslavia					
Origin country undetermined	16 076 000	24.9	17 388 100	28.3	8.2
Total non-OECD Countries	**16 076 000**	**24.9**	**17 388 100**	**28.3**	**8.2**
TOTAL	**64 644 800**	**100.0**	**61 444 000**	**100.0**	**−5.0**

1. Covers only commercial accommodation (ie excluding stays with friends/relatives).
2. United Kingdom includes Ireland.

AUSTRIA

ARRIVALS OF FOREIGN TOURISTS AT HOTELS

(by country of residence)

	1991	Relative share	1992	Relative share	% Variation over 1991
Austria	..	..	..	..	..
Belgium [1]	329 237	2.4	337 970	2.5	2.7
Denmark	128 751	0.9	117 530	0.9	−8.7
Finland	55 818	0.4	45 777	0.3	−18.0
France	666 335	4.9	576 589	4.2	−13.5
Germany	6 935 141	50.7	6 978 329	51.1	0.6
Greece	46 220	0.3	38 791	0.3	−16.1
Iceland [2]	..	..	169	0.0	..
Ireland	10 608	0.1	12 704	0.1	19.8
Italy	1 044 017	7.6	1 074 544	7.9	2.9
Luxembourg [1]	..	..	..	..	..
Netherlands	795 892	5.8	775 249	5.7	−2.6
Norway	46 384	0.3	47 396	0.3	2.2
Portugal	17 040	0.1	18 390	0.1	7.9
Spain	270 059	2.0	221 717	1.6	−17.9
Sweden	249 932	1.8	231 818	1.7	−7.2
Switzerland	673 355	4.9	644 493	4.7	−4.3
Turkey	25 739	0.2	21 462	0.2	−16.6
United Kingdom	675 168	4.9	652 332	4.8	−3.4
Other OECD-Europe	..	..	..	..	..
Total Europe	11 969 696	87.5	11 795 260	86.4	−1.5
Canada	62 626	0.5	65 933	0.5	5.3
United States	418 515	3.1	566 756	4.2	35.4
Total North America	481 141	3.5	632 689	4.6	31.5
Australia [3]	86 799	0.6	79 867	0.6	−8.0
New Zealand [3]	..	..	..	..	..
Japan	190 073	1.4	219 337	1.6	15.4
Total Australasia and Japan	276 872	2.0	299 204	2.2	8.1
Total OECD Countries	**12 727 709**	**93.0**	**12 727 153**	**93.3**	**−0.0**
Ex-Yugoslavia	179 083	1.3	136 724	1.0	−23.7
Other European countries [2]	435 133	3.2	390 238	2.9	−10.3
Bulgaria	12 576	0.1	14 704	0.1	16.9
Ex-Czechoslovakia	88 984	0.7	93 571	0.7	5.2
Hungary	152 582	1.1	157 377	1.2	3.1
Poland	60 788	0.4	65 737	0.5	8.1
Rumania	15 990	0.1	18 461	0.1	15.5
Ex-USSR	32 838	0.2	40 388	0.3	23.0
Latin America	71 375	0.5	75 262	0.6	5.4
Asia-Oceania	155 095	1.1	191 929	1.4	23.7
Africa	22 609	0.2	27 503	0.2	21.6
Origin country undetermined	96 361	0.7	98 368	0.7	2.1
Total non-OECD Countries	**959 656**	**7.0**	**920 024**	**6.7**	**−4.1**
TOTAL	**13 687 365**	**100.0**	**13 647 177**	**100.0**	**−0.3**

1. Belgium includes Luxembourg.
2. "Other European countries" includes Iceland.
3. Australia includes New Zealand.

AUSTRIA

ARRIVALS OF FOREIGN TOURISTS AT REGISTERED TOURIST ACCOMMODATION

(by country of residence)

	1991	Relative share	1992	Relative share	% Variation over 1991
Austria	..	..	..	..	..
Belgium[1]	450 111	2.4	468 264	2.5	4.0
Denmark	198 706	1.0	181 519	1.0	−8.6
Finland	55 818	0.3	45 777	0.2	−18.0
France	845 483	4.4	737 709	3.9	−12.7
Germany	10 613 343	55.6	10 664 269	55.8	0.5
Greece	49 995	0.3	41 696	0.2	−16.6
Iceland[2]			169	0.0	
Ireland	10 608	0.1	12 704	0.1	19.8
Italy	1 186 432	6.2	1 219 512	6.4	2.8
Luxembourg[1]	..	..	..	..	..
Netherlands	1 322 987	6.9	1 291 134	6.8	−2.4
Norway	46 384	0.2	47 396	0.2	2.2
Portugal	17 040	0.1	18 390	0.1	7.9
Spain	270 059	1.4	221 717	1.2	−17.9
Sweden	327 683	1.7	301 331	1.6	−8.0
Switzerland	782 365	4.1	752 532	3.9	−3.8
Turkey	25 739	0.1	21 462	0.1	−16.6
United Kingdom	786 300	4.1	752 918	3.9	−4.2
Other OECD-Europe	..	..	..	..	..
Total Europe	16 989 053	89.0	16 778 499	87.9	−1.2
Canada	77 774	0.4	82 638	0.4	6.3
United States	468 646	2.5	627 632	3.3	33.9
Total North America	546 420	2.9	710 270	3.7	30.0
Australia[3]	86 799	0.5	79 867	0.4	−8.0
New Zealand[3]	..	..	..	..	..
Japan	190 073	1.0	219 337	1.1	15.4
Total Australasia and Japan	276 872	1.5	299 204	1.6	8.1
Total OECD Countries	**17 812 345**	**93.3**	**17 787 973**	**93.1**	**−0.1**
Ex-Yugoslavia	212 205	1.1	154 927	0.8	−27.0
Other European countries[2]	538 838	2.8	577 501	3.0	7.2
Bulgaria	14 018	0.1	16 875	0.1	20.4
Ex-Czechoslovakia	147 884	0.8	153 291	0.8	3.7
Hungary	215 081	1.1	227 681	1.2	5.9
Poland	105 738	0.6	111 528	0.6	5.5
Rumania	19 159	0.1	21 191	0.1	10.6
Ex-USSR	36 958	0.2	46 935	0.2	27.0
Latin America	71 376	0.4	91 865	0.5	28.7
Asia-Oceania	163 355	0.9	198 907	1.0	21.8
Africa	22 609	0.1	27 503	0.1	21.6
Origin country undetermined	271 100	1.4	258 964	1.4	−4.5
Total non-OECD Countries	**1 279 483**	**6.7**	**1 309 667**	**6.9**	**2.4**
TOTAL	**19 091 828**	**100.0**	**19 097 640**	**100.0**	**0.0**

1. Belgium includes Luxembourg.
2. "Other European countries" includes Iceland.
3. Australia includes New Zealand.

AUSTRIA

NIGHTS SPENT BY FOREIGN TOURISTS IN HOTELS

(by country of residence)

	1991	Relative share	1992	Relative share	% Variation over 1991
Austria	..	..	..	..	..
Belgium[1]	1 983 728	3.1	2 065 705	3.2	4.1
Denmark	651 684	1.0	597 917	0.9	−8.3
Finland	235 233	0.4	196 307	0.3	−16.5
France	2 475 837	3.9	2 189 896	3.4	−11.5
Germany	38 172 969	59.4	38 519 615	60.0	0.9
Greece	128 042	0.2	122 300	0.2	−4.5
Iceland[2]	..	..	998	0.0	..
Ireland	55 764	0.1	64 335	0.1	15.4
Italy	2 806 764	4.4	3 037 178	4.7	8.2
Luxembourg[1]	..	..	..	..	..
Netherlands	5 153 046	8.0	4 998 214	7.8	−3.0
Norway	157 324	0.2	168 305	0.3	7.0
Portugal	34 108	0.1	40 236	0.1	18.0
Spain	563 629	0.9	466 291	0.7	−17.3
Sweden	1 050 578	1.6	1 016 497	1.6	−3.2
Switzerland	2 645 338	4.1	2 520 498	3.9	−4.7
Turkey	71 156	0.1	60 597	0.1	−14.8
United Kingdom	3 664 186	5.7	3 563 269	5.6	−2.8
Other OECD-Europe	..	..	..	..	..
Total Europe	59 849 386	93.2	59 628 158	92.9	−0.4
Canada	155 101	0.2	158 559	0.2	2.2
United States	1 063 374	1.7	1 369 969	2.1	28.8
Total North America	1 218 475	1.9	1 528 528	2.4	25.4
Australia[3]	203 224	0.3	194 135	0.3	−4.5
New Zealand[3]	..	..	..	..	..
Japan	413 186	0.6	453 099	0.7	9.7
Total Australasia and Japan	616 410	1.0	647 234	1.0	5.0
Total OECD Countries	**61 684 271**	**96.1**	**61 803 920**	**96.3**	**0.2**
Ex-Yugoslavia	500 254	0.8	374 444	0.6	−25.1
Other European countries[2]	1 107 134	1.7	1 018 688	1.6	−8.0
Bulgaria	33 357	0.1	38 555	0.1	15.6
Ex-Czechoslovakia	209 727	0.3	214 195	0.3	2.1
Hungary	359 468	0.6	384 010	0.6	6.8
Poland	159 941	0.2	176 046	0.3	10.1
Rumania	61 378	0.1	55 190	0.1	−10.1
Ex-USSR	132 833	0.2	150 692	0.2	13.4
Latin America	150 430	0.2	175 084	0.3	16.4
Asia-Oceania	410 712	0.6	451 067	0.7	9.8
Africa	87 097	0.1	102 551	0.2	17.7
Origin country undetermined	272 651	0.4	263 222	0.4	−3.5
Total non-OECD Countries	**2 528 278**	**3.9**	**2 385 056**	**3.7**	**−5.7**
TOTAL	**64 212 549**	**100.0**	**64 188 976**	**100.0**	**−0.0**

. Belgium includes Luxembourg.
. "Other European countries" includes Iceland.
. Australia includes New Zealand.

AUSTRIA

NIGHTS SPENT BY FOREIGN TOURISTS IN REGISTERED TOURIST ACCOMMODATION

(by country of residence)

	1991	Relative share	1992	Relative share	% Variation over 1991
Austria	..	..	..	..	..
Belgium [1]	2 889 874	2.9	3 010 297	3.0	4.2
Denmark	1 006 058	1.0	928 020	0.9	−7.8
Finland	235 233	0.2	196 307	0.2	−16.5
France	3 169 839	3.2	2 845 545	2.9	−10.2
Germany	64 285 539	64.5	64 715 088	64.9	0.7
Greece	144 773	0.1	135 223	0.1	−6.6
Iceland [2]	..	..	998	0.0	..
Ireland	55 764	0.1	64 335	0.1	15.4
Italy	3 307 567	3.3	3 609 209	3.6	9.1
Luxembourg [1]	..	..	..	..	..
Netherlands	9 242 866	9.3	8 998 720	9.0	−2.6
Norway	157 324	0.2	168 305	0.2	7.0
Portugal	34 108	0.0	40 236	0.0	18.0
Spain	563 629	0.6	466 291	0.5	−17.3
Sweden	1 414 429	1.4	1 355 865	1.4	−4.1
Switzerland	3 239 015	3.3	3 121 254	3.1	−3.6
Turkey	71 156	0.1	60 597	0.1	−14.8
United Kingdom	4 204 954	4.2	4 068 302	4.1	−3.2
Other OECD-Europe	..	..	..	..	..
Total Europe	94 022 128	94.4	93 784 592	94.0	−0.3
Canada	196 294	0.2	207 787	0.2	5.9
United States	1 191 496	1.2	1 526 478	1.5	28.1
Total North America	1 387 790	1.4	1 734 265	1.7	25.0
Australia [3]	203 224	0.2	194 135	0.2	−4.5
New Zealand [3]	..	..	..	..	..
Japan	413 186	0.4	453 099	0.5	9.7
Total Australasia and Japan	616 410	0.6	647 234	0.6	5.0
Total OECD Countries	**96 026 328**	**96.4**	**96 166 091**	**96.4**	**0.1**
Ex-Yugoslavia	708 816	0.7	488 248	0.5	−31.1
Other European countries [2]	1 444 333	1.4	1 613 246	1.6	11.7
Bulgaria	44 518	0.0	48 651	0.0	9.3
Ex-Czechoslovakia	344 798	0.3	373 006	0.4	8.2
Hungary	568 833	0.6	625 314	0.6	9.9
Poland	260 790	0.3	302 638	0.3	16.0
Rumania	75 926	0.1	68 555	0.1	−9.7
Ex-USSR	149 468	0.2	195 082	0.2	30.5
Latin America	150 430	0.2	175 084	0.2	16.4
Asia-Oceania	442 348	0.4	479 661	0.5	8.4
Africa	87 097	0.1	102 551	0.1	17.7
Origin country undetermined	782 371	0.8	728 594	0.7	−6.9
Total non-OECD Countries	**3 615 395**	**3.6**	**3 587 384**	**3.6**	**−0.8**
TOTAL	**99 641 723**	**100.0**	**99 753 475**	**100.0**	**0.1**

1. Belgium includes Luxembourg.
2. "Other European countries" includes Iceland.
3. Australia includes New Zealand.

BELGIUM

NIGHTS SPENT BY FOREIGN TOURISTS IN HOTELS

(by country of residence)

	1991	Relative share	1992	Relative share	% Variation over 1991
Austria	55 804	0.8	66 858	0.9	19.8
Belgium	..	..	..	..	..
Denmark	87 964	1.3	95 270	1.2	8.3
Finland [1]	..	..	..	..	..
France	827 427	12.6	1 009 516	13.1	22.0
Germany	963 992	14.7	1 130 757	14.7	17.3
Greece	70 922	1.1	85 994	1.1	21.3
Iceland [1]	..	..	..	..	..
Ireland	42 393	0.6	39 757	0.5	−6.2
Italy	339 048	5.2	392 560	5.1	15.8
Luxembourg	97 399	1.5	110 447	1.4	13.4
Netherlands	932 619	14.2	1 010 282	13.1	8.3
Norway	58 580	0.9	50 011	0.6	−14.6
Portugal	103 625	1.6	99 667	1.3	−3.8
Spain	209 784	3.2	271 205	3.5	29.3
Sweden	145 268	2.2	147 254	1.9	1.4
Switzerland	97 218	1.5	106 543	1.4	9.6
Turkey	21 257	0.3	22 664	0.3	6.6
United Kingdom	1 109 444	16.9	1 327 547	17.3	19.7
Other OECD-Europe	..	..	..	..	..
Total Europe	5 162 744	78.5	5 966 332	77.5	15.6
Canada	76 641	1.2	77 901	1.0	1.6
United States	486 811	7.4	602 921	7.8	23.9
Total North America	563 452	8.6	680 822	8.8	20.8
Australia [2]	..	..	..	..	..
New Zealand [2]	..	..	..	..	..
Japan	153 184	2.3	229 517	3.0	49.8
Total Australasia and Japan	153 184	2.3	229 517	3.0	49.8
Total OECD Countries	**5 879 380**	**89.4**	**6 876 671**	**89.4**	**17.0**
Ex-Yugoslavia	..	..	..	..	..
Other European countries [1]	278 792	4.2	234 001	3.0	−16.1
Ex-USSR	39 291	0.6	47 836	0.6	21.7
Latin America	44 740	0.7	50 449	0.7	12.8
Mexico [3]	22 177	0.3	19 962	0.3	−10.0
Asia-Oceania [2]	172 723	2.6	183 318	2.4	6.1
Africa	186 058	2.8	149 108	1.9	−19.9
Origin country undetermined	12 514	0.2	200 508	2.6	1502.3
Total non-OECD Countries	**694 827**	**10.6**	**817 384**	**10.6**	**17.6**
TOTAL	**6 574 207**	**100.0**	**7 694 055**	**100.0**	**17.0**

1. "Other European countries" includes Finland and Iceland.
2. "Asia-Oceania" includes Australia and New Zealand.
3. Mexico includes Central America.

BELGIUM

NIGHTS SPENT BY FOREIGN TOURISTS IN REGISTERED TOURIST ACCOMMODATION

(by country of residence)

	1991	Relative share	1992	Relative share	% Variation over 1991
Austria	62 242	0.5	72 216	0.6	16.0
Belgium	..	..	..	..	..
Denmark	116 656	1.0	136 864	1.1	17.3
Finland [1]	..	..	..	..	..
France	1 213 421	10.0	1 307 776	10.2	7.8
Germany	2 064 242	17.0	2 263 102	17.6	9.6
Greece	74 069	0.6	88 904	0.7	20.0
Iceland [1]	..	..	..	..	..
Ireland	47 242	0.4	44 699	0.3	–5.4
Italy	374 443	3.1	430 160	3.3	14.9
Luxembourg	194 041	1.6	153 534	1.2	–20.9
Netherlands	4 377 679	36.0	4 220 802	32.8	–3.6
Norway	69 818	0.6	53 378	0.4	–23.5
Portugal	123 680	1.0	112 106	0.9	–9.4
Spain	239 525	2.0	322 096	2.5	34.5
Sweden	159 140	1.3	160 060	1.2	0.6
Switzerland	107 408	0.9	114 678	0.9	6.8
Turkey	26 162	0.2	23 558	0.2	–10.0
United Kingdom	1 253 814	10.3	1 506 260	11.7	20.1
Other OECD-Europe	..	..	..	..	..
Total Europe	10 503 582	86.3	11 010 193	85.5	4.8
Canada	89 682	0.7	86 204	0.7	–3.9
United States	509 858	4.2	619 092	4.8	21.4
Total North America	599 540	4.9	705 296	5.5	17.6
Australia [2]	..	..	..	..	..
New Zealand [2]	..	..	..	..	..
Japan	157 954	1.3	233 368	1.8	47.7
Total Australasia and Japan	157 954	1.3	233 368	1.8	47.7
Total OECD Countries	**11 261 076**	**92.5**	**11 948 857**	**92.8**	**6.1**
Ex-Yugoslavia	..	..	..	..	..
Other European countries [1]	356 436	2.9	293 721	2.3	–17.6
Ex-USSR	47 958	0.4	54 795	0.4	14.3
Latin America	52 721	0.4	56 863	0.4	7.9
Mexico [3]	24 164	0.2	22 004	0.2	–8.9
Asia-Oceania [2]	196 823	1.6	202 944	1.6	3.1
Africa	217 157	1.8	161 313	1.3	–25.7
Origin country undetermined	86 711	0.7	216 284	1.7	149.4
Total non-OECD Countries	**909 848**	**7.5**	**931 125**	**7.2**	**2.3**
TOTAL	**12 170 924**	**100.0**	**12 879 982**	**100.0**	**5.8**

1. "Other European countries" includes Finland and Iceland.
2. "Asia-Oceania" includes Australia and New Zealand.
3. Mexico includes Central America.

CANADA

ARRIVALS OF FOREIGN TOURISTS AT FRONTIERS

(by country of residence)

	1991	Relative share	1992	Relative share	% Variation over 1991
Austria	21 800	0.1	26 500	0.2	21.6
Belgium [1]	32 400	0.2	34 800	0.2	7.4
Denmark	18 500	0.1	17 900	0.1	–3.2
Finland	15 200	0.1	12 400	0.1	–18.4
France [2]	306 600	2.1	310 000	2.1	1.1
Germany	272 800	1.8	290 300	2.0	6.4
Greece	14 800	0.1	14 300	0.1	–3.4
Iceland	1 200	0.0	1 400	0.0	16.7
Ireland	14 000	0.1	17 500	0.1	25.0
Italy	87 300	0.6	94 800	0.6	8.6
Luxembourg [1]	..	..	..	..	..
Netherlands	87 700	0.6	85 200	0.6	–2.9
Norway	12 600	0.1	13 300	0.1	5.6
Portugal	13 500	0.1	15 400	0.1	14.1
Spain	24 600	0.2	27 700	0.2	12.6
Sweden	26 400	0.2	25 900	0.2	–1.9
Switzerland	77 000	0.5	79 100	0.5	2.7
Turkey	3 600	0.0	3 400	0.0	–5.6
United Kingdom	530 400	3.6	536 400	3.6	1.1
Other OECD-Europe	..	..	..	..	..
Total Europe	1 560 400	10.5	1 606 300	10.9	2.9
Canada	..	..	..	..	..
United States	12 002 600	80.5	11 818 700	80.2	–1.5
Total North America	12 002 600	80.5	11 818 700	80.2	–1.5
Australia [4]	99 100	0.7	103 200	0.7	4.1
New Zealand	28 700	0.2	28 400	0.2	–1.0
Japan	393 000	2.6	392 300	2.7	–0.2
Total Australasia and Japan	520 800	3.5	523 900	3.6	0.6
Total OECD Countries	**14 083 800**	**94.4**	**13 948 900**	**94.6**	**–1.0**
Ex-Yugoslavia	12 100	0.1	7 900	0.1	–34.7
Other European countries	64 800	0.4	59 500	0.4	–8.2
Bulgaria [1]	3 600	0.0	4 100	0.0	13.9
Ex-Czechoslovakia	9 300	0.1	10 100	0.1	8.6
Hungary	7 800	0.1	7 500	0.1	–3.8
Poland	21 500	0.1	20 200	0.1	–6.0
Ex-USSR	22 600	0.2	17 600	0.1	–22.1
Latin America [3]	137 700	0.9	123 700	0.8	–10.2
Argentina	23 900	0.2	15 800	0.1	–33.9
Brazil	33 000	0.2	26 300	0.2	–20.3
Colombia	5 000	0.0	5 300	0.0	6.0
Mexico	65 100	0.4	65 100	0.4	0.0
Venezuela	10 700	0.1	11 200	0.1	4.7
Asia-Oceania	401 300	2.7	385 600	2.6	–3.9
China [6]	26 600	0.2	27 600	0.2	3.8
Hong Kong	121 000	0.8	119 400	0.8	–1.3
India [1]	50 900	0.3	47 400	0.3	–6.9
Israel	56 600	0.4	48 800	0.3	–13.8
Republic of Korea [1]	39 800	0.3	37 600	0.3	–5.5
Malaysia [1]	15 800	0.1	14 500	0.1	–8.2
Philippines [1]	19 800	0.1	18 300	0.1	–7.6
Singapore [1]	20 200	0.1	18 900	0.1	–6.4
Taiwan	41 200	0.3	40 900	0.3	–0.7
Thailand [1]	9 400	0.1	12 200	0.1	29.8
Africa	11 000	0.1	13 900	0.1	26.4
South Africa	11 000	0.1	13 900	0.1	26.4
Origin country undetermined [5]	201 400	1.4	201 300	1.4	–0.0
Total non-OECD Countries	**828 300**	**5.6**	**791 900**	**5.4**	**–4.4**
TOTAL [1]	**14 912 100**	**100.0**	**14 740 800**	**100.0**	**–1.1**

1. Estimate.
2. France includes Andorra and Monaco.
3. Latin America includes South America and Mexico.
4. Australia includes Papua New Guinea, Solomon, Caroline and Christmas islands.
5. Origin country undetermined includes Bermuda, Caribbean, Central America, Greenland and St. Pierre and Miquelon.
6. China includes Mongolia and Tibet.

CANADA

ARRIVALS OF FOREIGN VISITORS AT FRONTIERS

(by country of residence)

	1991	Relative share	1992	Relative share	% Variation over 1991
Austria	23 600	0.1	28 400	0.1	20.3
Belgium [1]	34 800	0.1	36 700	0.1	5.5
Denmark	20 300	0.1	20 400	0.1	0.5
Finland	16 700	0.0	13 600	0.0	−18.6
France [2]	324 900	0.9	328 300	0.9	1.0
Germany	312 300	0.8	339 900	0.9	8.8
Greece	16 400	0.0	16 000	0.0	−2.4
Iceland	1 300	0.0	1 500	0.0	15.4
Ireland	15 200	0.0	18 800	0.1	23.7
Italy	100 000	0.3	111 100	0.3	11.1
Luxembourg [1]	..	..	..	..	..
Netherlands	95 200	0.3	92 100	0.3	−3.3
Norway	13 600	0.0	14 500	0.0	6.6
Portugal	14 000	0.0	15 800	0.0	12.9
Spain	27 000	0.1	31 000	0.1	14.8
Sweden	28 600	0.1	28 100	0.1	−1.7
Switzerland	82 300	0.2	85 500	0.2	3.9
Turkey	3 900	0.0	3 800	0.0	−2.6
United Kingdom	580 700	1.6	595 600	1.6	2.6
Other OECD-Europe	..	..	..	..	..
Total Europe	1 710 800	4.6	1 781 100	4.9	4.1
Canada	..	..	..	..	..
United States	33 577 200	91.2	32 427 300	89.6	−3.4
Total North America	33 577 200	91.2	32 427 300	89.6	−3.4
Australia [4]	109 400	0.3	113 300	0.3	3.6
New Zealand	31 200	0.1	30 800	0.1	−1.3
Japan	480 300	1.3	495 800	1.4	3.2
Total Australasia and Japan	620 900	1.7	639 900	1.8	3.1
Total OECD Countries	**35 908 900**	**97.5**	**34 848 300**	**96.3**	**−3.0**
Ex-Yugoslavia	13 100	0.0	8 900	0.0	−32.1
Other European countries	67 600	0.2	62 800	0.2	−7.1
Bulgaria [1]	3 900	0.0	4 300	0.0	10.3
Ex-Czechoslovakia	10 100	0.0	11 000	0.0	8.9
Hungary	8 100	0.0	7 900	0.0	−2.5
Poland	22 500	0.1	21 600	0.1	−4.0
Ex-USSR	23 000	0.1	18 000	0.0	−21.7
Latin America [3]	153 900	0.4	142 100	0.4	−7.7
Argentina	25 600	0.1	19 100	0.1	−25.4
Brazil	36 300	0.1	28 600	0.1	−21.2
Colombia	5 700	0.0	6 200	0.0	8.8
Mexico	74 000	0.2	75 500	0.2	2.0
Venezuela	12 300	0.0	12 700	0.0	3.3
Asia-Oceania	448 400	1.2	440 400	1.2	−1.8
China [6]	30 300	0.1	32 200	0.1	6.3
Hong Kong	127 100	0.3	126 400	0.3	−0.6
India [1]	62 800	0.2	60 100	0.2	−4.3
Israel	65 900	0.2	59 100	0.2	−10.3
Republic of Korea [1]	46 500	0.1	46 200	0.1	−0.6
Malaysia [1]	18 400	0.0	16 900	0.0	−8.2
Philippines [1]	22 100	0.1	20 700	0.1	−6.3
Singapore [1]	21 700	0.1	21 900	0.1	0.9
Taiwan	43 100	0.1	43 600	0.1	1.2
Thailand [1]	10 500	0.0	13 300	0.0	26.7
Africa	11 600	0.0	14 800	0.0	27.6
South Africa	11 600	0.0	14 800	0.0	27.6
Origin country undetermined [5]	214 200	0.6	669 000	1.8	212.3
Total non-OECD Countries	**908 800**	**2.5**	**1 338 000**	**3.7**	**47.2**
TOTAL [1]	**36 817 700**	**100.0**	**36 186 300**	**100.0**	**−1.7**

1. Estimate.
2. France includes Andorra and Monaco.
3. Latin America includes South America and Mexico.
4. Australia includes Papua New Guinea, Solomon, Caroline and Christmas islands.
5. Origin country undetermined includes Bermuda, Caribbean, Central America, Greenland and St. Pierre and Miquelon.
6. China includes Mongolia and Tibet.

CANADA

NIGHTS SPENT BY FOREIGN TOURISTS IN TOURIST ACCOMMODATION[1]
(by country of residence)

	1991	Relative share	1992	Relative share	% Variation over 1991
Austria	279 500	0.3	305 000	0.4	9.1
Belgium	379 500	0.5	442 500	0.6	16.6
Denmark	194 200	0.2	195 900	0.2	0.9
Finland	122 900	0.1	103 500	0.1	−15.8
France	3 789 700	4.6	3 819 600	4.8	0.8
Germany	3 634 500	4.4	3 589 400	4.5	−1.2
Greece	214 200	0.3	279 600	0.4	30.5
Iceland	7 400	0.0	5 600	0.0	−24.3
Ireland	151 500	0.2	201 800	0.3	33.2
Italy	888 600	1.1	907 000	1.1	2.1
Luxembourg	..	..	..	..	..
Netherlands	1 058 700	1.3	1 058 700	1.3	0.0
Norway	108 800	0.1	144 700	0.2	33.0
Portugal	236 800	0.3	236 800	0.3	0.0
Spain	268 900	0.3	302 800	0.4	12.6
Sweden	256 600	0.3	222 100	0.3	−13.4
Switzerland	1 042 000	1.3	1 115 300	1.4	7.0
Turkey	51 600	0.1	44 700	0.1	−13.4
United Kingdom	6 313 200	7.6	6 118 700	7.7	−3.1
Other OECD-Europe	..	..	..	..	..
Total Europe	18 998 600	23.0	19 093 700	24.0	0.5
Canada	..	..	..	..	..
United States	49 365 500	59.6	46 289 400	58.3	−6.2
Total North America	49 365 500	59.6	46 289 400	58.3	−6.2
Australia	1 064 600	1.3	1 171 900	1.5	10.1
New Zealand	305 200	0.4	310 800	0.4	1.8
Japan	2 637 400	3.2	2 495 400	3.1	−5.4
Total Australasia and Japan	4 007 200	4.8	3 978 100	5.0	−0.7
Total OECD Countries	**72 371 300**	**87.4**	**69 361 200**	**87.3**	**−4.2**
Ex-Yugoslavia	206 600	0.2	148 700	0.2	−28.0
Other European countries	1 784 700	2.2	1 643 600	2.1	−7.9
Bulgaria	74 100	0.1	151 000	0.2	103.8
Ex-Czechoslovakia	210 700	0.3	204 300	0.3	−3.0
Hungary	178 200	0.2	204 600	0.3	14.8
Poland	616 500	0.7	631 800	0.8	2.5
Ex-USSR	705 200	0.9	451 900	0.6	−35.9
Latin America[2]	1 367 200	1.7	1 184 500	1.5	−13.4
Argentina	339 600	0.4	209 900	0.3	−38.2
Brazil	378 800	0.5	273 300	0.3	−27.9
Colombia	38 400	0.0	41 600	0.1	8.3
Mexico[2]	524 700	0.6	564 500	0.7	7.6
Venezuela	85 700	0.1	95 200	0.1	11.1
Asia-Oceania	4 199 100	5.1	3 908 900	4.9	−6.9
China	289 400	0.3	407 000	0.5	40.6
Hong Kong	289 400	0.3	407 000	0.5	40.6
India	518 100	0.6	443 100	0.6	−14.5
Israel	548 400	0.7	398 600	0.5	−27.3
Republic of Korea	214 200	0.3	237 100	0.3	10.7
Malaysia	131 800	0.2	151 900	0.2	15.3
Philippines	336 600	0.4	296 000	0.4	−12.1
Singapore	223 600	0.3	203 900	0.3	−8.8
Taiwan	376 700	0.5	450 600	0.6	19.6
Thailand	108 100	0.1	114 600	0.1	6.0
Africa	162 800	0.2	173 000	0.2	6.3
South Africa	162 800	0.2	173 000	0.2	6.3
Origin country undetermined	2 681 400	3.2	3 003 600	3.8	12.0
Total non-OECD Countries	**10 401 800**	**12.6**	**10 062 300**	**12.7**	**−3.3**
TOTAL	**82 773 100**	**100.0**	**79 423 500**	**100.0**	**−4.0**

1. Covers all forms of accommodation, including homes of friends or relatives.
2. Latin America includes Mexico.

DENMARK

NIGHTS SPENT BY FOREIGN TOURISTS IN HOTELS

(by country of nationality)

	1991	Relative share	1992	Relative share	% Variation over 1991
Austria [1]	..	..	..	..	..
Belgium [1]	..	..	..	..	..
Denmark	..	..	..	..	..
Finland	136 700	2.3	104 000	1.7	–23.9
France	85 200	1.4	81 200	1.3	–4.7
Germany	1 587 200	26.6	1 703 900	27.6	7.4
Greece [1]	..	..	..	..	..
Iceland [1]	..	..	..	..	..
Ireland [1]	..	..	..	..	..
Italy	142 300	2.4	157 700	2.6	10.8
Luxembourg [1]	..	..	..	..	..
Netherlands	156 700	2.6	194 700	3.2	24.3
Norway	746 800	12.5	793 800	12.8	6.3
Portugal [1]	..	..	..	..	..
Spain [1]	..	..	..	..	..
Sweden	1 746 200	29.3	1 724 900	27.9	–1.2
Switzerland [1]	..	..	..	..	..
Turkey [1]	..	..	..	..	..
United Kingdom	316 500	5.3	320 400	5.2	1.2
Other OECD-Europe [1]	308 200	5.2	317 600	5.1	3.0
Total Europe	5 225 800	87.6	5 398 200	87.4	3.3
Canada [2]	..	..	..	..	..
United States	291 500	4.9	305 200	4.9	4.7
Total North America	291 500	4.9	305 200	4.9	4.7
Australia [2]	..	..	..	..	..
New Zealand [2]	..	..	..	..	..
Japan	93 400	1.6	110 900	1.8	18.7
Total Australasia and Japan	93 400	1.6	110 900	1.8	18.7
Total OECD Countries	**5 610 700**	**94.1**	**5 814 300**	**94.1**	**3.6**
Ex-Yugoslavia	..	..	..	..	..
Origin country undetermined [2]	352 400	5.9	363 400	5.9	3.1
Total non-OECD Countries	**352 400**	**5.9**	**363 400**	**5.9**	**3.1**
TOTAL	**5 963 100**	**100.0**	**6 177 700**	**100.0**	**3.6**

1. Other OECD-Europe includes Austria, Belgium, Greece, Iceland, Ireland, Luxembourg, Portugal, Spain, Switzerland, Turkey as well as European non-member countries.
2. Origin country undetermined includes Australia, Canada and New Zealand.

DENMARK

NIGHTS SPENT BY FOREIGN TOURISTS IN REGISTERED TOURIST ACCOMMODATION

(by country of nationality)

	1991	Relative share	1992	Relative share	% Variation over 1991
Austria [1]	..	..	..	..	..
Belgium [1]	..	..	..	..	..
Denmark	..	..	..	..	..
Finland	232 634	2.2	191 600	1.7	−17.6
France	152 300	1.5	150 400	1.3	−1.2
Germany	3 928 400	37.7	4 573 000	39.5	16.4
Greece [1]	..	..	..	..	..
Iceland [1]	..	..	..	..	..
Italy	218 937	2.1	233 300	2.0	6.6
Luxembourg [1]	..	..	..	..	..
Netherlands	630 364	6.0	1 003 300	8.7	59.2
Norway	1 062 800	10.2	1 140 200	9.8	7.3
Portugal [1]	..	..	..	..	..
Spain [1]	..	..	..	..	..
Sweden	2 567 700	24.6	2 614 500	22.6	1.8
Switzerland [1]	..	..	..	..	..
Turkey [1]	..	..	..	..	..
United Kingdom	366 900	3.5	381 800	3.3	4.1
Other OECD-Europe [1]	428 888	4.1	442 400	3.8	3.2
Total Europe	9 588 923	91.9	10 730 500	92.6	11.9
Canada [2]	..	..	..	..	..
United States	311 000	3.0	324 200	2.8	4.2
Total North America	311 000	3.0	324 200	2.8	4.2
Australia [2]	..	..	..	..	..
New Zealand [2]	..	..	..	..	..
Japan [3]	93 400	0.9	110 900	1.0	18.7
Total Australasia and Japan	93 400	0.9	110 900	1.0	18.7
Total OECD Countries	**9 993 323**	**95.8**	**11 165 600**	**96.4**	**11.7**
Ex-Yugoslavia	..	..	..	..	..
Origin country undetermined [2]	438 077	4.2	422 500	3.6	−3.6
Total non-OECD Countries	**438 077**	**4.2**	**422 500**	**3.6**	**−3.6**
TOTAL	**10 431 400**	**100.0**	**11 588 100**	**100.0**	**11.1**

. Other OECD-Europe includes Austria, Belgium, Greece, Iceland, Ireland, Luxembourg, Portugal, Spain, Switzerland, Turkey as well as European non-member countries.
. Origin country undetermined includes Australia, Canada and New Zealand.
. Japan includes only nights spent in hotels.

FINLAND

NIGHTS SPENT BY FOREIGN TOURISTS IN HOTELS

(by country of residence)

	1991	Relative share	1992	Relative share	% Variation over 1991
Austria	22 123	1.0	23 164	1.0	4.7
Belgium	16 994	0.8	16 427	0.7	-3.3
Denmark	65 565	3.0	64 155	2.9	-2.2
Finland	..	..	..	..	..
France	80 840	3.7	83 679	3.7	3.5
Germany	351 017	15.9	376 700	16.8	7.3
Greece [1]	..	..	..	..	..
Iceland	5 434	0.2	7 806	0.3	43.7
Ireland [2]	..	..	..	..	..
Italy	81 830	3.7	76 557	3.4	-6.4
Luxembourg [1]	..	..	..	..	..
Netherlands	52 823	2.4	61 863	2.8	17.1
Norway	91 700	4.2	99 759	4.4	8.8
Portugal [3]	..	..	..	..	..
Spain [3]	31 607	1.4	32 966	1.5	4.3
Sweden	524 299	23.8	510 089	22.7	-2.7
Switzerland	62 271	2.8	59 327	2.6	-4.7
Turkey [1]	..	..	..	..	..
United Kingdom [2]	131 699	6.0	126 885	5.7	-3.7
Other OECD-Europe	..	..	..	..	..
Total Europe	1 518 202	69.0	1 539 377	68.6	1.4
Canada	24 895	1.1	21 033	0.9	-15.5
United States	144 098	6.5	151 137	6.7	4.9
Total North America	168 993	7.7	172 170	7.7	1.9
Australia	..	..	..	..	..
New Zealand	..	..	..	..	..
Japan	57 258	2.6	57 170	2.5	-0.2
Total Australasia and Japan	57 258	2.6	57 170	2.5	-0.2
Total OECD Countries	**1 744 453**	**79.3**	**1 768 717**	**78.9**	**1.4**
Ex-Yugoslavia	..	..	..	..	..
Other European countries [1]	279 412	12.7	283 227	12.6	1.4
Bulgaria [4]	11 178	0.5	9 163	0.4	-18.0
Ex-Czechoslovakia	14 448	0.7	10 976	0.5	-24.0
Hungary	12 313	0.6	13 383	0.6	8.7
Poland	19 624	0.9	19 342	0.9	-1.4
Ex-USSR	221 849	10.1	171 349	7.6	-22.8
Origin country undetermined [5]	177 005	8.0	190 797	8.5	7.8
Total non-OECD Countries	**456 417**	**20.7**	**474 024**	**21.1**	**3.9**
TOTAL	**2 200 870**	**100.0**	**2 242 741**	**100.0**	**1.9**

1. "Other European countries" includes Greece, Luxembourg and Turkey.
2. United Kingdom includes Ireland.
3. Spain includes Portugal.
4. Bulgaria includes Rumania.
5. "Origin country undetermined" includes Latin America Asia-Oceania and Africa.

FRANCE

ARRIVALS OF FOREIGN TOURISTS AT FRONTIERS[1]

(by country of residence)

	1991	Relative share	1992	Relative share	% Variation over 1991
Austria	409 000	0.7	457 000	0.8	11.7
Belgium	6 454 000	11.7	7 107 000	11.9	10.1
Denmark	662 000	1.2	722 000	1.2	9.1
Finland	106 000	0.2	89 000	0.1	−16.0
France	..	..	..	..	..
Germany	11 704 000	21.3	12 553 000	21.1	7.3
Greece	166 000	0.3	283 000	0.5	70.5
Iceland	20 000	0.0	27 000	0.0	35.0
Ireland	368 000	0.7	418 000	0.7	13.6
Italy	5 898 000	10.7	7 174 000	12.0	21.6
Luxembourg	285 000	0.5	313 000	0.5	9.8
Netherlands	5 932 000	10.8	6 197 000	10.4	4.5
Norway	289 000	0.5	325 000	0.5	12.5
Portugal	1 095 000	2.0	1 369 000	2.3	25.0
Spain	3 648 000	6.6	3 378 000	5.7	−7.4
Sweden	768 000	1.4	848 000	1.4	10.4
Switzerland	2 622 000	4.8	2 360 000	4.0	−10.0
Turkey	..	..	..	..	..
United Kingdom	8 099 000	14.7	8 196 000	13.8	1.2
Other OECD-Europe	..	..	..	..	..
Total Europe	48 525 000	88.2	51 816 000	87.0	6.8
Canada	493 000	0.9	581 000	1.0	17.8
United States	1 643 000	3.0	2 008 000	3.4	22.2
Total North America	2 136 000	3.9	2 589 000	4.3	21.2
Australia	..	..	..	..	..
New Zealand	..	..	..	..	..
Japan	422 000	0.8	435 000	0.7	3.1
Total Australasia and Japan	422 000	0.8	435 000	0.7	3.1
Total OECD Countries	**51 083 000**	**92.8**	**54 840 000**	**92.0**	**7.4**
Ex-Yugoslavia	..	..	..	..	..
Origin country undetermined	3 956 000	7.2	4 750 000	8.0	20.1
Total non-OECD Countries	**3 956 000**	**7.2**	**4 750 000**	**8.0**	**20.1**
TOTAL	**55 039 000**	**100.0**	**59 590 000**	**100.0**	**8.3**

1. Estimates of number of "trips", the same person coming perhaps several times in one year.

FRANCE[1]

ARRIVALS OF FOREIGN TOURISTS AT HOTELS

(by country of residence)

	1991	Relative share	1992	Relative share	% Variation over 1991
Austria[4]	..	..	..	..	..
Belgium[2]	1 719 837	6.8	1 764 431	6.2	2.6
Denmark[4]	..	..	221 305	0.8	..
Finland[4]	..	..	..	..	..
France	..	..	..	..	..
Germany	4 104 567	16.3	4 124 757	14.5	0.5
Greece[4, 8]	..	..	..	..	..
Iceland[4]	..	..	..	..	..
Ireland[3]	..	..	..	..	..
Italy[8]	3 137 722	12.4	3 722 894	13.1	18.6
Luxembourg[2]	..	..	..	..	..
Netherlands	1 337 046	5.3	1 293 800	4.6	−3.2
Norway[4]	..	..	..	..	..
Portugal[4, 9]	..	..	..	..	..
Spain[9]	1 413 675	5.6	1 933 124	6.8	36.7
Sweden[4]	..	..	..	..	..
Switzerland	1 128 411	4.5	1 199 975	4.2	6.3
Turkey[4]	..	..	..	..	..
United Kingdom[3]	5 137 632	20.4	5 556 868	19.6	8.2
Other OECD-Europe[4]	1 504 589	6.0	1 173 360	4.1	−22.0
Total Europe	19 483 479	77.2	20 990 514	73.9	7.7
Canada	360 630	1.4	399 387	1.4	10.7
United States	1 753 891	6.9	2 254 545	7.9	28.5
Total North America	2 114 521	8.4	2 653 932	9.3	25.5
Australia[5]	162 282	0.6	..	..	..
New Zealand[5]	..	..	..	..	..
Japan	1 016 778	4.0	1 551 074	5.5	52.5
Total Australasia and Japan	1 179 060	4.7	1 551 074	5.5	31.6
Total OECD Countries	**22 777 060**	**90.2**	**25 195 520**	**88.7**	**10.6**
Ex-Yugoslavia	..	..	..	..	..
Latin America[6]	313 934	1.2	376 648	1.3	20.0
Asia-Oceania[7]	332 956	1.3	573 141	2.0	72.1
Africa	479 083	1.9	371 572	1.3	−22.4
Origin country undetermined	1 335 008	5.3	1 873 571	6.6	40.3
Total non-OECD Countries	**2 460 981**	**9.8**	**3 194 932**	**11.3**	**29.8**
TOTAL	**25 238 041**	**100.0**	**28 390 452**	**100.0**	**12.5**

1. Data covering all France except 2 regions (Pays de la Loire and Champagne-Ardenne in 1991; Champagne-Ardenne and Corse in 1992).
2. Belgium includes Luxembourg.
3. United Kingdom includes Ireland.
4. "Other OECD-Europe" includes Austria, Denmark, Greece and Portugal (1991 only), Iceland, Finland, Norway, Sweden, Turkey and countries of Central and Eastern Europe.
5. Australia includes New Zealand and Oceania.
6. Latin America includes Central and South America.
7. Asia only.
8. Italy includes Greece in 1992.
9. Spain includes Portugal in 1992.

FRANCE[1]

NIGHTS SPENT BY FOREIGN TOURISTS IN HOTELS

(by country of residence)

	1991	Relative share	1992	Relative share	% Variation over 1991
Austria[4]	..	..	..	..	..
Belgium[2]	3 609 053	6.8	3 795 877	6.4	5.2
Denmark[4]	..	..	510 814	0.9	..
Finland[4]	..	..	..	..	..
France	..	..	..	..	..
Germany	8 502 236	16.0	8 308 398	13.9	-2.3
Greece[4, 8]	..	..	..	..	..
Iceland[4]	..	..	..	..	..
Ireland[3]	..	..	..	..	..
Italy[8]	7 000 617	13.2	8 380 527	14.1	19.7
Luxembourg[2]	..	..	..	..	..
Netherlands	2 421 424	4.6	2 424 585	4.1	0.1
Norway[4]	..	..	..	..	..
Portugal[4, 9]	..	..	..	..	..
Spain[9]	2 755 953	5.2	3 906 144	6.6	41.7
Sweden[4]	..	..	..	..	..
Switzerland	2 319 286	4.4	2 483 674	4.2	7.1
Turkey[4]	..	..	..	..	..
United Kingdom[3]	10 170 853	19.2	11 123 432	18.7	9.4
Other OECD-Europe[4]	3 699 926	7.0	2 717 209	4.6	-26.6
Total Europe	40 479 348	76.3	43 650 660	73.3	7.8
Canada	756 579	1.4	799 555	1.3	5.7
United States	3 917 294	7.4	4 976 852	8.4	27.0
Total North America	4 673 873	8.8	5 776 407	9.7	23.6
Australia[5]	341 490	0.6	..	..	..
New Zealand[5]	..	..	..	..	..
Japan	2 190 904	4.1	3 501 848	5.9	59.8
Total Australasia and Japan	2 532 394	4.8	3 501 848	5.9	38.3
Total OECD Countries	**47 685 615**	**89.9**	**52 928 915**	**88.8**	**11.0**
Ex-Yugoslavia	..	..	..	..	..
Latin America[6]	773 213	1.5	880 968	1.5	13.9
Asia-Oceania[7]	685 295	1.3	1 205 025	2.0	75.8
Africa	1 239 616	2.3	984 027	1.7	-20.6
Origin country undetermined	2 661 114	5.0	3 576 535	6.0	34.4
Total non-OECD Countries	**5 359 238**	**10.1**	**6 646 555**	**11.2**	**24.0**
TOTAL	**53 044 853**	**100.0**	**59 575 470**	**100.0**	**12.3**

1. Data covering all France except 2 regions (Pays de la Loire and Champagne-Ardenne in 1991; Champagne-Ardenne and Corse in 1992).
2. Belgium includes Luxembourg.
3. United Kingdom includes Ireland.
4. "Other OECD-Europe" includes Austria, Denmark, Greece and Portugal (1991 only), Iceland, Finland, Norway, Sweden, Turkey and countries of Central and Eastern Europe.
5. Australia includes New Zealand and Oceania.
6. Latin America includes Central and South America.
7. Asia only.
8. Italy includes Greece in 1992.
9. Spain includes Portugal in 1992.

FRANCE

NIGHTS SPENT BY FOREIGN TOURISTS IN TOURIST ACCOMMODATION[1]

(by country of residence)

	1991	Relative share	1992	Relative share	% Variation over 1991
Austria	2 300 000	0.6	2 477 000	0.6	7.7
Belgium	41 338 000	10.4	44 489 000	10.4	7.6
Denmark	5 565 000	1.4	6 123 000	1.4	10.0
Finland	1 966 000	0.5	1 832 000	0.4	−6.8
France	..	..	..	..	..
Germany	80 308 000	20.3	85 167 000	19.9	6.1
Greece	1 003 000	0.3	1 616 000	0.4	61.1
Iceland	143 000	0.0	189 000	0.0	32.2
Ireland	2 740 000	0.7	3 092 000	0.7	12.8
Italy	35 355 000	8.9	42 441 000	9.9	20.0
Luxembourg	1 825 000	0.5	1 958 000	0.5	7.3
Netherlands	55 859 000	14.1	59 351 000	13.9	6.3
Norway	2 175 000	0.5	2 413 000	0.6	10.9
Portugal	5 376 000	1.4	6 597 000	1.5	22.7
Spain	16 305 000	4.1	14 887 000	3.5	−8.7
Sweden	5 629 000	1.4	6 063 000	1.4	7.7
Switzerland	13 633 000	3.4	12 368 000	2.9	−9.3
Turkey	..	..	..	..	..
United Kingdom	60 399 000	15.3	60 695 000	14.2	0.5
Other OECD-Europe	..	..	..	..	..
Total Europe	331 919 000	83.8	351 758 000	82.1	6.0
Canada	4 647 000	1.2	5 336 000	1.2	14.8
United States	14 264 000	3.6	17 569 000	4.1	23.2
Total North America	18 911 000	4.8	22 905 000	5.3	21.1
Australia	..	..	..	..	..
New Zealand	..	..	..	..	..
Japan	1 976 000	0.5	1 959 000	0.5	−0.9
Total Australasia and Japan	1 976 000	0.5	1 959 000	0.5	−0.9
Total OECD Countries	**352 806 000**	**89.1**	**376 622 000**	**87.9**	**6.8**
Ex-Yugoslavia	..	..	..	..	..
Origin country undetermined	43 227 000	10.9	51 759 000	12.1	19.7
Total non-OECD Countries	**43 227 000**	**10.9**	**51 759 000**	**12.1**	**19.7**
TOTAL	**396 033 000**	**100.0**	**428 381 000**	**100.0**	**8.2**

1. The figures are based on an update of the findings of the 1991 frontier survey.

GERMANY[1]

ARRIVALS OF FOREIGN TOURISTS AT HOTELS[2]

(by country of residence)

	1991	Relative share	1992	Relative share	% Variation over 1991
Austria	549 730	4.2	532 616	4.2	−3.1
Belgium	483 699	3.7	485 936	3.8	0.5
Denmark	573 979	4.4	506 337	4.0	−11.8
Finland	164 201	1.3	134 543	1.1	−18.1
France	729 664	5.6	690 102	5.4	−5.4
Germany	..	..	..	..	..
Greece	104 304	0.8	98 603	0.8	−5.5
Iceland	18 765	0.1	17 405	0.1	−7.2
Ireland	33 961	0.3	31 423	0.2	−7.5
Italy	898 795	6.9	840 586	6.6	−6.5
Luxembourg	67 002	0.5	68 935	0.5	2.9
Netherlands	1 551 966	11.9	1 444 564	11.4	−6.9
Norway	256 382	2.0	237 308	1.9	−7.4
Portugal	49 971	0.4	45 231	0.4	−9.5
Spain	302 256	2.3	260 905	2.1	−13.7
Sweden	962 108	7.4	839 579	6.6	−12.7
Switzerland	709 493	5.4	688 501	5.4	−3.0
Turkey	93 685	0.7	88 148	0.7	−5.9
United Kingdom	1 221 558	9.4	1 213 410	9.6	−0.7
Other OECD-Europe	..	..	..	..	..
Total Europe	8 771 519	67.2	8 224 132	64.8	−6.2
Canada	141 292	1.1	140 589	1.1	−0.5
United States	1 538 400	11.8	1 607 951	12.7	4.5
Total North America	1 679 692	12.9	1 748 540	13.8	4.1
Australia	80 413	0.6	88 387	0.7	9.9
New Zealand	10 734	0.1	10 715	0.1	−0.2
Japan	639 365	4.9	696 937	5.5	9.0
Total Australasia and Japan	730 512	5.6	796 039	6.3	9.0
Total OECD Countries	**11 181 723**	**85.7**	**10 768 711**	**84.9**	**−3.7**
Ex-Yugoslavia	192 530	1.5	159 339	1.3	−17.2
Other European countries	555 838	4.3	581 991	4.6	4.7
Bulgaria	20 543	0.2	21 123	0.2	2.8
Ex-Czechoslovakia	117 387	0.9	138 405	1.1	17.9
Hungary	109 471	0.8	111 008	0.9	1.4
Poland	169 281	1.3	171 825	1.4	1.5
Rumania	27 201	0.2	28 139	0.2	3.4
Ex-USSR	111 955	0.9	111 491	0.9	−0.4
Latin America	130 692	1.0	130 048	1.0	−0.5
Argentina	26 591	0.2	27 651	0.2	4.0
Brazil	65 732	0.5	61 226	0.5	−6.9
Chile	8 368	0.1	9 332	0.1	11.5
Mexico	30 001	0.2	31 839	0.3	6.1
Asia-Oceania	107 018	0.8	99 889	0.8	−6.7
Israel	107 018	0.8	99 889	0.8	−6.7
Africa	38 737	0.3	38 870	0.3	0.3
South Africa	38 737	0.3	38 870	0.3	0.3
Origin country undetermined	838 083	6.4	910 146	7.2	8.6
Total non-OECD Countries	**1 862 898**	**14.3**	**1 920 283**	**15.1**	**3.1**
TOTAL	**13 044 621**	**100.0**	**12 688 994**	**100.0**	**−2.7**

1. The data relate to the territory of the Federal Republic of Germany prior to 3rd October 1990; as of 1990, tourists from the former German Democratic Republic will be regarded as domestic tourists.
2. Arrivals at hotels (including ''bed and breakfast''), boarding houses and inns.

GERMANY[1]

ARRIVALS OF FOREIGN TOURISTS AT REGISTERED TOURIST ACCOMMODATION[2]

(by country of residence)

	1991	Relative share	1992	Relative share	% Variation over 1991
Austria	596 363	3.8	580 828	3.8	−2.6
Belgium	568 096	3.6	576 834	3.8	1.5
Denmark	801 547	5.1	689 579	4.6	−14.0
Finland	219 847	1.4	184 641	1.2	−16.0
France	879 490	5.6	829 439	5.5	−5.7
Germany	..	..	..	..	..
Greece	108 908	0.7	103 067	0.7	−5.4
Iceland	21 981	0.1	20 010	0.1	−9.0
Ireland	49 114	0.3	48 031	0.3	−2.2
Italy	991 471	6.3	926 256	6.1	−6.6
Luxembourg	77 519	0.5	77 870	0.5	0.5
Netherlands	2 465 832	15.8	2 345 133	15.5	−4.9
Norway	293 583	1.9	272 651	1.8	−7.1
Portugal	56 712	0.4	50 521	0.3	−10.9
Spain	351 388	2.2	300 057	2.0	−14.6
Sweden	1 122 488	7.2	970 821	6.4	−13.5
Switzerland	772 768	4.9	751 300	5.0	−2.8
Turkey	100 806	0.6	94 029	0.6	−6.7
United Kingdom	1 416 252	9.1	1 388 045	9.2	−2.0
Other OECD-Europe	..	..	..	..	..
Total Europe	10 894 165	69.6	10 209 112	67.4	−6.3
Canada	167 619	1.1	166 685	1.1	−0.6
United States	1 635 523	10.5	1 709 312	11.3	4.5
Total North America	1 803 142	11.5	1 875 997	12.4	4.0
Australia	131 795	0.8	136 001	0.9	3.2
New Zealand	27 875	0.2	25 999	0.2	−6.7
Japan	666 317	4.3	728 195	4.8	9.3
Total Australasia and Japan	825 987	5.3	890 195	5.9	7.8
Total OECD Countries	**13 523 294**	**86.4**	**12 975 304**	**85.7**	**−4.1**
Ex-Yugoslavia	204 275	1.3	169 105	1.1	−17.2
Other European countries	700 501	4.5	715 795	4.7	2.2
Bulgaria	22 743	0.1	23 350	0.2	2.7
Ex-Czechoslovakia	148 607	0.9	168 298	1.1	13.3
Hungary	130 424	0.8	133 605	0.9	2.4
Poland	240 502	1.5	228 778	1.5	−4.9
Rumania	30 188	0.2	30 989	0.2	2.7
Ex-USSR	128 037	0.8	130 775	0.9	2.1
Latin America	150 061	1.0	149 900	1.0	−0.1
Argentina	31 143	0.2	33 157	0.2	6.5
Brazil	75 424	0.5	69 373	0.5	−8.0
Chile	10 259	0.1	12 176	0.1	18.7
Mexico	33 235	0.2	35 194	0.2	5.9
Asia-Oceania	115 065	0.7	106 813	0.7	−7.2
Israel	115 065	0.7	106 813	0.7	−7.2
Africa	46 873	0.3	46 814	0.3	−0.1
South Africa	46 873	0.3	46 814	0.3	−0.1
Origin country undetermined	906 918	5.8	983 344	6.5	8.4
Total non-OECD Countries	**2 123 693**	**13.6**	**2 171 771**	**14.3**	**2.3**
TOTAL	**15 646 987**	**100.0**	**15 147 075**	**100.0**	**−3.2**

1. The data relate to the territory of the Federal Republic of Germany prior to 3rd October 1990; as of 1990, tourists from the former German Democratic Republic will be regarded as domestic tourists. Since 1992, includes camping sites.
2. Arrivals at hotels and similar establishments, holiday villages, sanatoria and recreation and holiday homes.

GERMANY [1]

NIGHTS SPENT BY FOREIGN TOURISTS IN HOTELS [2]

(by country of residence)

	1991	Relative share	1992	Relative share	% Variation over 1991
Austria	1 113 448	4.0	1 097 345	4.1	−1.4
Belgium	1 154 343	4.2	1 137 104	4.2	−1.5
Denmark	1 084 394	3.9	956 477	3.6	−11.8
Finland	295 353	1.1	247 492	0.9	−16.2
France	1 403 608	5.1	1 322 317	4.9	−5.8
Germany	..	..	..	..	..
Greece	267 403	1.0	251 491	0.9	−6.0
Iceland	41 895	0.2	39 609	0.1	−5.5
Ireland	89 891	0.3	77 769	0.3	−13.5
Italy	1 735 885	6.3	1 637 150	6.1	−5.7
Luxembourg	190 830	0.7	195 297	0.7	2.3
Netherlands	3 494 580	12.6	3 178 529	11.8	−9.0
Norway	413 516	1.5	399 041	1.5	−3.5
Portugal	129 679	0.5	117 270	0.4	−9.6
Spain	603 097	2.2	555 494	2.1	−7.9
Sweden	1 515 960	5.5	1 337 408	5.0	−11.8
Switzerland	1 458 229	5.3	1 397 358	5.2	−4.2
Turkey	239 400	0.9	223 636	0.8	−6.6
United Kingdom	2 712 231	9.8	2 661 220	9.9	−1.9
Other OECD-Europe	..	..	..	..	..
Total Europe	17 943 742	64.6	16 832 007	62.6	−6.2
Canada	297 992	1.1	289 426	1.1	−2.9
United States	3 179 799	11.5	3 275 901	12.2	3.0
Total North America	3 477 791	12.5	3 565 327	13.3	2.5
Australia	164 855	0.6	177 974	0.7	8.0
New Zealand	26 218	0.1	23 964	0.1	−8.6
Japan	1 111 909	4.0	1 162 290	4.3	4.5
Total Australasia and Japan	1 302 982	4.7	1 364 228	5.1	4.7
Total OECD Countries	**22 724 515**	**81.8**	**21 761 562**	**80.9**	**−4.2**
Ex-Yugoslavia	504 533	1.8	515 182	1.9	2.1
Other European countries	1 724 788	6.2	1 831 583	6.8	6.2
Bulgaria	63 357	0.2	61 849	0.2	−2.4
Ex-Czechoslovakia	309 456	1.1	398 290	1.5	28.7
Hungary	301 623	1.1	313 030	1.2	3.8
Poland	558 425	2.0	583 601	2.2	4.5
Rumania	94 009	0.3	91 425	0.3	−2.7
Ex-USSR	397 918	1.4	383 388	1.4	−3.7
Latin America	311 408	1.1	308 739	1.1	−0.9
Argentina	65 703	0.2	66 207	0.2	0.8
Brazil	154 819	0.6	145 084	0.5	−6.3
Chile	22 275	0.1	23 059	0.1	3.5
Mexico	68 611	0.2	74 389	0.3	8.4
Asia-Oceania	306 968	1.1	275 527	1.0	−10.2
Israel	306 968	1.1	275 527	1.0	−10.2
Africa	103 223	0.4	93 603	0.3	−9.3
South Africa	103 223	0.4	93 603	0.3	−9.3
Origin country undetermined	2 092 797	7.5	2 112 367	7.9	0.9
Total non-OECD Countries	**5 043 717**	**18.2**	**5 137 001**	**19.1**	**1.8**
TOTAL	**27 768 232**	**100.0**	**26 898 563**	**100.0**	**−3.1**

1. The data relate to the territory of the Federal Republic of Germany prior to 3rd October 1990; as of 1990, tourists from the former German Democratic Republic will be regarded as domestic tourists.
2. Nights spent in hotels (including "bed and breakfast"), boarding houses and inns.

GERMANY [1]

NIGHTS SPENT BY FOREIGN TOURISTS IN REGISTERED TOURIST ACCOMMODATION [2]

(by country of residence)

	1991	Relative share	1992	Relative share	% Variation over 1991
Austria	1 244 726	3.3	1 237 722	3.4	−0.6
Belgium	1 502 023	4.0	1 521 246	4.2	1.3
Denmark	1 756 470	4.7	1 490 483	4.1	−15.1
Finland	389 293	1.0	333 537	0.9	−14.3
France	1 820 526	4.9	1 714 516	4.8	−5.8
Germany	..	..	..	..	..
Greece	284 396	0.8	270 259	0.7	−5.0
Iceland	53 486	0.1	48 809	0.1	−8.7
Ireland	144 474	0.4	127 323	0.4	−11.9
Italy	1 942 748	5.2	1 827 793	5.1	−5.9
Luxembourg	251 285	0.7	248 837	0.7	−1.0
Netherlands	8 333 968	22.3	7 831 158	21.7	−6.0
Norway	491 555	1.3	470 072	1.3	−4.4
Portugal	154 159	0.4	142 211	0.4	−7.8
Spain	722 751	1.9	659 946	1.8	−8.7
Sweden	1 860 721	5.0	1 612 905	4.5	−13.3
Switzerland	1 670 133	4.5	1 602 672	4.4	−4.0
Turkey	266 167	0.7	243 980	0.7	−8.3
United Kingdom	3 301 940	8.8	3 205 018	8.9	−2.9
Other OECD-Europe	..	..	..	..	..
Total Europe	26 190 821	70.0	24 588 487	68.1	−6.1
Canada	348 627	0.9	339 536	0.9	−2.6
United States	3 414 348	9.1	3 523 534	9.8	3.2
Total North America	3 762 975	10.1	3 863 070	10.7	2.7
Australia	249 655	0.7	254 405	0.7	1.9
New Zealand	56 974	0.2	49 134	0.1	−13.8
Japan	1 159 387	3.1	1 217 620	3.4	5.0
Total Australasia and Japan	1 466 016	3.9	1 521 159	4.2	3.8
Total OECD Countries	**31 419 812**	**84.0**	**29 972 716**	**83.1**	**−4.6**
Ex-Yugoslavia	547 730	1.5	559 085	1.5	2.1
Other European countries	2 330 025	6.2	2 440 765	6.8	4.8
Bulgaria	70 881	0.2	72 530	0.2	2.3
Ex-Czechoslovakia	376 135	1.0	468 981	1.3	24.7
Hungary	359 534	1.0	375 250	1.0	4.4
Poland	916 611	2.4	928 860	2.6	1.3
Rumania	106 110	0.3	103 316	0.3	−2.6
Ex-USSR	500 754	1.3	491 828	1.4	−1.8
Latin America	353 573	0.9	352 963	1.0	−0.2
Argentina	75 514	0.2	77 424	0.2	2.5
Brazil	173 056	0.5	162 994	0.5	−5.8
Chile	27 128	0.1	30 495	0.1	12.4
Mexico	75 875	0.2	82 050	0.2	8.1
Asia-Oceania	337 759	0.9	306 109	0.8	−9.4
Israel	337 759	0.9	306 109	0.8	−9.4
Africa	120 405	0.3	111 359	0.3	−7.5
South Africa	120 405	0.3	111 359	0.3	−7.5
Origin country undetermined	2 317 097	6.2	2 343 538	6.5	1.1
Total non-OECD Countries	**6 006 589**	**16.0**	**6 113 819**	**16.9**	**1.8**
TOTAL	**37 426 401**	**100.0**	**36 086 535**	**100.0**	**−3.6**

1. The data relate to the territory of the Federal Republic of Germany prior to 3rd October 1990; as of 1990, tourists from the former German Democratic Republic will be regarded as domestic tourists. Since 1992, includes camping sites.
2. Nights spent in hotels and similar establishments, holiday villages, sanatoria, and recreation and holiday homes.

GREECE

ARRIVALS OF FOREIGN TOURISTS AT FRONTIERS[1]

(by country of nationality)

	1991	Relative share	1992	Relative share	% Variation over 1991
Austria	288 317	3.6	345 259	3.7	19.7
Belgium[2]	179 754	2.2	225 099	2.4	25.2
Denmark	211 883	2.6	281 235	3.0	32.7
Finland	216 131	2.7	172 099	1.8	−20.4
France	470 945	5.9	542 222	5.8	15.1
Germany	1 561 113	19.4	1 944 704	20.8	24.6
Greece	..	..	..	..	..
Iceland[3]	..	..	..	..	..
Ireland	44 085	0.5	57 885	0.6	31.3
Italy	517 145	6.4	622 619	6.7	20.4
Luxembourg[2]	..	..	..	..	..
Netherlands	450 065	5.6	546 187	5.9	21.4
Norway	68 396	0.9	95 898	1.0	40.2
Portugal	16 586	0.2	26 245	0.3	58.2
Spain	104 655	1.3	119 964	1.3	14.6
Sweden	261 946	3.3	314 251	3.4	20.0
Switzerland	126 241	1.6	163 126	1.7	29.2
Turkey	53 531	0.7	73 650	0.8	37.6
United Kingdom	1 674 875	20.8	2 154 850	23.1	28.7
Other OECD-Europe	..	..	..	..	..
Total Europe	6 245 668	77.7	7 685 293	82.4	23.0
Canada	47 101	0.6	59 807	0.6	27.0
United States	180 429	2.2	278 941	3.0	54.6
Total North America	227 530	2.8	338 748	3.6	48.9
Australia	66 566	0.8	69 658	0.7	4.6
New Zealand[4]	8 489	0.1	8 035	0.1	−5.3
Japan	57 902	0.7	109 680	1.2	89.4
Total Australasia and Japan	132 957	1.7	187 373	2.0	40.9
Total OECD Countries	**6 606 155**	**82.2**	**8 211 414**	**88.0**	**24.3**
Ex-Yugoslavia	518 644	6.5	93 413	1.0	−82.0
Other European countries[3]	703 672	8.8	..	..	..
Bulgaria	157 910	2.0	140 725	1.5	−10.9
Ex-Czechoslovakia	130 129	1.6	191 585	2.1	47.2
Hungary	107 685	1.3	107 403	1.2	−0.3
Poland	47 535	0.6	43 788	0.5	−7.9
Rumania	17 919	0.2	19 683	0.2	9.8
Ex-USSR	78 194	1.0	100 058	1.1	28.0
Argentina	5 092	0.1	8 655	0.1	70.0
Brazil	8 523	0.1	8 999	0.1	5.6
Mexico	3 642	0.0	6 535	0.1	79.4
Asia-Oceania[4]	106 852	1.3	..	..	..
Iran	4 226	0.1	6 794	0.1	60.8
Israel	36 989	0.5	35 065	0.4	−5.2
Lebanon	15 637	0.2	15 922	0.2	1.8
Africa	83 547	1.0	..	..	..
Egypt	20 020	0.2	19 525	0.2	−2.5
South Africa	13 527	0.2	16 944	0.2	25.3
Origin country undetermined	17 257	0.2	1 026 533	11.0	5848.5
Total non-OECD Countries	**1 429 972**	**17.8**	**1 119 946**	**12.0**	**−21.7**
TOTAL	**8 036 127**	**100.0**	**9 331 360**	**100.0**	**16.1**

1. Excluding Greek nationals residing abroad and cruise passengers.
2. Belgium includes Luxembourg.
3. "Other European countries" includes Iceland.
4. "Asia-Oceania" includes New Zealand.

ICELAND

ARRIVALS OF FOREIGN TOURISTS AT FRONTIERS[1]

(by country of nationality)

	1991	Relative share	1992	Relative share	% Variation over 1991
Austria	4 036	2.8	3 123	2.2	−22.6
Belgium	1 060	0.7	1 223	0.9	15.4
Denmark	13 777	9.6	14 396	10.1	4.5
Finland	4 079	2.8	4 866	3.4	19.3
France	10 071	7.0	7 925	5.6	−21.3
Germany	22 477	15.7	24 520	17.2	9.1
Greece	183	0.1	181	0.1	−1.1
Iceland	..	..	..	..	..
Ireland	491	0.3	542	0.4	10.4
Italy	4 808	3.4	4 158	2.9	−13.5
Luxembourg	508	0.4	332	0.2	−34.6
Netherlands	2 952	2.1	3 808	2.7	29.0
Norway	10 391	7.2	11 218	7.9	8.0
Portugal	248	0.2	361	0.3	45.6
Spain	1 173	0.8	1 154	0.8	−1.6
Sweden	16 295	11.4	16 050	11.3	−1.5
Switzerland	7 003	4.9	5 852	4.1	−16.4
Turkey	82	0.1	55	0.0	−32.9
United Kingdom	14 662	10.2	13 900	9.8	−5.2
Other OECD-Europe	..	..	..	..	..
Total Europe	114 296	79.7	113 664	79.7	−0.6
Canada	943	0.7	1 153	0.8	22.3
United States	22 506	15.7	21 706	15.2	−3.6
Total North America	23 449	16.3	22 859	16.0	−2.5
Australia	465	0.3	436	0.3	−6.2
New Zealand	144	0.1	178	0.1	23.6
Japan	1 254	0.9	1 431	1.0	14.1
Total Australasia and Japan	1 863	1.3	2 045	1.4	9.8
Total OECD Countries	**139 608**	**97.3**	**138 568**	**97.2**	**−0.7**
Ex-Yugoslavia	339	0.2	221	0.2	−34.8
Other European countries	39	0.0	72	0.1	84.6
Bulgaria	31	0.0	35	0.0	12.9
Ex-Czechoslovakia	253	0.2	220	0.2	−13.0
Hungary	136	0.1	157	0.1	15.4
Poland	645	0.4	396	0.3	−38.6
Rumania	16	0.0	11	0.0	−31.3
Ex-USSR	420	0.3	583	0.4	38.8
Latin America	131	0.1	147	0.1	12.2
Argentina	45	0.0	38	0.0	−15.6
Brazil	89	0.1	68	0.0	−23.6
Chile	46	0.0	34	0.0	−26.1
Colombia	28	0.0	14	0.0	−50.0
Mexico	94	0.1	140	0.1	48.9
Venezuela	17	0.0	16	0.0	−5.9
Asia-Oceania	108	0.1	146	0.1	35.2
China	127	0.1	129	0.1	1.6
Hong Kong	14	0.0	8	0.0	−42.9
India	83	0.1	85	0.1	2.4
Iran	17	0.0	21	0.0	23.5
Israel	167	0.1	249	0.2	49.1
Republic of Korea	75	0.1	71	0.0	−5.3
Lebanon	19	0.0	18	0.0	−5.3
Malaysia	27	0.0	23	0.0	−14.8
Pakistan	12	0.0	11	0.0	−8.3
Philippines	123	0.1	120	0.1	−2.4
Saudi Arabia	5	0.0	8	0.0	60.0
Singapore	26	0.0	23	0.0	−11.5
Taiwan	184	0.1	453	0.3	146.2
Thailand	143	0.1	138	0.1	−3.5
Africa	125	0.1	151	0.1	20.8
Algeria	26	0.0	8	0.0	−69.2
Egypt	25	0.0	31	0.0	24.0
Morocco	12	0.0	19	0.0	58.3
South Africa	174	0.1	115	0.1	−33.9
Origin country undetermined	3 108	2.2	3 254	2.3	4.7
Total non-OECD Countries	**3 850**	**2.7**	**3 991**	**2.8**	**3.7**
TOTAL	**143 458**	**100.0**	**142 559**	**100.0**	**−0.6**

1. Excluding shore excursionists.

IRELAND

ARRIVALS OF FOREIGN VISITORS AT FRONTIERS[1]

(by country of residence)

	1991	Relative share	1992	Relative share	% Variation over 1991
Austria[4]	..	..	..	..	..
Belgium[4]	..	..	..	..	..
Denmark[4]	..	..	..	..	..
Finland[4]	..	..	..	..	..
France	219 000	7.3	217 000	6.9	–0.9
Germany	194 000	6.5	221 000	7.1	13.9
Greece[4]	..	..	..	..	..
Iceland[4]	..	..	..	..	..
Ireland	..	..	..	..	..
Italy[4]	..	..	..	..	..
Luxembourg[4]	..	..	..	..	..
Netherlands[4]	..	..	..	..	..
Norway[4]	..	..	..	..	..
Portugal[4]	..	..	..	..	..
Spain[4]	..	..	..	..	..
Sweden[4]	..	..	..	..	..
Switzerland[4]	..	..	..	..	..
Turkey[4]	..	..	..	..	..
United Kingdom	1 729 000	57.7	1 758 000	56.3	1.7
Other OECD-Europe[4]	411 000	13.7	417 000	13.3	1.5
Total Europe	2 553 000	85.2	2 613 000	83.6	2.4
Canada	30 000	1.0	39 000	1.2	30.0
United States	313 000	10.4	366 000	11.7	16.9
Total North America	343 000	11.4	405 000	13.0	18.1
Australia[2]	50 000	1.7	53 000	1.7	6.0
New Zealand[2]	..	..	..	..	..
Japan[3]	..	..	..	..	..
Total Australasia and Japan	50 000	1.7	53 000	1.7	6.0
Total OECD Countries	**2 946 000**	**98.3**	**3 071 000**	**98.3**	**4.2**
Ex-Yugoslavia	..	..	..	..	..
Origin country unspecified[3]	52 000	1.7	53 000	1.7	1.9
Total non-OECD Countries	**52 000**	**1.7**	**53 000**	**1.7**	**1.9**
TOTAL	**2 998 000**	**100.0**	**3 124 000**	**100.0**	**4.2**

1. Visitors arrivals on overseas routes only.
2. Australia includes New Zealand.
3. Origin country unspecified includes Japan.
4. Included in Other OECD-Europe.

IRELAND

ARRIVALS OF FOREIGN TOURISTS AT HOTELS

(by country of residence)

	1991	Relative share	1992	Relative share	% Variation over 1991
Austria	..	..	..	..	..
Belgium [2]	18 000	1.1	26 000	1.4	44.4
Denmark	..	..	..	..	..
Finland	..	..	..	..	..
France	138 000	8.1	139 000	7.7	0.7
Germany	110 000	6.4	125 000	7.0	13.6
Greece	..	..	..	..	..
Iceland	..	..	..	..	..
Ireland	..	..	..	..	..
Italy	79 000	4.6	80 000	4.4	1.3
Luxembourg [2]					
Netherlands	50 000	2.9	45 000	2.5	−10.0
Norway	..	..	..	..	..
Portugal	..	..	..	..	..
Spain	..	..	..	..	..
Sweden	..	..	..	..	..
Switzerland	29 000	1.7	38 000	2.1	31.0
Turkey					
United Kingdom [1]	795 000	46.4	789 000	43.9	−0.8
Other OECD-Europe	98 000	5.7	100 000	5.6	2.0
Total Europe	1 317 000	76.9	1 342 000	74.6	1.9
Canada	29 000	1.7	28 000	1.6	−3.4
United States	288 000	16.8	341 000	19.0	18.4
Total North America	317 000	18.5	369 000	20.5	16.4
Australia [3]	41 000	2.4	35 000	1.9	−14.6
New Zealand [3]	..	..	..	..	..
Japan	..	..	..	..	..
Total Australasia and Japan	41 000	2.4	35 000	1.9	−14.6
Total OECD Countries	**1 675 000**	**97.8**	**1 746 000**	**97.1**	**4.2**
Ex-Yugoslavia	..	..	..	..	..
Origin country undetermined	38 000	2.2	52 000	2.9	36.8
Total non-OECD Countries	**38 000**	**2.2**	**52 000**	**2.9**	**36.8**
TOTAL	**1 713 000**	**100.0**	**1 798 000**	**100.0**	**5.0**

1. Excludes Northern Ireland.
2. Belgium includes Luxembourg.
3. Australia includes New Zealand.

IRELAND

ARRIVALS OF FOREIGN TOURISTS IN TOURIST ACCOMMODATION

(by country of residence)

	1991	Relative share	1992	Relative share	% Variation over 1991
Austria	..	..	..	..	..
Belgium[3]	33 000	1.1	40 000	1.3	21.2
Denmark	19 000	0.6	18 000	0.6	−5.3
Finland	..	..	..	..	..
France	220 000	7.3	220 000	7.1	0.0
Germany	203 000	6.7	23 000	0.7	−88.7
Greece	..	..	..	..	..
Iceland	..	..	..	..	..
Ireland	..	..	..	..	..
Italy	96 000	3.2	101 000	3.2	5.2
Luxembourg[3]	..	..	..	..	..
Netherlands	83 000	2.8	73 000	2.3	−12.0
Norway[4]	27 000	0.9	26 000	0.8	−3.7
Portugal	..	..	..	..	..
Spain	62 000	2.1	56 000	1.8	−9.7
Sweden[4]	..	..	..	..	..
Switzerland	46 000	1.5	52 000	1.7	13.0
Turkey	..	..	..	..	..
United Kingdom[1]	1 710 000	56.7	1 707 000	54.8	−0.2
Other OECD-Europe	..	..	..	..	..
Total Europe	2 499 000	82.9	2 316 000	74.3	−7.3
Canada	35 000	1.2	43 000	1.4	22.9
United States	321 000	10.6	374 000	12.0	16.5
Total North America	356 000	11.8	417 000	13.4	17.1
Australia[2]	..	..	..	..	..
New Zealand[2]	54 000	1.8	57 000	1.8	5.6
Japan	..	..	14 000	0.4	..
Total Australasia and Japan	54 000	1.8	71 000	2.3	31.5
Total OECD Countries	**2 909 000**	**96.5**	**2 804 000**	**90.0**	**−3.6**
Ex-Yugoslavia	..	..	..	..	..
Origin country undetermined	106 000	3.5	312 000	10.0	194.3
Total non-OECD Countries	**106 000**	**3.5**	**312 000**	**10.0**	**194.3**
TOTAL	**3 015 000**	**100.0**	**3 116 000**	**100.0**	**3.3**

1. Excludes Northern Ireland.
2. New Zealand includes Australia.
3. Belgium includes Luxembourg.
4. Norway includes Sweden.

IRELAND

NIGHTS SPENT BY FOREIGN TOURISTS IN HOTELS

(by country of residence)

	1991	Relative share	1992	Relative share	% Variation over 1991
Austria	..	..	..	..	..
Belgium [2]	85 000	0.9	176 000	1.9	107.1
Denmark	..	..	..	..	..
Finland	..	..	..	..	..
France	892 000	9.5	890 000	9.5	−0.2
Germany	817 000	8.7	808 000	8.7	−1.1
Greece	..	..	..	..	..
Iceland	..	..	..	..	..
Ireland	..	..	..	..	..
Italy	571 000	6.1	509 000	5.5	−10.9
Luxembourg [2]	..	..	..	..	..
Netherlands	302 000	3.2	273 000	2.9	−9.6
Norway	..	..	..	..	..
Portugal	..	..	..	..	..
Spain	..	..	..	..	..
Sweden	..	..	..	..	..
Switzerland	189 000	2.0	312 000	3.3	65.1
Turkey	..	..	..	..	..
United Kingdom [1]	3 562 000	37.8	3 316 000	35.5	−6.9
Other OECD-Europe	..	..	..	..	..
Total Europe	6 418 000	68.1	6 284 000	67.3	−2.1
Canada	164 000	1.7	209 000	2.2	27.4
United States	1 793 000	19.0	1 890 000	20.3	5.4
Total North America	1 957 000	20.8	2 099 000	22.5	7.3
Australia [3]	253 000	2.7	167 000	1.8	−34.0
New Zealand [3]	..	..	..	..	..
Japan	..	..	..	..	..
Total Australasia and Japan	253 000	2.7	167 000	1.8	−34.0
Total OECD Countries	**8 628 000**	**91.6**	**8 550 000**	**91.6**	**−0.9**
Ex-Yugoslavia	..	..	..	..	..
Origin country undetermined	795 000	8.4	783 000	8.4	−1.5
Total non-OECD Countries	**795 000**	**8.4**	**783 000**	**8.4**	**−1.5**
TOTAL	**9 423 000**	**100.0**	**9 333 000**	**100.0**	**−1.0**

1. Excludes Northern Ireland.
2. Belgium includes Luxembourg.
3. Australia includes New Zealand.

IRELAND

NIGHTS SPENT BY FOREIGN TOURISTS IN TOURIST ACCOMMODATION

(by country of residence)

	1991	Relative share	1992	Relative share	% Variation over 1991
Austria	..	..	..	..	..
Belgium [3]	336 000	1.0	472 000	1.4	40.5
Denmark	177 000	0.5	..	..	..
Finland	..	..	..	..	..
France	3 029 000	9.1	3 324 000	9.8	9.7
Germany	3 218 000	9.7	3 420 000	10.1	6.3
Greece	..	..	..	..	..
Iceland	..	..	..	..	..
Ireland	..	..	..	..	..
Italy	1 310 000	3.9	1 340 000	4.0	2.3
Luxembourg [3]	..	..	..	..	..
Netherlands	984 000	3.0	827 000	2.4	−16.0
Norway [4]	227 000	0.7	..	..	..
Portugal	..	..	..	..	..
Spain	..	..	..	..	..
Sweden [4]	..	..	..	..	..
Switzerland	629 000	1.9	689 000	2.0	9.5
Turkey	..	..	..	..	..
United Kingdom [1]	14 723 000	44.2	14 373 000	42.6	−2.4
Other OECD-Europe	..	..	..	..	..
Total Europe	24 633 000	74.0	24 445 000	72.4	−0.8
Canada	437 000	1.3	569 000	1.7	30.2
United States	3 874 000	11.6	4 256 000	12.6	9.9
Total North America	4 311 000	13.0	4 825 000	14.3	11.9
Australia [2]	..	..	..	..	..
New Zealand [2]	873 000	2.6	566 000	1.7	−35.2
Japan	..	..	..	..	..
Total Australasia and Japan	873 000	2.6	566 000	1.7	−35.2
Total OECD Countries	**29 817 000**	**89.6**	**29 836 000**	**88.3**	**0.1**
Ex-Yugoslavia	..	..	..	..	..
Origin country undetermined	3 469 000	10.4	3 941 000	11.7	13.6
Total non-OECD Countries	**3 469 000**	**10.4**	**3 941 000**	**11.7**	**13.6**
TOTAL	**33 286 000**	**100.0**	**33 777 000**	**100.0**	**1.5**

1. Excludes Northern Ireland.
2. New Zealand includes Australia.
3. Belgium includes Luxembourg.
4. Norway includes Sweden.

ITALY

ARRIVALS OF FOREIGN VISITORS AT FRONTIERS[1]

(by country of nationality)

	1991	Relative share	1992	Relative share	% Variation over 1991
Austria	5 540 654	10.8	5 325 611	10.6	−3.9
Belgium	953 229	1.9	781 892	1.6	−18.0
Denmark	421 444	0.8	371 260	0.7	−11.9
Finland	220 537	0.4	210 170	0.4	−4.7
France	9 114 554	17.8	8 798 740	17.6	−3.5
Germany	9 205 658	17.9	8 782 614	17.5	−4.6
Greece	521 864	1.0	509 582	1.0	−2.4
Iceland [2]	..	..	..	..	..
Ireland	136 410	0.3	143 520	0.3	5.2
Italy	..	..	..	..	..
Luxembourg	135 443	0.3	184 889	0.4	36.5
Netherlands	1 533 360	3.0	1 205 676	2.4	−21.4
Norway	215 136	0.4	218 539	0.4	1.6
Portugal	179 060	0.3	201 986	0.4	12.8
Spain	601 966	1.2	606 680	1.2	0.8
Sweden	469 974	0.9	417 465	0.8	−11.2
Switzerland	10 228 678	19.9	10 083 072	20.1	−1.4
Turkey	169 639	0.3	198 678	0.4	17.1
United Kingdom	1 711 634	3.3	1 612 803	3.2	−5.8
Other OECD-Europe	..	..	..	..	..
Total Europe	41 359 240	80.6	39 653 177	79.2	−4.1
Canada	350 056	0.7	357 692	0.7	2.2
United States	1 137 441	2.2	1 294 423	2.6	13.8
Total North America	1 487 497	2.9	1 652 115	3.3	11.1
Australia	199 877	0.4	215 637	0.4	7.9
New Zealand	..	..	..	..	..
Japan	559 665	1.1	741 984	1.5	32.6
Total Australasia and Japan	759 542	1.5	957 621	1.9	26.1
Total OECD Countries	**43 606 279**	**85.0**	**42 262 913**	**84.4**	**−3.1**
Ex-Yugoslavia	4 367 181	8.5	4 100 526	8.2	−6.1
Other European countries [2]	1 962 826	3.8	2 189 838	4.4	11.6
Ex-USSR	73 675	0.1	91 709	0.2	24.5
Latin America	578 389	1.1	670 819	1.3	16.0
Argentina	137 193	0.3	144 412	0.3	5.3
Brazil	144 218	0.3	147 613	0.3	2.4
Mexico	74 152	0.1	127 397	0.3	71.8
Venezuela	79 102	0.2	99 861	0.2	26.2
Asia-Oceania	150 558	0.3	178 877	0.4	18.8
Israel	69 956	0.1	74 495	0.1	6.5
Africa	90 599	0.2	121 895	0.2	34.5
Egypt	43 333	0.1	60 816	0.1	40.3
South Africa	47 266	0.1	61 079	0.1	29.2
Origin country undetermined	561 359	1.1	563 842	1.1	0.4
Total non-OECD Countries	**7 710 912**	**15.0**	**7 825 797**	**15.6**	**1.5**
TOTAL	**51 317 191**	**100.0**	**50 088 710**	**100.0**	**−2.4**

1. Includes about 53% of excursionists.
2. "Other European countries" includes Iceland.

ITALY

ARRIVALS OF FOREIGN TOURISTS AT HOTELS

(by country of nationality)

	1991	Relative share	1992	Relative share	% Variation over 1991
Austria	896 715	5.3	822 974	4.7	−8.2
Belgium	411 596	2.4	410 883	2.4	−0.2
Denmark	123 123	0.7	113 115	0.7	−8.1
Finland	89 030	0.5	64 860	0.4	−27.1
France	1 713 251	10.0	1 585 031	9.1	−7.5
Germany	5 115 542	30.0	4 780 006	27.5	−6.6
Greece	195 980	1.1	193 263	1.1	−1.4
Iceland [1]	..	..	..	..	..
Ireland	52 673	0.3	58 404	0.3	10.9
Italy	..	..	..	..	..
Luxembourg	27 693	0.2	25 215	0.1	−8.9
Netherlands	344 431	2.0	322 190	1.9	−6.5
Norway	62 619	0.4	63 130	0.4	0.8
Portugal	90 276	0.5	94 024	0.5	4.2
Spain	789 833	4.6	800 370	4.6	1.3
Sweden	214 430	1.3	200 073	1.2	−6.7
Switzerland	933 671	5.5	875 383	5.0	−6.2
Turkey	69 148	0.4	60 451	0.3	−12.6
United Kingdom	1 098 423	6.4	1 151 684	6.6	4.8
Other OECD-Europe	..	..	..	..	..
Total Europe	12 228 434	71.7	11 621 056	66.9	−5.0
Canada	189 091	1.1	206 297	1.2	9.1
United States	1 419 656	8.3	1 846 323	10.6	30.1
Total North America	1 608 747	9.4	2 052 620	11.8	27.6
Australia	208 450	1.2	233 194	1.3	11.9
New Zealand	..	..	..	..	..
Japan	657 574	3.9	905 784	5.2	37.7
Total Australasia and Japan	866 024	5.1	1 138 978	6.6	31.5
Total OECD Countries	**14 703 205**	**86.2**	**14 812 654**	**85.3**	**0.7**
Ex-Yugoslavia	218 405	1.3	185 302	1.1	−15.2
Other European countries [1]	582 945	3.4	635 759	3.7	9.1
Ex-USSR	93 554	0.5	185 302	1.1	98.1
Latin America	535 582	3.1	603 536	3.5	12.7
Argentina	120 753	0.7	157 491	0.9	30.4
Brazil	198 794	1.2	180 256	1.0	−9.3
Mexico	74 168	0.4	101 245	0.6	36.5
Venezuela	30 506	0.2	35 044	0.2	14.9
Asia-Oceania	201 687	1.2	196 471	1.1	−2.6
Israel	127 854	0.7	121 322	0.7	−5.1
Africa	54 945	0.3	52 361	0.3	−4.7
Egypt	19 809	0.1	18 394	0.1	−7.1
South Africa	35 136	0.2	33 967	0.2	−3.3
Origin country undetermined	764 187	4.5	879 766	5.1	15.1
Total non-OECD Countries	**2 357 751**	**13.8**	**2 553 195**	**14.7**	**8.3**
TOTAL	**17 060 956**	**100.0**	**17 365 849**	**100.0**	**1.8**

1. "Other European countries" includes Iceland.

ITALY

ARRIVALS OF FOREIGN TOURISTS AT REGISTERED TOURIST ACCOMMODATION

(by country of nationality)

	1991	Relative share	1992	Relative share	% Variation over 1991
Austria	1 108 755	5.5	1 036 988	5.1	−6.5
Belgium	480 402	2.4	478 458	2.3	−0.4
Denmark	192 328	1.0	173 001	0.8	−10.0
Finland	102 954	0.5	75 882	0.4	−26.3
France	1 965 068	9.7	1 801 753	8.8	−8.3
Germany	6 453 361	31.9	6 046 075	29.6	−6.3
Greece	202 387	1.0	199 127	1.0	−1.6
Iceland [1]	..	..	..	..	..
Ireland	61 510	0.3	67 044	0.3	9.0
Italy	..	..	..	..	..
Luxembourg	30 739	0.2	28 105	0.1	−8.6
Netherlands	571 945	2.8	527 305	2.6	−7.8
Norway	76 431	0.4	75 201	0.4	−1.6
Portugal	104 489	0.5	105 674	0.5	1.1
Spain	860 284	4.3	854 644	4.2	−0.7
Sweden	268 713	1.3	244 406	1.2	−9.0
Switzerland	1 066 687	5.3	1 022 621	5.0	−4.1
Turkey	75 120	0.4	64 001	0.3	−14.8
United Kingdom	1 246 522	6.2	1 292 347	6.3	3.7
Other OECD-Europe	..	..	..	..	..
Total Europe	14 867 695	73.5	14 092 632	69.0	−5.2
Canada	215 255	1.1	234 163	1.1	8.8
United States	1 489 358	7.4	1 926 351	9.4	29.3
Total North America	1 704 613	8.4	2 160 514	10.6	26.7
Australia	254 626	1.3	279 787	1.4	9.9
New Zealand	..	..	..	..	..
Japan	669 973	3.3	921 431	4.5	37.5
Total Australasia and Japan	924 599	4.6	1 201 218	5.9	29.9
Total OECD Countries	**17 496 907**	**86.4**	**17 454 364**	**85.5**	**−0.2**
Ex-Yugoslavia	230 931	1.1	196 928	1.0	−14.7
Other European countries [1]	845 971	4.2	934 992	4.6	10.5
Ex-USSR	97 231	0.5	96 619	0.5	−0.6
Latin America	578 687	2.9	650 244	3.2	12.4
Argentina	132 495	0.7	171 730	0.8	29.6
Brazil	215 175	1.1	194 864	1.0	−9.4
Mexico	78 187	0.4	106 988	0.5	36.8
Venezuela	31 925	0.2	36 114	0.2	13.1
Asia-Oceania	211 354	1.0	205 367	1.0	−2.8
Israel	133 661	0.7	126 230	0.6	−5.6
Africa	63 644	0.3	58 841	0.3	−7.5
Egypt	21 052	0.1	18 883	0.1	−10.3
South Africa	42 592	0.2	39 958	0.2	−6.2
Origin country undetermined	813 723	4.0	924 246	4.5	13.6
Total non-OECD Countries	**2 744 310**	**13.6**	**2 970 618**	**14.5**	**8.2**
TOTAL	**20 241 217**	**100.0**	**20 424 982**	**100.0**	**0.9**

1. "Other European countries" includes Iceland.

ITALY

NIGHTS SPENT BY FOREIGN TOURISTS IN HOTELS

(by country of nationality)

	1991	Relative share	1992	Relative share	% Variation over 1991
Austria	3 839 373	5.8	3 418 193	5.4	−11.0
Belgium	1 856 932	2.8	1 846 198	2.9	−0.6
Denmark	556 316	0.8	520 445	0.8	−6.4
Finland	482 626	0.7	312 815	0.5	−35.2
France	5 099 186	7.7	4 564 715	7.2	−10.5
Germany	26 165 156	39.7	23 979 885	37.8	−8.4
Greece	464 439	0.7	453 007	0.7	−2.5
Iceland [1]	..	..	..	..	..
Ireland	178 428	0.3	209 070	0.3	17.2
Italy	..	..	..	..	..
Luxembourg	180 095	0.3	165 189	0.3	−8.3
Netherlands	1 408 547	2.1	1 265 965	2.0	−10.1
Norway	241 438	0.4	232 738	0.4	−3.6
Portugal	233 990	0.4	252 257	0.4	7.8
Spain	1 774 574	2.7	1 787 743	2.8	0.7
Sweden	864 674	1.3	744 496	1.2	−13.9
Switzerland	4 045 814	6.1	3 579 837	5.6	−11.5
Turkey	205 954	0.3	169 939	0.3	−17.5
United Kingdom	4 545 966	6.9	4 571 866	7.2	0.6
Other OECD-Europe	..	..	..	..	..
Total Europe	52 143 508	79.2	48 074 358	75.8	−7.8
Canada	485 844	0.7	510 908	0.8	5.2
United States	3 627 778	5.5	4 550 965	7.2	25.4
Total North America	4 113 622	6.2	5 061 873	8.0	23.1
Australia	485 599	0.7	538 195	0.8	10.8
New Zealand	..	..	..	..	..
Japan	1 367 867	2.1	1 853 210	2.9	35.5
Total Australasia and Japan	1 853 466	2.8	2 391 405	3.8	29.0
Total OECD Countries	**58 110 596**	**88.3**	**55 527 636**	**87.6**	**−4.4**
Ex-Yugoslavia	755 015	1.1	761 428	1.2	0.8
Other European countries [1]	2 207 274	3.4	2 223 512	3.5	0.7
Ex-USSR	367 906	0.6	373 101	0.6	1.4
Latin America	1 584 779	2.4	1 676 251	2.6	5.8
Argentina	338 673	0.5	429 295	0.7	26.8
Brazil	562 680	0.9	490 633	0.8	−12.8
Mexico	187 931	0.3	241 534	0.4	28.5
Venezuela	90 487	0.1	95 923	0.2	6.0
Asia-Oceania	592 028	0.9	534 587	0.8	−9.7
Israel	293 231	0.4	270 943	0.4	−7.6
Africa	192 024	0.3	177 497	0.3	−7.6
Egypt	90 044	0.1	76 265	0.1	−15.3
South Africa	101 980	0.2	101 232	0.2	−0.7
Origin country undetermined	2 401 074	3.6	2 514 548	4.0	4.7
Total non-OECD Countries	**7 732 194**	**11.7**	**7 887 823**	**12.4**	**2.0**
TOTAL	**65 842 790**	**100.0**	**63 415 459**	**100.0**	**−3.7**

. "Other European countries" includes Iceland.

ITALY

NIGHTS SPENT BY FOREIGN TOURISTS IN REGISTERED TOURIST ACCOMMODATION

(by country of nationality)

	1991	Relative share	1992	Relative share	% Variation over 1991
Austria	5 357 557	6.2	4 902 375	5.9	−8.5
Belgium	2 441 621	2.8	2 415 602	2.9	−1.1
Denmark	1 088 660	1.3	971 774	1.2	−10.7
Finland	562 600	0.6	378 392	0.5	−32.7
France	6 256 610	7.2	5 571 214	6.7	−11.0
Germany	36 027 508	41.5	33 205 307	39.7	−7.8
Greece	492 792	0.6	490 056	0.6	−0.6
Iceland [1]	..	..	..	..	..
Ireland	208 254	0.2	244 192	0.3	17.3
Italy	..	..	..	..	..
Luxembourg	204 068	0.2	191 200	0.2	−6.3
Netherlands	3 206 802	3.7	2 864 264	3.4	−10.7
Norway	337 431	0.4	315 519	0.4	−6.5
Portugal	280 352	0.3	286 292	0.3	2.1
Spain	1 994 859	2.3	1 979 930	2.4	−0.7
Sweden	1 261 545	1.5	1 059 458	1.3	−16.0
Switzerland	5 098 646	5.9	4 775 053	5.7	−6.3
Turkey	241 440	0.3	197 552	0.2	−18.2
United Kingdom	5 387 131	6.2	5 398 815	6.5	0.2
Other OECD-Europe	..	..	..	..	..
Total Europe	70 447 876	81.2	65 246 995	78.0	−7.4
Canada	599 741	0.7	632 043	0.8	5.4
United States	3 955 794	4.6	4 936 644	5.9	24.8
Total North America	4 555 535	5.3	5 568 687	6.7	22.2
Australia	592 333	0.7	653 397	0.8	10.3
New Zealand	..	..	..	..	..
Japan	1 415 473	1.6	1 911 799	2.3	35.1
Total Australasia and Japan	2 007 806	2.3	2 565 196	3.1	27.8
Total OECD Countries	**77 011 217**	**88.8**	**73 380 878**	**87.7**	**−4.7**
Ex-Yugoslavia	853 087	1.0	904 299	1.1	6.0
Other European countries [1]	3 505 558	4.0	3 853 226	4.6	9.9
Ex-USSR	391 380	0.5	432 823	0.5	10.6
Latin America	1 778 501	2.1	1 886 180	2.3	6.1
Argentina	393 684	0.5	485 126	0.6	23.2
Brazil	625 806	0.7	655 774	0.8	4.8
Mexico	201 452	0.2	264 284	0.3	31.2
Venezuela	106 286	0.1	107 666	0.1	1.3
Asia-Oceania	645 167	0.7	601 935	0.7	−6.7
Israel	309 641	0.4	291 172	0.3	−6.0
Africa	229 864	0.3	211 472	0.3	−8.0
Egypt	104 209	0.1	89 057	0.1	−14.5
South Africa	125 655	0.1	122 415	0.1	−2.6
Origin country undetermined	2 711 523	3.1	2 804 577	3.4	3.4
Total non-OECD Countries	**9 723 700**	**11.2**	**10 261 689**	**12.3**	**5.5**
TOTAL	**86 734 917**	**100.0**	**83 642 567**	**100.0**	**−3.6**

1. "Other European countries" includes Iceland.

JAPAN

ARRIVALS OF FOREIGN TOURISTS AT FRONTIERS

(by country of nationality)

	1991	Relative share	1992	Relative share	% Variation over 1991
Austria	3 544	0.2	3 746	0.2	5.7
Belgium	3 368	0.2	3 282	0.2	−2.6
Denmark	2 992	0.1	4 136	0.2	38.2
Finland	4 110	0.2	3 348	0.2	−18.5
France	20 851	1.0	20 490	1.0	−1.7
Germany	24 091	1.1	27 640	1.3	14.7
Greece	1 994	0.1	2 066	0.1	3.6
Iceland	..	..	..	..	..
Ireland	1 870	0.1	1 718	0.1	−8.1
Italy	12 935	0.6	11 038	0.5	−14.7
Luxembourg	..	..	..	..	..
Netherlands	6 314	0.3	6 229	0.3	−1.3
Norway	1 918	0.1	1 862	0.1	−2.9
Portugal	3 790	0.2	4 374	0.2	15.4
Spain	7 156	0.3	7 085	0.3	−1.0
Sweden	6 190	0.3	6 273	0.3	1.3
Switzerland	7 150	0.3	7 169	0.3	0.3
Turkey	1 520	0.1	1 604	0.1	5.5
United Kingdom	122 626	5.8	143 341	6.8	16.9
Other OECD-Europe	..	..	..	..	..
Total Europe	232 419	11.0	255 401	12.1	9.9
Canada	37 296	1.8	43 661	2.1	17.1
United States	289 951	13.8	298 049	14.2	2.8
Total North America	327 247	15.6	341 710	16.2	4.4
Australia	25 082	1.2	28 412	1.4	13.3
New Zealand	8 886	0.4	10 936	0.5	23.1
Japan	..	..	..	..	..
Total Australasia and Japan	33 968	1.6	39 348	1.9	15.8
Total OECD Countries	**593 634**	**28.2**	**636 459**	**30.3**	**7.2**
Ex-Yugoslavia	994	0.0	524	0.0	−47.3
Poland	919	0.0	724	0.0	−21.2
Ex-USSR	18 510	0.9	14 848	0.7	−19.8
Argentina	3 283	0.2	3 330	0.2	1.4
Brazil	64 164	3.0	36 325	1.7	−43.4
Chile	1 086	0.1	877	0.0	−19.2
Colombia	1 956	0.1	2 092	0.1	7.0
Mexico	6 465	0.3	7 161	0.3	10.8
Venezuela	965	0.0	839	0.0	−13.1
China	24 864	1.2	29 147	1.4	17.2
Hong Kong	26 560	1.3	28 619	1.4	7.8
India	6 241	0.3	5 801	0.3	−7.1
Iran	41 851	2.0	10 597	0.5	−74.7
Israel	6 654	0.3	5 788	0.3	−13.0
Republic of Korea	504 099	24.0	502 871	23.9	−0.2
Lebanon	121	0.0	91	0.0	−24.8
Malaysia	50 897	2.4	35 670	1.7	−29.9
Pakistan	1 958	0.1	1 873	0.1	−4.3
Philippines	23 552	1.1	20 734	1.0	−12.0
Singapore	27 138	1.3	25 433	1.2	−6.3
Taiwan	565 882	26.9	622 707	29.6	10.0
Thailand	69 004	3.3	58 583	2.8	−15.1
Africa	4 155	0.2	3 896	0.2	−6.2
Egypt	457	0.0	573	0.0	25.4
South Africa	637	0.0	1 107	0.1	73.8
Origin country undetermined	1 505 208	71.5	1 462 167	69.5	−2.9
Total non-OECD Countries	**1 510 357**	**71.8**	**1 466 587**	**69.7**	**−2.9**
TOTAL	**2 103 991**	**100.0**	**2 103 046**	**100.0**	**−0.0**

JAPAN

ARRIVALS OF FOREIGN VISITORS AT FRONTIERS

(by country of nationality)

	1991	Relative share	1992	Relative share	% Variation over 1991
Austria	7 957	0.2	8 024	0.2	0.8
Belgium	8 013	0.2	7 812	0.2	-2.5
Denmark	7 806	0.2	9 254	0.3	18.5
Finland	9 192	0.3	7 901	0.2	-14.0
France	50 119	1.4	48 605	1.4	-3.0
Germany	61 227	1.7	63 930	1.8	4.4
Greece	3 970	0.1	3 578	0.1	-9.9
Iceland	554	0.0	342	0.0	-38.3
Ireland	5 221	0.1	5 176	0.1	-0.9
Italy	30 199	0.9	26 866	0.7	-11.0
Luxembourg	442	0.0	396	0.0	-10.4
Netherlands	18 044	0.5	18 253	0.5	1.2
Norway	5 263	0.1	5 316	0.1	1.0
Portugal	5 539	0.2	6 180	0.2	11.6
Spain	16 554	0.5	13 580	0.4	-18.0
Sweden	14 763	0.4	14 888	0.4	0.8
Switzerland	15 385	0.4	15 237	0.4	-1.0
Turkey	3 175	0.1	3 511	0.1	10.6
United Kingdom	219 425	6.2	241 893	6.8	10.2
Other OECD-Europe	..	..	..	..	
Total Europe	482 848	13.7	500 742	14.0	3.7
Canada	62 306	1.8	69 620	1.9	11.7
United States	543 075	15.4	560 940	15.7	3.3
Total North America	605 381	17.1	630 560	17.6	4.2
Australia	54 520	1.5	59 844	1.7	9.8
New Zealand	18 120	0.5	21 014	0.6	16.0
Japan	..	..	..	..	
Total Australasia and Japan	72 640	2.1	80 858	2.3	11.3
Total OECD Countries	**1 160 869**	**32.8**	**1 212 160**	**33.8**	**4.4**
Ex-Yugoslavia	1 756	0.0	1 225	0.0	-30.2
Other European countries	37 962	1.1	32 739	0.9	-13.8
Bulgaria	623	0.0	579	0.0	-7.1
Hungary	2 038	0.1	2 456	0.1	20.5
Poland	2 182	0.1	2 196	0.1	0.6
Rumania	609	0.0	719	0.0	18.1
Ex-USSR	31 828	0.9	26 765	0.7	-15.9
Latin America	121 691	3.4	87 202	2.4	-28.3
Argentina	5 025	0.1	4 980	0.1	-0.9
Brazil	69 503	2.0	41 987	1.2	-39.6
Chile	1 954	0.1	1 935	0.1	-1.0
Colombia	2 708	0.1	2 772	0.1	2.4
Mexico	9 216	0.3	10 045	0.3	9.0
Venezuela	1 699	0.0	1 428	0.0	-16.0
Asia-Oceania	2 197 095	62.2	2 234 931	62.4	1.7
China	130 487	3.7	183 220	5.1	40.4
Hong Kong	38 526	1.1	40 174	1.1	4.3
India	26 978	0.8	26 159	0.7	-3.0
Iran	48 901	1.4	14 999	0.4	-69.3
Israel	9 010	0.3	8 411	0.2	-6.6
Republic of Korea	861 820	24.4	864 052	24.1	0.3
Lebanon	488	0.0	479	0.0	-1.8
Malaysia	77 423	2.2	60 894	1.7	-21.3
Pakistan	6 575	0.2	6 711	0.2	2.1
Philippines	114 383	3.2	105 195	2.9	-8.0
Saudi Arabia	1 126	0.0	1 217	0.0	8.1
Singapore	42 882	1.2	40 956	1.1	-4.5
Taiwan	658 106	18.6	715 487	20.0	8.7
Thailand	107 770	3.0	97 234	2.7	-9.8
Africa	12 915	0.4	12 677	0.4	-1.8
Algeria	436	0.0	334	0.0	-23.4
Egypt	1 405	0.0	1 861	0.1	32.5
Morocco	395	0.0	427	0.0	8.1
South Africa	2 433	0.1	3 016	0.1	24.0
Origin country undetermined	2 119	0.1	1 831	0.1	-13.6
Total non-OECD Countries	**2 373 538**	**67.2**	**2 370 605**	**66.2**	**-0.1**
TOTAL	**3 534 407**	**100.0**	**3 582 765**	**100.0**	**1.4**

NETHERLANDS

ARRIVALS OF FOREIGN TOURISTS AT HOTELS

(by country of residence)

	1991	Relative share	1992	Relative share	% Variation over 1991
Austria [3]		..		..	..
Belgium	159 800	4.3	170 000	4.3	6.4
Denmark	60 800	1.6	63 100	1.6	3.8
Finland	31 800	0.9	26 900	0.7	−15.4
France	259 800	7.0	287 800	7.3	10.8
Germany	798 600	21.7	813 900	20.7	1.9
Greece [3]	..	..	..	..	..
Iceland [3]	..	..	..	..	..
Ireland	27 200	0.7	25 900	0.7	−4.8
Italy	246 800	6.7	244 200	6.2	−1.1
Luxembourg	13 100	0.4	14 600	0.4	11.5
Netherlands	..	..	..	..	..
Norway	46 000	1.2	49 800	1.3	8.3
Portugal [1]	..	..	..	..	..
Spain [1]	154 200	4.2	146 800	3.7	−4.8
Sweden	113 100	3.1	118 800	3.0	5.0
Switzerland	95 000	2.6	92 500	2.4	−2.6
Turkey [3]	..	..	..	..	..
United Kingdom	703 400	19.1	745 500	19.0	6.0
Other OECD-Europe [3]	189 400	5.1	229 400	5.8	21.1
Total Europe	2 899 000	78.6	3 029 200	77.0	4.5
Canada	63 100	1.7	64 200	1.6	1.7
United States	366 200	9.9	408 800	10.4	11.6
Total North America	429 300	11.6	473 000	12.0	10.2
Australia [2]	39 900	1.1	53 000	1.3	32.8
New Zealand [2]	..	..			
Japan	87 300	2.4	111 700	2.8	27.9
Total Australasia and Japan	127 200	3.5	164 700	4.2	29.5
Total OECD Countries	**3 455 500**	**93.7**	**3 666 900**	**93.3**	**6.1**
Ex-Yugoslavia	..	..	..	..	..
Latin America	51 600	1.4	64 900	1.7	25.8
Asia-Oceania	134 700	3.7	157 200	4.0	16.7
Africa	44 900	1.2	42 900	1.1	−4.5
Total non-OECD Countries	**231 200**	**6.3**	**265 000**	**6.7**	**14.6**
TOTAL	**3 686 700**	**100.0**	**3 931 900**	**100.0**	**6.7**

. Spain includes Portugal.
. Australia includes New Zealand.
. Other OECD-Europe includes Austria, Greece, Iceland, Turkey and all non-OECD European countries.

NETHERLANDS

ARRIVALS OF FOREIGN TOURISTS AT REGISTERED TOURIST ACCOMMODATION

(by country of residence)

	1991	Relative share	1992	Relative share	% Variation over 1991
Austria[3]	..	..	..	..	..
Belgium	353 000	6.0	342 500	5.6	–3.0
Denmark	95 400	1.6	96 700	1.6	1.4
Finland	40 000	0.7	34 700	0.6	–13.3
France	370 600	6.3	396 000	6.5	6.9
Germany	2 068 700	35.4	2 146 700	35.3	3.8
Greece[3]	..	..	..	..	..
Iceland[3]					
Ireland	34 600	0.6	32 400	0.5	–6.4
Italy	309 300	5.3	301 800	5.0	–2.4
Luxembourg	14 400	0.2	16 000	0.3	11.1
Netherlands					
Norway	56 400	1.0	59 700	1.0	5.9
Portugal[1]	..	..	..	..	..
Spain[1]	201 000	3.4	187 400	3.1	–6.8
Sweden	144 500	2.5	146 400	2.4	1.3
Switzerland	131 800	2.3	122 000	2.0	–7.4
Turkey[3]	..	..	..	..	..
United Kingdom	831 800	14.2	871 200	14.3	4.7
Other OECD-Europe[3]	270 500	4.6	299 600	4.9	10.8
Total Europe	4 922 000	84.3	5 053 100	83.1	2.7
Canada	79 500	1.4	79 300	1.3	–0.3
United States	409 600	7.0	451 200	7.4	10.2
Total North America	489 100	8.4	530 500	8.7	8.5
Australia[2]	70 900	1.2	81 100	1.3	14.4
New Zealand[2]	..	..	..	..	..
Japan	90 600	1.6	116 100	1.9	28.1
Total Australasia and Japan	161 500	2.8	197 200	3.2	22.1
Total OECD Countries	**5 572 600**	**95.4**	**5 780 800**	**95.0**	**3.7**
Ex-Yugoslavia					
Latin America	62 900	1.1	75 200	1.2	19.6
Asia-Oceania	150 900	2.6	174 200	2.9	15.4
Africa	55 500	1.0	52 700	0.9	–5.0
Total non-OECD Countries	**269 300**	**4.6**	**302 100**	**5.0**	**12.2**
TOTAL	**5 841 900**	**100.0**	**6 082 900**	**100.0**	**4.1**

1. Spain includes Portugal.
2. Australia includes New Zealand.
3. Other OECD-Europe includes Austria, Greece, Iceland, Turkey and non-OECD European countries.

NETHERLANDS

NIGHTS SPENT BY FOREIGN TOURISTS IN HOTELS

(by country of residence)

	1991	Relative share	1992	Relative share	% Variation over 1991
Austria [3]	..	..	..	..	..
Belgium	305 600	3.8	322 400	3.8	5.5
Denmark	128 300	1.6	129 200	1.5	0.7
Finland	69 000	0.9	56 400	0.7	−18.3
France	495 500	6.2	549 900	6.5	11.0
Germany	1 857 900	23.2	1 935 200	22.8	4.2
Greece [3]	..	..	..	..	..
Iceland [3]	..	..	..	..	..
Ireland	59 800	0.7	55 300	0.7	−7.5
Italy	538 600	6.7	517 100	6.1	−4.0
Luxembourg	27 400	0.3	29 100	0.3	6.2
Netherlands	..	..	..	..	..
Norway	92 600	1.2	101 200	1.2	9.3
Portugal [1]	..	..	..	..	..
Spain [1]	331 100	4.1	311 700	3.7	−5.9
Sweden	228 800	2.9	234 800	2.8	2.6
Switzerland	202 300	2.5	199 500	2.3	−1.4
Turkey [3]	..	..	..	..	..
United Kingdom	1 519 000	19.0	1 633 300	19.2	7.5
Other OECD-Europe [3]	425 600	5.3	492 600	5.8	15.7
Total Europe	6 281 500	78.6	6 567 700	77.3	4.6
Canada	134 200	1.7	132 000	1.6	−1.6
United States	764 600	9.6	861 200	10.1	12.6
Total North America	898 800	11.2	993 200	11.7	10.5
Australia [2]	87 000	1.1	112 600	1.3	29.4
New Zealand [2]	..	..	..	..	..
Japan	174 300	2.2	220 500	2.6	26.5
Total Australasia and Japan	261 300	3.3	333 100	3.9	27.5
Total OECD Countries	**7 441 600**	**93.1**	**7 894 000**	**92.9**	**6.1**
Ex-Yugoslavia	..	..	..	..	..
Latin America	121 300	1.5	143 900	1.7	18.6
Asia-Oceania	324 900	4.1	356 100	4.2	9.6
Africa	105 700	1.3	102 000	1.2	−3.5
Total non-OECD Countries	**551 900**	**6.9**	**602 000**	**7.1**	**9.1**
TOTAL	**7 993 500**	**100.0**	**8 496 000**	**100.0**	**6.3**

1. Spain includes Portugal.
2. Australia includes New Zealand.
3. Other OECD-Europe includes Austria, Greece, Iceland, Turkey and all non-OECD European countries.

NETHERLANDS

NIGHTS SPENT BY FOREIGN TOURISTS IN REGISTERED TOURIST ACCOMMODATION

(by country of residence)

	1991	Relative share	1992	Relative share	% Variation over 1991
Austria [3]	..	..	..	..	..
Belgium	1 219 500	7.1	1 130 700	6.2	−7.3
Denmark	246 600	1.4	237 100	1.3	−3.9
Finland	85 900	0.5	73 300	0.4	−14.7
France	763 500	4.4	791 600	4.4	3.7
Germany	8 364 100	48.6	9 067 700	50.1	8.4
Greece [3]	..	..	..	..	..
Iceland [3]	..	..	..	..	..
Ireland	80 500	0.5	74 900	0.4	−7.0
Italy	691 900	4.0	644 500	3.6	−6.9
Luxembourg	32 600	0.2	34 400	0.2	5.5
Netherlands					
Norway	116 200	0.7	124 100	0.7	6.8
Portugal [1]	..	..	..	..	..
Spain [1]	452 400	2.6	408 200	2.3	−9.8
Sweden	296 500	1.7	296 700	1.6	0.1
Switzerland	313 200	1.8	299 900	1.7	−4.2
Turkey [3]					
United Kingdom	1 940 900	11.3	2 061 200	11.4	6.2
Other OECD-Europe [3]	625 800	3.6	666 500	3.7	6.5
Total Europe	15 229 600	88.5	15 910 800	87.9	4.5
Canada	165 500	1.0	161 700	0.9	−2.3
United States	844 100	4.9	944 000	5.2	11.8
Total North America	1 009 600	5.9	1 105 700	6.1	9.5
Australia [2]	154 100	0.9	176 900	1.0	14.8
New Zealand [2]					
Japan	179 900	1.0	228 400	1.3	27.0
Total Australasia and Japan	334 000	1.9	405 300	2.2	21.3
Total OECD Countries	**16 573 200**	**96.3**	**17 421 800**	**96.3**	**5.1**
Ex-Yugoslavia	..	..	..	..	..
Latin America	142 900	0.8	163 000	0.9	14.1
Asia-Oceania	362 000	2.1	390 700	2.2	7.9
Africa	127 800	0.7	123 500	0.7	−3.4
Total non-OECD Countries	**632 700**	**3.7**	**677 200**	**3.7**	**7.0**
TOTAL	**17 205 900**	**100.0**	**18 099 000**	**100.0**	**5.2**

1. Spain includes Portugal.
2. Australia includes New Zealand.
3. Other OECD-Europe includes Austria, Greece, Iceland, Turkey and all non-OECD European countries.

NEW ZEALAND

ARRIVALS OF FOREIGN TOURISTS AT FRONTIERS

(by country of residence)

	1991	Relative share	1992	Relative share	% Variation over 1991
Austria	2 839	0.3	3 507	0.3	23.5
Belgium	824	0.1	1 135	0.1	37.7
Denmark	3 342	0.3	4 174	0.4	24.9
Finland	2 011	0.2	1 388	0.1	−31.0
France	4 643	0.5	5 325	0.5	14.7
Germany	34 298	3.6	45 705	4.3	33.3
Greece	295	0.0	303	0.0	2.7
Iceland	32	0.0	..		..
Ireland	1 632	0.2	1 724	0.2	5.6
Italy	3 580	0.4	3 766	0.4	5.2
Luxembourg	111	0.0	153	0.0	37.8
Netherlands	7 584	0.8	9 734	0.9	28.3
Norway	2 037	0.2	1 962	0.2	−3.7
Portugal	203	0.0	205	0.0	1.0
Spain	925	0.1	1 528	0.1	65.2
Sweden	7 992	0.8	6 700	0.6	−16.2
Switzerland	11 717	1.2	12 457	1.2	6.3
Turkey	192	0.0	379	0.0	97.4
United Kingdom	87 944	9.1	96 523	9.1	9.8
Other OECD-Europe	..	..	..	..	..
Total Europe	172 201	17.9	196 668	18.6	14.2
Canada	30 276	3.1	25 849	2.4	−14.6
United States	132 690	13.8	131 357	12.4	−1.0
Total North America	162 966	16.9	157 206	14.9	−3.5
Australia	338 509	35.1	363 642	34.4	7.4
New Zealand [1]	7 062	0.7	6 484	0.6	−8.2
Japan	114 718	11.9	128 962	12.2	12.4
Total Australasia and Japan	460 289	47.8	499 088	47.3	8.4
Total OECD Countries	**795 456**	**82.6**	**852 962**	**80.8**	**7.2**
Ex-Yugoslavia	231	0.0	219	0.0	−5.2
Bulgaria	32	0.0	..		..
Ex-Czechoslovakia	149	0.0	142	0.0	−4.7
Hungary	180	0.0	216	0.0	20.0
Poland	94	0.0	393	0.0	318.1
Rumania	83	0.0	68	0.0	−18.1
Ex-USSR	2 807	0.3	2 830	0.3	0.8
Argentina	1 715	0.2	2 320	0.2	35.3
Brazil	1 143	0.1	1 046	0.1	−8.5
Chile	478	0.0	344	0.0	−28.0
Colombia	184	0.0	283	0.0	53.8
Mexico	735	0.1	1 099	0.1	49.5
Venezuela	144	0.0	160	0.0	11.1
China	2 596	0.3	3 612	0.3	39.1
Hong Kong	18 564	1.9	19 327	1.8	4.1
India	1 495	0.2	1 810	0.2	21.1
Iran	191	0.0	143	0.0	−25.1
Israel	1 172	0.1	1 047	0.1	−10.7
Republic of Korea	6 369	0.7	12 757	1.2	100.3
Lebanon	29	0.0	..		..
Malaysia	8 776	0.9	10 110	1.0	15.2
Pakistan	173	0.0	305	0.0	76.3
Philippines	2 237	0.2	2 370	0.2	5.9
Saudi Arabia	483	0.1	944	0.1	95.4
Singapore	17 342	1.8	19 044	1.8	9.8
Taiwan	14 811	1.5	25 060	2.4	69.2
Thailand	6 897	0.7	9 905	0.9	43.6
Egypt	84	0.0	66	0.0	−21.4
Morocco	10	0.0	..		..
South Africa	2 045	0.2	3 586	0.3	75.4
Origin country undetermined	167 783	17.4	202 500	19.2	20.7
Total non-OECD Countries	**168 014**	**17.4**	**202 719**	**19.2**	**20.7**
TOTAL	**963 470**	**100.0**	**1 055 681**	**100.0**	**9.6**

1. New Zealanders who have lived abroad for less than 12 months and who return for a short stay.

NEW ZEALAND

NIGHTS SPENT BY FOREIGN TOURISTS IN REGISTERED TOURIST ACCOMMODATION

(by country of residence)

	1991	Relative share	1992	Relative share	% Variation over 1991
Austria	73 665	0.4	94 295	0.5	28.0
Belgium	23 759	0.1	24 079	0.1	1.3
Denmark	142 158	0.7	170 025	0.8	19.6
Finland	42 654	0.2	27 547	0.1	−35.4
France	94 571	0.5	103 560	0.5	9.5
Germany	1 133 327	5.9	1 375 924	6.7	21.4
Greece	..	..	..	..	..
Iceland					
Ireland	54 613	0.3	45 489	0.2	−16.7
Italy	51 238	0.3	57 817	0.3	12.8
Luxembourg	..	..	..	..	..
Netherlands	320 272	1.7	367 003	1.8	14.6
Norway	..	..	..	..	..
Portugal	..	..	..	..	..
Spain	21 499	0.1	31 194	0.2	45.1
Sweden	215 757	1.1	163 173	0.8	−24.4
Switzerland	489 306	2.5	484 951	2.4	−0.9
Turkey	5 064	0.0	5 138	0.0	1.5
United Kingdom	3 137 433	16.3	3 169 126	15.5	1.0
Other OECD-Europe	..	..	..	..	..
Total Europe	5 805 316	30.1	6 119 321	29.8	5.4
Canada	666 285	3.5	620 000	3.0	−6.9
United States	1 903 738	9.9	1 973 664	9.6	3.7
Total North America	2 570 023	13.3	2 593 664	12.6	0.9
Australia	5 204 779	27.0	5 357 289	26.1	2.9
New Zealand [1]	252 094	1.3	192 501	0.9	−23.6
Japan	1 298 393	6.7	1 456 413	7.1	12.2
Total Australasia and Japan	6 755 266	35.0	7 006 203	34.2	3.7
Total OECD Countries	**15 130 605**	**78.4**	**15 719 188**	**76.6**	**3.9**
Ex-Yugoslavia	13 150	0.1	8 999	0.0	−31.6
Ex-USSR	444 591	2.3	431 372	2.1	−3.0
Argentina	21 604	0.1	31 856	0.2	47.5
Brazil	21 037	0.1	18 531	0.1	−11.9
China	107 451	0.6	129 209	0.6	20.2
Hong Kong	271 740	1.4	290 215	1.4	6.8
India	46 298	0.2	66 310	0.3	43.2
Israel	44 525	0.2	39 159	0.2	−12.1
Republic of Korea	125 363	0.6	160 941	0.8	28.4
Malaysia	178 279	0.9	224 344	1.1	25.8
Singapore	273 655	1.4	..	..	..
Taiwan	203 736	1.1	350 894	1.7	72.2
Thailand	114 696	0.6	153 912	0.8	34.2
Origin country undetermined	4 144 840	21.5	4 780 097	23.3	15.3
Total non-OECD Countries	**4 157 990**	**21.6**	**4 789 096**	**23.4**	**15.2**
TOTAL	**19 288 595**	**100.0**	**20 508 284**	**100.0**	**6.3**

1. New Zealanders who have lived abroad for less than 12 months and who return for a short stay.

NORWAY

NIGHTS SPENT BY FOREIGN TOURISTS IN HOTELS

(by country of nationality)

	1991	Relative share	1992	Relative share	% Variation over 1991
Austria [1]	..	..	..	..	..
Belgium [1]	..	..	..	..	..
Denmark	701 634	17.9	714 750	16.7	1.9
Finland	118 141	3.0	95 414	2.2	−19.2
France	208 419	5.3	242 475	5.7	16.3
Germany	713 212	18.2	850 587	19.9	19.3
Greece [1]	..	..	..	..	..
Iceland [1]	..	..	..	..	..
Italy [1]	157 003	4.0	157 252	3.7	0.2
Luxembourg [1]	..	..	..	..	..
Netherlands	150 398	3.8	174 272	4.1	15.9
Norway [1]	..	..	..	..	..
Portugal [1]	..	..	..	..	..
Spain [1]	40 201	1.0	42 775	1.0	6.4
Sweden	680 972	17.4	661 670	15.5	−2.8
Switzerland [1]	47 404	1.2	50 970	1.2	7.5
Turkey [1]	..	..	..	..	..
United Kingdom	347 278	8.9	428 593	10.0	23.4
Other OECD-Europe	154 193	3.9	152 268	3.6	−1.2
Total Europe	3 318 855	84.7	3 571 026	83.5	7.6
Canada [1]	..	..	..	..	..
United States	280 250	7.2	351 528	8.2	25.4
Total North America	280 250	7.2	351 528	8.2	25.4
Australia [1]	..	..	..	..	..
New Zealand [1]	..	..	..	..	..
Japan	85 001	2.2	99 840	2.3	17.5
Total Australasia and Japan	85 001	2.2	99 840	2.3	17.5
Total OECD Countries	**3 684 106**	**94.1**	**4 022 394**	**94.1**	**9.2**
Yugoslavia (S.F.R.) [1]	..	..	..	..	..
Origin country undetermined [1]	232 667	5.9	252 769	5.9	8.6
Total non-OECD Countries	**232 667**	**5.9**	**252 769**	**5.9**	**8.6**
TOTAL	**3 916 773**	**100.0**	**4 275 163**	**100.0**	**9.2**

. Included in "Origin country undetermined".

PORTUGAL

ARRIVALS OF FOREIGN TOURISTS AT FRONTIERS

(by country of nationality)

	1991	Relative share	1992	Relative share	% Variation over 1991
Austria	41 439	0.5	42 706	0.5	3.1
Belgium	188 296	2.2	191 122	2.2	1.5
Denmark	107 486	1.2	115 768	1.3	7.7
Finland	148 154	1.7	83 661	0.9	−43.5
France	667 122	7.7	647 807	7.3	−2.9
Germany	786 496	9.1	812 310	9.1	3.3
Greece [1]	..	..	..	..	..
Iceland [1]	..	..	..	..	..
Ireland	73 783	0.9	88 877	1.0	20.5
Italy	250 478	2.9	258 443	2.9	3.2
Luxembourg	16 010	0.2	17 615	0.2	10.0
Netherlands	325 586	3.8	337 427	3.8	3.6
Norway	23 509	0.3	29 480	0.3	25.4
Portugal	..	..	..	..	..
Spain	4 111 089	47.5	4 225 746	47.6	2.8
Sweden	105 188	1.2	101 158	1.1	−3.8
Switzerland	73 366	0.8	64 257	0.7	−12.4
Turkey [1]	..	..	..	..	..
United Kingdom	1 161 863	13.4	1 276 001	14.4	9.8
Other OECD-Europe	..	..	..	..	..
Total Europe	8 079 865	93.3	8 292 378	93.3	2.6
Canada	62 872	0.7	66 276	0.7	5.4
United States	143 459	1.7	156 583	1.8	9.1
Total North America	206 331	2.4	222 859	2.5	8.0
Australia [2]	19 322	0.2	19 908	0.2	3.0
New-Zealand [2]	..	..	..	..	..
Japan	26 587	0.3	25 569	0.3	−3.8
Total Australasia and Japan	45 909	0.5	45 477	0.5	−0.9
Total OECD Countries	**8 332 105**	**96.2**	**8 560 714**	**96.4**	**2.7**
Yugoslavia (S.F.R.) [1]	..	..	..	..	..
Other European countries [1]	57 295	0.7	..	..	..
Africa	101 006	1.2	..	..	..
Origin country undetermined	166 550	1.9	323 411	3.6	94.2
Total non-OECD Countries	**324 851**	**3.8**	**323 411**	**3.6**	**−0.4**
TOTAL	**8 656 956**	**100.0**	**8 884 125**	**100.0**	**2.6**

1. "Other European countries" includes Greece, Iceland, Turkey and Ex-Yugoslavia.
2. Australia includes New Zealand.

PORTUGAL

ARRIVALS OF FOREIGN VISITORS AT FRONTIERS

(by country of nationality)

	1991	Relative share	1992	Relative share	% Variation over 1991
Austria	48 745	0.2	45 220	0.2	−7.2
Belgium	198 434	1.0	207 272	1.0	4.5
Denmark	112 220	0.6	119 587	0.6	6.6
Finland	149 205	0.8	85 682	0.4	−42.6
France	711 493	3.6	685 682	3.3	−3.6
Germany	851 858	4.3	877 456	4.2	3.0
Greece	16 068	0.1	17 645	0.1	9.8
Iceland	3 251	0.0	5 197	0.0	59.9
Ireland	76 182	0.4	92 864	0.4	21.9
Italy	290 971	1.5	283 063	1.4	−2.7
Luxembourg	17 521	0.1	18 840	0.1	7.5
Netherlands	360 452	1.8	366 674	1.8	1.7
Norway	26 393	0.1	33 589	0.2	27.3
Portugal	..	..	..	..	..
Spain	14 583 216	74.2	15 553 444	75.0	6.7
Sweden	114 315	0.6	108 417	0.5	−5.2
Switzerland	79 890	0.4	72 534	0.3	−9.2
Turkey	3 365	0.0	3 207	0.0	−4.7
United Kingdom	1 307 312	6.7	1 435 346	6.9	9.8
Other OECD-Europe	..	..	..	..	..
Total Europe	18 950 891	96.5	20 011 719	96.5	5.6
Canada	69 299	0.4	73 955	0.4	6.7
United States	178 133	0.9	220 452	1.1	23.8
Total North America	247 432	1.3	294 407	1.4	19.0
Australia	16 457	0.1	17 498	0.1	6.3
New Zealand	4 966	0.0	4 711	0.0	−5.1
Japan	28 422	0.1	27 234	0.1	−4.2
Total Australasia and Japan	49 845	0.3	49 443	0.2	−0.8
Total OECD Countries	**19 248 168**	**98.0**	**20 355 569**	**98.1**	**5.8**
Ex-Yugoslavia	6 777	0.0	8 450	0.0	24.7
Other European countries	64 012	0.3	58 962	0.3	−7.9
Bulgaria	2 509	0.0	2 445	0.0	−2.6
Ex-Czechoslovakia	6 487	0.0	10 329	0.0	59.2
Hungary	3 407	0.0	5 880	0.0	72.6
Poland	12 262	0.1	11 326	0.1	−7.6
Rumania	1 155	0.0	1 483	0.0	28.4
Ex-USSR	36 435	0.2	25 155	0.1	−31.0
Latin America	161 525	0.8	162 529	0.8	0.6
Argentina	10 694	0.1	10 497	0.1	−1.8
Brazil	114 053	0.6	106 080	0.5	−7.0
Chile	3 009	0.0	3 214	0.0	6.8
Colombia	2 319	0.0	2 583	0.0	11.4
Mexico	4 578	0.0	7 314	0.0	59.8
Venezuela	17 902	0.1	22 745	0.1	27.1
Asia-Oceania	52 993	0.3	55 626	0.3	5.0
China	2 469	0.0	2 397	0.0	−2.9
Hong Kong	950	0.0	767	0.0	−19.3
India	9 435	0.0	6 993	0.0	−25.9
Iran	845	0.0	937	0.0	10.9
Israel	7 284	0.0	8 049	0.0	10.5
Republic of Korea	5 444	0.0	5 000	0.0	−8.2
Lebanon	556	0.0	486	0.0	−12.6
Malaysia	1 012	0.0	1 453	0.0	43.6
Pakistan	1 627	0.0	1 406	0.0	−13.6
Philippines	17 124	0.1	20 010	0.1	16.9
Saudi Arabia	362	0.0	317	0.0	−12.4
Singapore	989	0.0	1 180	0.0	19.3
Thailand	1 143	0.0	1 728	0.0	51.2
Africa	105 837	0.5	98 876	0.5	−6.6
Algeria	1 287	0.0	1 164	0.0	−9.6
Egypt	1 115	0.0	800	0.0	−28.3
Morocco	4 255	0.0	4 413	0.0	3.7
South Africa	14 503	0.1	14 925	0.1	2.9
Origin country undetermined	2 017	0.0	1 867	0.0	−7.4
Total non-OECD Countries	**393 161**	**2.0**	**386 310**	**1.9**	**−1.7**
TOTAL	**19 641 329**	**100.0**	**20 741 879**	**100.0**	**5.6**

PORTUGAL

ARRIVALS OF FOREIGN TOURISTS AT HOTELS[1]

(by country of residence)

	1991	Relative share	1992	Relative share	% Variation over 1991
Austria	45 622	1.2	42 794	1.2	−6.2
Belgium	101 959	2.6	94 596	2.6	−7.2
Denmark	62 208	1.6	58 518	1.6	−5.9
Finland	126 322	3.2	67 377	1.8	−46.7
France	350 410	9.0	301 913	8.2	−13.8
Germany	534 237	13.7	549 600	15.0	2.9
Greece	9 647	0.2	9 470	0.3	−1.8
Iceland	2 744	0.1	3 337	0.1	21.6
Ireland	47 337	1.2	53 028	1.4	12.0
Italy	232 422	5.9	232 420	6.3	−0.0
Luxembourg	6 143	0.2	5 577	0.2	−9.2
Netherlands	228 008	5.8	204 772	5.6	−10.2
Norway	23 198	0.6	26 981	0.7	16.3
Portugal	..	..	..	..	..
Spain	734 127	18.8	651 846	17.8	−11.2
Sweden	104 888	2.7	90 424	2.5	−13.8
Switzerland	96 881	2.5	81 240	2.2	−16.1
Turkey	1 154	0.0	1 488	0.0	28.9
United Kingdom	718 435	18.4	702 502	19.1	−2.2
Other OECD-Europe	..	..	..	..	..
Total Europe	3 425 742	87.5	3 177 883	86.6	−7.2
Canada	63 328	1.6	54 444	1.5	−14.0
United States	186 020	4.8	202 938	5.5	9.1
Total North America	249 348	6.4	257 382	7.0	3.2
Australia	9 169	0.2	9 987	0.3	8.9
New Zealand	1 758	0.0	1 365	0.0	−22.4
Japan	31 904	0.8	34 663	0.9	8.6
Total Australasia and Japan	42 831	1.1	46 015	1.3	7.4
Total OECD Countries	**3 717 921**	**95.0**	**3 481 280**	**94.8**	**−6.4**
Ex-Yugoslavia	2 282	0.1	1 620	0.0	−29.0
Other European countries	12 311	0.3	13 802	0.4	12.1
Bulgaria	755	0.0	1 087	0.0	44.0
Ex-Czechoslovakia	2 008	0.1	2 080	0.1	3.6
Hungary	1 702	0.0	1 635	0.0	−3.9
Poland	1 499	0.0	1 903	0.1	27.0
Rumania	718	0.0	550	0.0	−23.4
Ex-USSR	4 654	0.1	4 718	0.1	1.4
Latin America	106 745	2.7	104 655	2.9	−2.0
Argentina	6 895	0.2	6 856	0.2	−0.6
Brazil	85 821	2.2	76 955	2.1	−10.3
Chile	1 142	0.0	1 646	0.0	44.1
Colombia	810	0.0	1 070	0.0	32.1
Mexico	3 778	0.1	5 075	0.1	34.3
Venezuela	5 350	0.1	9 582	0.3	79.1
Asia-Oceania	19 286	0.5	18 168	0.5	−5.8
China	1 405	0.0	1 601	0.0	14.0
Iran	129	0.0	83	0.0	−35.7
Israel	9 709	0.2	7 585	0.2	−21.9
Lebanon	244	0.0	177	0.0	−27.5
Philippines	1 103	0.0	1 428	0.0	29.5
Saudi Arabia	600	0.0	614	0.0	2.3
Africa	54 521	1.4	52 014	1.4	−4.6
Egypt	623	0.0	488	0.0	−21.7
Morocco	2 458	0.1	3 341	0.1	35.9
South Africa	18 105	0.5	11 852	0.3	−34.5
Total non-OECD Countries	**195 145**	**5.0**	**190 259**	**5.2**	**−2.5**
TOTAL	**3 913 066**	**100.0**	**3 671 539**	**100.0**	**−6.2**

1. Includes arrivals at hotels, studio-hotels, holiday-flats, villages, motels, inns and boarding-houses.

PORTUGAL

ARRIVALS OF FOREIGN TOURISTS AT REGISTERED TOURIST ACCOMMODATION[1]

(by country of residence)

	1991	Relative share	1992	Relative share	% Variation over 1991
Austria	58 100	1.2	53 174	1.2	−8.5
Belgium	140 401	2.9	127 118	2.9	−9.5
Denmark	75 732	1.6	67 071	1.5	−11.4
Finland	128 641	2.7	68 818	1.6	−46.5
France	535 406	11.2	459 327	10.6	−14.2
Germany	750 039	15.7	700 490	16.1	−6.6
Greece	10 000	0.2	9 729	0.2	−2.7
Iceland	2 768	0.1	3 355	0.1	21.2
Ireland	49 491	1.0	54 931	1.3	11.0
Italy	270 509	5.7	260 621	6.0	−3.7
Luxembourg	6 756	0.1	6 118	0.1	−9.4
Netherlands	342 131	7.2	291 256	6.7	−14.9
Norway	24 395	0.5	27 924	0.6	14.5
Portugal	..	..	..	..	..
Spain	886 357	18.6	777 190	17.9	−12.3
Sweden	108 218	2.3	92 906	2.1	−14.1
Switzerland	107 663	2.3	89 606	2.1	−16.8
Turkey	1 261	0.0	1 598	0.0	26.7
United Kingdom	750 236	15.7	729 221	16.8	−2.8
Other OECD-Europe	..	..	..	..	..
Total Europe	4 248 104	89.1	3 820 453	87.9	−10.1
Canada	67 003	1.4	57 814	1.3	−13.7
United States	191 100	4.0	207 664	4.8	8.7
Total North America	258 103	5.4	265 478	6.1	2.9
Australia	15 551	0.3	15 564	0.4	0.1
New Zealand	5 938	0.1	4 494	0.1	−24.3
Japan	32 550	0.7	35 127	0.8	7.9
Total Australasia and Japan	54 039	1.1	55 185	1.3	2.1
Total OECD Countries	**4 560 246**	**95.6**	**4 141 116**	**95.3**	**−9.2**
Ex-Yugoslavia	2 950	0.1	2 054	0.0	−30.4
Other European countries	17 082	0.4	18 200	0.4	6.5
Bulgaria	842	0.0	1 115	0.0	32.4
Ex-Czechoslovakia	2 717	0.1	2 878	0.1	5.9
Hungary	2 930	0.1	2 928	0.1	−0.1
Poland	3 806	0.1	3 950	0.1	3.8
Rumania	877	0.0	657	0.0	−25.1
Ex-USSR	4 873	0.1	4 809	0.1	−1.3
Latin America	111 255	2.3	109 627	2.5	−1.5
Argentina	7 280	0.2	7 344	0.2	0.9
Brazil	89 244	1.9	80 260	1.8	−10.1
Chile	1 246	0.0	1 865	0.0	49.7
Colombia	883	0.0	1 135	0.0	28.5
Mexico	3 916	0.1	5 231	0.1	33.6
Venezuela	5 476	0.1	9 864	0.2	80.1
Asia-Oceania	19 951	0.4	18 740	0.4	−6.1
China	1 429	0.0	1 652	0.0	15.6
Iran	155	0.0	141	0.0	−9.0
Israel	9 906	0.2	7 736	0.2	−21.9
Lebanon	248	0.0	186	0.0	−25.0
Philippines	1 106	0.0	1 437	0.0	29.9
Saudi Arabia	644	0.0	614	0.0	−4.7
Africa	57 606	1.2	54 810	1.3	−4.9
Egypt	634	0.0	494	0.0	−22.1
Morocco	3 503	0.1	4 301	0.1	22.8
South Africa	19 118	0.4	12 669	0.3	−33.7
Total non-OECD Countries	**208 844**	**4.4**	**203 431**	**4.7**	**−2.6**
TOTAL	**4 769 090**	**100.0**	**4 344 547**	**100.0**	**−8.9**

1. Includes arrivals at hotels, studio-hotels, holiday-flats, villages, motels, inns, boarding-houses, recreation centres for children and camping-sites.

PORTUGAL

NIGHTS SPENT BY FOREIGN TOURISTS IN HOTELS[1]

(by country of residence)

	1991	Relative share	1992	Relative share	% Variation over 1991
Austria	189 455	1.0	176 477	1.0	–6.9
Belgium	457 021	2.4	419 049	2.3	–8.3
Denmark	384 222	2.0	371 470	2.1	–3.3
Finland	898 993	4.7	399 973	2.2	–55.5
France	980 151	5.1	784 594	4.4	–20.0
Germany	3 233 873	16.9	3 297 973	18.4	2.0
Greece	25 511	0.1	27 458	0.2	7.6
Iceland	21 236	0.1	32 514	0.2	53.1
Ireland	372 567	2.0	416 055	2.3	11.7
Italy	598 905	3.1	573 061	3.2	–4.3
Luxembourg	41 469	0.2	30 624	0.2	–26.2
Netherlands	1 693 066	8.9	1 494 667	8.4	–11.7
Norway	141 375	0.7	184 159	1.0	30.3
Portugal	..	..	..	..	..
Spain	1 870 917	9.8	1 625 356	9.1	–13.1
Sweden	698 078	3.7	593 717	3.3	–14.9
Switzerland	360 374	1.9	291 886	1.6	–19.0
Turkey	4 183	0.0	4 585	0.0	9.6
United Kingdom	5 618 270	29.4	5 696 672	31.9	1.4
Other OECD-Europe	..	..	..	..	..
Total Europe	17 589 666	92.1	16 420 290	91.9	–6.6
Canada	278 760	1.5	216 555	1.2	–22.3
United States	485 490	2.5	538 840	3.0	11.0
Total North America	764 250	4.0	755 395	4.2	–1.2
Australia	25 427	0.1	24 322	0.1	–4.3
New Zealand	4 096	0.0	3 151	0.0	–22.8
Japan	72 679	0.4	74 686	0.4	2.8
Total Australasia and Japan	102 202	0.5	102 169	0.6	–0.0
Total OECD Countries	**18 456 118**	**96.7**	**17 277 854**	**96.6**	**–6.4**
Ex-Yugoslavia	9 854	0.1	8 229	0.0	–16.5
Other European countries	42 312	0.2	50 838	0.3	20.2
Bulgaria	3 422	0.0	3 133	0.0	–8.4
Ex-Czechoslovakia	7 393	0.0	6 522	0.0	–11.8
Hungary	5 138	0.0	6 728	0.0	30.9
Poland	6 025	0.0	6 446	0.0	7.0
Rumania	1 980	0.0	5 093	0.0	157.2
Ex-USSR	15 419	0.1	17 368	0.1	12.6
Latin America	287 295	1.5	254 861	1.4	–11.3
Argentina	20 250	0.1	16 459	0.1	–18.7
Brazil	226 645	1.2	188 284	1.1	–16.9
Chile	3 740	0.0	4 413	0.0	18.0
Colombia	2 336	0.0	2 305	0.0	–1.3
Mexico	8 953	0.0	13 597	0.1	51.9
Venezuela	16 713	0.1	19 912	0.1	19.1
Asia-Oceania	55 618	0.3	50 397	0.3	–9.4
China	4 641	0.0	5 172	0.0	11.4
Iran	426	0.0	369	0.0	–13.4
Israel	25 847	0.1	17 048	0.1	–34.0
Lebanon	720	0.0	723	0.0	0.4
Philippines	2 811	0.0	3 185	0.0	13.3
Saudi Arabia	2 146	0.0	1 858	0.0	–13.4
Africa	237 731	1.2	234 852	1.3	–1.2
Egypt	2 589	0.0	1 652	0.0	–36.2
Morocco	7 170	0.0	10 623	0.1	48.2
South Africa	65 947	0.3	41 750	0.2	–36.7
Total non-OECD Countries	**632 810**	**3.3**	**599 177**	**3.4**	**–5.3**
TOTAL	**19 088 928**	**100.0**	**17 877 031**	**100.0**	**–6.3**

1. Includes nights spent at hotels, studio-hotels, holiday-flats, villages, motels, inns and boarding-houses.

PORTUGAL

NIGHTS SPENT BY FOREIGN TOURISTS IN REGISTERED TOURIST ACCOMMODATION[1]

(by country of residence)

	1991	Relative share	1992	Relative share	% Variation over 1991
Austria	224 875	1.0	205 135	1.0	−8.8
Belgium	584 922	2.7	527 174	2.6	−9.9
Denmark	436 316	2.0	403 841	2.0	−7.4
Finland	915 288	4.2	408 088	2.0	−55.4
France	1 484 551	6.8	1 195 064	6.0	−19.5
Germany	3 966 162	18.1	3 825 534	19.1	−3.5
Greece	27 228	0.1	27 996	0.1	2.8
Iceland	21 299	0.1	32 561	0.2	52.9
Ireland	381 733	1.7	422 616	2.1	10.7
Italy	709 291	3.2	646 027	3.2	−8.9
Luxembourg	43 664	0.2	32 189	0.2	−26.3
Netherlands	2 152 918	9.8	1 844 244	9.2	−14.3
Norway	147 844	0.7	188 416	0.9	27.4
Portugal	..	..	..	..	..
Spain	2 365 405	10.8	2 012 404	10.0	−14.9
Sweden	711 686	3.2	603 733	3.0	−15.2
Switzerland	390 295	1.8	316 002	1.6	−19.0
Turkey	4 625	0.0	5 322	0.0	15.1
United Kingdom	5 782 887	26.3	5 824 570	29.0	0.7
Other OECD-Europe	..	..	..	..	..
Total Europe	20 350 989	92.7	18 520 916	92.3	−9.0
Canada	287 805	1.3	224 440	1.1	−22.0
United States	500 018	2.3	550 449	2.7	10.1
Total North America	787 823	3.6	774 889	3.9	−1.6
Australia	42 163	0.2	37 947	0.2	−10.0
New Zealand	13 822	0.1	10 267	0.1	−25.7
Japan	74 152	0.3	75 595	0.4	1.9
Total Australasia and Japan	130 137	0.6	123 809	0.6	−4.9
Total OECD Countries	**21 268 949**	**96.9**	**19 419 614**	**96.8**	**−8.7**
Ex-Yugoslavia	12 244	0.1	9 377	0.0	−23.4
Other European countries	55 662	0.3	61 369	0.3	10.3
Bulgaria	3 833	0.0	3 188	0.0	−16.8
Ex-Czechoslovakia	9 214	0.0	8 495	0.0	−7.8
Hungary	8 860	0.0	10 127	0.1	14.3
Poland	10 671	0.0	10 657	0.1	−0.1
Rumania	3 001	0.0	5 671	0.0	89.0
Ex-USSR	16 943	0.1	17 608	0.1	3.9
Latin America	303 892	1.4	271 721	1.4	−10.6
Argentina	21 435	0.1	17 536	0.1	−18.2
Brazil	240 140	1.1	201 004	1.0	−16.3
Chile	4 073	0.0	5 067	0.0	24.4
Colombia	2 478	0.0	2 515	0.0	1.5
Mexico	9 312	0.0	13 888	0.1	49.1
Venezuela	17 082	0.1	20 577	0.1	20.5
Asia-Oceania	58 003	0.3	51 682	0.3	−10.9
China	4 774	0.0	5 315	0.0	11.3
Iran	516	0.0	565	0.0	9.5
Israel	27 173	0.1	17 348	0.1	−36.2
Lebanon	730	0.0	752	0.0	3.0
Philippines	2 817	0.0	3 198	0.0	13.5
Saudi Arabia	2 264	0.0	1 858	0.0	−17.9
Africa	258 589	1.2	250 702	1.2	−3.1
Egypt	2 610	0.0	1 661	0.0	−36.4
Morocco	11 890	0.1	15 369	0.1	29.3
South Africa	68 803	0.3	43 616	0.2	−36.6
Total non-OECD Countries	**688 390**	**3.1**	**644 851**	**3.2**	**−6.3**
TOTAL	**21 957 339**	**100.0**	**20 064 465**	**100.0**	**−8.6**

1. Includes nights spent at hotels, studio-hotels, holiday-flats, villages, motels, inns, boarding-houses, recreation centres for children and camping-sites.

SPAIN

ARRIVALS OF FOREIGN VISITORS AT FRONTIERS[1]

(by country of nationality)

	1991	Relative share	1992	Relative share	% Variation over 1991
Austria	320 040	0.6	325 961	0.6	1.9
Belgium	1 369 365	2.6	1 361 774	2.5	-0.6
Denmark	412 702	0.8	437 037	0.8	5.9
Finland	411 762	0.8	289 764	0.5	-29.6
France	12 052 767	22.5	11 792 108	21.3	-2.2
Germany	7 663 223	14.3	7 762 127	14.0	1.3
Greece	94 787	0.2	95 096	0.2	0.3
Iceland	19 854	0.0	15 786	0.0	-20.5
Ireland	177 339	0.3	207 899	0.4	17.2
Italy	1 767 599	3.3	1 852 567	3.3	4.8
Luxembourg	79 818	0.1	90 683	0.2	13.6
Netherlands	2 157 079	4.0	2 117 030	3.8	-1.9
Norway	301 541	0.6	285 696	0.5	-5.3
Portugal	10 535 848	19.7	11 567 533	20.9	9.8
Spain[2]	3 471 896	6.5	..	..	..
Sweden	781 837	1.5	745 491	1.3	-4.6
Switzerland	1 167 088	2.2	1 109 871	2.0	-4.9
Turkey	17 041	0.0	17 370	0.0	1.9
United Kingdom	6 145 003	11.5	6 515 540	11.8	6.0
Other OECD-Europe[3]	372 904	0.7	..	..	..
Total Europe	49 319 493	92.2	46 589 333	84.2	-5.5
Canada	137 950	0.3	146 429	0.3	6.1
United States	652 338	1.2	825 387	1.5	26.5
Total North America	790 288	1.5	971 816	1.8	23.0
Australia	48 709	0.1	52 247	0.1	7.3
New Zealand	18 539	0.0	21 605	0.0	16.5
Japan	186 485	0.3	222 243	0.4	19.2
Total Australasia and Japan	253 733	0.5	296 095	0.5	16.7
Total OECD Countries	**50 363 514**	**94.1**	**47 857 244**	**86.5**	**-5.0**
Ex-Yugoslavia	57 287	0.1	37 110	0.1	-35.2
Other European countries	306 285	0.6	..	..	..
Bulgaria	12 596	0.0	24 287	0.0	92.8
Ex-Czechoslovakia	36 389	0.1	61 120	0.1	68.0
Hungary	18 215	0.0	28 747	0.1	57.8
Poland	47 167	0.1	35 456	0.1	-24.8
Rumania	15 134	0.0	100 635	0.2	565.0
Ex-USSR	176 784	0.3	91 479	0.2	-48.3
Latin America	479 850	0.9	..	..	..
Argentina	102 684	0.2	128 713	0.2	25.3
Brazil	104 047	0.2	107 135	0.2	3.0
Chile	24 111	0.0	30 536	0.1	26.6
Colombia	31 378	0.1	37 764	0.1	20.4
Mexico	62 334	0.1	89 882	0.2	44.2
Venezuela	51 509	0.1	60 869	0.1	18.2
Asia-Oceania	211 944	0.4	..	..	..
China	8 193	0.0	8 543	0.0	4.3
India	28 497	0.1	24 587	0.0	-13.7
Iran	4 259	0.0	3 717	0.0	-12.7
Israel	25 595	0.0	30 454	0.1	19.0
Republic of Korea	22 755	0.0	19 175	0.0	-15.7
Lebanon	4 123	0.0	4 134	0.0	0.3
Malaysia	2 912	0.0	4 362	0.0	49.8
Pakistan	4 803	0.0	4 367	0.0	-9.1
Philippines	66 199	0.1	66 839	0.1	1.0
Saudi Arabia	5 065	0.0	4 525	0.0	-10.7
Singapore	3 228	0.0	3 607	0.0	11.7
Taiwan	..	..	647	0.0	..
Thailand	3 030	0.0	4 459	0.0	47.2
Africa	2 067 996	3.9	..	..	..
Algeria	149 388	0.3	148 726	0.3	-0.4
Egypt	7 868	0.0	9 800	0.0	24.6
Morocco	1 851 017	3.5	2 034 737	3.7	9.9
Origin country undetermined	8 088	0.0	7 436 362	13.4	91843.2
Total non-OECD Countries	**3 131 450**	**5.9**	**7 473 472**	**13.5**	**138.7**
TOTAL	**53 494 964**	**100.0**	**55 330 716**	**100.0**	**3.4**

1. Includes about 34% of arrivals of excursionists.
2. Spanish nationals residing abroad.
3. "Other OECD-Europe" includes Andorra, Cyprus, Malta, Monaco, and the Vatican States.

SPAIN

ARRIVALS OF FOREIGN TOURISTS AT HOTELS[1]
(by country of nationality)

	1991	Relative share	1992	Relative share	% Variation over 1991
Austria	..	..	121 426	1.0	..
Belgium	432 358	3.6	471 337	3.8	9.0
Denmark	130 780	1.1	125 602	1.0	−4.0
Finland	..	..	60 178	0.5	..
France	1 582 876	13.1	1 592 851	12.8	0.6
Germany	2 916 982	24.2	2 862 211	22.9	−1.9
Greece	31 595	0.3	34 047	0.3	7.8
Iceland	..	..	..	..	..
Ireland	33 610	0.3	56 247	0.5	67.4
Italy	1 118 199	9.3	1 114 892	8.9	−0.3
Luxembourg	26 961	0.2	37 446	0.3	38.9
Netherlands	357 129	3.0	352 787	2.8	−1.2
Norway	59 325	0.5	87 024	0.7	46.7
Portugal	325 444	2.7	330 066	2.6	1.4
Spain	..	..	..	..	..
Sweden	180 619	1.5	239 691	1.9	32.7
Switzerland	339 093	2.8	303 556	2.4	−10.5
Turkey	..	..	..	..	..
United Kingdom	2 339 168	19.4	2 365 488	18.9	1.1
Other OECD-Europe	..	..	..	..	..
Total Europe	9 874 139	82.0	10 154 849	81.3	2.8
Canada	51 014	0.4	50 116	0.4	−1.8
United States	579 414	4.8	679 834	5.4	17.3
Total North America	630 428	5.2	729 950	5.8	15.8
Australia	..	..	..	..	..
New Zealand	..	..	..	..	..
Japan	341 745	2.8	340 567	2.7	−0.3
Total Australasia and Japan	341 745	2.8	340 567	2.7	−0.3
Total OECD Countries	**10 846 312**	**90.0**	**11 225 366**	**89.9**	**3.5**
Ex-Yugoslavia	..	..	..	..	..
Other European countries	357 219	3.0	234 672	1.9	−34.3
Latin America	406 744	3.4	..	..	..
Argentina	89 932	0.7	149 300	1.2	66.0
Mexico	63 118	0.5	111 519	0.9	76.7
Venezuela	20 504	0.2	38 809	0.3	89.3
Origin country undetermined	438 628	3.6	1 026 842	8.2	134.1
Total non-OECD Countries	**1 202 591**	**10.0**	**1 261 514**	**10.1**	**4.9**
TOTAL	**12 048 903**	**100.0**	**12 486 880**	**100.0**	**3.6**

1. Arrivals recorded in hotels with "estrellas de oro" (golden stars) and "estrellas de plata" (silver stars).

SPAIN

NIGHTS SPENT BY FOREIGN TOURISTS IN HOTELS[1]

(by country of nationality)

	1991	Relative share	1992	Relative share	% Variation over 1991
Austria	..	..	940 379	1.2	..
Belgium	3 226 737	4.3	3 365 281	4.4	4.3
Denmark	816 016	1.1	790 218	1.0	–3.2
Finland			528 703	0.7	
France	6 727 747	9.0	6 064 101	7.9	–9.9
Germany	25 975 175	34.9	25 216 078	32.8	–2.9
Greece	68 231	0.1	96 545	0.1	41.5
Iceland					
Ireland	171 090	0.2	507 172	0.7	196.4
Italy	4 631 878	6.2	5 261 600	6.8	13.6
Luxembourg	237 371	0.3	287 392	0.4	21.1
Netherlands	2 434 054	3.3	2 357 636	3.1	–3.1
Norway	297 735	0.4	655 631	0.9	120.2
Portugal	792 452	1.1	831 040	1.1	4.9
Spain	..	..	..	..	..
Sweden	1 072 574	1.4	1 696 897	2.2	58.2
Switzerland	2 254 496	3.0	2 106 203	2.7	–6.6
Turkey					
United Kingdom	19 045 083	25.6	19 331 397	25.1	1.5
Other OECD-Europe	..	..	..	..	..
Total Europe	67 750 639	91.0	70 036 273	91.0	3.4
Canada	122 489	0.2	142 662	0.2	16.5
United States	1 293 788	1.7	1 499 247	1.9	15.9
Total North America	1 416 277	1.9	1 641 909	2.1	15.9
Australia	..	..	..	..	..
New Zealand	..		..		..
Japan	616 909	0.8	702 352	0.9	13.9
Total Australasia and Japan	616 909	0.8	702 352	0.9	13.9
Total OECD Countries	**69 783 825**	**93.7**	**72 380 534**	**94.1**	**3.7**
Ex-Yugoslavia					
Other European countries	2 355 504	3.2	1 053 177	1.4	–55.3
Latin America	959 712	1.3	..	..	..
Argentina	216 550	0.3	314 577	0.4	45.3
Mexico	152 515	0.2	266 944	0.3	75.0
Venezuela	54 877	0.1	92 885	0.1	69.3
Origin country undetermined	1 340 390	1.8	3 500 607	4.6	161.2
Total non-OECD Countries	**4 655 606**	**6.3**	**4 553 784**	**5.9**	**–2.2**
TOTAL	**74 439 431**	**100.0**	**76 934 318**	**100.0**	**3.4**

1. Nights recorded in hotels with "estrellas de oro" (golden stars) and "estrellas de plata" (silver stars).

SWEDEN

NIGHTS SPENT BY FOREIGN TOURISTS IN HOTELS
(by country of nationality)

	1991	Relative share	1992	Relative share	% Variation over 1991
Austria [1]	..	..	..	..	..
Belgium [1]	..	..	..	..	..
Denmark	189 246	6.7	184 603	6.6	−2.5
Finland	367 849	13.0	278 589	9.9	−24.3
France	92 503	3.3	92 599	3.3	0.1
Germany	450 697	15.9	486 464	17.4	7.9
Greece [1]	..	..	..	..	..
Iceland [1]	..	..	..	..	..
Ireland [1]	..	..	..	..	..
Italy	118 347	4.2	115 680	4.1	−2.3
Luxembourg [1]	..	..	..	..	..
Netherlands	68 784	2.4	83 804	3.0	21.8
Norway	370 781	13.1	356 298	12.7	−3.9
Portugal [1]	..	..	..	..	..
Spain [1]	..	..	..	..	..
Sweden	..	..	..	..	..
Switzerland	57 027	2.0	56 358	2.0	−1.2
Turkey [1]	..	..	..	..	..
United Kingdom	228 135	8.1	238 579	8.5	4.6
Other OECD-Europe	..	..	..	..	..
Total Europe	1 943 369	68.8	1 892 974	67.5	−2.6
Canada	15 959	0.6	15 967	0.6	0.1
United States	238 495	8.4	267 328	9.5	12.1
Total North America	254 454	9.0	283 295	10.1	11.3
Australia [2]	..	..	..	..	..
New Zealand [2]	..	..	..	..	..
Japan	84 110	3.0	81 528	2.9	−3.1
Total Australasia and Japan	84 110	3.0	81 528	2.9	−3.1
Total OECD Countries	**2 281 933**	**80.7**	**2 257 797**	**80.5**	**−1.1**
Ex-Yugoslavia	..	..	..	..	..
Other European countries [1]	230 840	8.2	252 599	9.0	9.4
Origin country undetermined [2]	313 387	11.1	293 315	10.5	−6.4
Total non-OECD Countries	**544 227**	**19.3**	**545 914**	**19.5**	**0.3**
TOTAL	**2 826 160**	**100.0**	**2 803 711**	**100.0**	**−0.8**

1. Included in "Other European countries".
2. Included in "Origin country undetermined".

SWEDEN

NIGHTS SPENT BY FOREIGN TOURISTS IN REGISTERED TOURIST ACCOMMODATION

(by country of nationality)

	1991	Relative share	1992	Relative share	% Variation over 1991
Austria [1]	..	..	..	..	..
Belgium [1]	..	..	..	..	..
Denmark	519 934	9.3	537 121	9.2	3.3
Finland	556 958	9.9	440 486	7.6	−20.9
France	164 724	2.9	167 108	2.9	1.4
Germany	1 319 398	23.6	1 512 494	26.0	14.6
Greece [1]	..	..	..	..	..
Iceland [1]	..	..	..	..	..
Ireland [1]	..	..	..	..	..
Italy	134 119	2.4	130 178	2.2	−2.9
Luxembourg [1]	..	..	..	..	..
Netherlands	321 133	5.7	337 636	5.8	5.1
Norway	1 083 756	19.4	1 134 597	19.5	4.7
Portugal [1]	..	..	..	..	..
Spain [1]	..	..	..	..	..
Sweden					
Switzerland	72 733	1.3	69 767	1.2	−4.1
Turkey [1]	..	..	..	..	..
United Kingdom	275 157	4.9	288 183	5.0	4.7
Other OECD-Europe	..	..	..	..	..
Total Europe	4 447 912	79.4	4 617 570	79.4	3.8
Canada	18 376	0.3	18 463	0.3	0.5
United States	252 448	4.5	281 476	4.8	11.5
Total North America	270 824	4.8	299 939	5.2	10.8
Australia [2]	..	..	..	..	..
New Zealand [2]	..	..	..	..	..
Japan	89 841	1.6	85 901	1.5	−4.4
Total Australasia and Japan	89 841	1.6	85 901	1.5	−4.4
Total OECD Countries	**4 808 577**	**85.9**	**5 003 410**	**86.1**	**4.1**
Ex-Yugoslavia	..	..	..	..	..
Other European countries [1]	389 292	7.0	434 473	7.5	11.6
Origin country undetermined [2]	402 504	7.2	376 639	6.5	−6.4
Total non-OECD Countries	**791 796**	**14.1**	**811 112**	**13.9**	**2.4**
TOTAL	**5 600 373**	**100.0**	**5 814 522**	**100.0**	**3.8**

1. Included in ''Other European countries''.
2. Included in ''Origin country undetermined''.

SWITZERLAND

ARRIVALS OF FOREIGN TOURISTS AT HOTELS

(by country of residence)

	1991	Relative share	1992	Relative share	% Variation over 1991
Austria	175 759	2.4	157 632	2.1	−10.3
Belgium	225 038	3.0	231 039	3.1	2.7
Denmark	43 764	0.6	41 016	0.5	−6.3
Finland	32 836	0.4	29 090	0.4	−11.4
France	558 860	7.6	527 755	7.0	−5.6
Germany	2 244 199	30.3	2 190 223	29.1	−2.4
Greece	58 566	0.8	54 245	0.7	−7.4
Iceland [1]	..	..	..	..	..
Ireland	15 092	0.2	14 338	0.2	−5.0
Italy	659 526	8.9	651 364	8.7	−1.2
Luxembourg	32 646	0.4	32 144	0.4	−1.5
Netherlands	273 230	3.7	264 555	3.5	−3.2
Norway	30 110	0.4	29 443	0.4	−2.2
Portugal	37 578	0.5	33 758	0.4	−10.2
Spain	251 835	3.4	217 446	2.9	−13.7
Sweden	109 527	1.5	104 507	1.4	−4.6
Switzerland	..	..	..	..	..
Turkey	31 750	0.4	29 365	0.4	−7.5
United Kingdom	536 230	7.2	548 076	7.3	2.2
Other OECD-Europe	..	..	..	..	..
Total Europe	5 316 546	71.8	5 155 996	68.5	−3.0
Canada	77 036	1.0	78 549	1.0	2.0
United States	715 637	9.7	887 431	11.8	24.0
Total North America	792 673	10.7	965 980	12.8	21.9
Australia [2]	70 051	0.9	72 794	1.0	3.9
New Zealand [2]	..	..	..	..	..
Japan	414 987	5.6	502 796	6.7	21.2
Total Australasia and Japan	485 038	6.6	575 590	7.6	18.7
Total OECD Countries	**6 594 257**	**89.1**	**6 697 566**	**89.0**	**1.6**
Ex-Yugoslavia	55 173	0.7	30 598	0.4	−44.5
Other European countries [1]	126 879	1.7	134 788	1.8	6.2
Ex-USSR	24 054	0.3	27 151	0.4	12.9
Latin America	131 865	1.8	140 641	1.9	6.7
Argentina	20 549	0.3	24 927	0.3	21.3
Brazil	53 432	0.7	46 919	0.6	−12.2
Mexico	16 026	0.2	19 523	0.3	21.8
Asia-Oceania	378 448	5.1	417 959	5.6	10.4
India	29 292	0.4	28 833	0.4	−1.6
Iran	10 089	0.1	8 629	0.1	−14.5
Israel	120 149	1.6	104 454	1.4	−13.1
Africa	113 670	1.5	106 446	1.4	−6.4
Egypt	17 600	0.2	17 810	0.2	1.2
South Africa	25 403	0.3	24 064	0.3	−5.3
Total non-OECD Countries	**806 035**	**10.9**	**830 432**	**11.0**	**3.0**
TOTAL	**7 400 292**	**100.0**	**7 527 998**	**100.0**	**1.7**

1. "Other European countries" includes Iceland.
2. Australia includes New Zealand.

SWITZERLAND

ARRIVALS OF FOREIGN TOURISTS AT REGISTERED TOURIST ACCOMMODATION

(by country of residence)

	1991	Relative share	1992	Relative share	% Variation over 1991
Austria	221 745	2.2	203 085	2.0	−8.4
Belgium	360 783	3.6	376 870	3.7	4.5
Denmark	64 089	0.6	61 098	0.6	−4.7
Finland	42 323	0.4	37 364	0.4	−11.7
France	753 089	7.4	715 778	7.0	−5.0
Germany	3 522 334	34.8	3 485 649	34.0	−1.0
Greece	61 699	0.6	56 685	0.6	−8.1
Iceland [1]	..	..	..	..	..
Ireland	19 945	0.2	18 398	0.2	−7.8
Italy	775 812	7.7	772 149	7.5	−0.5
Luxembourg	42 799	0.4	41 911	0.4	−2.1
Netherlands	593 317	5.9	593 752	5.8	0.1
Norway	35 830	0.4	35 161	0.3	−1.9
Portugal	44 356	0.4	40 105	0.4	−9.6
Spain	334 828	3.3	285 008	2.8	−14.9
Sweden	131 721	1.3	127 158	1.2	−3.5
Switzerland	..	..	..	..	..
Turkey	32 940	0.3	30 555	0.3	−7.2
United Kingdom	670 793	6.6	681 851	6.6	1.6
Other OECD-Europe	..	..	..	..	..
Total Europe	7 708 403	76.2	7 562 577	73.7	−1.9
Canada	96 629	1.0	98 698	1.0	2.1
United States	783 467	7.7	961 355	9.4	22.7
Total North America	880 096	8.7	1 060 053	10.3	20.4
Australia [2]	121 713	1.2	113 795	1.1	−6.5
New Zealand [2]	..	..	..	..	..
Japan	429 318	4.2	519 525	5.1	21.0
Total Australasia and Japan	551 031	5.4	633 320	6.2	14.9
Total OECD Countries	**9 139 530**	**90.4**	**9 255 950**	**90.2**	**1.3**
Ex-Yugoslavia	62 393	0.6	33 901	0.3	−45.7
Other European countries [1]	206 666	2.0	235 529	2.3	14.0
Latin America	149 017	1.5	159 016	1.5	6.7
Argentina	23 672	0.2	29 404	0.3	24.2
Brazil	60 503	0.6	52 937	0.5	−12.5
Mexico	17 876	0.2	22 221	0.2	24.3
Asia-Oceania	422 558	4.2	460 829	4.5	9.1
India	31 301	0.3	30 667	0.3	−2.0
Iran	10 615	0.1	9 208	0.1	−13.3
Israel	131 114	1.3	114 824	1.1	−12.4
Africa	130 922	1.3	120 198	1.2	−8.2
Egypt	18 412	0.2	18 670	0.2	1.4
South Africa	32 934	0.3	31 702	0.3	−3.7
Total non-OECD Countries	**971 556**	**9.6**	**1 009 473**	**9.8**	**3.9**
TOTAL	**10 111 086**	**100.0**	**10 265 423**	**100.0**	**1.5**

1. "Other European countries" includes Iceland.
2. Australia includes New Zealand.

SWITZERLAND

NIGHTS SPENT BY FOREIGN TOURISTS IN HOTELS

(by country of residence)

	1991	Relative share	1992	Relative share	% Variation over 1991
Austria	414 303	2.0	364 379	1.8	−12.1
Belgium	924 226	4.5	970 615	4.8	5.0
Denmark	104 856	0.5	100 347	0.5	−4.3
Finland	78 523	0.4	65 051	0.3	−17.2
France	1 545 634	7.6	1 442 258	7.1	−6.7
Germany	6 961 061	34.2	6 838 980	33.8	−1.8
Greece	138 616	0.7	126 809	0.6	−8.5
Iceland [1]	..	..	..	..	..
Ireland	38 821	0.2	34 268	0.2	−11.7
Italy	1 407 635	6.9	1 397 301	6.9	−0.7
Luxembourg	120 624	0.6	124 845	0.6	3.5
Netherlands	892 630	4.4	881 383	4.4	−1.3
Norway	69 843	0.3	65 161	0.3	−6.7
Portugal	80 933	0.4	72 647	0.4	−10.2
Spain	460 630	2.3	410 304	2.0	−10.9
Sweden	252 161	1.2	233 927	1.2	−7.2
Switzerland	..	..	..	..	..
Turkey	104 820	0.5	81 712	0.4	−22.0
United Kingdom	1 847 021	9.1	1 847 948	9.1	0.1
Other OECD-Europe	..	..	..	..	..
Total Europe	15 442 337	75.8	15 057 935	74.4	−2.5
Canada	177 402	0.9	174 388	0.9	−1.7
United States	1 576 724	7.7	1 889 289	9.3	19.8
Total North America	1 754 126	8.6	2 063 677	10.2	17.6
Australia [2]	158 954	0.8	158 401	0.8	−0.3
New Zealand [2]	..	..	..	..	..
Japan	724 962	3.6	815 392	4.0	12.5
Total Australasia and Japan	883 916	4.3	973 793	4.8	10.2
Total OECD Countries	**18 080 379**	**88.8**	**18 095 405**	**89.4**	**0.1**
Ex-Yugoslavia	180 702	0.9	99 814	0.5	−44.8
Other European countries [1]	373 446	1.8	355 994	1.8	−4.7
Ex-USSR	95 401	0.5	92 170	0.5	−3.4
Latin America	326 654	1.6	326 028	1.6	−0.2
Argentina	49 201	0.2	56 905	0.3	15.7
Brazil	126 426	0.6	108 474	0.5	−14.2
Mexico	37 405	0.2	41 519	0.2	11.0
Asia-Oceania	986 081	4.8	1 006 384	5.0	2.1
India	82 244	0.4	67 067	0.3	−18.5
Iran	37 026	0.2	29 174	0.1	−21.2
Israel	296 310	1.5	268 654	1.3	−9.3
Africa	418 222	2.1	352 313	1.7	−15.8
Egypt	65 856	0.3	61 289	0.3	−6.9
South Africa	70 451	0.3	62 254	0.3	−11.6
Total non-OECD Countries	**2 285 105**	**11.2**	**2 140 533**	**10.6**	**−6.3**
TOTAL	**20 365 484**	**100.0**	**20 235 938**	**100.0**	**−0.6**

1. "Other European countries" includes Iceland.
2. Australia includes New Zealand.

SWITZERLAND

NIGHTS SPENT BY FOREIGN TOURISTS IN REGISTERED TOURIST ACCOMMODATION

(by country of residence)

	1991	Relative share	1992	Relative share	% Variation over 1991
Austria	580 989	1.6	533 109	1.4	−8.2
Belgium	2 026 277	5.5	2 152 529	5.8	6.2
Denmark	199 236	0.5	197 345	0.5	−0.9
Finland	104 004	0.3	88 898	0.2	−14.5
France	2 494 172	6.7	2 346 388	6.3	−5.9
Germany	16 133 407	43.6	15 964 680	43.2	−1.0
Greece	149 415	0.4	136 118	0.4	−8.9
Iceland [1]	..	..	..	..	..
Ireland	52 292	0.1	46 875	0.1	−10.4
Italy	1 977 390	5.3	2 028 631	5.5	2.6
Luxembourg	208 595	0.6	209 861	0.6	0.6
Netherlands	3 394 502	9.2	3 405 046	9.2	0.3
Norway	90 549	0.2	84 328	0.2	−6.9
Portugal	97 395	0.3	89 510	0.2	−8.1
Spain	715 817	1.9	627 089	1.7	−12.4
Sweden	344 024	0.9	342 439	0.9	−0.5
Switzerland	..	..	..	..	..
Turkey	111 889	0.3	87 586	0.2	−21.7
United Kingdom	2 551 296	6.9	2 608 563	7.1	2.2
Other OECD-Europe	..	..	..	..	..
Total Europe	31 231 249	84.3	30 948 995	83.7	−0.9
Canada	223 162	0.6	218 355	0.6	−2.2
United States	1 802 749	4.9	2 114 320	5.7	17.3
Total North America	2 025 911	5.5	2 332 675	6.3	15.1
Australia [2]	263 111	0.7	239 470	0.6	−9.0
New Zealand [2]	..	..	..	..	..
Japan	755 149	2.0	847 811	2.3	12.3
Total Australasia and Japan	1 018 260	2.7	1 087 281	2.9	6.8
Total OECD Countries	**34 275 420**	**92.5**	**34 368 951**	**92.9**	**0.3**
Ex-Yugoslavia	209 461	0.6	116 130	0.3	−44.6
Other European countries [1]	554 601	1.5	577 119	1.6	4.1
Latin America	372 581	1.0	369 034	1.0	−1.0
Argentina	56 217	0.2	64 705	0.2	15.1
Brazil	144 122	0.4	122 865	0.3	−14.7
Mexico	41 490	0.1	46 611	0.1	12.3
Asia-Oceania	1 134 322	3.1	1 147 185	3.1	1.1
India	88 927	0.2	71 963	0.2	−19.1
Iran	39 889	0.1	31 592	0.1	−20.8
Israel	361 266	1.0	333 520	0.9	−7.7
Africa	491 954	1.3	417 261	1.1	−15.2
Egypt	72 242	0.2	69 713	0.2	−3.5
South Africa	95 880	0.3	90 235	0.2	−5.9
Total non-OECD Countries	**2 762 919**	**7.5**	**2 626 729**	**7.1**	**−4.9**
TOTAL	**37 038 339**	**100.0**	**36 995 680**	**100.0**	**−0.1**

1. "Other European countries" includes Iceland.
2. Australia includes New Zealand.

TURKEY

ARRIVALS OF FOREIGN TRAVELLERS AT FRONTIERS

(by country of nationality)

	1991	Relative share	1992	Relative share	% Variation over 1991
Austria	102 071	1.8	204 662	2.9	100.5
Belgium	33 763	0.6	75 071	1.1	122.3
Denmark	32 320	0.6	64 016	0.9	98.1
Finland	80 511	1.5	104 190	1.5	29.4
France	117 070	2.1	247 603	3.5	111.5
Germany	779 882	14.1	1 165 164	16.5	49.4
Greece	138 918	2.5	147 174	2.1	5.9
Iceland [1]	..	..	2 470	0.0	..
Ireland [1]	..	..	22 997	0.3	..
Italy	64 134	1.2	158 185	2.2	146.6
Luxembourg [1]	..	..	1 743	0.0	..
Netherlands	107 018	1.9	204 802	2.9	91.4
Norway	24 590	0.4	42 482	0.6	72.8
Portugal [1]	..	..	5 811	0.1	..
Spain	24 944	0.5	47 318	0.7	89.7
Sweden	69 344	1.3	120 248	1.7	73.4
Switzerland	41 606	0.8	78 735	1.1	89.2
Turkey	..	..	..	..	..
United Kingdom	200 813	3.6	314 608	4.4	56.7
Other OECD-Europe [1]	19 939	0.4	..	..	..
Total Europe	1 836 923	33.3	3 007 279	42.5	63.7
Canada	17 680	0.3	26 355	0.4	49.1
United States	79 256	1.4	182 429	2.6	130.2
Total North America	96 936	1.8	208 784	3.0	115.4
Australia	20 707	0.4	30 907	0.4	49.3
New Zealand	6 950	0.1	7 337	0.1	5.6
Japan	18 479	0.3	36 398	0.5	97.0
Total Australasia and Japan	46 136	0.8	74 642	1.1	61.8
Total OECD Countries	**1 979 995**	**35.9**	**3 290 705**	**46.5**	**66.2**
Ex-Yugoslavia	158 699	2.9	155 559	2.2	−2.0
Other European countries	2 751 666	49.9	3 027 090	42.8	10.0
Bulgaria	943 250	17.1	818 895	11.6	−13.2
Ex-Czechoslovakia	217 232	3.9	126 773	1.8	−41.6
Hungary	164 903	3.0	148 131	2.1	−10.2
Poland	184 008	3.3	111 931	1.6	−39.2
Rumania	503 785	9.1	566 665	8.0	12.5
Ex-USSR	731 869	13.3	1 241 010	17.5	69.6
Latin America	11 428	0.2	26 275	0.4	129.9
Argentina	2 218	0.0	5 053	0.1	127.8
Brazil	3 094	0.1	4 838	0.1	56.4
Chile	523	0.0	2 109	0.0	303.3
Colombia	..	..	1 852	0.0	..
Mexico	2 100	0.0	5 260	0.1	150.5
Venezuela	..	..	1 318	0.0	..
Asia-Oceania	552 913	10.0	503 547	7.1	−8.9
China	..	..	5 500	0.1	..
India	..	..	4 431	0.1	..
Iran	253 260	4.6	150 168	2.1	−40.7
Israel	46 043	0.8	49 858	0.7	8.3
Republic of Korea	..	..	3 959	0.1	..
Lebanon	14 140	0.3	14 776	0.2	4.5
Malaysia	..	..	1 711	0.0	..
Pakistan	9 370	0.2	10 223	0.1	9.1
Philippines	..	..	3 966	0.1	..
Saudi Arabia	15 083	0.3	19 423	0.3	28.8
Singapore	..	..	2 279	0.0	..
Africa	59 943	1.1	69 320	1.0	15.6
Algeria	6 286	0.1	5 735	0.1	−8.8
Egypt	8 343	0.2	11 181	0.2	34.0
Morocco	2 621	0.0	5 165	0.1	97.1
Origin country undetermined [2]	3 253	0.1	3 600	0.1	10.7
Total non-OECD Countries	**3 537 902**	**64.1**	**3 785 391**	**53.5**	**7.0**
TOTAL	**5 517 897**	**100.0**	**7 076 096**	**100.0**	**28.2**

1. "Other OECD-Europe" includes Iceland, Ireland, Luxembourg and Portugal.
2. "Origin country undetermined" includes Other North America and Stateless persons.

TURKEY

ARRIVALS OF FOREIGN TOURISTS AT HOTELS

(by country of nationality)

	1991	Relative share	1992	Relative share	% Variation over 1991
Austria	56 650	2.6	87 597	2.6	54.6
Belgium [1]	110 029	5.0	231 348	6.8	110.3
Denmark [2]	89 246	4.0	154 180	4.5	72.8
Finland [2]	..	..	..	..	..
France	183 950	8.3	434 260	12.7	136.1
Germany	563 870	25.4	889 630	26.1	57.8
Greece	21 920	1.0	25 877	0.8	18.1
Iceland	..	..	..	..	..
Ireland	..	..	..	..	..
Italy	115 068	5.2	217 119	6.4	88.7
Luxembourg [1]	..	..	..	..	..
Netherlands [1]	..	..	..	..	..
Norway [2]	..	..	..	..	..
Portugal	..	..	..	..	..
Spain	80 674	3.6	133 396	3.9	65.4
Sweden [2]	..	..	..	..	..
Switzerland	30 708	1.4	41 725	1.2	35.9
Turkey	..	..	..	..	..
United Kingdom	94 170	4.2	158 533	4.6	68.3
Other OECD-Europe	..	..	..	..	..
Total Europe	1 346 285	60.7	2 373 665	69.6	76.3
Canada	7 950	0.4	14 544	0.4	82.9
United States	91 288	4.1	158 048	4.6	73.1
Total North America	99 238	4.5	172 592	5.1	73.9
Australia	10 299	0.5	12 082	0.4	17.3
New Zealand	..	..	..	..	..
Japan	49 623	2.2	123 402	3.6	148.7
Total Australasia and Japan	59 922	2.7	135 484	4.0	126.1
Total OECD Countries	**1 505 445**	**67.9**	**2 681 741**	**78.6**	**78.1**
Ex-Yugoslavia	39 387	1.8	36 178	1.1	−8.1
Other European countries	315 646	14.2	320 063	9.4	1.4
Bulgaria	92 607	4.2	49 741	1.5	−46.3
Hungary	38 816	1.8	45 826	1.3	18.1
Poland	75 641	3.4	34 703	1.0	−54.1
Rumania	37 700	1.7	56 555	1.7	50.0
Ex-USSR	70 882	3.2	133 238	3.9	88.0
Asia-Oceania [3]	100 403	4.5	100 576	2.9	0.2
Iran	44 098	2.0	23 070	0.7	−47.7
Lebanon	6 528	0.3	5 610	0.2	−14.1
Pakistan	4 527	0.2	8 384	0.2	85.2
Saudi Arabia	20 459	0.9	25 673	0.8	25.5
Africa	14 721	0.7	14 816	0.4	0.6
Egypt	5 957	0.3	7 476	0.2	25.5
Origin country undetermined	240 976	10.9	256 815	7.5	6.6
Total non-OECD Countries	**711 133**	**32.1**	**728 448**	**21.4**	**2.4**
TOTAL	**2 216 578**	**100.0**	**3 410 189**	**100.0**	**53.8**

1. Belgium includes Luxembourg and Netherlands.
2. Denmark includes Finland, Norway and Sweden.
3. Asia-Oceania includes Iraq, Kuwait, Lebanon, Syria, Saudi Arabia, Jordan, Iran and Pakistan.

TURKEY

ARRIVALS OF FOREIGN TOURISTS AT REGISTERED TOURIST ACCOMMODATION

(by country of nationality)

	1991	Relative share	1992	Relative share	% Variation over 1991
Austria	69 762	2.9	115 891	3.1	66.1
Belgium [1]	121 197	5.1	247 473	6.7	104.2
Denmark [2]	91 781	3.8	160 964	4.3	75.4
Finland [2]	..	..	..	..	..
France	206 269	8.6	487 120	13.1	136.2
Germany	661 497	27.6	1 038 062	27.9	56.9
Greece	22 093	0.9	26 100	0.7	18.1
Iceland	..	..	..	..	..
Ireland	..	..	..	..	..
Italy	124 941	5.2	233 962	6.3	87.3
Luxembourg [1]	..	..	..	..	..
Netherlands [1]	..	..	..	..	..
Norway [2]	..	..	..	..	..
Portugal	..	..	..	..	..
Spain	81 349	3.4	133 859	3.6	64.5
Sweden [2]	..	..	..	..	..
Switzerland	37 788	1.6	51 581	1.4	36.5
Turkey	..	..	..	..	..
United Kingdom	102 374	4.3	168 803	4.5	64.9
Other OECD-Europe	..	..	..	..	..
Total Europe	1 519 051	63.3	2 663 815	71.6	75.4
Canada	8 286	0.3	14 829	0.4	79.0
United States	92 496	3.9	159 848	4.3	72.8
Total North America	100 782	4.2	174 677	4.7	73.3
Australia	10 470	0.4	12 842	0.3	22.7
New Zealand	..	..	..	..	..
Japan	49 707	2.1	123 504	3.3	148.5
Total Australasia and Japan	60 177	2.5	136 346	3.7	126.6
Total OECD Countries	**1 680 010**	**70.0**	**2 974 838**	**80.0**	**77.1**
Ex-Yugoslavia	39 588	1.7	36 633	1.0	–7.5
Other European countries	317 763	13.2	324 315	8.7	2.1
Bulgaria	92 713	3.9	50 059	1.3	–46.0
Hungary	39 578	1.7	46 901	1.3	18.5
Poland	76 530	3.2	35 608	1.0	–53.5
Rumania	37 930	1.6	56 923	1.5	50.1
Ex-USSR	71 012	3.0	134 834	3.6	89.9
Asia-Oceania [3]	100 935	4.2	103 653	2.8	2.7
Iran	44 187	1.8	23 879	0.6	–46.0
Lebanon	6 879	0.3	5 863	0.2	–14.8
Pakistan	4 534	0.2	8 485	0.2	87.1
Saudi Arabia	20 474	0.9	26 284	0.7	28.4
Africa	14 763	0.6	14 936	0.4	1.2
Egypt	5 967	0.2	7 533	0.2	26.2
Origin country undetermined	245 607	10.2	266 252	7.2	8.4
Total non-OECD Countries	**718 656**	**30.0**	**745 789**	**20.0**	**3.8**
TOTAL	**2 398 666**	**100.0**	**3 720 627**	**100.0**	**55.1**

1. Belgium includes Luxembourg and Netherlands.
2. Denmark includes Finland, Norway and Sweden.
3. Asia-Oceania includes Iraq, Kuwait, Lebanon, Syria, Saudi Arabia, Jordan, Iran and Pakistan.

TURKEY

NIGHTS SPENT BY FOREIGN TOURISTS IN HOTELS

(by country of nationality)

	1991	Relative share	1992	Relative share	% Variation over 1991
Austria	295 750	3.6	596 726	4.4	101.8
Belgium[1]	435 325	5.4	971 027	7.2	123.1
Denmark[2]	500 365	6.2	940 934	6.9	88.0
Finland[2]	..	..	..	..	..
France	467 794	5.8	1 030 526	7.6	120.3
Germany	3 458 776	42.5	5 699 323	42.0	64.8
Greece	52 451	0.6	84 255	0.6	60.6
Iceland	..	..	..	..	..
Ireland	..	..	..	..	..
Italy	293 218	3.6	507 873	3.7	73.2
Luxembourg[1]	..	..	..	..	..
Netherlands[1]	..	..	..	..	..
Norway[2]	..	..	..	..	..
Portugal	..	..	..	..	..
Spain	146 571	1.8	284 740	2.1	94.3
Sweden[2]	..	..	..	..	..
Switzerland	129 740	1.6	257 867	1.9	98.8
Turkey	..	..	..	..	..
United Kingdom	378 702	4.7	787 486	5.8	107.9
Other OECD-Europe	..	..	..	..	..
Total Europe	6 158 692	75.7	11 160 757	82.3	81.2
Canada	19 522	0.2	29 546	0.2	51.3
United States	282 437	3.5	386 880	2.9	37.0
Total North America	301 959	3.7	416 426	3.1	37.9
Australia	20 418	0.3	28 861	0.2	41.4
New Zealand	..	..	..	..	..
Japan	90 890	1.1	214 535	1.6	136.0
Total Australasia and Japan	111 308	1.4	243 396	1.8	118.7
Total OECD Countries	**6 571 959**	**80.8**	**11 820 579**	**87.2**	**79.9**
Ex-Yugoslavia	64 856	0.8	72 765	0.5	12.2
Other European countries	647 200	8.0	698 778	5.2	8.0
Bulgaria	134 755	1.7	76 830	0.6	−43.0
Hungary	77 163	0.9	97 743	0.7	26.7
Poland	190 010	2.3	107 743	0.8	−43.3
Rumania	84 919	1.0	112 836	0.8	32.9
Ex-USSR	160 353	2.0	304 112	2.2	89.7
Asia-Oceania[3]	245 534	3.0	259 602	1.9	5.7
Iran	110 289	1.4	72 444	0.5	−34.3
Lebanon	15 379	0.2	13 474	0.1	−12.4
Pakistan	9 527	0.1	17 237	0.1	80.9
Saudi Arabia	49 398	0.6	65 438	0.5	32.5
Africa	45 922	0.6	46 592	0.3	1.5
Egypt	19 287	0.2	24 682	0.2	28.0
Origin country undetermined	555 627	6.8	661 843	4.9	19.1
Total non-OECD Countries	**1 559 139**	**19.2**	**1 739 580**	**12.8**	**11.6**
TOTAL	**8 131 098**	**100.0**	**13 560 159**	**100.0**	**66.8**

1. Belgium includes Luxembourg and Netherlands.
2. Denmark includes Finland, Norway and Sweden.
3. Asia-Oceania includes Iraq, Kuwait, Lebanon, Syria, Saudi Arabia, Jordan, Iran and Pakistan.

TURKEY

NIGHTS SPENT BY FOREIGN TOURISTS IN REGISTERED TOURIST ACCOMMODATION
(by country of nationality)

	1991	Relative share	1992	Relative share	% Variation over 1991
Austria	421 862	4.3	921 678	5.5	118.5
Belgium [1]	500 657	5.2	1 118 657	6.7	123.4
Denmark [2]	514 268	5.3	985 526	5.9	91.6
Finland [2]	..	..	..	..	..
France	631 272	6.5	1 447 251	8.6	129.3
Germany	4 448 640	45.9	7 573 318	45.1	70.2
Greece	52 862	0.5	85 033	0.5	60.9
Iceland	..	..	..	..	..
Ireland	..	..	..	..	..
Italy	366 916	3.8	642 069	3.8	75.0
Luxembourg [1]	..	..	..	..	..
Netherlands [1]	..	..	..	..	..
Norway [2]	..	..	..	..	..
Portugal	..	..	..	..	..
Spain	147 729	1.5	288 342	1.7	95.2
Sweden [2]	..	..	..	..	..
Switzerland	188 880	1.9	368 719	2.2	95.2
Turkey	..	..	..	..	..
United Kingdom	419 471	4.3	870 592	5.2	107.5
Other OECD-Europe	..	..	..	..	..
Total Europe	7 692 557	79.3	14 301 185	85.2	85.9
Canada	20 181	0.2	30 466	0.2	51.0
United States	287 511	3.0	393 281	2.3	36.8
Total North America	307 692	3.2	423 747	2.5	37.7
Australia	21 048	0.2	30 792	0.2	46.3
New Zealand	..	..	..	..	..
Japan	91 097	0.9	214 770	1.3	135.8
Total Australasia and Japan	112 145	1.2	245 562	1.5	119.0
Total OECD Countries	**8 112 394**	**83.6**	**14 970 494**	**89.2**	**84.5**
Ex-Yugoslavia	65 323	0.7	73 670	0.4	12.8
Other European countries	651 883	6.7	714 809	4.3	9.7
Bulgaria	134 907	1.4	77 743	0.5	−42.4
Hungary	78 098	0.8	99 285	0.6	27.1
Poland	192 765	2.0	111 123	0.7	−42.4
Rumania	85 321	0.9	114 100	0.7	33.7
Ex-USSR	160 792	1.7	312 558	1.9	94.4
Asia-Oceania [3]	246 496	2.5	266 725	1.6	8.2
Iran	110 675	1.1	74 260	0.4	−32.9
Lebanon	15 786	0.2	14 418	0.1	−8.7
Pakistan	9 549	0.1	17 586	0.1	84.2
Saudi Arabia	49 431	0.5	67 284	0.4	36.1
Africa	46 160	0.5	46 971	0.3	1.8
Egypt	19 331	0.2	24 951	0.1	29.1
Origin country undetermined	576 841	5.9	712 786	4.2	23.6
Total non-OECD Countries	**1 586 703**	**16.4**	**1 814 961**	**10.8**	**14.4**
TOTAL	**9 699 097**	**100.0**	**16 785 455**	**100.0**	**73.1**

1. Belgium includes Luxembourg and Netherlands.
2. Denmark includes Finland, Norway and Sweden.
3. Asia-Oceania includes Iraq, Kuwait, Lebanon, Syria, Saudi Arabia, Jordan, Iran and Pakistan.

UNITED KINGDOM

ARRIVALS OF FOREIGN VISITORS AT FRONTIERS

(by country of residence)

	1991	Relative share	1992	Relative share	% Variation over 1991
Austria	158 000	0.9	179 000	1.0	13.3
Belgium	662 000	3.9	768 000	4.2	16.0
Denmark	273 000	1.6	309 000	1.7	13.2
Finland	112 000	0.7	96 000	0.5	−14.3
France	2 289 000	13.4	2 477 000	13.6	8.2
Germany	2 134 000	12.5	2 257 000	12.4	5.8
Greece	118 000	0.7	127 000	0.7	7.6
Iceland	32 000	0.2	52 000	0.3	62.5
Ireland	1 314 000	7.7	1 299 000	7.1	−1.1
Italy	722 000	4.2	777 000	4.3	7.6
Luxembourg	27 000	0.2	31 000	0.2	14.8
Netherlands	1 118 000	6.5	994 000	5.5	−11.1
Norway	283 000	1.7	289 000	1.6	2.1
Portugal	101 000	0.6	101 000	0.6	0.0
Spain	623 000	3.6	678 000	3.7	8.8
Sweden	502 000	2.9	493 000	2.7	−1.8
Switzerland	434 000	2.5	430 000	2.4	−0.9
Turkey	62 000	0.4	42 000	0.2	−32.3
United Kingdom	..	..	..	..	..
Other OECD-Europe	..	..	..	..	..
Total Europe	10 964 000	64.0	11 399 000	62.7	4.0
Canada	547 000	3.2	613 000	3.4	12.1
United States	2 320 000	13.5	2 690 000	14.8	15.9
Total North America	2 867 000	16.7	3 303 000	18.2	15.2
Australia	467 000	2.7	492 000	2.7	5.4
New Zealand	110 000	0.6	111 000	0.6	0.9
Japan	458 000	2.7	534 000	2.9	16.6
Total Australasia and Japan	1 035 000	6.0	1 137 000	6.3	9.9
Total OECD Countries	**14 866 000**	**86.8**	**15 839 000**	**87.1**	**6.5**
Ex-Yugoslavia	39 000	0.2	26 000	0.1	−33.3
Other European countries	388 000	2.3	417 000	2.3	7.5
Latin America	200 000	1.2	232 000	1.3	16.0
Asia-Oceania	1 032 000	6.0	1 086 000	6.0	5.2
Africa	536 000	3.1	526 000	2.9	−1.9
Origin country undetermined	63 000	0.4	53 000	0.3	−15.9
Total non-OECD Countries	**2 258 000**	**13.2**	**2 340 000**	**12.9**	**3.6**
TOTAL	**17 124 000**	**100.0**	**18 179 000**	**100.0**	**6.2**

UNITED KINGDOM

NIGHTS SPENT BY FOREIGN TOURISTS IN TOURIST ACCOMMODATION[1]

(by country of residence)

	1991	Relative share	1992	Relative share	% Variation over 1991
Austria	1 389 000	0.7	1 690 000	0.9	21.7
Belgium	2 786 000	1.5	2 868 000	1.6	2.9
Denmark	1 924 000	1.0	1 986 000	1.1	3.2
Finland	826 000	0.4	795 000	0.4	−3.8
France	14 790 000	7.9	14 936 000	8.2	1.0
Germany	19 452 000	10.4	19 212 000	10.5	−1.2
Greece	1 445 000	0.8	2 032 000	1.1	40.6
Iceland	303 000	0.2	392 000	0.2	29.4
Ireland	10 165 000	5.5	10 032 000	5.5	−1.3
Italy	9 075 000	4.9	8 807 000	4.8	−3.0
Luxembourg	124 000	0.1	120 000	0.1	−3.2
Netherlands	6 492 000	3.5	5 770 000	3.2	−11.1
Norway	2 048 000	1.1	1 573 000	0.9	−23.2
Portugal	1 459 000	0.8	995 000	0.5	−31.8
Spain[2]	9 460 000	5.1	8 726 000	4.8	−7.8
Sweden	4 149 000	2.2	4 233 000	2.3	2.0
Switzerland	4 400 000	2.4	4 227 000	2.3	−3.9
Turkey	1 562 000	0.8	1 030 000	0.6	−34.1
United Kingdom	..	..	..	..	..
Other OECD-Europe	..	..	..	..	..
Total Europe	91 849 000	49.3	89 424 000	49.0	−2.6
Canada	7 622 000	4.1	7 385 000	4.0	−3.1
United States	24 935 000	13.4	26 448 000	14.5	6.1
Total North America	32 557 000	17.5	33 833 000	18.5	3.9
Australia	12 066 000	6.5	11 346 000	6.2	−6.0
New Zealand	3 588 000	1.9	2 408 000	1.3	−32.9
Japan	4 216 000	2.3	4 045 000	2.2	−4.1
Total Australasia and Japan	19 870 000	10.7	17 799 000	9.8	−10.4
Total OECD Countries	**144 276 000**	**77.4**	**141 056 000**	**77.3**	**−2.2**
Ex-Yugoslavia	710 000	0.4	580 000	0.3	−18.3
Other European countries	6 640 000	3.6	8 856 000	4.9	33.4
Latin America	2 546 000	1.4	2 178 000	1.2	−14.5
Asia-Oceania	19 317 000	10.4	17 396 000	9.5	−9.9
Africa	10 829 000	5.8	10 947 000	6.0	1.1
Origin country undetermined	2 058 000	1.1	1 400 000	0.8	−32.0
Total non-OECD Countries	**42 100 000**	**22.6**	**41 357 000**	**22.7**	**−1.8**
TOTAL	**186 376 000**	**100.0**	**182 413 000**	**100.0**	**−2.1**

1. Estimates of total number of nights spent in all forms of accommodation, including stays with friends and relatives. Excluding: visitors in transit, visits of merchant seamen, airline personnel and military on duty.
2. Spain includes Canary Islands.

UNITED STATES

ARRIVALS OF FOREIGN TOURISTS AT FRONTIERS

(by country of residence)

	1991	Relative share	1992	Relative share	% Variation over 1991
Austria	121 000	0.3	150 663	0.3	24.5
Belgium	149 099	0.3	171 146	0.4	14.8
Denmark	95 399	0.2	100 363	0.2	5.2
Finland	93 151	0.2	83 716	0.2	−10.1
France	770 230	1.8	795 444	1.8	3.3
Germany	1 430 193	3.3	1 691 663	3.8	18.3
Greece	49 429	0.1	55 321	0.1	11.9
Iceland	15 183	0.0	16 221	0.0	6.8
Ireland	101 980	0.2	118 229	0.3	15.9
Italy	478 853	1.1	589 837	1.3	23.2
Luxembourg	11 910	0.0	13 738	0.0	15.3
Netherlands	316 609	0.7	342 034	0.8	8.0
Norway	93 691	0.2	103 863	0.2	10.9
Portugal	36 206	0.1	45 378	0.1	25.3
Spain	291 646	0.7	343 922	0.8	17.9
Sweden	260 424	0.6	261 728	0.6	0.5
Switzerland	304 541	0.7	321 725	0.7	5.6
Turkey	32 064	0.1	35 241	0.1	9.9
United Kingdom	2 495 354	5.8	2 823 983	6.3	13.2
Other OECD-Europe	..	..	..	..	..
Total Europe	7 146 962	16.6	8 064 215	18.1	12.8
Canada	19 113 000	44.5	18 578 461	41.6	−2.8
United States	..	..	..	..	..
Total North America	19 113 000	44.5	18 578 461	41.6	−2.8
Australia	470 595	1.1	486 851	1.1	3.5
New Zealand	145 306	0.3	139 515	0.3	−4.0
Japan	3 319 934	7.7	3 652 828	8.2	10.0
Total Australasia and Japan	3 935 835	9.2	4 279 194	9.6	8.7
Total OECD Countries	**30 195 797**	**70.3**	**30 921 870**	**69.3**	**2.4**
Ex-Yugoslavia	27 637	0.1	15 395	0.0	−44.3
Other European countries	208 719	0.5	207 000	0.5	−0.8
Ex-Czechoslovakia	17 651	0.0	24 100	0.1	36.5
Hungary	20 311	0.0	24 475	0.1	20.5
Poland	51 650	0.1	45 831	0.1	−11.3
Rumania	12 664	0.0	10 267	0.0	−18.9
Ex-USSR	100 233	0.2	90 763	0.2	−9.4
Latin America[1]	10 720 700	25.0	11 513 000	25.8	7.4
Argentina	280 504	0.7	342 008	0.8	21.9
Brazil	459 384	1.1	475 266	1.1	3.5
Chile	88 673	0.2	104 550	0.2	17.9
Colombia	160 755	0.4	188 808	0.4	17.5
Mexico	7 718 000	18.0	8 258 000	18.5	7.0
Venezuela	310 735	0.7	372 313	0.8	19.8
Asia-Oceania	1 258 818	2.9	..	..	..
China	344 263	0.8	411 131	0.9	19.4
Hong Kong	178 381	0.4	191 237	0.4	7.2
India	109 557	0.3	105 790	0.2	−3.4
Israel	169 912	0.4	160 051	0.4	−5.8
Republic of Korea	278 182	0.6	341 311	0.8	22.7
Philippines	103 463	0.2	117 031	0.3	13.1
Saudi Arabia	51 148	0.1	60 966	0.1	19.2
Singapore	57 309	0.1	64 953	0.1	13.3
Africa	138 101	0.3	150 000	0.3	8.6
South Africa	40 924	0.1	58 161	0.1	42.1
Origin country undetermined[2]	386 137	0.9	1 820 196	4.1	371.4
Total non-OECD Countries	**12 740 112**	**29.7**	**13 705 591**	**30.7**	**7.6**
TOTAL	**42 935 909**	**100.0**	**44 627 461**	**100.0**	**3.9**

1. Latin America includes Central America, Carribean, South America and Mexico.
2. Origin country undetermined includes Middle East only.

MAIN SALES OUTLETS OF OECD PUBLICATIONS
PRINCIPAUX POINTS DE VENTE DES PUBLICATIONS DE L'OCDE

ARGENTINA – ARGENTINE
Carlos Hirsch S.R.L.
Galería Güemes, Florida 165, 4° Piso
1333 Buenos Aires   Tel. (1) 331.1787 y 331.2391
                        Telefax: (1) 331.1787

AUSTRALIA – AUSTRALIE
D.A. Information Services
648 Whitehorse Road, P.O.B 163
Mitcham, Victoria 3132   Tel. (03) 873.4411
                        Telefax: (03) 873.5679

AUSTRIA – AUTRICHE
Gerold & Co.
Graben 31
Wien I   Tel. (0222) 533.50.14

BELGIUM – BELGIQUE
Jean De Lannoy
Avenue du Roi 202
B-1060 Bruxelles   Tel. (02) 538.51.69/538.08.41
                        Telefax: (02) 538.08.41

CANADA
Renouf Publishing Company Ltd.
1294 Algoma Road
Ottawa, ON K1B 3W8   Tel. (613) 741.4333
                        Telefax: (613) 741.5439
Stores:
61 Sparks Street
Ottawa, ON K1P 5R1   Tel. (613) 238.8985
211 Yonge Street
Toronto, ON M5B 1M4   Tel. (416) 363.3171
                        Telefax: (416)363.59.63

Les Éditions La Liberté Inc.
3020 Chemin Sainte-Foy
Sainte-Foy, PQ G1X 3V6   Tel. (418) 658.3763
                        Telefax: (418) 658.3763

Federal Publications Inc.
165 University Avenue, Suite 701
Toronto, ON M5H 3B8   Tel. (416) 860.1611
                        Telefax: (416) 860.1608

Les Publications Fédérales
1185 Université
Montréal, QC H3B 3A7   Tel. (514) 954.1633
                        Telefax : (514) 954.1635

CHINA – CHINE
China National Publications Import
Export Corporation (CNPIEC)
16 Gongti E. Road, Chaoyang District
P.O. Box 88 or 50
Beijing 100704 PR   Tel. (01) 506.6688
                        Telefax: (01) 506.3101

DENMARK – DANEMARK
Munksgaard Book and Subscription Service
35, Nørre Søgade, P.O. Box 2148
DK-1016 København K   Tel. (33) 12.85.70
                        Telefax: (33) 12.93.87

FINLAND – FINLANDE
Akateeminen Kirjakauppa
Keskuskatu 1, P.O. Box 128
00100 Helsinki

Subscription Services/Agence d'abonnements :
P.O. Box 23
00371 Helsinki   Tel. (358 0) 12141
                        Telefax: (358 0) 121.4450

FRANCE
OECD/OCDE
Mail Orders/Commandes par correspondance:
2, rue André-Pascal
75775 Paris Cedex 16   Tel. (33-1) 45.24.82.00
Telefax: (33-1) 45.24.81.76 or (33-1) 45.24.85.00
                        Telex: 640048 OCDE

OECD Bookshop/Librairie de l'OCDE :
33, rue Octave-Feuillet
75016 Paris   Tel. (33-1) 45.24.81.67
                        (33-1) 45.24.81.81

Documentation Française
29, quai Voltaire
75007 Paris   Tel. 40.15.70.00

Gibert Jeune (Droit-Économie)
6, place Saint-Michel
75006 Paris   Tel. 43.25.91.19

Librairie du Commerce International
10, avenue d'Iéna
75016 Paris   Tel. 40.73.34.60

Librairie Dunod
Université Paris-Dauphine
Place du Maréchal de Lattre de Tassigny
75016 Paris   Tel. (1) 44.05.40.13

Librairie Lavoisier
11, rue Lavoisier
75008 Paris   Tel. 42.65.39.95

Librairie L.G.D.J. - Montchrestien
20, rue Soufflot
75005 Paris   Tel. 46.33.89.85

Librairie des Sciences Politiques
30, rue Saint-Guillaume
75007 Paris   Tel. 45.48.36.02

P.U.F.
49, boulevard Saint-Michel
75005 Paris   Tel. 43.25.83.40

Librairie de l'Université
12a, rue Nazareth
13100 Aix-en-Provence   Tel. (16) 42.26.18.08

Documentation Française
165, rue Garibaldi
69003 Lyon   Tel. (16) 78.63.32.23

Librairie Decitre
29, place Bellecour
69002 Lyon   Tel. (16) 72.40.54.54

GERMANY – ALLEMAGNE
OECD Publications and Information Centre
August-Bebel-Allee 6
D-53175 Bonn 2   Tel. (0228) 959.120
                        Telefax: (0228) 959.12.17

GREECE – GRÈCE
Librairie Kauffmann
Mavrokordatou 9
106 78 Athens   Tel. (01) 32.55.321
                        Telefax: (01) 36.33.967

HONG-KONG
Swindon Book Co. Ltd.
13–15 Lock Road
Kowloon, Hong Kong   Tel. 366.80.31
                        Telefax: 739.49.75

HUNGARY – HONGRIE
Euro Info Service
POB 1271
1464 Budapest   Tel. (1) 111.62.16
                        Telefax : (1) 111.60.61

ICELAND – ISLANDE
Mál Mog Menning
Laugavegi 18, Pósthólf 392
121 Reykjavik   Tel. 162.35.23

INDIA – INDE
Oxford Book and Stationery Co.
Scindia House
New Delhi 110001   Tel.(11) 331.5896/5308
                        Telefax: (11) 332.5993
17 Park Street
Calcutta 700016   Tel. 240832

INDONESIA – INDONÉSIE
Pdii-Lipi
P.O. Box 269/JKSMG/88
Jakarta 12790   Tel. 583467
                        Telex: 62 875

IRELAND – IRLANDE
TDC Publishers – Library Suppliers
12 North Frederick Street
Dublin 1   Tel. (01) 874.48.35
                        Telefax: (01) 874.84.16

ISRAEL
Electronic Publications only
Publications électroniques seulement
Sophist Systems Ltd.
71 Allenby Street
Tel-Aviv 65134   Tel. 3-29.00.21
                        Telefax: 3-29.92.39

ITALY – ITALIE
Libreria Commissionaria Sansoni
Via Duca di Calabria 1/1
50125 Firenze   Tel. (055) 64.54.15
                        Telefax: (055) 64.12.57
Via Bartolini 29
20155 Milano   Tel. (02) 36.50.83

Editrice e Libreria Herder
Piazza Montecitorio 120
00186 Roma   Tel. 679.46.28
                        Telefax: 678.47.51

Libreria Hoepli
Via Hoepli 5
20121 Milano   Tel. (02) 86.54.46
                        Telefax: (02) 805.28.86

Libreria Scientifica
Dott. Lucio de Biasio 'Aeiou'
Via Coronelli, 6
20146 Milano   Tel. (02) 48.95.45.52
                        Telefax: (02) 48.95.45.48

JAPAN – JAPON
OECD Publications and Information Centre
Landic Akasaka Building
2-3-4 Akasaka, Minato-ku
Tokyo 107   Tel. (81.3) 3586.2016
                        Telefax: (81.3) 3584.7929

KOREA – CORÉE
Kyobo Book Centre Co. Ltd.
P.O. Box 1658, Kwang Hwa Moon
Seoul   Tel. 730.78.91
                        Telefax: 735.00.30

MALAYSIA – MALAISIE
Co-operative Bookshop Ltd.
University of Malaya
P.O. Box 1127, Jalan Pantai Baru
59700 Kuala Lumpur
Malaysia   Tel. 756.5000/756.5425
                        Telefax: 757.3661

MEXICO – MEXIQUE
Revistas y Periodicos Internacionales S.A. de C.V.
Florencia 57 - 1004
Mexico, D.F. 06600   Tel. 207.81.00
                        Telefax : 208.39.79

NETHERLANDS – PAYS-BAS
SDU Uitgeverij Plantijnstraat
Externe Fondsen
Postbus 20014
2500 EA's-Gravenhage   Tel. (070) 37.89.880
Voor bestellingen: Telefax: (070) 34.75.778

**NEW ZEALAND
NOUVELLE-ZÉLANDE**
Legislation Services
P.O. Box 12418
Thorndon, Wellington   Tel. (04) 496.5652
                              Telefax: (04) 496.5698

NORWAY – NORVÈGE
Narvesen Info Center – NIC
Bertrand Narvesens vei 2
P.O. Box 6125 Etterstad
0602 Oslo 6   Tel. (022) 57.33.00
                              Telefax: (022) 68.19.01

PAKISTAN
Mirza Book Agency
65 Shahrah Quaid-E-Azam
Lahore 54000   Tel. (42) 353.601
                              Telefax: (42) 231.730

PHILIPPINE – PHILIPPINES
International Book Center
5th Floor, Filipinas Life Bldg.
Ayala Avenue
Metro Manila   Tel. 81.96.76
                              Telex 23312 RHP PH

PORTUGAL
Livraria Portugal
Rua do Carmo 70-74
Apart. 2681
1200 Lisboa   Tel.: (01) 347.49.82/5
                              Telefax: (01) 347.02.64

SINGAPORE – SINGAPOUR
Gower Asia Pacific Pte Ltd.
Golden Wheel Building
41, Kallang Pudding Road, No. 04-03
Singapore 1334   Tel. 741.5166
                              Telefax: 742.9356

SPAIN – ESPAGNE
Mundi-Prensa Libros S.A.
Castelló 37, Apartado 1223
Madrid 28001   Tel. (91) 431.33.99
                              Telefax: (91) 575.39.98

Libreria Internacional AEDOS
Consejo de Ciento 391
08009 – Barcelona   Tel. (93) 488.30.09
                              Telefax: (93) 487.76.59
Llibreria de la Generalitat
Palau Moja
Rambla dels Estudis, 118
08002 – Barcelona
             (Subscripcions) Tel. (93) 318.80.12
             (Publicacions) Tel. (93) 302.67.23
                              Telefax: (93) 412.18.54

SRI LANKA
Centre for Policy Research
c/o Colombo Agencies Ltd.
No. 300-304, Galle Road
Colombo 3   Tel. (1) 574240, 573551-2
                              Telefax: (1) 575394, 510711

SWEDEN – SUÈDE
Fritzes Information Center
Box 16356
Regeringsgatan 12
106 47 Stockholm   Tel. (08) 690.90.90
                              Telefax: (08) 20.50.21
Subscription Agency/Agence d'abonnements :
Wennergren-Williams Info AB
P.O. Box 1305
171 25 Solna   Tel. (08) 705.97.50
                              Téléfax : (08) 27.00.71

SWITZERLAND – SUISSE
Maditec S.A. (Books and Periodicals - Livres
et périodiques)
Chemin des Palettes 4
Case postale 266
1020 Renens   Tel. (021) 635.08.65
                              Telefax: (021) 635.07.80

Librairie Payot S.A.
4, place Pépinet
CP 3212
1002 Lausanne   Tel. (021) 341.33.48
                              Telefax: (021) 341.33.45

Librairie Unilivres
6, rue de Candolle
1205 Genève   Tel. (022) 320.26.23
                              Telefax: (022) 329.73.18

Subscription Agency/Agence d'abonnements :
Dynapresse Marketing S.A.
38 avenue Vibert
1227 Carouge   Tel.: (022) 308.07.89
                              Telefax : (022) 308.07.99

See also – Voir aussi :
OECD Publications and Information Centre
August-Bebel-Allee 6
D-53175 Bonn 2 (Germany)   Tel. (0228) 959.120
                              Telefax: (0228) 959.12.17

TAIWAN – FORMOSE
Good Faith Worldwide Int'l. Co. Ltd.
9th Floor, No. 118, Sec. 2
Chung Hsiao E. Road
Taipei   Tel. (02) 391.7396/391.7397
                              Telefax: (02) 394.9176

THAILAND – THAÏLANDE
Suksit Siam Co. Ltd.
113, 115 Fuang Nakhon Rd.
Opp. Wat Rajbopith
Bangkok 10200   Tel. (662) 225.9531/2
                              Telefax: (662) 222.5188

TURKEY – TURQUIE
Kültür Yayinlari Is-Türk Ltd. Sti.
Atatürk Bulvari No. 191/Kat 13
Kavaklidere/Ankara   Tel. 428.11.40 Ext. 2458
Dolmabahce Cad. No. 29
Besiktas/Istanbul   Tel. 260.71.88
                              Telex: 43482B

UNITED KINGDOM – ROYAUME-UNI
HMSO
Gen. enquiries   Tel. (071) 873 0011
Postal orders only:
P.O. Box 276, London SW8 5DT
Personal Callers HMSO Bookshop
49 High Holborn, London WC1V 6HB
                              Telefax: (071) 873 8200
Branches at: Belfast, Birmingham, Bristol, Edin-
burgh, Manchester

UNITED STATES – ÉTATS-UNIS
OECD Publications and Information Centre
2001 L Street N.W., Suite 700
Washington, D.C. 20036-4910 Tel. (202) 785.6323
                              Telefax: (202) 785.0350

VENEZUELA
Libreria del Este
Avda F. Miranda 52, Aptdo. 60337
Edificio Galipán
Caracas 106   Tel. 951.1705/951.2307/951.1297
                   Telegram: Libreste Caracas

Subscription to OECD periodicals may also be
placed through main subscription agencies.

Les abonnements aux publications périodiques de
l'OCDE peuvent être souscrits auprès des
principales agences d'abonnement.

Orders and inquiries from countries where Distribu-
tors have not yet been appointed should be sent to:
OECD Publications Service, 2 rue André-Pascal,
75775 Paris Cedex 16, France.

Les commandes provenant de pays où l'OCDE n'a
pas encore désigné de distributeur devraient être
adressées à : OCDE, Service des Publications,
2, rue André-Pascal, 75775 Paris Cedex 16, France.

2-1994

OECD PUBLICATIONS, 2 rue André-Pascal, 75775 PARIS CEDEX 16
PRINTED IN FRANCE
(78 94 01 1) ISBN 92-64-14091-3 - No. 47003 1994
ISSN 0256-7598